Praise for M.G. Vassanji

"A novelist at the height of his powers. . . . Vassanji leaves his readers with dazzling images." — *Books in Canada*

"The quiet lyricism . . . the careful evocation of place, the writer's obvious warmth for his characters, the sense of compassion layered into the story—these are all Vassanji's." — *The Washington Post Book World*

"[Vassanji] writes with bedazzling charm and shrewd insight. . . . [He] subtly and cannily negotiates the gap between spirituality and religious fundamentalism, traces the arduous path to enlightenment, and illuminates the continuity of human experience." — *Booklist*

"Strikingly written . . . beautifully observed, filled with myths, stories, legends, history, journal entries and family narratives. It is an expertly stitched collage and, as much as it reveals about India, it is a great portrait of Vassanji himself." — *The Globe and Mail*

"What Vassanji does wonderfully well, with zero hectoring and unsettling calm, is describe the complexity of race relations in post-colonial, multi-cultural societies." — *National Post*

"[Vassanji] is an important inheritor of the tradition in Canadian literature started by Austin Clarke. As the immigrant narrative becomes more and more the dominant one, we're fortunate that its telling is in such good hands." — *The Gazette* (Montreal)

M. G. Vassanji

A PLACE WITHIN

Rediscovering India

 ANCHOR CANADA

LIBRARY AND ARCHIVES OF CANADA CATALOGUING IN PUBLICATION HAS BEEN APPLIED FOR.

ISBN 978-0-385-66179-9

Grateful acknowledgement is made to reprint the following:
Folio from a Khamsa (Quintet) by Amir Khusrau Dihlavi; verso: Amir Khusrau Presents a Book of Poetry to Ala'uddin Khalji
Ala'uddin Muhammad al-Harawi
Amir Khusrau Dihlawi, (1253–1324)
Safavid dynasty, 1503–1504
Opaque watercolor, ink and gold on paper
Origin: Balkh, Afghanistan / Historical Region: Iran
Courtesy of the Arthur M. Sackler Gallery, Smithsonian Institution, Washington, D.C.

Jacket images: (front) © Walter Crump / CORBIS, (back) Panoramic Images / Getty Images
Jacket and book design: CS Richardson
Map illustrator: Adam Hilborn
Printed and bound in the USA

Published in Canada by Anchor Canada,
a division of Random House of Canada Limited

Visit Random House of Canada Limited's website: www.randomhouse.ca

BVG 10 9 8 7 6 5 4 3

*To my friends
of the Puri Express*

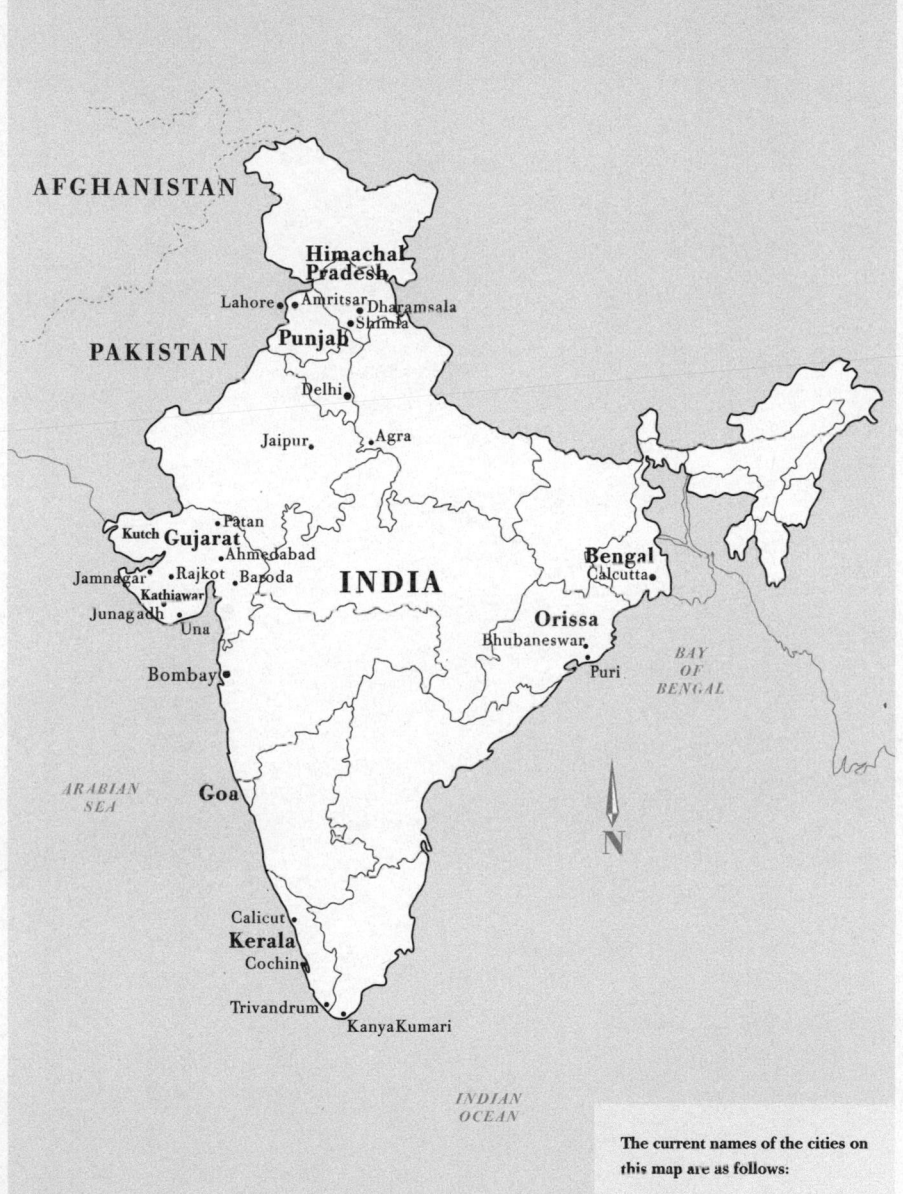

AFGHANISTAN

PAKISTAN

Lahore • • Amritsar

Himachal Pradesh

Dharamsala

• Shimla

Punjab

Delhi •

Jaipur •

Agra •

Patan •

Kutch Gujarat

Ahmedabad •

Jamnagar •

Kathiawar • Rajkot • Baroda

Junagadh •

Una •

Bombay •

INDIA

Bengal

Calcutta •

Orissa

Bhubaneswar •

Puri •

BAY OF BENGAL

ARABIAN SEA

Goa

N

Calicut •

Kerala

Cochin •

Trivandrum •

Kanya Kumari •

INDIAN OCEAN

The current names of the cities on this map are as follows:

Baroda: Vadodara
Bombay: Mumbai
Calcutta: Kolkata
Calicut: Khozhikode
Cochin: Kochi
Trivandrum: Thiruvananthapuram

Introduction

It would take many lifetimes, it was said to me during my first visit, to see all of India. It was January 1993. The desperation must have shown on my face to take in all I possibly could. This was not something I had articulated or resolved, and yet I recall an anxiety as I travelled the length and breadth of the country, senses raw to every new experience, that even in the distraction of a blink I might miss something profoundly significant.

I was not born in India, nor were my parents; that might explain much in my expectation of that visit. Yet how many people go to the birthplace of their grandparents with such a heartload of expectation and momentousness, such a desire to find themselves in everything they see? Is it only India that clings thus, to those who've forsaken it; is this why Indians in a foreign land seem always so desperate to seek each other out?

What was India to me? I must put this in the past, because by now I have returned many times and my relationship to the country has evolved. Ever since that first visit, there has been the irrepressible urge to describe my experience of India; yet in spite of copious notes this was not easy, because that experience was deeply subjective, my India was essentially my own creation, what

I put of myself in it. I grew up in Dar es Salaam, on the coast of East Africa; the memory and sight of that city, of that continent, evoke in me a deep nostalgia and love of place. India, on the other hand, seemed to do something to the soul; give it a certain ease, a sense of homecoming, quite another kind of nostalgia. During each visit I sought it more, as intensely as ever. There was no satisfaction.

I recall my maternal grandmother relating how one day as a child back in Gujarat in India she was lost, having gone out with her sister to bring home water. I also recall not paying any particular attention to this story set in a foreign land as it was being told to my elder siblings, who sat on the floor around her. But I seem to have paid more attention than I thought I did, for I always carried a picture of two Indian girls sitting under a tree in an open land, waiting to be rescued. And that was all there was to the story: getting lost and rescued somewhere in India.

The East African countries became independent from Britain in the early 1960s. But by then to my generation and in my community of people, our spiritual home, so we naively thought, was already England. We believed we could shed our ancestral connections for a thin veneer of colonialness, an ersatz sophistication. And so we chose to imagine India as poor, backward, and laughable—the past. It seems evident now that all that laughing and jeering was at ourselves, our colonial, racial insecurity; we were both the clown and its audience. It did not take long to be disillusioned.

There were always stories about India. One of them concerned my orphaned father, who apparently was something of a wanderer as a young man. All his travels were within the territory of East Africa, but once, according to my mother, he took it upon himself to board a ship bound from Mombasa to Bombay, without papers or much money. When he reached the great city, he was not allowed to disembark. He returned disappointed. I always imagine him watching Bombay wistfully through the portholes of that ship, until it finally turned around and crossed the Indian Ocean back to Africa. Another Bombay story, and repeated more often for its comic value, involved one of my uncles, my mother's older brother, so excessively pious as to be considered nicely crazy. Apparently he reached Bombay and disembarked, but upon seeing the extreme poverty in evidence, he returned home on the same ship. I would picture him seated in misery atop his luggage outside the harbour, having given all his money to the swarm of beggars that had plagued him.

My mother held blithely contradictory views about India. On one hand it was the land of ruthless cunning and violence—which she could illustrate with colourful and often morbid tales heard from passersby in our shop. On the other hand, India was the land of primal morality—which was why she would allow us to go to the cinema, sometimes, to watch a tearful Bollywood social drama offering lessons in fortitude, piety, and family values, and songs to remember afterwards. In a grand gesture for our meagre means, she sent us all to the Odeon to watch the blockbuster *Mother India*: a widow brings up her two sons against much hardship, and triumphs at the end. My mother too was a widow, which was also why I could never hear firsthand the full story of my dad's fruitless trip to Bombay. *Mother India* was perhaps the only film she herself saw in a decade.

There was, finally, the ancestral mythical memory of India. According to a founding legend of my people, the Gujarati Khojas, a Muslim holy man arrives in medieval times at a remote village in western Gujarat and joins the people in a traditional dance called the garba. As he dances, he sings them a song. The villagers and the mystic—for such he is—go around in circles, clapping hands in rhythm and singing. The people are poor and desperate, for the land is prone to drought; the visitor is new and charismatic and hopeful. They are Krishna devotees, whom he teaches to expect an incarnation of the god to come from the west. You should sing day and night, he sings to them—meaning, I am not sure what, but perhaps this was how they should express their new expectation and joy. Meanwhile they continued worshipping their beloved Krishna. These spiritual dance songs are called the garbi and belong to a larger corpus called ginans.

That syncretism, a happy combination of mystical and devotional Hinduism and Islam, without a thought to internal contradictions or to the mainstream traditions, inevitably defined my relationship with India. The existence of such inclusive systems of belief was proof of an essential historical quality of India, that of tolerance and flexibility, a certain laissez faire in matters of the spirit, at least at the local level, far away from the watchful eyes of orthodoxy. Therefore today I can only find the labels "Hindu" and "Muslim" too exacting, too excluding; I resist them. They carry the charge of recent history and a consequent bitterness, to which I refuse to subscribe. In my travels in India I would simply let people assume "what" I was, since according to them I had to be something. My two initials were my mask.

"What is this India?" asks Jawaharlal Nehru, in his book *The Discovery of India*, in a chapter titled, significantly, "The Quest." For Nehru, India was a discovery, a reclamation. "What is this India, apart from her physical and geographical aspects? . . . India was in my blood and there was much in her that instinctively thrilled me. And yet I approached her almost as an alien critic . . ."

My first serious engagement with India began when as a student strolling along the aisles of a university book sale one spring in Cambridge, Massachusetts, I happened upon a remaindered copy of Jawaharlal Nehru's autobiography and quickly—though I cannot say with what expectation—picked it up. Something of the liberal expansiveness of the author, educated in Harrow and that other Cambridge, in England, and his generosity of spirit, appealed to this expatriate student barely out of his teens and foundering upon questions of identity on alien shores. I was of Indian descent, born in East Africa, had recently seen the independence of my country, amidst great euphoria and hope for Africa. Nehru wrote his autobiography (as he did his *Discovery*) during one of his several terms in jail during India's own struggle for independence. Reading him I became aware of India as a real, modern country—as opposed to a mythical one—a recent phenomenon, having achieved its independence a decade and a half before East Africa did, after a long struggle. I was reading, for the first time after a colonial education, words written by an Indian, and I felt a swell of pride in that. After Nehru I read Gandhi, in English at first, then later, falteringly, in what seemed a difficult Gujarati. (I grew up speaking this language, in addition to Kutchi, a more regional language, a smattering of Hindi, and of course Swahili.) Gandhi brought India even closer: he had lived many years in South Africa, and he had given an opinion regarding the so-called Indian Question in East Africa; and he was a Gujarati, from the same city, as I was to discover, as my maternal grandfather.

In the early 1970s, a time still of the hippies and the counterculture and the antiwar movement, India had a certain *outré* glamour for young people, denoting spirituality, austerity, and a Lucy-in-the-sky exoticism. The Beatles had visited India, all manner of gurus did their rounds of North America, books on spiritualism flourished. Louis Malle's dense personal documentary *Phantom India* evoked the exotic and the mysterious at a time when the material and the rational, as symbols of weapons and war, were under attack by the young. To think that my roots were there, amidst all that magic of India. A Satyajit Ray retrospective, showing all his films in a college hall, was another revelation. In Ray's sparsely drawn India, full of pithy reality, the characters reached out to me in all my Indian-ness. I did not have to speak Bengali to understand them. I could catch the fleeting shadow of sadness as it crossed the face of a mother, laugh at the banter of city youths out on a picnic, exult in the catchy, triumphant smile of a young father carrying his son on his shoulders.

I had long harboured a desire to visit India, ever since this youthful romance, but more immediate and mundane and adult concerns soon took the greater priority. The possibility receded in some back drawer of the mind, an experience put off indefinitely; its time would come. It did, two decades later, when through a fortuitous contact I published a novel in India. Finally, I told myself, I had made that visit, albeit symbolically. Soon after, as a corollary, came an invitation to go to India for a conference. Arrangements would be made for me to tour various places; just come, said my hosts. The current outbreak of riots in the country was of no concern, I was assured, they would not affect me. Yes, I replied promptly, in case they changed their minds, I will come to India. The significance of the journey that awaited seemed as profound as possible for a single human life.

And so to that first arrival. It was 3 a.m. in New Delhi's airport; if I had not actually rehearsed this moment, I had thought of it many times. A return after three generations, if one wanted to lend it epic proportions, an element of drama. I recall African Americans arriving in Nairobi or Dar es Salaam in the sixties, a decade of intense black pride and consciousness, and kissing the sun-drenched earth of their forefathers. I was not of so dramatic an inclination, and my people had not been away as long as theirs had. And besides, I stepped out not onto the earth of India but upon the rubber mat of a covered portal and found myself walking through musty corridors into a dingy immigration hall, where I was hit by an overwhelmingly wretched sense of the familiar. Long lines, people jumping queues, patient, bemused officials. A tired and valiantly grinning host met me finally and took me to a hostel through dark Delhi streets; shown my room, I fell straight asleep.

At six the desk clerk woke me up to ask what my initials stood for. I had barely shut my eyes. Indulgently, I answered him, and reminded myself that I was here to garner impressions, not to make touristic scenes of outrage. Happily, that most wonderful of concoctions, "morning tea," was brought for me on a tray and, the buses groaning on the road outside making it impossible to sleep, I was ready to begin my first day in India. Downstairs in the lobby, attendants and waiters went by wishing guests a happy New Year, murmuring the words with embarrassed religiosity every time they passed.

"A country you've seen in films; you're linked to by tradition, culture, language. Where is it?" I asked myself, and kept asking throughout that visit.

Having postponed from the airport that moment of epiphany, I now awaited it anew. I remember contemplating the glass doors leading outside. There was a gate and a guardhouse beyond a yard, and farther, a few taxis at the street; the sun was bright, city life bustling. Should I walk out and experience the city, that first moment, by myself or simply await my escort for a guided tour? First impressions were surely important, even more for so momentous a visit. Inside, other visitors, Europeans and North Americans wearing thick-belted theft-proof fanny packs, had gathered for breakfast in the room adjoining the lobby, also ready to take on the city. I myself had been advised to wear a wallet inside my shirt, around my neck, and had dutifully and much to my later embarrassment done so, prepared for the numerous and cunning thieves of India. Newspapers lay around for those who had to wait. "Fight the menace politically," began a grim editorial in the current edition of a *Time*-format newsmagazine, commenting on the recent demolition of the Babri Mosque by Hindu fanatics. More than half the issue analyzed the current crisis in the country—the communal divide that was widening, and the emerging threats to the secular ideals of the past. The forecasts were discouraging, except to those given to India's eternal prayer of hope: Life goes on, it will be all right. But this was not the India I had come to experience; there was so much more of it, and anyway, I did not see myself as Hindu or Muslim.

The reception desk was now under the command of a tall, straight-backed Bengali woman in sari; she talked in clear accentless tones heard across the hall, sounding firm with foreigner and local alike. She was, I heard her say, on her way to Saudi Arabia to join her husband, was keen to know about the schools there for her three children.

She directed me, when I asked her where I could briefly walk to, to a place called the Jantar Mantar down the road. Winter weather had not set in; it was balmy outside. The Jantar Mantar is an eighteenth-century observatory situated in the midst of a park, consisting of geometric stone constructions which were used for making astronomical observations. There had been a political demonstration in the area the day before, and the site was littered all over. A few people walked about, a young couple sat self-consciously together. The structure, built by a king of Jaipur, was an extraordinary feat in its time. But as it lay there, out of context, out of place and time, it failed to impress. Its descriptions meagre and unhelpful, you made of it what you could. All around, traffic was thick and fast. On the way back I bought a map of Delhi from a street vendor, partly so I could talk to someone in my broken Hindi. An angry man was abusing a young well-dressed youth in the most explicit language imaginable. To my surprise, I understood it; the rough street Kutchi of Dar es Salaam evidently was not far removed from the more vulgar brogue of Delhi.

As I waited in the lobby once again, my local host, Krishan Chander, drove up in his Maruti, grinning from ear to ear, and led me into the streets of his city, into India.

The India I would find, on this and later trips, seemed at once so startlingly familiar and yet so alien; so frustrating and yet so enlightening and humbling; so warm and friendly and yet so inhumanly cruel and callous. But above all, it spoke to me; I found myself responding to it, it mattered to me. It was as if a part of me which had lain dormant all the while had awakened and reclaimed me.

The First Visit

What am I in for now?
Whose country have I come to this time?

HOMER, The Odyssey, XXIII

This Is India. Where Is It?

Of course the first thing to do was to make a grand survey of the country she was going to travel through.

LEWIS CARROLL, *Through the Looking-Glass*

I WOULD BE ASKED IF I PLANNED to visit my ancestral village; I would say no. I did not even know then what my ancestral village or villages were, though I did not tell them this; for me, India was the ancestral homeland, the village, if you will. If I needed more detail, then a visit to Gujarat would suffice, where they spoke my language. But India for now was one single continuous experience, twenty-eight days in duration, seven thousand miles long, travelled mostly on land, eyes wide open.

It was as if, during that visit, I was in some sort of a bubble, all my senses peeled to take in this world around me. On one hand I stood at an objective distance, watching and observing; and yet everything I saw I took personally, conscious all the time, This is India, this is the homeland, to which I am returning on behalf of my family after seventy, eighty, a hundred years. My great-grandfather Nanji Lalji left Gujarat, in the west, in about 1885, there is a plaque at the Nairobi Khoja khano (our prayer house and community centre) to prove this. Some thirty years later, my mother's parents, too, crossed the Indian Ocean for Africa. These people around me, in this screeching bustle in the heat and

3
–

dust, I told myself, are Indians, like me; I could be in their shoes, they in mine. I could not understand this reaction of mine, this deep communion I felt with the place. It was more natural to be the haughty returnee (this was still possible then), in sunglasses and expensive clothes, clutching my bottle of purified water, disdainfully stepping aside from a cowpat or a beggar, impatient of Third World inefficient ways, disgusted by smell and filth. Even those born in India could do that, so why couldn't I? Here I was, taking things in stride. What I did not understand, I was curious about; what was familiar comforted me; what seemed to disturb, I filed away for contemplation. In return I was treated like a long-lost cousin, a genuine returnee. I was given a chance to see, amidst all the bustle, a place of friendship and hospitality, love and romance, song and laughter.

There was one fatal flaw to this scenario. India was undergoing an upheaval; my visit to the homeland also coincided with a barbaric blight which afflicts it periodically. Its disturbing reverberations followed me in my journeys, making themselves felt dimly and distantly, until finally the reality of the horrors of the "riots" became impossible to ignore. To be as resigned to the violence as many of my new Indian friends and acquaintances were, I realized, I would have to be born here. I was not.

I spent the day after my arrival with my host while recovering from my long flight. I do not much remember that day; I drove around a lot with him, asked many questions. Early the next morning I headed off to the railway station in a rickshaw and caught a train for Bhubaneswar, a distant city on the east coast. Thus I began a tour of India that over its course took on the aspect partly of a pilgrimage and partly a revelatory voyage. And because it was a single, continuous experience, here I describe it whole, in an edited form of the journal I kept.

The Puri Express: A Train Journey

Indian Airlines is on strike, private airlines are irregular and few. Krishan Chander has booked us seats on the train for the conference in Bhubaneswar, Orissa, on the east coast. Privately, I feel somewhat pleased at this turn of events, though thousands of middle-class Indians are practically hostage to the strike—and the tourist industry is suffering badly. But travelling across India by train is how I have always imagined seeing the country. City-hopping by plane was how I was advised to travel by my hosts. On my last visit to East Africa, I came upon the realization that there's nothing like an extended journey on land for thoroughly purging the spirit of North American puritanical cleanliness, of the fears acquired abroad: fear of disease at every corner and therefore of every food; fear of contact, fear ultimately of the smell of people.

And so the Puri Express, second-class AC (air-conditioned).

Second AC is how the middle class travel; it provides a modicum of privacy, compared to ordinary second. There is no third class. There are four berths to a compartment, each of which can be closed off at night by a blue curtain. Across from each compartment along the aisle are two seats facing each other next to the window, under an upper bunk. This is where I find myself. The back rests of the seats are folded when required to form the lower bunk. Each of these bunks can also be closed off with a blue curtain. At night you either worry about your shoes and luggage, which you've left in the dark on the floor, or you take in the shoes and your small bag with you and tie your larger bag to the leg of a seat using a thick metal chain with a padlock, a contraption which apparently can be bought at the station.

I drink in every sight. What I see, however, seems rather plain. I have been spoilt by land journeys in childhood: African plains covered with giraffe, zebra, wildebeest; elephants crossing the road; the roar of a lion; roads climbing up geological faults and craters. It seems, in comparison, that the cameras that have filmed India have been kind. We roll through drab, yellow plains; pass the backsides of occasional towns and villages; sun and languor and empty fields. A few men crouching among the dry grass, presumably to relieve themselves; a slow walk upon a trail; closer to town boys play cricket; hovels huddled together. Once, an open-air classroom, in a half-built or ruined house. And then more plains, the rocking of the train, the clackety-clack.

Opposite me, a young cameraman sulking because the airline strike has forced him to take the train; his large suitcases block the gangway. Periodically his producers, a young man and woman, come by to pamper him. Across the aisle from us, in the four-berth compartment, the party I belong to: a group of academic women, knitting, holding *Reader's Digest*s in their laps, discussing trips to Austria, the United States. I am known to be from "there." These people have a sense of the overseas, they know (they think) what I am used to. Sympathy is offered me for the discomfort of train travel. No mention of the recent disturbances here, in the wake of the mosque demolition in Ayodhya, though the papers are full of diagnoses of the country's current sickness.

I watch the hovels flying past, dark gaping mouths housing extreme poverty. How can these sights horrify, surprise, raise any emotion, if you've seen Ray's *Pather Panchali* and already responded appropriately? This is India that's passing me by, that moved me many years ago as a student. One wishes one could shut out the chit-chat (and yet that is also India) and somehow look inside these huts, spend time in their barren yards, touch the life there. A fatuous thought. Do I simply yearn for the exotic, for its shock, to tell myself I have now *been* in India, *really* seen it? I wonder, as I watch these hovels, which is Hindu, which Muslim. Once in a while, a Muslim shrine, a built-up grave, alone under a tree, whitewashed, flat upon the earth; and sometimes a Hindu shrine in a field, a little temple housing a deity. Would these simple people that we pass get up and kill their neighbours in a frenzy of hatred? What would they be like, at such times?

At Allahabad, Krishan Chander takes me out to the station platform, tells me of the claim to fame of this city: the Nehru family residence. He treats me to some guavas from a vendor's cart, a specialty of the city, he says; sweeter than the sweetmeats, he grins. Have you had them before? he asks. We had them in Africa, I tell him, though they were somewhat smaller there. They were considered a wild fruit and we ate them with red chillies and salt. Everything is bigger here.

Later on, a fellow passenger, a Jain mathematics professor making a pilgrimage, is bade goodbye. My host is ebullient, generous. "You Jains are hard-working," he patronizes in his innocent manner. "My father used to say the Jains have contributed the most to this country. We Brahmins haven't done much."

"You didn't have to, did you?" retorts one of the women in our party, evidently also a Jain, thus exposing a raw nerve.

There is so much of India, I tell myself. How does one get to it? I would like to reach out and touch it, it feels so close and familiar, yet there seems a glass cage around me.

Even I know when we reach a Bengali station. It is dawn, but there is noise, there is colour, there are signs of life outside of the railway. The station is Kharagpur, a junction for trains going south. Every wall is covered with slogans and messages, posted or painted in large black letters: calls to demonstrate in Calcutta or Delhi; Communist Party meetings; women's demonstrations; marches against communalism (as the Hindu-Muslim conflicts are called). The hammer and sickle is evident, comfortable in a way I've never noticed before. The ruling party in Bengal is communist. On the platform, the air is cool, humid; a pleasant feeling. There is the ubiquitous tea and newspaper stall. A beggar touches my feet;

somewhat surreptitiously I slip him a coin. Very soon three of them surround me, I race inside.

And then, when the train gets on its way, suddenly there comes a song in Bengali, from inside a curtained compartment nearby, so beautifully sung and spontaneous that a feeling of joy has stirred inside me. A morning raga on a train in Kharagpur station. So unbroken and clear is the voice, I fear that against my dearest wish it might be from a recording. I inquire. No, I am told. It's a real voice. Bengali homes have a long tradition of providing singing lessons for girls, Krishan Chander tells me proudly. He himself is Punjabi.

If I were looking for an epiphany of the genuine India, outside of the spoilt and pouting cameraman from Delhi who is going to film temples, outside of the city banter of the four foreign-travelled academic women across from me, outside of the homilies of my genial host, then this child's singing is it. I realize that I have to let India happen and respond to it accordingly; I cannot go anxiously searching for it, seeking nuance under every stone and behind every wall.

The train reaches our destination, Bhubaneswar, thirty hours after departure and some hours late, and we are met by frenzied local hosts and transported by taxi to our residences. I am to stay at the state guest house.

Bhubaneswar, Orissa: Premonitions of Fire in a Land of Temples

Orissa lies on the Bay of Bengal, south of West Bengal state. It is poor and rural, though more than two millennia ago the strong Kalinga kingdom had domain here, whose influence spread all the way across the sea to Java, Bali, Sumatra, and the Philippines, and perhaps, speculation has it, to East Africa, for the Sun Temple at Konark has a giraffe among its carvings of animals. The emperor Asoka attacked and conquered this land in 261 BC in a war so terrible, it is said, the rivers flowed red with blood. A remorseful Asoka soon after became a Buddhist.

The first impression of this capital city, Bhubaneswar, is dusty streets, brown earth in a glaring sunlight, stray dogs quietly scampering about, looking busy over, it seems, nothing.

There is overwhelming warmth shown me here, the visitor from abroad but one of us. People want to talk, confide, be of service. The young men are respectful, the older ones friendly, the women charming. Then there is something else in the air, like smoke from charred remains . . .

A sign in large letters high on the wall of a university residence: "OH MUSLIMS LOVE INDIA OR LEAVE INDIA." Who painted the sign? It could not have been done without being noticed. Why is it still there, day after day?

There is sadness and resignation at the state of the country. Many foreign delegates have stayed away because of the troubles. The federal government is blamed for failing to deal with them. An elderly professor wonders if Nehru had not made a mistake in his idealism, in his dreams of democracy. What does he mean, I wonder. A secular dictatorship as in China? A religious state like Pakistan?

Mohamed is a professor from Gujarat. I meet him at four in the morning when he knocks on my door, having just arrived. He has come to the wrong room, he is supposed to be sharing with Krishan Chander. The next morning Mohamed and I meet again. Instantly, past the first introduction, he starts talking to me in Kutchi, and we speak as if we have spoken this way all our lives. I was brought up speaking both Kutchi and Gujarati. A Muslim, Mohamed feels victimized, a little afraid. He is married to a Hindu woman and wants to remain aloof from the subject, but every time the troubles get mentioned, he cannot resist an outburst, for his is an excitable nature, with a lot of humour, I think, to hide the bitterness. He is from the Memon community and tells me in his typical manner that when he was little, in his village, he would be warned to stay away from the vicinity of the Khoja khano; for it was believed that the Khojas (my people) would catch a child and drive a nail through its head to drink its blood. We laugh, but I push back a nudge of discomfort inside me. I, too, was brought up with prejudices, though none as blood-red as this one.

The rest of the delegation from Gujarat arrives twenty-four hours late due to the riots. Oh yes, they say nonchalantly, Ahmedabad is still burning. And yes, they tell me, please come to Gujarat, but not on kite day, a Gujarati festival; it might provide just the opportunity for a riot.

Am I *not* supposed to be afraid? These are moments when I feel pushed away; on one hand I receive the confidences and treatment due an insider, one of them; then I become the outsider, someone who doesn't know and has to be protected, someone who hasn't lived close to the fire and felt the heat.

There exists a sentimental though powerful notion of this country as Mother India, an object of worship. The sixties' film of that name was the mega tear-jerker of all time, you had no heart if you emerged from the cinema dry-eyed. It tells the story of a mother's sacrifice for her children and her nation. Of the few scenes I have always been able to recall from this film, one is of a wedding, a beautiful bride bidding farewell to the paradise that has been her home, a gut-wrenching song in the background; another has the young woman, played by the actress Nargis, searching from village to village and door to door for her husband, singing a lament; and finally a less vivid but still unforgettable scene of a raging fire. Fire, that most potent and ubiquitous Indian symbol: fire of the Vedic sacrifice, the cremation, the wedding ritual, the bride-burning; and the fires of the riots. Fire, the agent of destruction.

"City people are like biscuits," he says. "They are the same everywhere."

He's a lecturer in nearby Berhampur, a newspaper man, an Oriya poet. A short stocky man in bush shirt, whose brown even teeth look as if they've had a dip in jaggery. He believes in folk motifs, he tells me, a people's poetry. He writes of the hungry and the displaced, of those who have to sell their children to survive in the arid, undeveloped waste of Orissa. "You should see a village, visit the tribals." "Tribals" are the aborigines of the country, also called the "Adivasis." I never knew such people existed. I had known of the canonical four Hindu castes, and then there were the Muslims, Sikhs, and Christians. Now these. Having given me his confidences and opinions for a good part of a day, my new friend finally takes me and a few others to a jatra, which he translates as "opera."

The jatra starts at eleven and goes on for most of the night. The reason for these hours, explains our host, is so that people who live far don't have to walk back home in the middle of the night. We have also acquired by now another host, a retired police inspector general. We've been told he comes from an accomplished literary family, his brother is a well-known dramatist in Delhi. It is perhaps because of him that we receive our VIP treatment, seats close to the stage.

The jatra is a travelling show, therefore thoroughly professional. It is also the poor people's night entertainment. It takes place inside a large tent on dusty ground on the city outskirts. As we arrive, there are crowds waiting to get inside. Outside the entrance: stalls of food, tea, paan, cigarettes. The crowd is predominantly men, youths or a little older, in shirts and trousers, a shawl draped across the shoulder for the chill. They are, I am told, working people, living mostly in shanties. Women are not present—except for the few young companions brought along—because someone has to stay behind to mind the children and the home. Among the middle classes, it appears, this mode of entertainment is not respectable. My host has moved up, but misses his village, has had to convince his wife that this nocturnal and lower-class outing is only because the visitors want to go.

Inside the tent are three stages in a row. The main one is in the centre, colourful and brilliant with lights, a diaphanous curtain going all around it. This arrangement allows all portions of the crowd a close view. Five thousand people sit in the tent, the chairs arranged around the three stages in sections separated by aisles. The seating is numbered, according to a code only the ushers seem to know.

Not many years ago the program consisted of a musical prelude followed by the main drama, which used to be based on the Indian epics, the *Mahabharata* and the *Ramayana*. But today the prelude consists of dances of the Hindi-film mode, very sexually suggestive with hip shakes and crotch thrusts from the boys (about twelve years old) directed at sweetly smiling girls. The audience whistles and shouts. The dance is on the main stage; thematic screen projections and solo dancing appear on the second stage, where the manager also makes loud announcements and introductions. The lit gangway between these two stages serves as the third performing space.

The drama now begins, with a dance to the spring season performed by girls in bright colours playing the roles of flowers; in the midst of this performance arrive the bees, boys dressed in black costumes with wings attached, fluttering from flower to flower. The bees and flowers dance together. Watching them, among an audience, is a greasy politician.

The plot is typical, filmic. Girl, poor parents, wealthy boy with unscrupulous father demanding dowry, the villain of the piece the politician-crook who wants the girl; a good police inspector under a corrupt police chief; and so on. The aficionados among us can see through this entertainment into the realistic message. The villain in such plots used to be the moneylender; now he is the politician. The crooked policeman is only too familiar. And the message of the dowry is clear.

Some of the girls in the dances are in fact boys. My host, grinning cheerfully, tells me they get regularly buggered by their managers. What to make of this, my mind racing through cries of child abuse? What to make of his grin: is he seeking male approval or is he apologetic? I don't think even he knows, perhaps he is testing my response.

We leave at 2:15, a little after the intermission.

On the last night of the conference it is decided to hold a mushaira, a session of poetry recitals. The readings, in English, on the terrace of a hotel earlier in the evening amidst vegetarian fare, have gone well but left a sense of incompleteness. Something stronger for the heart and soul is required, something more nourishing in Hindi and Punjabi. And so we gather in the square courtyard of the state-run guest house called Yatri Nivas. The rooms open directly into this space. No Mughal prince could have asked for a better venue for a mushaira than this mellow, subdued night under a star-studded sky. A circle is formed, everyone is invited to join in, including the Oriya watchman, who, deeply touched, goes to ask permission from his manager; it is denied. A contingent of high school teenagers, boys and girls, have arrived from Punjab and sit in the distance against the walls, eyeing us adults with bored sleepy looks on their faces.

And so: ghazals, kavitas, film songs. A line recited, a phrase offered up to savour; repeated for effect. The verse completed, ending with a repetition. The audience under stars and moon resay the words, the phrases they enjoy. The reciter becomes a poet among an audience of poets. It is wonderful to see how many of the poems and songs are commonly known among this audience, from Punjab, Delhi, Shimla, Gujarat. One of the teenagers, a boy, has surreptitiously drawn closer to our circle, charmed no doubt by poetry's magic. He is invited to recite. Unabashedly, and much to my surprise, he does so, two verses from a poem. Wah! they respond. Well done! They're my own, he says modestly.

A Punjabi scholar working in Gujarat sings a poem by Shiv Kumar Batalvi, perhaps (I am told) the greatest Punjabi poet of modern times. When he starts to sing, Raj Kumar closes his eyes, makes a gesture as if he were taking over the place, or entering some private space of his own. His voice is so rich, so full of feeling and melody, it is enough in itself. But after a few verses he is ready to quit: I see darkness, he says. A cave. Someone should assist you, it is suggested. Yes. Who but the boy gets up and approaches, and between the two—a shaky yet not unintimidated boy, and the master—they take it away.

A girl sings plaintively: I don't know you, and neither do you know me, but our love has happened.

It's an old song that I know. To whom does she sing those words?

This is still a land of romance, I tell myself, of song and love. Hearts still are given and taken away. It's a place of signals, with looks, and handkerchiefs, and small gestures. A place of laughter. How well do I recognize these, how utterly have I lost them. The cynicism is reserved for politicians, among this middle-class crowd, the irony for foreign consumption.

The Jagannath temple complex in Puri is one of the four major dhams, or holy centres of Hinduism. Even the self-proclaimed non-believers must have a go at it, get the darshanas, if not for them-selves then at least for their neighbours, their friends, their mothers. The reigning deity of this temple is Jagannath, Lord of the Universe, the All-Seeing One, worshipped by followers of Vishnu and Shiva, Buddhists and Jains, and even Muslims. In the middle of every July, pilgrims pour into town for the annual chariot festival, in which chariots forty feet high and more, red and yellow, bearing Jagannath and his sister and brother, are conveyed in a symbolic procession round the universe. But it is January and we are not so lucky as to witness such a spectacle.

Shoes are not allowed in the temple, and some therefore alight from our two buses enthusiastic and already barefoot, and walk the grimy, sandy, squelchy way to the temple. It's a longish walk, along a busy commercial street crowded with pedestrians and pil-grims and lined with shoe stands where one may remove one's shoes and take a token as a receipt. Only Hindus are allowed into the temple, a sign says, but who is to check and how? What exactly is a Hindu? I have not denied any Hindu god.

The temples are famous for their intricate architecture, patient work of decades, details into which one could get easily lost. But few here are conscious of this, the atmosphere is one of a fete—no, a market—crowds of worshippers, gangs of hustlers. It seems like an offence, to the outsider, that a visit to such historic sites, national monuments, iconographic representations of mankind's spiritual strivings, should be greeted by beggars and hustlers, self-proclaimed guides, who simply cling and cling, are not, are never, shaken off until the end of the visit when you get back on your bus.

And then the sheer uncanniness of it: amidst the sordidness, the hustling, the thieving, the bargaining with the priests, a professor covers her head, goes for, tolerates, the darshana—because she has to; something deserves respect, only she can tell what that something is for her. The humility, the grace of such a worshipper is astounding, before the Brahmins with the blessings, and the icon of Shiva, and the attendants who make space for her by pushing others aside because she's a "Madam," a respectable lady, who has brought rupees, and they are merely the poor supplicants with nothing but endless woes.

A beggar woman calls out, Help a poor woman, Bhagwan will give you a boy. A boy and girl in rags, of about five, come to beg. The heart melts. What will you buy with the money? Come on, tell, my companion, who's just prayed, says in mock sternness. The two break into fits of giggles. They get a rupee. As we walk away, a pulling match. The boy gets to hold the coin.

Back in the bus, a box of prasad arrives, sweetmeats blessed at the temple. Yes, I remember, it has to be taken with the right hand. One crumbles in my hand: an exploding ladoo, I exclaim. Everyone laughs. But the spilt crumbs have to be carefully collected and thrown away, not stepped upon. There are some who would not even throw them away but consume them; but this is an educated crowd.

Orissa is a land of temples, profusely ornamented on the outside and plain and dark inside. They were built between the sixth and thirteenth centuries AD, by artisans who remain unknown. Bhubaneswar alone boasts more than five hundred temples of this period. The Rajarani temple is a tourist site, surrounded by a well-tended lawn. A magnificent temple of red sandstone, completely covered on the exterior with intricately carved nymphs inside stone niches; but it is unused, there is no deity here. We take walks and group photographs, undisturbed, unmolested. The sense of mystery within the hollow, empty interior is deep, the imagination free to roam. A short walk away is the Lingaraja temple complex, dedicated to the deity Shiva. Outside, shoe and prasad stalls, catering to the pilgrims. This is a shrine in use and crowded. Inside the compound a single priest also accepts homage to the god Vishnu.

One can visit temple after temple here. At a simple one in the middle of a busy street, two women at a shrine, eyes beseeching, pleading to a god. This human sight, so private a moment so publicly displayed, is the one that ultimately touches the most, leaves one humbled, feeling ignorant, superfluous. Universal mysteries aside, what domestic calamity, what private problems do these two bring? How would they be resolved? How mysterious, unreachable, the secret pains of another heart. I, too, recall women of my family, similarly beseeching, utterly helpless (they thought); some resolutions come, but never that elusive happiness, even in old age.

Scenes outside the temple at Puri·

A boy walking, his hands thrust inside his shorts, clutching at his crotch; a mangy dog limping along with bloody testicles. In the crowd outside the temple, outside the curio shops and tea stalls and clothing stores for visitors, a pigtailed girl of about eighteen in trouser suit weaving in and out on a bicycle, her school books on the carrier at the back. A scene so much from my own experience growing up in Dar es Salaam, I feel I could trace the rest of the girl's day.

A Sense of the Private: The Governor's Special Quota

At this point I would have preferred to make Calcutta my next stop. It is the closest large city. I have a recommendation from Toronto to a literary, not an academic, group. I suspect I will see a more intellectual, more left, and certainly very different crowd from the career academics I have so far been with. It seems like time to get that other perspective—a sharp jolt as it were, and a different, more open view of what is happening in India. With the happy, satisfied crowd I am with, the sense of emergency and crisis seems far away.

But Trivandrum, Kerala, needs me; there are two emissaries from the south to tell me that, to beseech me to come; there is a workshop there they would like me to attend. Trivandrum it has to be, except that with the airline strike on, trains are booked solid, weeks in advance. There seems no hope. But in India, as I am learning, there is always a way.

One of the guests happens to know the Governor of Orissa's aide-de-camp personally. Off we drive to Government House, but we find there that the ADC has gone home for lunch. With great pains, a sentry and a woman, perhaps a secretary, direct us to the eminence's house. After a few wrong turns we find it. As we walk up a garden path, the ADC is putting his relatives into his Maruti wagon, to take them to the train station. He is a tall and youngish military man, a captain, and a north Indian. My case is explained to him: foreign visitor, a conference in Trivandrum. When does he want to go? the ADC asks. Tomorrow, they tell him, by the Coromandel Express; he has to give the inaugural lecture. The ADC could have hummed and hawed, he could have asked to see my passport. But he simply writes a chit, tells my companions, Buy a ticket and take it to the station master; I'm on my way there, I'll meet you.

And so, within an hour, a ticket on the Coromandel Express, on the Governor of Orissa's Emergency Quota.

Bhubaneswar–Coimbatore

I remember musing, many years ago when I was a student and would often find myself between cities on a train in North America, that it could go on forever, this journey, for all I cared, I could give my life to this long moment of rolling and roaring, of endless rhythm. I was a displaced person, like Zeno's arrow going some place else even as I was stationary in another, and a train ride vivified the feeling of constant motion, going somewhere endlessly.

Trains here in India are the next best thing to endless constant motion. The Puri Express of a few days before, though it seems months away now, so intense have been my experiences, was some nine hundred miles long, thirty hours in duration. This present journey is even longer, from the northeast to the bottom of India, Bay of Bengal to the Arabian Sea. What better way than to sit in a train responding to the ancestral homeland, every scene and every moment full of meaning and possibility, blooming epiphany? The only torment: the wet washrooms.

A woman sleeps in the seat-bunk across from me, her husband, without a sleeping berth of his own, sits near her feet. She hardly says a word, doesn't eat, even when she sits up. Eat, he says several times. She declines. A tear in her eye. Why is she crying? No, I realize, she seems to have a cold. Finally she opens her box, brings out puris, pickle, and something else—but I give them their privacy, I look away.

The Coromandel goes up to Madras, arrives twenty-four hours after departure, in the evening. From here I have to catch another train, on which I don't have a reservation. The station is teeming with people, India in motion. You have to know where you are going, you have to have a ticket. It all looks hopeless. With me is an escort, on his way to Trivandrum, who has a reservation on ordinary second class. Out of desperation for my case we take a rickshaw to the bus station; perhaps I can catch a bus. The bus station, too, is packed. We return to the train station. My companion, Hussein, goes to look around, comes back with the information, having peeked at the reservation chart for the train, that four berths are vacant in second-class AC. Get into one of them, he instructs me, and I do just that. We encounter the TC, ticket collector, and declare my Emergency Quota status. But the Orissa governor's influence does not extend this far. First-class passengers have priority, says the TC, what can he do? Hussein goes away with him to have a chat in private and returns. Go and give him fifty rupees, he advises me. Tell him it's for his trouble. I go outside on the platform, where the TC awaits, and mumble something about the emergency quota and hand him the fifty rupees. The TC is embarrassed, says, If you need anything let me know. And on the way, he does inquire after me, in the morning brings me a cup of coffee.

In the middle of the night he brings a woman to the berth opposite mine. A young woman in red sari, with a child, and a family elsewhere in the compartment that comes to see her occasionally. Perhaps they, too, have paid off the TC. A young man comes several times—husband or brother? Later in the night a young woman sits on my berth, at the edge, and watches over the girl. Definitely not a sister, I think, she is too formal; and definitely not her husband's sister. Must be a bhabhi, her brother's wife. It's the girl's *own* family. The young woman leaves after a while.

The girl's brought her bedding with her, and neatly makes up the bed, and makes a bed for the baby, too—nice, frilly, pink and yellow with a plastic sheet. I know exactly how she's going to sleep, I tell myself. On her side, back towards me, the baby (a quiet, obliging type) in the concave in her front.

But first she feeds the child; I turn away. Later, after one more visitor to inquire after her, she prepares to sleep. Shall we turn off the light? I ask. She does it. A relation soon comes by and partly draws the curtain to her berth.

There is a certain humbleness bred out of a common humanity that one experiences in such situations. How in close proximity one does one's thing, retaining a sense of modesty and dignity, a sense of private self. The woman feeds the child some more, on her side, then sleeps on her back.

I'm trying to say that now I'm in India. And I feel an empathy I cannot fully understand.

"Eleven Burnt Alive in Bombay"—headline, *Deccan Herald.*

And so, somewhere, the "disturbance," or the "communal violence," goes on, the fire rages. Once more a glimpse of the dark side behind the warm embrace, the familiarity. An unease descends upon the soul. There is a real mystery to these mob violences, something truly unfathomable.

We get off at Coimbatore to change trains. The station has rooms for resting, each with a bed, a shower, and a toilet, at one hundred rupees a day. My companion, Hussein, finds it scandalous that we should pay that much for only an hour or two. But at this point I'm willing to pay five times that much, though I don't tell him this. After a shower and coffee I tell him I'm ready to go the twelve more hours to our destination. It's been thirty-six hours since we left Bhubaneswar and I don't know whether I am coming or going, what day of the week it is, Toronto seems far far away.

The station is crowded with dozens of men who look like some kind of mendicants: clad in black dhotis going round the waist and black shirts, with marks on the forehead. They are all barefoot and carry cloth bundles which they tend to hold on their heads. Some have bells tinkling at the waist, most also carry water flasks; two exceptions among them wear trousers instead of dhoti, and two others have canvas shoulder bags. Sometimes a line of them passes by, chanting. I'm told they come from all places and are on their way to a pilgrimage to Lord Ayyappan, a form of the god Vishnu.

Coimbatore–Trivandrum

I did not catch the name of this train, but it is crowded. No space, says the TC. People get in anyway, even find places to sit. I feel bold enough by now to do the same. On the train from Delhi, and later the one from Bhubaneswar, sitting with strangers, facing each other for hours, watching and being watched all the time, I felt intolerably overexposed. Now I feel I can sit anywhere. Almost.

The pilgrims, it appears, cannot find seats or a place to pause on the train, lines of them pass through our compartment, clutching their bundles, looking very cheerful. The scenery outside is pleasant—the Western Ghats in the distance to my right, a lot of lush greenery all around, with a profusion of coconut and banana trees. Colourful yellow, blue, and pink houses. Not much sign of the kind of poverty of the north, not close to the track at least. Halfway to Trivandrum, the pilgrims all get off, hang around the station platform. From here they will proceed on foot to a pilgrimage site up a mountain. As I watch, a few of them take to the adjacent tracks to attend to nature, facing away. One can only look away in return.

Scootering through the Countryside in Search of Lost History

"Our Martyrs are the fountainhead of our sorrows," says a somewhat puzzling slogan written in English on a public fence. There are signs and slogans all over Trivandrum; as in Bengal, the hammer and sickle is prominently present. Kerala has had elected communist governments on and off for many years, although at present it's Congress that holds office. The student movement is a force to be reckoned with. It will provide the next generation of political leaders and has to be indulged. Currently they are holding the university vice-chancellor under siege in his residence; only the police can see him, important business (such as that relating to the workshop I am attending) has to be smuggled in to him. He has been charged with possessing a fraudulent degree from Sussex. A previous vice-chancellor, who returned from America to take up the post, I am told, died of a heart attack. Such are the strains of this office.

Kerala is a long stretch of lush green land between the Arabian Sea and the Western Ghats; next to it, in the east, lies Tamil Nadu. The landscape is dominated by coconut trees, rivers, and canals; the language spoken is Malayalam. This is the real south; Hindi is almost a foreign tongue, and the English spoken is hard to understand. I was asked, upon arrival, to see a Yum Yum Thomas, influential journalist; it took me two days of asking and considerable embarrassment before I realized that M. M. Thomas was meant. There is a certain reserve in the people. Whereas in the north people come at you, tell you things, are curious about you, thrust their books into your hands, here they hold back. This reserve they attribute to their sense of personal pride. It is for me a little like going from Brussels to Antwerp, as I happened to do once, many years ago. But there are no beggars here to touch your feet or thrust their hands at you inside a rickshaw. The long-distance STD booths are full in the evenings, with people making calls worth a few rupees to one wonders where, until one is told that all villages are connected to telephone lines. Traffic is orderly; unlike in Delhi, cars actually drive behind one another, they wait at stop signs, and signal before turning. And there is more colour here, houses look freshly painted, blue, pink, yellow, with attention to detail in their construction.

Because it faces the Arabian Sea, Kerala has ancient links with Arabia. The population is divided between Hindus, Muslims, and Christians; one is taken with pride to the city centre, where a mosque, a temple, and a church stand facing each other. The first Christians were converted by Saint Thomas in the first century. But the recent disturbances in the north have made people conscious of who they are, in a way they weren't before, they say.

The slogans in evidence everywhere in the city are due to a national students' congress that is about to open. On the afternoon of the opening parade, the city promises to come to a standstill; ordinary people start off early for their homes, to leave the city centre to the students. I take up an invitation by Hussein to go to his home for dinner (and therefore spend a night there). He is honoured, and so am I.

On the way to the village by bus, we pass dozens of loud honking buses racing to the city full of students shouting, "Inqalab Zindabad," Long live the Revolution!

We stop at a town where my host teaches at a small college. It dispenses B.A.s. A somewhat bleak place, looking more like a slum apartment building—a block with dirty yellow paint, no grounds, many windows. I am taken to the principal, introduced in the most effusive terms. The office: long empty tables arranged in a U, at the head of which sits the weary-looking principal with no work in front of him. He's tired simply being there. He's not very old, has been recently transferred here from the city. His is a government job. At one end of the almost empty room are bundles of paper, tied with string and piled up; I understand from a similar pile at the University of Kerala, though upon a table there, that this is the filing system, a century old, perhaps even regressed since then. The only prominent items in the principal's room: a row of five formal photographs of former principals on one wall; on another wall, Gandhi, Nehru, and Swami Vivekananda. As I sit somewhat uncomfortably at a table, there takes place a long exchange between Hussein and the principal. The outcome is that the principal signs five copies of a letter which turns out to grant three weeks' unpaid leave to Hussein for having participated in the conference in Orissa. Hussein is very disappointed; he had been granted permission, commended for his initiative to further his qualifications; and now this bureaucratic betrayal. He had hoped my presence would convince the principal to cooperate, but that strategy has obviously failed. He has only lost face.

After lunch—the students have filled up most of the restaurants—we take another bus, to Hussein's local town, Varkala. Here he picks up his scooter parked at a friend's house, and we ride it to his village ten miles away. He parks outside a shop and takes me home.

The village consists of a small row of shops on one side of the road, a few side streets, and across the road some houses scattered

next to the beach. To get to his house, which is on the beach side, we walk along a narrow path at the edge of an aqueduct said to be built by the British, a short stream at which some womenfolk are washing. At the end of the path we walk up onto the bank, cutting across an uneven landscape full of coconut trees and other vegetation, until we reach the house. In the old days, Hussein explains, one was considered to have a lower status if one's house was close to the highway.

The coconuts, he says, bring in one thousand rupees a month, a considerable sum. The land belongs to his wife through her father, the adjacent land with an empty house belongs to his sister, who is in the Gulf.

The traditional occupations of the village are selling copra and coir—both coconut products—and fishing. As we look upon the Arabian Sea, the beach is empty, there are a few boats in the distance. They are from a Christian village up the road, Hussein says. Nowadays the fishermen of his village—generally men of over forty years in age—fish from 4 a.m. to 8 a.m., and collect some two hundred rupees, of which they spend half on occasional household expenses, half on drink.

And yes, a truth emerges: most young men are away working in the Gulf at low-status jobs but earning high wages by local standards. Most of the wives and children remain behind. The men return once a year on leave. A lot of money comes in (the monthly wage there is two thousand dirhams, or sixteen thousand rupees; a lecturer here makes five thousand rupees) and gets squandered on useless consumer items. Any problems? You can't buy fish, he says. You can't buy land. But people build larger houses, "better than you would see in New York." A mosque has almost been completed on his wife's property, using donations from Gulf-earned money. It is an impressive, towering, gleaming white structure with domes and arches, like some alien spaceship looking upon, from the top of a hill, the ramshackle village.

Through this hill site, the local British administration had started building a tunnel. But when the workers reached a certain spot, now on the grounds of the mosque, they came upon a body in sitting posture; the land around was soaked in blood. The tunnel was quickly diverted. A shrine was later constructed where the body was buried. The mosque, almost completed, stands at the site of a landslide. But the land, according to local belief, is hallowed and free from the danger of another slide—which the unbeliever, however, has no hesitation in predicting.

I am interested in the history of the community—their conversion to Islam, their folklore regarding this event, their indigenous responses to Islam. Muslim communities in Gujarat, Sindh, Punjab, even Bengal, I am aware, have their own folklore and songs, their saints and shrines. There are long syncretistic traditions in those parts. The subject has interested me, has become a passion, and so I ask my questions brashly. Hussein is somewhat at a loss—it's something he doesn't quite know about. He takes me to the mullah at the new mosque.

The mullah, in white robe and cap, has a black beard and appears quite young when one begins to focus on his face, which is very fair. To answer my question, he tells us the story of the first Muslims who came to Kerala, at about the time of the Prophet (in the sixth century). As these visitors arrived on shore, the local people offered them coconuts to eat. Instead of straightaway accepting the gift, the shaikhs asked the people if the coconuts belonged to them to give away. The locals were impressed by this response. Are you from the Prophet across the sea? they asked. Yes, the visitors replied. What is the proof, then? At this, the Arabs pointed up above to the sky. When the locals looked up, they saw the crescent moon broken into two, a sign which according to Islamic legend had appeared to the Prophet himself in Arabia. And so Islam spread in Kerala.

I ask the mullah about local Muslim literature, in Malayalam. He speaks of translations from Arabic. In them, he says, nothing has been changed since the time of the Prophet. To him that obviously makes them purer, better. Arabic Islam is the purest; next comes the translated one. Indigenous responses are adulterated. I cannot help thinking that unless these Muslims have their own responses to their lives here, they will always be out of the mainstream, watching wistfully as their neighbours carry out their exuberant celebrations and festivals. Many of these festivals, like Onam, as Hussein tells me, they do still celebrate. But what do they mean to them?

Hussein is as aware of my dissatisfaction as he is flattered by my interest; and disconcerted by his ignorance. The story we heard about the arrival of the Arabs was set elsewhere on the Kerala coast, it does not say anything about his own community here. After tea, therefore, he takes me around. We scooter through town and countryside looking for someone Hussein says who knows some village history—the first conversions, the local lore, and so on. We are directed to the Rotary Club, a shack, which is closed.

We drive around, and he shows me some of the newer houses outside the town, built out of Gulf money. We alight at the town centre, inquire about the party we are looking for, but nobody knows where he is. The town is quite lively in the evening, buses plying the road, dropping passengers off, men standing around, everyone known to each other. At around eight, all go home, as do we.

This search for local Muslim history and lore has turned out not only fruitless but also somewhat disquieting. Hussein promises to send me some information by mail. That very promise says a lot. I suspect the conversions in this area to be recent, class and caste reactions, a seeking out to break the bonds of ancient barriers—and what better way than to deny everything and start afresh? But what to replace the everyday culture with? What songs to sing?

We return to the village on the scooter, my heart in my mouth, a bus in front of us and another behind. The shops are closed. Hussein puts the scooter in an empty store he rents, pulling out the door panels in the same way they did in my grandmother's shop in Dar es Salaam long ago.

Hussein's wife is a shy woman, and bigger than him. She hardly talks, makes gestures to him from another room that he easily translates for me. Even as we eat at the table, he and I, the food appears from the kitchen area brought by the son. I sense a certain embarrassment in my host.

(To eat with the hand: one only has to do it once to feel comfortable with it again, it is quite natural, easily reacquired. But there is no point in trying to eat curd and condiments—served in their separate plates—the way they do here, in one swift motion following the helping of rice and chicken, with the quickness of an assembly-line operation, the flick of a hand or finger; and trying to roll down a boll of rice to the palm and involving the whole hand is a habit that's been lost for more than a generation and had better stay that way.)

By this time I'm wearing a lunghi and borrowed shirt; we sit watching news; he shows me paragraphs from Raja Rao's *The Serpent and the Rope.*

To get a job in a Muslim college, Hussein tells me, he was asked to give a fifteen-thousand-rupee "donation" to the institution, which he could not afford. So he had worked in an office until he found a job at a government college. Now he's doing a Ph.D. on the work of Michael Ondaatje. He's desperately looking for a copy of *The English Patient.* Ondaatje, I tell myself, should feel honoured to be the object of study of this dedicated academic who's just lost three weeks' pay in pursuit of his study.

The older son is in college, studying botany—not out of interest but because he had no choice. A more popular subject would have required an unaffordable "donation." The middle child, a girl, goes to the village school, where the language of instruction is Malayalam. The youngest, a boy, goes three miles away to an English medium school and to perhaps better prospects than his sister. All the children have Malayalam names, unlike their father and mother, who have Arabic ones; one begins to wonder.

Morning: crows crowing, rooster calling; waves pounding on the shore as the tide comes in barely a hundred yards away; coconut leaves rustling; a song on the radio welcoming dawn, another comparing dawn to the child Krishna. A young rooster makes bold to walk in through the open front door, looks left and right, walks out.

It is a beautiful, peaceful, rural scene. My host contemplates leaving it, he's told me, wants to sell it to buy a house in urban Trivandrum. He feels embarrassed by this rural setting, the village life. He has academic aspirations. How long, I tell myself, before someone builds a tourist hotel here?

Morning ablutions: cleaning teeth with charcoal powder, the kind we bought back home for economic reasons, called Monkey Brand, made in India. A shred of coconut leaf to clean the tongue.

A frog leaps out of the bathroom.

It is not easy, after so many years, to get used to getting up from a crouch in the privy.

In the morning the wife, still extremely shy, comes to say goodbye. It's all smiles and shakes of the head. She asks me to enquire to my mother, my wife—meaning, in local usage, convey regards to them.

While Bombay Burns: The Calcutta Intellectuals

Bombay burns, the newspapers tell us. Riots rampage through the city. My hosts there have sent a message to Trivandrum: Don't send him. If he comes, it's at his own risk. My hosts in Baroda, Gujarat: Under no circumstances come before the kite festival (which could be used as a pretext for violence). I go to Delhi by plane.

It is a singular piece of irony for me that my father saw Bombay only through a porthole; I see it also from a porthole, of a plane, as we fly over it. I see it desolate, the streets and highways empty, except for a few places with thin, tentative crowds.

From Delhi to Calcutta I also travel by plane, and learn that the express train on which I had originally made my booking has crashed, with a few people dead.

A local communist party official has been murdered—the body had lain outside in the street the whole night before police arrived—so traffic on the way to the airport is at a standstill. My host Pranab has had to walk part of the way to fetch me. It takes us a while to get a taxi, and a long time to get to town.

Calcutta: one has heard so much about it. But this stop is going to be short, I'm here only because I made a prior arrangement to come. Smoky, foggy, wet, grimy streets that seem weirdly Dickensian. Cabbies who have their own ideas about where they want to go, so that where you go, and if you go anywhere at all, seems to depend on their whims and convenience. Nowhere else have I seen cab drivers so reluctant.

Calcutta is the intellectual capital. Book fairs here are attended by the hundreds of thousands. This is the state of Rabindranath Tagore and Satyajit Ray. At Independence a large part of Bengal broke away to form East Pakistan, later Bangladesh. Pranab is a professor of literature and has translated African writers into Bengali. Middle aged and somewhat ailing, he is simple, modest, and generous, but possessed with an unsettling intransigence in his views, a readiness to condemn. He arranges a meeting for me with fellow intellectuals.

A smoke-filled room, young people sitting on the floor, the scene very reminiscent of a campus radical group of the sixties or early seventies. If the mood in the rest of the country is resigned fatalism—What is happening to the country? Times are bad, but they will go away—here it is, There is no hope. It is finished. The end is coming. *We told you so!*

They are the opposition. They have always been the opposition. A young professor commands the room, rake-thin and dark, smoking incessantly, hoarse-voiced—a rising star, with an attitude of, *See! We know the types: fascists, Nazis, racists, the bourgeoisie*—and possessing a sense about him of gloating at the troubles wracking the nation, at having been on the right side all the time. This could be a room from Dostoevsky's *The Possessed.* With someone like him, it's all or nothing. You either speak his language or you don't. If you speak it, you have to know his political facts, and moreover have the right interpretations. With him he has two chelas, students simmering with the anxiety of wanting to say the appropriate thing, quickly and sharply enough to impress, and the exhilaration of having a cause, at being on the right side of things, on the path of the good ones.

Of course there is a brilliance here, compared to the simple career-mindedness that I've seen elsewhere. These people here are not merely climbers, with wives or families to answer to, status to aspire to. They do not yearn for trips abroad. They are well informed, up-to-date not only on the news but also on global events and history; and they know literature. This is Calcutta. They can quote freely from Bengali writings (as well as Derrida and Foucault), and unlike Indians elsewhere lapse easily into the mother tongue in front of a nonspeaker even as they apologize for this; they relish the language, love it, so it's easy to understand, excuse the lapse. And there is a genuine sympathy for the oppressed: after all, there exists a caste system, and the multitudes are poor beyond imagination.

But with them there are no two ways. The world is divided neatly between the oppressed and the oppressors. There is right, and there is wrong. They are on the side of the right. They see fast approaching a fascist government under the BJP, the right-wing Bharatiya Janata Party. I remind them that a recent issue of *India Today* had warned of just that possibility. The media, they proclaim, were the first to embrace the BJP. There is no room for adjustments: the media belong to right-wing elements. Hinduism is an oppressive religion; it allows the caste system to flourish; its most sacred book, the *Gita*, justifies war; it has fascistic ideas and its proponents massacred the Buddhists in the past, and now are oppressing the Muslims and other minorities.

It occurs to me that the Muslims are merely a handy cause for these rebels of the privileged classes. They are too convenient, and I say so. And moreover, the Muslims are a diverse lot, culturally, socially, economically, historically. The Muslims do not want to be patronized by the Calcutta intellectuals.

From the perspective of this smoke-filled room, the whole country seems to be rotten. I cannot help thinking that the despair of these people is superficial, that they seem to be celebrating.

But I leave Calcutta not untouched by that mood of imminent disaster. All weekend, details of the violence in Bombay keep pouring in through the newspapers. It is worse than I thought, worse than anyone had thought. Here I quote straight from these newspaper accounts, because it seems to me nothing more needs to be said.

Last week we saw the future in Bombay and it was a kaleidoscope brimming with blood. An inquisition launched against India's Muslims for a series of crimes beginning with 700 years of imperial rule and ending with the usurpation of street space for Friday prayers took on a fresh range of practical dimensions: raw communal violence with almost computerised targeting, very well defined economic aggression and ethnic cleansing. . . .

The fascist cross was marked on every Muslim door and there was escape for neither the anonymous toiler condemned to a life of darkness of 15 square feet of a chawl nor the influential senior executive of a multinational floating in 3000 square feet of the sky. Both became victims of a trapped identity.

The Daily Telegraph, January 17, 1993

The intensity with which the rioters have murdered people and destroyed property suggests that the violence was premeditated and carefully designed to look like intercommunal hysteria.

Indian Express, January 17, 1993

MERCHANTS OF DEATH CAME IN AN AMBULANCE

Surat (Gujarat) 12:30 p.m.

An ambulance van labelled "Emergency Hospital" came to a screeching halt near Vishramnagar locality on the slum-dominated Ved Road. One by one emerged from the van the merchants of death who were within hours to burn alive some 32 innocent people. . . .

Around 6 p.m., having laid the dragnet, the group suddenly raced menacingly towards some houses in Vishramnagar. Swords, daggers, kerosene lamps, hammers and lathis in their hands. Some of them held the residents while others dragged out whatever was contained in the house and threw it in large pits. . . .

In the presence of scores of slum-dwellers, some 32 residents of Vishramnagar were stabbed and pushed into pyres in the pits. Some were torched and pushed into a manhole.

Indian Express, January 1993

Surat mobs strip women as camera unit films rapes.

Indian Express, December 1992

The enormity of what happened still escapes the city and its residents.

There is Mr. D. A. Desai. A retired judge of the Supreme Court. A Surti by birth and inclination. He laments: "This year I simply could not bring myself to sending New Year greetings. The screams of women raped are still ringing in my ears."

An IPS officer. A veteran of riots in Ahmedabad and Baroda. He simply shudders: "I have never seen atrocities of this kind visited by one group of human beings on another."

At a primary school, the headmaster pretends to be puzzled about why the Muslim students have not returned to the classrooms.

When the arsonists were done for the day, they had 32 victims to their credit. All first killed, then dumped in a nullah and torched. One school teacher recalled how a young girl was raped, then an iron rod shoved up her vagina, and, finally, killed.

The Times of India, January 16, 1993

Acid Bulbs, Ghalib, and Sweetmeats: The Homeland

Paschim Express: New Delhi–Baroda
A gentle rhythmic ride, the roll of the train, the rumble. One would not trade this for any plane trip. The compartment has four berths,

with curtains, night lights . . . such palatial luxury after the night-marishly slow, crowded, and dirty Toofan Express I had to take from Calcutta, because the express route had been closed due to an accident. In the adjoining compartment men and women, young couples, chatting and laughing; an atmosphere of togetherness that for a group makes such a ride so memorable. I feel uncontrollably happy.

The young couple with child, in the two berths across from me, are on their way to Bombay. The child is a boy, his name Aman Kumar. "All boys are kumars," I say stupidly in a sentimental moment.

In this AC compartment are young families, each with a child, speaking combinations of Hindi and English to their offspring: How are you? What is your name? Would you like a biscuit? Usko kaho, Thank you.

Aren't you afraid to go to Bombay? I ask the couple. Oh, it's all right now, they say. Bombay can't stay closed for long. What kind of family are they, I wonder, to feel so confident? The wife is a teacher. I can see my Calcutta friends sneering: Government-wallahs, rich folks, police and army connections—nothing happens to such as these. True, most likely. Yet I can't help empathizing with this young couple with infant, can't help wishing them well.

With me is a bureaucrat from Canada. He is formerly from India. He has on a newly bought Indian-made leather jacket. A bargain, he says, you can't beat local prices for leather goods. Four times cheaper than the same stuff in Canada. He makes sure everyone around knows where he is from. There is of course a practical advantage to this, it does make a difference wherever you go. Diligently he eats only the fruit and biscuits he's brought with him, holds onto the bottled water as to dear life, doesn't touch train food or tea. For him India is old hat, he is grateful to have escaped its strangling bureaucracy, which he experienced while teaching in a college; he feels no nostalgia.

"A proud Canadian," he now calls himself, "from the best country in the world."

I am going to the state of my ancestors, Gujarat, where people speak a language I speak. How do I feel? On the train I strain my ears for Gujarati. I see a man counting beads, tasbih. A Hindu or a Muslim, fundamentalist or just pious and tolerant? It is in that state that the violence has raged for the longest time, in a manner that defies reason, defies everything I thought Gujarat was: the land of Gandhi, of peaceful though clever shopkeepers. At the stations where we stop, I feel a tremor of discomfort, fear. How am I looked upon? Would people see me as something other than what I am and feel, what label would they put on me? There are reports of trains stopped, people being stripped to check if they were one or the other, circumcised or not, Muslim or Hindu; then slaughtered or let go.

And so, in spite of my euphoria, I feel a trauma after all.

In Baroda station I am received warmly by Mohamed and Raj Kumar, both of whom I had met in Orissa, a little more than two weeks before; we now meet like old friends. There had been some anxiety about my making it, ever since I got diverted from Trivandrum to Calcutta via Delhi.

Whereas Delhi seems to run on the tiny Indian-made Maruti cars, Baroda seems to run in large part on scooters. I am taken to my room in an auto-rickshaw.

Baroda

Mohamed takes me to a shopping centre to meet a young man who is a Khoja Ismaili like me. It is late afternoon, and the three of us head by rickshaw towards the khano, the prayer hall. We pass through a busy street, apparently the most prone to riots, first the Hindu section and then the Muslim section. It is difficult not to feel a twinge of nervousness, imagine being attacked, when told that Baroda, known for its excellent university, is one of the cities most prone to communal violence.

In the Khoja community of Surat, the young man says, some eighty people were killed: a pregnant woman made to watch her entire family being slaughtered, then left alive with her two arms hacked off; a boy of five, head smashed with a field-hockey stick; and so on with the horrors . . .

I ask him what they actually do if they see a mob approach. Do they simply pray? Watch? What? Surely the young men have provisions for defence, as young men would everywhere?

He could understandably have refused to answer, but he tells me.

We make acid bulbs, he says, bottles filled with acid and topped with a wick, and we throw them when the mobs approach. If that doesn't work, then about four or five of the young men go out with knives and swords. It has been a miracle so far, he adds, that four or five youths have been able to defend their area.

The khano is modest—a grey concrete square block of a place. It is Thursday, the poorest members of the community are present. A girl recites a ginan, in Gujarati. I notice that it is sung to a different tune from the one I am familiar with, though it does not sound completely strange. A young man stands up to offer a prayer in Gujarati—O Lord, bring peace and prosperity to this nation—a prayer almost identical to one we recited in East Africa. Finally a prayer in Arabic, in a peculiarly Gujarati accent, recited by a girl while the people sit cross-legged on the floor.

The mukhi, the leader of the congregation, invites Mohamed (who waited outside the khano, being from another sect) and me to his home. It is a modest bungalow in a housing colony behind the grey khano. Both the khano and the colony face an open side street that leads to the main thoroughfare on which we came.

This area is safe, says the mukhi to Mohamed, who of course knows the city and its ways. Behind the colony is an entirely Muslim area. Behind that is a Hindu area. But the area is so open, says Mohamed, you could be attacked from the street; which is exactly what I am thinking. They can't do it, says the mukhi, and I wonder at his confidence. His wife brings water, but Mohamed cautions me against drinking it—not from a bottle, it might be unsafe for a visitor. But how to refuse a drink of water, and from a mukhi? I drink some.

–

One always deplores violence, one shudders, but one has also become cold to it. It happens *there*, on the other side of the television screen, to other people. To see it so close, however, among people so close, is different . . . Can I not shrug off this kind of bestiality, this brutalization of innocents, as something happening *there*, without involving my feelings in it? But after all I did come here, saw it as a kind of return, could identify with so many things: so do I simply shun, reject as not mine, what I cannot cope with, while accepting gratefully what I can? Aren't we at some level connected, this mukhi, this other young man, and I? If my family had stayed here, what would I have become, a victim or a thug? A defender with acid bulbs and swords?

I say as much at a seminar I have come ostensibly to give here in Baroda. Let me tell you something about myself. I was brought up Gujarati, to some degree. We spoke the language, we played dandia raas during festivals. Sure, we had communal fights, but at the level of fisticuffs, or competition in business, cricket, academic achievement. This is the first time I have been in a place where Gujarati is the main language. I came here expecting to take back mithai, sweetmeats, with me, this being the traditional way, when you would upon your return present a little of the mithai to neighbours and relatives. But I came to Gujarat actually feeling afraid. *This* in the land of Gandhi?

Perhaps I get a bit carried away.

Is it possible to sound boorish talking about senseless violence and butchery? I think in India it's possible. Such barbarity as I have read and heard about seems part of accepted life. Don't worry, someone told me my first day here, the violence is elsewhere, a couple of miles away . . . Mobs burning homes, mobs setting people aflame; rape and hacking of limbs; smashing children to death. Not violence in the abstract or at a distance, not a bullet or a rocket, but atrocity inflicted at the individual level, while making eye contact. Cannibalism seems more civilized. Horror: Conrad didn't know the full meaning of the term.

I feel enraged because I cannot detach and disinfect myself from this horror.

My last two hours in Baroda. I have been treated well, with love and respect, and with sympathy and understanding at the gut response I displayed at the seminar.

Gujarat is a "dry" state, meaning you cannot buy alcohol. My friend Raj Kumar wants to quench his "thirst" and read from his poetry. And so, in his living room, as a child struggles with a Lego set, a few of us sit around, watching the clock for my departure time, listening to Raj first reciting Ghalib. They are in love with Ghalib, those who know his poetry, can recite it by heart: Arré what is mere Shakespeare compared to Ghalib, they will say. Raj then recites a poem he wrote the other day about the current violence wracking parts of India. Another person recites Ghalib, and Raj recites a second poem, another of his compositions, in Hindi. And then, on three motorbikes, I behind Raj on his twenty-five-year-old Czech-designed Java, we race to the railway station for me to catch the Rajdhani Express back to Delhi.

It is an emotional send-off. So much had been expected of this visit, but it's too short. This has been a meeting of minds, but even more a meeting of hearts. This was India's embrace, its kiss, to an Indian however many times removed.

And yes, someone gave me a box of mithai to take back with me.

On the train intercom, a taped voice says, "Laugh and let the world laugh with you." The tape is a tribute to the legendary film actor Raj Kapoor, who always played the part of the oddball, the man of the people. A song comes on:

> *We live in this land*
> *on which the Ganges flows*
> *in which honesty flows from lips*
> *and purity lives in souls . . .*

Ah, poor Raj Kapoor, always the innocent idealist, the anari.

Horn Please!

Marriage season in New Delhi. Every block it seems has a wedding on. Buildings strung with coloured lights, marquees set up on lawns with softly glowing fluorescent-lit interiors, for the wedding ceremonies of the rich. We see one about the size of a large hall—almost a block wide—which Krishan Chander parks his car to contemplate. The wedding must be of a minister's daughter, he concludes. Look at the cars outside.

We make our way to a wedding reception. A very middle-class crowd. The bride and groom sit looking lost and alone on one side, all around them people milling about, getting introduced.

"We would like our daughter to marry abroad," says a woman. "She is educated, na. Boys over there like girls from India who are educated. They like to dominate." Perhaps the wrong word? I press with a query. "Women need men," she says. "All women need the assistance of men. And husbands wouldn't eat, they can't take care of themselves. They need their wives, too." I ask if the girls bred in the Western countries wouldn't resent this—Indian boys going out with them and then turning around and marrying girls from India. "They don't like Indian boys," she says categorically of such girls. "They think they are too orthodox. They marry the others—white boys. And Indian boys like to marry girls from India only."

"I would like one family member to be abroad," says her husband, to whom another man has just revealed a modern miracle: a pocket electronic diary.

Later, another home, this one waiting to say goodbye to its daughter, recently married, on her way in a few hours to join her husband in Toronto.

The men sit in the front living room. The scene is a little reminiscent of a wake. They look sombre, dejected, martyred, but liven up when we arrive with my jolly host. The father of the girl: sitting with a shawl around him, morose, making one-line statements that one doesn't quite know how to respond to, indulging the many younger children with tender reminders to go to sleep, finally taking a boy under his shawl. He's almost a child himself, with a daughter going away: and daughters are often called "mother" by their fathers.

In the other room the women are more relaxed and jovial. The bride appears in the front room once, can't be more than twenty-two; she wears a red shalwar-kameez and is very beautiful. B.A., M.Sc., Krishan Chander tells me. He borrows ten Canadian dollars from me to give her as a present. She is his niece.

My last impressions of India, in New Delhi in the wedding season, are fleeting. I have seen so much in the last four weeks, I feel numbed. I visit the Gandhi memorial and the tombs of the great Sufi Nizamuddin Auliya and his disciple, the poet and musician Amir Khusrau. I walk through Old Delhi and realize that here is another world I have not seen. But I know I am going to return, India has taken me back.

At a reception given by the British Council, finally I meet that institution of a man, the writer Khushwant Singh, who had written glowingly and generously of my first novel when it appeared in India. He gives me a warm embrace. Here I also meet the writer and journalist M. J. Akbar, who has written of these recent and previous occurrences of ethnic violence. He compares it to Bosnia. It is now that Krishan Chander becomes aware of the extent of what has been going on in Surat and Bombay. So busy has he been organizing Canadian-studies affairs, he has not had time to look at the papers. I didn't know, he says. He tells me of an incident he witnessed on his street after the assassination of Indira Gandhi, when the Sikhs of Delhi were victimized. He saw a corner store belonging to a Sikh being torched. And it turns out, he himself is a refugee from some part of current Pakistan.

Krishan Chander and his wife drive me to the airport in their white Maruti. He tells me that he now awaits a relation of his who is coming from England on the express purpose of going to his village and having a twenty-year-old curse lifted from his daughter, also in England. Indians are tribal, says Krishan Chander's wife, a school principal; all except the educated ones, she adds.

Ahead of us, a commercial vehicle. On its back a decorated sign: "Horn please!"

Delhi:
The Burden of History

Think now
History has many cunning passages, contrived corridors
And issues, deceives with whispering ambitions,
Guides us by vanities. Think now
She gives when our attention is distracted
And what she gives, gives with such supple confusions
That the giving famishes the craving. Gives too late
What's not believed in, or if still believed,
In memory only, reconsidered passion.

T. S. ELIOT, "Gerontion"

Enigmas to Uncover

Think, in this batter'd Caravanserai
Whose Doorways are alternate Night and Day,
How Sultan after Sultan with his Pomp
Abode his Hour or two, and went his way.

EDWARD FITZGERALD, *The Rubaiyat of Omar Khayyam*

BECAUSE DELHI WAS THE FIRST CITY where I landed, I have always returned to it; from here I have departed for various places, and here I always return, before heading back to Canada. I am unsettled by nature, and yet I am a creature of habit. I abhor changes and moving, yet I long to get away. My continual returning to India through Delhi reflects perhaps, in some convoluted way, this dual nature.

Bombay, which was the traditional landing place for my people and synonymous with India in my childhood, and the setting of many a popular film and song, has an infectious rhythm and colour; it is a city cluttered with life and a pleasure to walk in; much is written about it. Delhi, on the other hand, more open and expansive, is not the stuff of movies; it is both older and newer, has been so for at least a thousand years. And the more recent newer Delhi has all the character of a suburban sprawl. But Delhi in its traditional sense, said the right way, evokes the mystique of history, and old poetry, reminders of empires rising and falling; it carries images of wars and marauding armies, echoes dimly with the clash of steel, the roll of cannon, the thunder of horses. It was the seat of the so-called Muslim rule in India and, recently, of a modern right-wing nationalist government drawing much rhetorical strength, if not the poison of communal hatred, from allusions to that rule. Not only were the last Mughals defeated here by the British, the last emperor exiled ignominiously to faraway Burma and his family destined to live in poverty, but thousands of Muslims fled Delhi during the partition of India (called, simply, "Partition," all its horrors implied), headed for the newly formed nation of Pakistan. Hindus travelled the opposite way, bringing the bitterness of exile and loss and violence with them into the new developments of Delhi. Up to half a million Hindus, Muslims, and Sikhs are said to have perished in the slaughter that accompanied Partition. Every monument here therefore gives pause for thought, a squirm of the mind: How does one respond? Does that put a label on one? Isn't there a neutral, intellectual, dispassionate way to respond to the history? Delhi, for me, always raises questions. Once, upon telling a taxi driver to take me to the Mughal emperor Humayun's tomb, a grand monument amidst a splendid garden, all of it recently renovated, he lied, "Why go there, there's nothing there but an empty roundabout." Immediately I craned my neck to identify the telltale markers of his faith in the stickers on his dashboard, the hangings on his mirror. And felt guilty afterwards for my suspicion.

Within the area now called Delhi, many an old Delhi (the canonical number is seven) rose and fell into neglect and ruin, a monument to a ruler's ambition, a lesson in the transience of empire and dynasty. The heroes of the great Indian epic the *Mahabharata*, the five Pandava brothers, are thought to have held court here, some three thousand years ago, in a city they had built called Indraprastha. The city is described in great detail in the *Mahabharata*, as grand and wonderful, with "well-planned streets, magnificent white buildings, pavilions, pleasure hillocks, ponds, lakes, and tanks [reservoirs]. It was surrounded by beautiful gardens where trees of many kinds blossomed and bore fruit and where the air resounded with the call of peacocks and cuckoos. . . . From here Yudhisthira [the eldest of the Pandavas] ruled over his realm, cultivating among his subjects *dharma* (righteousness), *artha* (material well-being), and *kama* (the satisfaction of sensual pleasure)." Among the magnificent buildings was a great hall which had golden pillars and was studded with precious stones. The details seem fantastical, but that might well be poetic licence. Did the descriptions have a basis in fact? Apparently not. A covered archaeological dig at Purana Qila, the Old Fort, is perhaps the site of ancient Indraprastha. Archaeologists who have dug at this site and at others connected with or mentioned in the epic have indeed found ancient artifacts— shards of fine pottery called Painted Grey Ware—dating to about 1000 BC, but nothing so exotically wonderful as to have belonged to the Indraprastha of the *Mahabharata*. But then, what inspired the poet who described Indraprastha so opulently, and when did he write?

Lying alongside the Jumna river, at the end of a corridor between the Himalayan range to the north and the Rajasthan desert to the south and west, Delhi became the prize of many an invader from the north and west. The rest of India lay before it, so to speak, inviting conquest and plunder. In Delhi, the Turks from Central Asia began the long era of Muslim rule over India, the great Mughal empire reached its zenith, declined, and fell, and the British ruled over the jewel of an empire over which the sun finally set. Here Mahatma Gandhi, still grieving the breakup of the country in the horror of Partition following the country's independence from Britain, was assassinated; and from here the charismatic public-school and Cambridge-educated Jawaharlal Nehru presided as India's first prime minister during the heyday of Nonalignment and the Cold War.

A growing metropolis of increasing millions, streets packed with buses, auto-rickshaws, Marutis, and other, newer car models, the air heavily polluted, immense hoardings looming over the traffic, advertising the two competing colas, Bollywood films, computers, wireless providers, the focus here is on the now and the future.

And so if one came expecting history to leap out from the sidewalks, as I did first, as one might in London or Paris—where history is organized and preserved and documented for the visitor not only in the public buildings but also in the grand museums—one is disappointed. I recall my visit to the Jantar Mantar observatory on my first day in Delhi and coming out feeling empty. Monuments there are in plenty, a thousand years' worth of them, a few of them prized and showcased, but most decaying or lost or known only to a few, and all surrounded with an ironic sense of detachment from much of the populace.

Perhaps this is because Delhi has always been seen as a city invaded, in wave after wave of conquest, and built over and extended and moved over time; perhaps also because it is a city of recent refugees—and one could argue that the most recent invasion of Delhi was by the Punjabi refugees who bitterly left their ancestral homes in the land that became Pakistan and arrived in trainloads in this city and radically changed its nature. So Delhi's past is not what everyone takes pride in, claims as his or her own. History is selective, discontinuous. If you see the city as having been invaded by foreign Muslim conquerors whose descendants are now Pakistanis, then its monuments, if they don't bring up bile, mean nothing to you.

❦

"We're living off an inheritance," a well-respected restoration architect tells me. "We've inherited many buildings but built few ourselves." An unfair assessment, perhaps, and dated, in this rapidly changing city. But as if to illustrate that statement, during my first visit I was driven through the "New Delhi" built by the British, in an area of lush lawns and gardens and wide tree-lined avenues, past Rashtrapati Bhavan, the once viceregal now presidential palace, the parliament buildings ("gift of the Britishers," a guidebook explained), Claridges Hotel, and residences of the ruling elite. "In this area Indians were not allowed once," my host, Krishan Chander, smiled. I wondered if there was any method in his choice of only these sites for me to see. None of the Mughal monuments, nothing pre-British, apparently, excited him. This was his fixed itinerary for visitors from abroad, what he thought would impress them. He was, as I later learned, one of the refugees of Partition. For his pièce de résistance he took me to the Diplomatic Enclave, in the posh area called Chanakya Puri, containing broad leafy streets named after grand rulers of the past and grand philosophies, and showed me the Canadian High Commission. "Home!" he announced with a wide grin. It could be a touch of irony, cruel, but it wasn't. He seemed sincere in his belief that the place would remind me of home. If only home were such a simple matter. During my second day in the country, as I recall, he had taken me for a returned Indian and left me to negotiate on my own the vast, bewildering New Delhi railway station.

On a train to Shimla, once, I sat across from two young women very diligently eating chappati and daal with their hands, from a package bought at a station. Something in their accent, something in their reserve, suggested they could only be Canadian. Yet they did not have that ubiquitous badge that many Canadian travellers carry, a Canadian flag, a red maple leaf sewn prominently on their luggage somewhere. A family of Gujarati tourists with two very indulged kids tried to convince one of the girls that it was all right to throw trash out the window, and she, after hesitating for some time, finally chucked her refuse out. I am not used to it, she explained, we are taught to throw garbage only in bins. The Gujarati woman smiled. We have a lot to learn from you, she said. The girl came from Canada, she said. Only then, I, who am usually reticent with strangers, felt I had a claim to them. I spoke to them about where they came from, where I lived. They were students in Kingston, in fact, which city I had to visit immediately after my return. But I was right in another respect also: very soon the girls produced Canadian pins, with the maple leaf at the head, and handed them out. They were eagerly accepted by all the passengers around.

But here in Delhi, excepting the monuments and the size of the city, so much actually reminds me of another home, in East Africa, across the Indian Ocean. The residential streets in many areas look exactly like those in the Indian areas of the Nairobi and Dar es Salaam of my childhood: the flower bushes in bungalow gardens, the mango trees giving wide shade; the two-storey apartment blocks of brick and cement, painted a simple white or light colour; the people outside them, vegetable sellers and their customers, the school kids. The pace of life, the background sounds. And inside the houses, the one- or two-bedroom cluttered interiors, the photo of a deceased family elder in prime place, objects displayed in glass cabinets, the essentially modest furniture and facilities. All this, so familiar as to take the breath away.

I recall a scene in suburban Delhi; this was later, during a family visit to India. We had taken a bus from our guest house in South Delhi to go to Connaught Circus, the heart of New Delhi. On the way we passed certain residential areas of the city, and glancing at my wife I saw a sudden emotion come over her face. She, who had not been back to Dar es Salaam in over twenty years, was reminded of it by the neighbourhoods we passed through. Such is the meaning of home. How could I possibly explain this to Krishan Chander, whose one ambition seems to be to send at least one of his children "there"? And if he succeeds, would he then go and stare nostalgically at the Canadian High Commission or the American Embassy?

Krishan Chander teaches English at one of the colleges that make up the massive University of Delhi system, though speaking to him one might not quite guess his specialty, and watching him operate reminds one more of a broker. Krishan Chander is an organizer, a doer, conferences are his métier, and although he complains that they take away from his scholarship, one is hard put to believe that. This occupation gives him privilege and status. His specialty is Canada, and to prove his loyalty he wears a maple-leaf pin in the manner of many Ontario civil servants, identical to the ones I saw the two Canadian girls giving away on the train to Shimla. He goes about from city to city all over the country, a latter-day evangelist for a little-known faith, offering as ultimate prize a trip to that paradise in the north. Many a hapless scholar has been caught in his honey trap

Every evening after nine the telephone will start ringing in Krishan Chander's cluttered living room, and picking it up he is connected to the world. I have often imagined him as a minor Indian god, sitting cross-legged like Gandhi, cheerful as a Ganesh, well-worn address book on his lap, telephone to his ear. Calls will come from other "centres" all across the country; from stranded foreign visitors; from would-be conference participants; from his typist or travel agent; even from the Canadian High Commission. You can call him at any hour of the day or night, certain of his attention. He will settle quarrels, budgets, itineraries. Every morning before he leaves the house he will again pick up his phone and his tattered book and begin dialing. He will not be rushed, attending to every item on his agenda one at a time. It is the only way, with his harried schedule. Finally he will come out of the house, looking distracted, his clothes already crumpled, his oiled hair curling up at the ears. A man with a passion, and a smile on his face.

He will get out his Maruti, close the iron gate of the house (with its special "Canadian" guest room), and, toot-tooting, speed away past cows and pedestrians to the day's appointments.

He goes by a simple principle, driving the Maruti around on the clogged streets of Delhi. He uses this system, as every other driver seems to do, in place of a rear-view mirror, right and left turn signals, stop lights: oblivious to any danger, he will scoot through a turn as I hold my breath, or through a crossroads, his horn happily blaring; this happy-fierce toot-toot gives him licence, a right, and he uses it effectively, though I wonder for how long. The car already has several dents, blamed on his family learning to drive. There is a simple method, apparently, to negotiating Delhi traffic, and it involves pushing through, struggling ahead as best as you can. Every space of likely advantage, however small, is contended for. At every instant a victor emerges, goes forward, the loser relents, is at it again. The horn is a welcome sign, warning others and announcing yourself, deafening to the visitor. Trucks cheerfully tell you on their backs, "Blow Horn," in addition to a prayer to the Mother Goddess, and a pithy proverb: "O you with the dirty look, your face be black."

"Whom do the cows belong to?" I asked Krishan Chander on my first visit. A great smile came over his face. The question had been put to him before. One of his foreign visitors had written a poem to the cows of Delhi, he said. I had guessed that perhaps they belonged to homes in the neighbourhood. They belonged to no one, Krishan told me. They are simply tolerated. One finds them plodding along in the thick of traffic, getting the blare of horns like everything else on the road, very much of the place and belonging. One finds them sitting right in the middle of a street, cars going past on either side, in both directions. One finds them scavenging the garbage dumps. At times they are angrily pushed aside, shouted at, as when one of them picks up an onion outside a store and ambles innocently away. They are a part of street life, as much as a beggar, a stray dog, a rickshaw, a man or woman crossing the road at a construction site bearing a load of bricks, traffic patiently waiting. And one sees cow droppings all over the residential streets, seemingly unnoticed and prudently avoided, like a rock or stump on the road.

In recent times, though, a globalized Krishan has moved on to consultancy and world travelling. He's recently been to Pakistan, seen the place of his birth. A grownup child is already "there," in the U.S. But while in Delhi he is still always available to assist, now on his cell phone, at home and on the road.

><

History is addictive, is an obsession, I've discovered. There's so much around, layers to peel back, enigmas to uncover. I've seen the monuments, the Qutb complex, Humayun's tomb, Red Fort; been driven past the odd mound or dome, remnants of a lost age; read bits of description and history. All dutifully accomplished. Registered in passing. But the urge persists, and grows, to step into the past, look behind the ruin, the beauty, the enigma—and find coherence, impute meaning and relevance. It's risky, I know, a little like walking into a dream.

Why this obsession with the past? I can only conclude that it reflects the deep dissatisfaction of unfinished, incomplete migrations, a perpetual homelessness in my life. My colonial existence—in which memory and the past were trampled upon in a rush to better our lot—and the insecurities of an unorthodox communal culture, in the process of extinction and reinvention by the exigencies of globalized living and modern politics, have both created an uncontrollable and perhaps vain desire to know and record who I am. There are the ways of the mystic and the scientist, to answer this question; and there is the way of history and fiction, which I find more compelling. In how I connect to the history I learn about myself.

The axis of Delhi is oriented north-south. The legendary many cities of Delhi were often simply extensions one of another, in proximity to the Jumna river, each new Delhi generally to the north of the previous one, so as to benefit first from the cooling winds during the torrid dry summer. And so some of the oldest surviving monuments, the earliest Delhis, can be found among the suburbs in the south. The British, however, after much debate reversed this trend and built their Imperial Indian capital, New Delhi, in 1912, adjacent to what was then the current Delhi (called Shahjahanabad) and to its south. Since then the southwards trend has continued.

54
–

The noted English surgeon Frederick Treves, famous for his friendship with Joseph Merrick, the Elephant Man, and also imperial traveller, happened to visit Delhi in 1906 and gave a fine panoramic description of the landscape, looking out from the then Delhi, southwards from Delhi Gate:

There lies, to the south of Delhi . . . a desolate plain covered with the ruin and wreckage of many cities. For miles it wanders, telling ever the one woeful story of the hand of the destroyer. This country of things-that-were has been swept by a hundred armies, has heard the roar of a thousand battles, and none can tell the number of the dead who have lain stark among its stones. . . .

From the Delhi Gate a road starts across this desert and reaches to a kindly and wholesome land beyond. The road is straight, and it leads through a country of stones and dust. . . .

Those who follow this melancholy track will pass by miles of ruins, by walls with breaches, shreds of turrets and relics of gates, by crumbling domes rent with cracks . . . , by tottering pillars and half-seen vaults, and by prostrate blocks of matted stone which were bastions or buttresses.

Only six years later, on this landscape of broken old cities and a few straggling villages, was built New Delhi, covering incidentally much of the site of the ancient capital Indraprastha. After Independence, the growth of the city has continued southwards, on and around the ruins, and people will tell you that the newest Delhi is far south of the oldest Delhi, in the burgeoning modern satellite towns of Gurgaon and Noida, beneficiaries of India's new globalized economy, with their spanking-new air-conditioned industrial parks, shopping malls, and housing developments, where the nouveau riche professionals can live in (Western) style.

But it is not the modern glass, steel, and concrete—which could be transplants from anywhere—but those silent ancient stone structures and their haunting echoes of tumultuous times past that draw the breath, at least of this visitor. Are they relevant? Of course they are; history is always relevant. An awareness of the past runs like lava beneath the surface of life here. The prompt for the outbreak of communal violence that took place in 1993 in Bombay and parts of Gujarat, and its follow-up, the one in Gujarat in 2002, was the destruction of a sixteenth-century mosque built by the Mughal emperor Babur, allegedly upon the site of the birthplace of the Hindu god Rama. During communal conflicts Muslims are to this day anachronistically and erroneously jeered with cries of "Babur's progeny" and "Turk." In a happier, secular vein, modern India needs a capital worthy of its status and ambitions, and where else to look for the requisite imperial grandeur and gravity than in the abundant evidence of its rich history. No wonder, then, that restorers can be seen toiling away at the monuments as never before. "Heritage building" is a term gaining currency, and not only in Delhi.

>◁

In 1192, Delhi, then a city in a Rajput kingdom of the north, fell to the armies of Muhammad of Ghur, a region in the western part of the area we now know as Afghanistan, and the era of so-called Muslim rule began in Delhi, from whence it proceeded to the rest of India. There were, to be sure, Muslims living in various parts of India before 1192: Arab traders and settlers in the cities all along the western coast, having arrived by sea; ambassadors at various courts; Sufis from Persia and Central Asia. There had been other incursions by Muslim rulers from the north. But this particular conflict changed everything, for the conquerors had come to stay. The remains of the medieval Rajput city can be found in a few fragments of a rubble wall in southern Delhi; those of the conquerors' city are at the Qutb complex, at which the red sandstone tower called Qutb Minar rises resplendently.

It is always instructive to remind oneself of this obvious fact: The boundaries and names of many places are only recent in origin and often hide richer, more complex truths than one might imagine; the past then becomes inconvenient and slippery, far less easy to generalize.

In this respect it is useful to know that southeastern Afghanistan was culturally and politically closer to South Asia than to the Near East, a fact evident to this day in its chaotic porous mountain border with Pakistan; Kabul is less than a hundred miles from Peshawar. Before the partition of India it was not unusual to see Afghans plying their trades in northern India. Kipling's famous spy on the road, Mahbub Ali, was an Afghan horse trader. At the same time, many of India's peoples have originated in the north. And in ancient times, the Maurya empire, based in present-day north India, had embraced parts of Afghanistan, where it brought Buddhism, which survived many centuries. The great Buddhist statues at Bamiyan, destroyed by the Taliban in 2001 as un-Islamic, were from the fifth century AD.

Islam arrived in the region of Afghanistan in the seventh century, but it took a slow hold on the land, as people still clung to their pre-Islamic traditions. Politically the region consisted of changing frontiers and fortunes under rival Turkish dynasties often at war. Descended from the nomadic tribes of the lands north of the Oxus river, the Turks had been brought into the Islamic domains as slaves and converted, and rose among the ranks in the armies. From Baghdad in the west to Bukhara (in central Asia) in the east, they were the warrior class of the Islamic world, just as the Kshatriyas were the warrior caste among the Indians. From the tenth century onwards, most of the ruling dynasties of the Muslim world were Turkish in origin, just as the ruling dynasties of northern India were Rajput Kshatriya. The battles for Delhi (1191–92) were therefore fought by these two warrior peoples, the Turks and the Rajputs.

The story of the "Muslim conquest" of India must begin, however, with a larger-than-life character called Mahmud of Ghazna (a city on the Kabul–Kandahar road). In a chaotic, fragmented Afghanistan, in 998 AD, Mahmud came to power and began a series of conquests to build up a large empire stretching from Persia to present-day Pakistan. In his homeland he is celebrated as a great conqueror—he never lost a battle in forty years of ceaseless warfare—and as a pious and cultured ruler, who brought the best poets, artists, and scholars to his court. (One of his acquisitions was Alberuni, a Persian scientist and scholar, who spent ten years in India, learned Sanskrit, and wrote one of the most important and comprehensive accounts ever attempted of life in India.) In India, however, Mahmud of Ghazna's reputation derives largely from his conquests. In 999, Mahmud was designated a sultan by the Caliph of Islam, considered the representative of the Prophet, whose seat was in Baghdad. Upon this prestigious endorsement the Turk took a vow to wage holy war against the Hindus every year. Starting in the year 1000, up to 1030, when he died, Mahmud made at least seventeen incursions into India; his most infamous act was the destruction and plunder of the wealthy temple of Somnath by the Arabian Sea. The name of Mahmud of Ghazna, therefore, is emblematic of the destructiveness of temple-razing Muslim sultans and tops the historical hate list of present-day Hindu nationalists. Only after him on that list comes Muhammad of Ghur.

Mahmud never stayed in India; his base remained at Ghazna, capital of his empire and (now known as Ghazni) still important today. His empire was finally overrun in 1150 by the sultans of Ghur.

The background of Ghur, too, defies easy generalization. Lying in the central west of the region amidst high mountain ranges, Ghur was a land not easily accessible to conquest. The intrepid Mahmud subdued it only by feigning a retreat. Orthodox Islam also faced hard going against a residual Buddhism, and Mahmud had to appoint teachers to bring an acceptable Islam to the people of Ghur. A sect called Karami, with beliefs and practices strongly influenced by centuries of Buddhism, was prevalent in the region. In their newly Islamic beliefs, the Karamis substituted the idea of Buddha on his lotus throne with a similar, corporeal Allah. Even the notoriously unorthodox Ismailis tried to gain a foothold here.

It might be argued that their idea of a godlike Imam bore resemblance to the Karamis' God. Muhammad of Ghur, the eventual conqueror of northern India, was possibly a Karami before converting to the Hanafi Sunni school.

In 1191, after a series of military campaigns in the north, Muhammad of Ghur arrived on the plains of Tarain, some ninety miles from Delhi, where he faced a confederacy of Rajput Indian forces which had gathered to check his advance.

The Rajputs had dominated northern India through a number of independent, competing kingdoms. At the time of Muhammad's invasion, Delhi was a city in an important Rajput kingdom based at Ajmer and ruled by Prithviraj III, also called Rai Pithora. In the First Battle of Tarain, Muhammad of Ghur was roundly defeated, and suffered a severe wound as well. A graphic description of a key confrontation in the battle seems almost to leap out of a miniature painting of the period. Imagine the dust of the north Indian plains, the blinding, deafening clash of steel, the cries of soldiers, the Turks on their steeds, the Rajputs relying on elephants. And then,

> the Sultan attacked the elephant on which the ruler of Delhi, Govind Rai, was riding. . . . He struck his lance at the face of the Rai with such force that two of his teeth fell into his mouth. The Rai threw a javelin at him and severely wounded his arm. The Sultan turned round his charger's head and retreated. Due to the agony of the wound, he was unable to remain seated on horseback and was about to fall on the ground when a lion-hearted warrior, a Khalji stripling, recognized him, sprang up (on the horse) behind the Sultan and, supporting him in his arms, urged the horse with his voice and brought him out of the field of battle.

Back in the mountains of Ghur, Muhammad began preparations to avenge his defeat, not without punishing first the amirs who had somewhat ignominiously fled the battlefield of Tarain. So great was his grief at his humiliation, it is said, that he would refuse to eat or drink.

At about the time when Muhammad was licking his wounds in Ghur and preparing his comeback, a young mystic called Muinuddin, of a Sufi order founded in the nearby town of Chisht saw the Prophet of Islam in a dream and left for Ajmer in the kingdom of Rai Pithora, where he founded what would become the greatest Sufi movement in India. That Muinuddin Chishti, as the young shaikh was called, could carry out his activities in a kingdom that was at war with his compatriots and coreligionists is something to ponder over. To this day, long after the Turkish dynasties have passed into oblivion, hundreds of thousands of pilgrims of all faiths visit Ajmer on the anniversary of Muinuddin of Chisht's death.

In 1192, at the Second Battle of Tarain, Rai Pithora was defeated by Muhammad. According to some sources the Rajput king was executed; according to others he was allowed to function at Ajmer as a vassal and later put to death for treason. Rai Pithora's son was allowed to rule in Ajmer for a while. Govind Rai, the ruler of Delhi and hero of the first battle, was killed in the second one, but his successor ruled for some time, acknowledging the authority of Muhammad.

From here on, the fate of India took a sharp turn. A new culture, based on a new faith, grew, receiving royal patronage and sometimes guiding the rulers using precepts that were foreign to this already highly cultured land. Architecture, music, language, law, and politics were all affected. Mosque minarets and domes, the muezzin's prayer call five times a day, the Arabic script, and the Persian language symbolized this new order. The Turks had distinctly Oriental features, with fair skin, dark hair, and high cheekbones. They brought with them different court and civil rituals, alien personal manners and prejudices. Their racist epithet for the dark Indian was "crow." They imported army mercenaries and civilian immigrants. And the seed of resentment and division was sown on the subcontinent to last to the present day. The Partition of 1947 was not a resolution; it simply amplified the resentments. Its violence and ravages were in effect another war. Since then, three conventional wars have already been fought by India and Pakistan.

The Rajput king Prithviraj—Rai Pithora—is a figure of a romantic and ultimately tragic legend, a gallant and noble king, whose story has come down to us in an epic poem titled *Prithvirajaraso*, composed by his court poet and friend Chand Bardai but thoroughly embellished over the generations. His dashing courage is illustrated by a bravura public act: at a ceremony held in a neighbouring and rival Rajput kingdom, in which its princess, Sanyogita, would select her groom from a number of suitors, Prithviraj had suddenly emerged from behind a statue and rode away with the princess, who all the time had been his secret lover. Prithviraj had purposely not been invited to the ceremony. His defiance proved the downfall of the Rajputs, for whereas they had united in the First Battle of Tarain, in the second confrontation Prithviraj went without the previous level of support and was crushed.

According to a Rajput legend, Prithviraj was taken in chains by his conqueror all the way to Ghur. There, having dared to look Muhammad in the eye, he was blinded. But he had his beloved Chand Bardai at hand. Chand contrived a ruse to avenge Rajput humiliation. Presented before the sultan, he boasted that his lord, though blinded, was so skilled an archer that he could take aim and shoot his target merely from hearing a sound. An archery competition was called to test this claim, at which Chand caused the foolish, arrogant sultan to utter an inopportune word. Prithviraj turned, at once took aim, and slew the conqueror of Delhi.

In contrast, the Turkish Afghan sultans hardly cut romantic figures. They seem hard, hungry, and restless. According to some accounts, their horses were swifter and their fighting tactics faster against the cumbersome but lavishly decorated elephants of the Rajputs. They were on the offence, and on the chessboard that was the battlefield the knight had outdone the rook.

Not surprisingly, Chand Bardai, and those who interpolated the text of his tragic romance afterwards, portray Muhammad as a treacherous thug and torturer. The Muslim chroniclers, who wrote in Persian, were not writing nostalgic heroic paeans but historical narrative, but they, too, naturally had their biases, arising from the arrogance of the conqueror and the necessity to demonstrate Islamic piety and superiority, as well as abject loyalty to their benefactors the sultans. According to them, Muhammad of Ghur was assassinated on the evening of March 15, 1206, in his tent on the bank of the Indus river while returning from a military campaign. The identity of the assassins is a matter of debate. Among the suspects are the Ismailis, of Assassin notoriety, and Rajput loyalists. Within fourteen years of his death, his birthplace, Ghur, had been razed by the Mongols, its inhabitants massacred. The independent sultanates of Central Asia disappeared. Only Delhi remained to resist the Mongol onslaught, and it did so valiantly.

Muhammad of Ghur had left behind in Delhi his viceroy Qutbuddin Aibak, who in 1206 declared himself the independent sultan of Delhi. His capital was at the site of the old Rajput city, called Qila Rai Pithora, in the present-day suburb of South Delhi. The thick rubble-built walls of this old city are still visible in some places. In the new city, Aibak built the magnificent Quwwatul Islam mosque and began construction of the tower called Qutb Minar, both of which stand today at the Qutb complex among a dazzling array of red sandstone structures in various stages of ruin. The Qutb Minar was completed by later sultans and stands at 238 feet, with five storeys. The tower and the mosque symbolize the triumph of the new order and, more relevant for modern times, the beginning of a clash of cultures. An inscription on the mosque tells us it was built out of materials taken from twenty-seven Hindu and Jain temples, the evidence of which is still visible in the rows of pillars in the mosque decorated with typically Indian floral motifs and animal and human figures, some of which have been disfigured so as not to offend the piety of the Muslim prayer house. A great screen wall with arched openings stands in front of the mosque. The arches of this early mosque are of the indigenous style (succeeding layers of brick projecting a distance outwards from the one below, to form an arched opening), found in many ancient cultures. The "true arch" of the Roman and Islamic world would come to predominate later. Each of the storeys of the Qutb Minar had a balcony, the balustrades of which are now missing. It was perhaps a tower of victory; its sides are embellished by Quranic texts, and it has been claimed that it might also have been used by the muezzin to call the faithful to prayer.

Not surprisingly, taking into account the bitter humiliation, not to say hatred, that some still draw from the result of the eight-hundred-year-old Second Battle of Tarain, the Qutb Minar has been the subject of some controversy. A tradition claims that the tower was originally built by Prithviraj for his beloved wife Sanyogita to catch a glimpse of the Jumna river every morning, but this has been dismissed by archaeologists. In 1957, a 213-foot brick tower, the Minar-e Jam was discovered in the Ghur region in Afghanistan and is believed to be a direct inspiration for the Qutb Minar. Recently and more significantly, Hindu militants have claimed the site as Hindu, on the basis that temple materials were used there; an attempted worship was aborted by authorities. The tower has also been struck by lightning and been restored and repaired over the centuries.

A certain Major Smith has earned a reputation for his indiscriminate interference with the Indian monuments. Among his dubious achievements is the removal of the balustrades from the Qutb and building a superstructure upon it in 1803 that was so hideous that in 1848 the governor general, Lord Hardinge, had it removed.

Eight centuries later, oblivious to all this history and controversy, visitors come in great numbers to stroll inside the grounds that house the pink and white structures, for this is a popular site, spacious, beautiful, and mysterious, away from the buzz of the main city. Vendors ply limp postcards and packaged snacks, a snake charmer plays to a lethargic snake.

The Sultan and the Sufi

There is joy today
I have found my pir
Nizamuddin Auliya, Nizamuddin Auliya!

AMIR KHUSRAU

IN THE MIDDLE OF THE AFTERNOON one time in Delhi, a few of us decide to go visit the ancient tank, a water reservoir, called Hauz Khas in suburban South Delhi. It is my last day in the city, until the next time, so there is a sense of farewell in our outing and conversations. By now I have made close friends in Delhi, and we will have our final lunch together. For me the day will be painfully long, for planes heading west to Europe and North America leave awfully late, and Delhi airport is a nightmare not worth contemplating.

We park at the shopping centre of Hauz Khas Village, visit the bookstore first. Mahesh, my host during my more recent few visits, introduces me to the owner. He ran a newspaper stand when I was still in college, says my boisterous friend. Now he owns a chain of bookstores! The man, in his early sixties perhaps, is on his way out and feels embarrassed, as do I. But his is another of Delhi's rags-to-riches stories, post-Independence.

A quiet street leads from the shopping centre towards the Hauz Khas. First comes a rustic-looking restaurant partly hidden by the woods, exclusive merely by its location. After a Punjabi lunch we

65
–

walk into the park and come upon a small lake, at the sight of which my friend goes ballistic. Not long ago this was still a conventional though defunct water tank, a rectangular reservoir with steps leading down for Delhi's inhabitants of olden times to fetch water. A historical site. Now it is a suburban lake in a park. When he was young, Mahesh says, he could walk straight across from here to the Qutb; now a grid of busy roads girdles the area in between. To our right, a posh apartment complex abutting an ancient wall looks down upon the lake. The wall is part of an imposing structure. We stroll towards it, find ourselves at the bottom of an archaeological site. The climb up is unorthodox and a little risky, accomplished partly on all fours, with assistance from an attendant at the top. To our amazement he assumes the two middle-aged greybeards and two ladies to be out for hanky-panky, like teenagers, among the ruins and expects a large tip. He is disappointed. But there are teenagers out from school locked together intimately on the wide windowsills, exhibiting the arrogance of the young, rich, and Westernized.

The Hauz Khas reservoir was built by Sultan Alauddin of the Khilji dynasty in the early fourteenth century. The ruins overlooking it, where we've arrived, belong to a large madrassa, a school, attached to the mausoleum of Firoz Shah Tughlaq who followed Alauddin some decades later. Firoz's marble tomb lies alongside three others in a grimy hall gutted of all ornament. In Firoz's time lived the man of letters Ziauddin Barni, who in his old age undertook to write an engaging history of Delhi's rulers, which includes a gripping account of Alauddin's tumultuous long reign, from the terrible betrayal that brought him his kingship to the horrifying murders that ended it.

Thus the ghosts haunting Delhi's ruins, a cast of characters seen as through a mist, mystifying, awe-inspiring, ultimately too alien. A Shakespeare might have infused life into these shades, made them speak and feel. But no such creative genius sprang up here sufficiently detached from his narrative to render it timeless, less alien.

Did they feel like us, these sultans who lived here, paraded their victories, built towers of enemy skulls? Their customary treachery and cruelty make the blood curdle; and yet they administered and defended a vast empire; and they professed profound piety, patronized scholars and scientists, and favoured poets who produced beauty we still marvel at, composed songs that move us to tears. Consider Alauddin.

About a century after the conquest of Delhi and the inauguration of the Turkish dynasty by Qutbuddin Aibak, a new dynasty began in 1290 in Delhi, with Jalaluddin Firuz Khilji. Himself an Afghan, Jalaluddin ended Turkish chauvinism in the ruling and administration of the state. Well on in his years when he ascended the throne, he came to be admired—and repudiated—as a good man, almost to the point of idiocy. Rarely has a ruler of those times been described, and criticized, for his goodness. Jalaluddin simply did not fit the mould of the ruler, and the noblemen were intensely frustrated with him. When some of these nobles broke out into an insurgency, the sultan, instead of punishing them brutally in exemplary fashion, had them clothed, wined, and dined. When thieves were caught in Delhi, he extracted promises of good behaviour from them and freed them. When Thugs (the notorious robbers of the night who strangled their victims with knotted kerchiefs) were captured in Delhi, he had them exiled. He tolerated the Hindus in their un-Islamic beliefs. He was therefore considered weak and an idiot. Says Ziauddin Barni, "Men complained of the clemency and humanity of the sultan."

Jalaluddin had a beloved nephew, his brother's son, Alauddin, who was also his son-in-law, but his exact opposite in nature: ambitious, cruel, and unscrupulous. One day in the holy month of Ramadan, against all advice, the old sultan set off on his royal barge down the Ganges, which was swollen by the monsoon rains, to greet his nephew, who awaited at a place called Kara (present-day Allahabad) loaded with booty after a brilliant military victory in the south. Thereby Jalaluddin sailed into a trap, "his doom pulling him by the hair," as Barni puts it. Alauddin had plotted meticulously. Through the ruse of a letter, the sultan had been led to believe he was going to meet and comfort a contrite nephew who had disobeyed him and, depressed, was on the verge of taking poison. To hasten his journey, Jalaluddin went with a small retinue. In the last stage of the journey, on a small boat, the sultan's attendants were convinced to disarm. When the two met on the bank of the river at Kara, the nephew fell at his uncle's feet, who raised him and kissed him on the eyes and cheeks, as he would a son, and stroked his beard. "I have brought you up from infancy, why are you afraid of me?" the old man said, at which moment the stone-hearted Alauddin gave the signal and the first of several blows from the hand of an assassin fell upon the sultan. Wounded, Jalaluddin ran towards the river, crying, "Oh, you villain Alauddin, what have you done?" Another of Alauddin's men ran after the sultan, threw him to the ground, cut off his head, and presented it dripping to the nephew. Says Barni, "Villainy and treachery, and murderous feelings, covetousness and desire of riches, thus did their work." It was the afternoon of Wednesday, July 19, 1296.

Thus the accession of Alauddin Khilji, who went on to become one of the great rulers of India, in the manner the nobles had demanded of Jalaluddin the Good. But with Alauddin's spies around, reportedly the nobles now found it necessary to speak in whispers or even in gestures. He was ruthless and ambitious, his rule was long and stable. Among his achievements was a strong central administration and an effective system of collecting revenue, which enabled him to establish a large standing army. This Second Alexander, as he styled himself, made numerous conquests, including that of Gujarat, and brought most of India under his dominion or vassalage. Delhi became one of the major Islamic centres, attracting scholars, teachers, artists, traders, and administrators from all over the Islamic world.

But there prevailed a constant state of war with the Mongols, the descendants of Chinghiz Khan, "the accursed"—so-called because he had already laid waste the Islamic lands to the north and west, including Afghanistan, the ancestral homeland of Delhi's rulers. The Mongols, considered uncouth, non-Muslim, and uncivilized, made regular raids in the northwest. In 1303 they almost conquered Delhi.

A force of tens of thousands of Mongol horsemen proceeded towards the capital, raising dust and mayhem along the highway, and camped some six miles outside the city, which had overflowed meanwhile with terrified refugees from the countryside. From their positions the Mongols controlled the vital river crossings and the highways. Alauddin's forces, after recent engagements, were weak in number. Water and supplies were short in the city. "Utmost terror prevailed," says Barni. The sultan fixed his camp at a place called Siri outside the city gates and the two armies faced off. The Mongols, finding no way to breach the Hindustan line after a siege of two months, at last departed. And Delhi's denizens shouted their thanks to their one and many gods for this miracle. "If Targhi [the

Mongol commander] had remained another month upon the Jumna," Barni writes, "the panic would have reached to such a height that a general flight would have taken place and Delhi would have been lost."

Following this siege, Alauddin moved his capital to Siri, where he built his "palace of a thousand columns." It stood two miles to the north of the previous capital; its meagre ruins, now a grazing ground for bullocks, lie behind a market next to the well-heeled neighbourhood of Asian Games Village. Its recently restored walls form a backdrop to the Panchsheel Park in the same area. The Hauz Khas was built in its northern limits to provide water to the new city. Meanwhile in the old city the Quwwatul Islam mosque was extended, as well as the Qutb area around it; and a new brick tower, proposed to be double the size of the Qutb Minar, was begun to celebrate Alauddin's reign. It was never finished.

><

While the monuments of the sultans lie silent, some of them abject, neglected ruins, those of the poets and mystics live on and sing and perhaps mock to this day. Shrines are an important part of worship in India, and even the acknowledged agnostic in the currently "cool India," of whatever faith, will not mind placing a basket of roses upon a grave, standing back, and joining hands to pay respects to a mystic of the past.

The Nizamuddin area of Delhi is named after the great Sufi Hazrat Nizamuddin Auliya (1238–1325), who lived and died and is buried here, at the outskirts of the once thriving old Delhis, now close to the heart of the modern city. The Sufi's shrine is one of Delhi's most visited sites. The railway station nearby also bears his name.

Nizamuddin was born in a small town outside Delhi, his paternal grandfather having emigrated from Bukhara. When he was twenty years old he went to visit the famous Sufi Baba Fariduddin

Ganj-e-Shakar in Pakpattan (now in Pakistan). Baba Farid belonged to the Chishti order, which was brought to India, it will be recalled, just prior to the conquest of Delhi. Baba Farid was so ascetic in his practices, he reputedly hung himself by the feet from a well to say his prayers. Impressed by the young visitor from Delhi, however, he installed Nizamuddin as the khalifa, the leader, of the order in that city. Here Nizamuddin established his khanqah, his centre, "in a corner apart from the men of the City," where he lived and taught his disciples until his death.

The Chishti order took a keen interest in music and poetry, and because it preached and practised a classless society and a simple devotion to God, it attracted many followers. Indeed, it appears that Sufism was primarily responsible for the conversions to Islam in northern India. In a typical khanqah, the master and his disciples lived in one large room, where time was spent on prayers and studying. All were welcome, and whatever food was there was shared out. Of course not everyone became a Sufi mystic; most would simply have paid homage to the holy man and come to listen to his teachings and participate in the devotional sessions. But such was the influence of Nizamuddin in Delhi, it has been said, that it became the fashion to buy and study devotional classics.

Stories are, of course, oft repeated about this beloved character, and a good number of them involve the sultans of Delhi. In the Muslim world, the relationships of sultans with the Sufi masters in their domains were always precarious, for the Sufis were arrogant and defiant, and the kings no less arrogant but also wary about the influence of the mystics on the people and nervous about their spiritual powers. Many an eminent Sufi has been martyred by his earthly sultan.

It is said that Delhi was saved from the Mongols, in that crucial encounter with Alauddin outside Siri, by the prayers of Nizamuddin, its beloved mystic. And yet, when the sultan wished to see Nizamuddin, the shaikh declined. Alauddin's heir, Khizr, was however a disciple. One day the prince brought a letter from Alauddin, but the shaikh did not open it. If he wants me to leave the city, he retorted, I will do so. There is enough room in God's world for the two of us.

Surely Alauddin knew he was doomed?

✕

If there was ever a case of just retribution in the bloody annals of medieval Delhi, it was made manifest in the final days of Alauddin, who had so heinously murdered his uncle to usurp the throne. In our imagination, as the macabre denouement of his life unfolds, it is as if Fellini had collaborated with Shakespeare to write the script.

At the centre of the tragic drama that was Alauddin's miserable end stood the figure of an evil genius called Malik Kafur, a former eunuch slave who had been bought in a Baghdad market, brought to India, and captured by Alauddin's generals in the port city of Khambat (Cambay) during the Gujarat campaigns. He went on to become the victor of several military campaigns on behalf of Alauddin and, at the end, his close confidant. He was a handsome man, and suggestions of a homosexual relationship with his master add spice to their story. Because he had been bought for a thousand ("hazar" in Persian and Hindi) dinars at the market, Malik Kafur was also known as Malik Hazar-dinari.

Alauddin lay in bed sick with dropsy, weak and only partly conscious, suffering unbearable bouts of pain and flashes of temper, and neglected by his family: the queen devoted to participating in celebrations, the sultan's mother to her social functions, his beloved but spoilt heir Khizr Khan to his many amusements, including women, wine, and sports. "The locks of beautiful girls were constantly in his hands," said his friend Amir Khusrau, the court poet, "as rosaries are in the hands of the pious." Malik Kafur was recalled from the south to give comfort to the suffering sultan in his sick bed. When Khizr Khan, having sworn to go on foot to pray for his father at the graves of the saints, was reported to have gone on horseback instead, and moreover in the company of musicians and dancing girls, the deeply disappointed sultan, under Kafur's malign influence, reluctantly divested him of his status as heir and agreed to send him to prison. But Alauddin nevertheless extracted a promise from the faithless Kafur not to harm the prince. This episode only worsened Alauddin's condition, and he died a few days later, his end hastened, some said, by the attentions of Kafur. Subsequently the former thousand-dinar slave had Khizr Khan blinded in a dungeon. And he sent his barber to blind Shadi Khan, Khizr's brother, which the barber accomplished by "cutting his eyes from their sockets with a razor, like slices of melon." He proceeded to remove all the wives and children of the sultan who had claims upon the throne and set up his own favourite as the successor. It was January 1316. Malik Kafur's intrigues ultimately caught up with him, and he died by the sword shortly afterwards, ungrieved.

Alauddin's incomplete tower, a gigantic brick stump, stands eighty feet high. His dynasty petered out shortly after his death, following a number of bloody disputes over the succession to the throne.

Khizr Khan's tomb supposedly lies at Nizamuddin, in the vicinity of that of his friend Amir Khusrau, who would devote an epic poem to his passion for a Gujarati princess. But that is another tale.

Another stone testimony to the thwarted vanity of kings stands five miles to the east of Alauddin's stump: the massive, severe, red and grey ruins of Tughlaqabad Fort, still immensely imposing and awesome, on the Badarpur Road at the edge of the modern city, overlooking the highway headed south to Mathura and Agra. Built by Ghiyasuddin Tughlaq, who started his own dynasty in 1320, it was abandoned not long afterwards; reflecting the grim, austere personality of its designer, it stands in sharp contrast to the graceful buildings of his predecessors. Only the odd awestruck tourist or a band of goats taking a shortcut over the massive collapsed structure visits it today. It was once, one learns, a four-mile-perimeter city, octagonal in shape, its thirty-foot walls enclosing a citadel, some palaces, and streets laid out in a grid.

Across the road, equally forlorn, lies the tomb of the sultan.

><

Nizamuddin's final resting place, on the other hand, is visited every year by thousands of people of all faiths, bearing baskets of roses as offerings and desires to be fulfilled.

You enter an alley from the main Mathura Road where it meets Lodi Road, then walk into a long, slightly winding, narrow corridor lined by stalls all clamouring for custom, selling Muslim devotional music and videos, wall hangings, food, and roses by the heaps, chaddars (shawls to spread over a grave) and bags of prasad for you to take inside to the shrine as offerings; a dozen or more stalls offer to keep your shoes. You buy your rose tray and remove your shoes, but not the socks (as other places demand), and enter a paved courtyard fairly busy with a quiet sort of activity. Prominently in front is the grand mausoleum of Nizamuddin Auliya, a colourful, partly gilded square structure capped with a dome, and possessed with a low, arched entrance and latticed green and white walls. A steady stream of men, their heads covered with caps or kerchiefs, walk in and out. Women, who are not allowed inside, sit devoutly on the verandah. The interstices of the lattice walls are filled with strips of cloth, left by them as tokens to the saint for wishes to be fulfilled. The grave of the Sufi lies in the centre of a small inner room, a narrow aisle going around it so that if you do not wish to stand for long before it, as many do, their palms raised open before them in prayer, you have to squeeze your way past. The grave is covered with layers of chaddars and flowers, to which you add your offering. A chandelier hangs above the grave, its light dim, but unlike other shrines, there is no lamp burning to symbolize the nur, or spirit, of the saint. It is a brief experience, and as you emerge into the bright sunlight and feel the hot pavement under your feet you do not quite know how to respond. What moves is the sight of the people who believe so fervently, who need so desperately, the devotion so open on their faces; and an awareness of the different backgrounds and faiths they belong to. An attendant comes to take down your name and address, accepts a donation. He claims descent from Nizamuddin, hands you a card, shows you around. Adjoining the shrine compound is a mosque, where some people are at prayer, and a madrassa, not in session at this time. The kids who come here, my informant is quick to tell me, anticipating my question, also go to regular school.

Behind Nizamuddin's shrine, across the courtyard, lies the slightly less opulent mausoleum of his disciple Amir Khusrau, a prolific poet and one of the chief historians of his time. He wrote both in Persian, the literary and scholarly language of the time, and the local Hindustani, which he quite adored, and his poetry is loved and performed to this day. He was born in northern India in 1254, to a family of Turkish immigrants (or refugees) from central Asia, and died in 1325, six months after his master. So devoted was Khusrau to Nizamuddin that it is said he would lick the plate the master had eaten from. But Khusrau spent much of his time in court, where he was required to entertain the sultan with his clever compositions. A man surviving on a tightrope between the two worlds.

Outside the poet's mausoleum three singers have appeared, seated on the ground with their instruments, to give a performance of his work. You ask your informant about the prince Khizr Khan's grave, which according to your reading is somewhere on this site, close to that of his friend. He doesn't know, but across from Khusrau's mausoleum he points out a modest unmarked

grave that he says belongs to Ziauddin Barni. Like many such graves, it is raised a few inches above the ground and painted an olive green. History tells us this servant of Clio spent his last years in this area, a pauper. This naked grave could well be his. You go over and place a few flowers upon it.

Finally you depart, pick up your shoes. The beggars are at your back now as you make your way out the long narrow corridor. The eating stalls hustle for money to feed the needy, five rupees a person. The video stalls show pious movies, in one of them uniformed young boys in formation singing praises to the Prophet, looking ominously militaristic. A beggar woman runs after you pleading. Another takes over from her and gives you a glimpse of the baby in her arms. Give me something to feed the child. Those eyes. You pay and you flee.

Another time. It's a warm Thursday night, holy Jumé-raat, when the devout and the needy visit the graves of the Sufis everywhere. Here at Nizamuddin, a mandap, a makeshift auditorium under a cloth canopy, has been set up between the mausoleums of the master and his disciple. The only light is at Khusrau's shrine, to enter which the devotees silently line up, dressed up for this special occasion. In contrast to these silent—and perhaps desperate—devotions, on the ground outside, under the canopy, sit some hundred people rapt with attention, listening to four qawali singers belting out praises to the Prophet. The tabla beats, the harmonium wails. It is holy clamour in the perfumed smoky air of the shrine. Fill my beggar's pouch, Ya Muhammad! shout the singers as fresh people come in, look for places to squeeze into. Occasionally someone from the audience stands up, goes and drops a bill or two before the singers.

As you sit in the dark listening to the music, and watch as one group of singers yields its place to another, and you notice how they toss up their frenzied lines into the air and catch them, the voices rising and falling, and as you let your gaze wander and take in the black caps and the green caps denoting status, the embroidered ones denoting regions, and the simple skull caps of the majority of those here and the freshly pressed kurta-pyjamas and the handful of tourists hovering at the edges, their heads also covered, you can't help thinking, What a memorial to a poet.

>⊂<

The story is told that when Sultan Ghiyasuddin Tughlaq, the builder of Tughlaqabad, was returning once from a campaign in the east, he sent a message in advance to the Shaikh Nizamuddin telling him to leave the city before he arrived. Why he would do so is not clear, but certainly there was no love lost between sultan and Sufi. To the sultan's message, the shaikh replied, *"Hanouz Delhi dur ast,"* meaning, Delhi is still far off. Ghiyasuddin did not make it to Delhi, dying in an accident on the way. This story, pitting a beloved mystic against a vain sultan, people love to tell. Historians discard it with disdain, but repeat it all the same. As I cannot help but do.

When Nizamuddin died, his disciple Khusrau wrote, in the Sufi vein, "*Gori soyi sej par, mukh par daale kes / Chal Khusro ghar aapne, raen bhai chanhu des*," singing which lines at a restaurant table, my friend Mahesh wipes his eyes with emotion. The bride lies in the bed, Mahesh translates, her face covered by her (black) hair / Come away Khusrau to your home, night falls in the four directions. Simple lines depicting the death of a beloved, and of a spiritual master, when his light forsakes the world. The Sufi, or any mystic, of course, is a bride of God.

Such poetry, such yearning, lives on in the romantic heart of the nation, even as the airwaves and newsprint dazzle and bewitch with the transitory magic of the material. But the poetry thrills the heart, it is one's link to here; surely, you think, India cannot let it all go in its frantic race to superpowerdom?

They Walked with Loud Lamentations

Delhi . . . [is] the metropolis of India, a vast and magnificent city, uniting beauty with strength. It is surrounded by a wall that has no equal in the world, and is the largest city in India, nay rather the largest city in the entire Muslim world.

IBN BATTUTA (1304-1368)

AMIR KHUSRAU'S LIFE PRESENTS a familiar conundrum. His greatness as a poet was unquestioned in his own time. Seven hundred years later, his compositions continue to thrill audiences, which in our electronic age have become worldwide. Not many who listen to his verses must be aware that Khusrau was also Alauddin's historian, describing his achievements in glowing terms. And this is where our problem emerges. As the modern historian M. Habib wrote, "The statesmen of the middle ages patronised poets as their modern successors patronise the printing press"–and, one might add, more recently television and the Internet. Khusrau could not but help write propaganda when required. He may have licked the spit of his spiritual master, and sung Ali! Ali! in ecstasy at the Sufi gatherings at Nizamuddin's centre, but he was also a courtier who dined with sultans, ate their salt, as we say. He was the poet who survived when his sultans–first Jalaluddin, then Alauddin–were betrayed. The dreadful Malik Kafur did not touch him, though Khusrau was around the court at the time of Alauddin's death and as his friend Khizr Khan languished in the dungeons, soon to be blinded and murdered. What do we make of his silences, and of his jingoistic pronouncements? Was the Sufi in him only playing games? The one who knows doesn't tell, he says in one of his songs, and the teller doesn't know.

When he writes with such relish about the destruction of an important temple by Alauddin's forces, what does he not tell? Thus—

> The foundations of this golden temple, which was the holy temple of the Hindus, were dug up with the greatest care. The glorifiers of God broke the infidel building, so that spiritual birds descended on it like pigeons from the air. The ears of the wall opened at the sound of the spade. At its call the sword also raised its head from the scabbard; and the heads of Brahmans and idol worshippers came dancing from their trunks at the flashes of the sword . . . the stench of blood was emitted by ground once fragrant with musk. And at this smell the men of Faith were intoxicated and the men of infidelity ruined.

Amir Khusrau presents a poem to Sultan Alauddin.

Is there a trace of irony in these words? asks Habib. "[Was] this the trumpet of a bloated fanaticism or the excruciating melody of the tragic muse? Was Amir Khusrau praising the idol-breakers or bewailing their lack of true faith?" Such questions are not academic, they test our own attitudes, our biases.

No one who reads accounts of the early Muslim historians of India would fail to feel uneasy at the bigotry and the arrogance they reveal among the ruling classes and in the behaviour of the sultans. Accounts of temple destructions so casually fill the histories they become embarrassing to read. They remind us, let's be honest, of Muslim fanatics of today. Says Alauddin to his qadi (judge), according to Barni, "Now you tell me that it is all in accordance with law that the Hindus should be reduced to the most abject obedience." Says the much nicer Firoz Shah in his memoir, "I forbade the infliction of any severe punishment on the Hindus in general, but I destroyed their idol temples, and instead thereof raised mosques." Surely we must acknowledge this past, which casts a shadow upon our lives even today, when a politician can invoke it to create discord and mayhem in the nation. Surely we must ask if we can turn away from those aspects of it that disturb us while allowing others to move us. We must come to terms with it.

Lest we judge the past too harshly and easily, several mitigating factors have been pointed out by modern scholars regarding such historical accounts. First, the historians of the time often were at the mercy of their sultans in whose employ they were, and none was more so than Amir Khusrau, receiving his thousand-tanka stipend from Alauddin (thirty could fetch a concubine or a handsome lad) to produce flattery and bombast upon demand. Furthermore, descriptions of temple destructions were often merely a formula used to extol a ruler as a pious Muslim (even when he was far from it) and therefore prone to exaggeration if not outright manufacture. The sultans also often helped to build temples. They were practical men who administered a vast, diverse territory and population, and well knew that stability within their kingdoms depended on the wealth and cooperation of that population, the great majority of which were Hindus, happy or unhappy with the rule of the day, as people are everywhere with their governments. When the sultans were infected by excessive zeal or bigotry, their victims often included nonorthodox Muslims. And finally, what seems obvious but is often overlooked in the translations is that the terms "Hindu" and "Muslim" should be understood in historical context and always be qualified. After all, who was a "Hindu"? The term itself is modern. What must have been meant in the original Persian accounts, especially in the earlier periods, is a person of Hindustan who was not an immigrant. Though, of course, a temple was a temple.

Nevertheless, even with these cautions against oversimplification, the arrogance and bigotry, the discrimination against Hindus and the destruction of their temples, cannot be wished away from our historical consciousness. They were the reality of the day, and we must acknowledge them, albeit as reflecting the values of the Muslim elites of a long-gone past—a time in which, to take one example, the punishment for selling goods that were underweight was to have the difference in weight cut from the haunches of the culprit. As for Khusrau, even great artists bear the prejudices of their age. We do not have to look hard in our own times to find them. And it must not be forgotten that fanatical intolerance has existed everywhere, India's caste system being but one example that still persists, sometimes in grotesque forms.

I always cringe at the terms "Hindu" and "Muslim"; they are so final, so unequivocal. So exclusive. For "Hindu"—itself derived not from the name of a founder, as "Christian" is, or a philosophy or attitude (of submission), as "Muslim" is, but from a geographical marker, the river Indus—I often substitute "Indian," for India's primary identity is rooted in its ancient history and culture, which preceded these religious divisions. I imagined India as my ancestral homeland; to witness, upon my arrival, its divisions running so deep was profoundly unsettling. It was to be asked to carry an open wound where perhaps only an itch had existed; to accept difference at the profoundest level.

There was a prevalent tendency, I found, to essentialize—and therefore, in a certain way, to exclude. If you were a Muslim you ate meat, could not possibly be vegetarian; you spoke Urdu (the cultured language of poetry that evolved from old Hindi under the influence of Persian), which would be wonderful were it true, but it is not my language. As a Muslim, the understanding was, you naturally felt closer to a Muslim from another corner of the country, and even from a foreign country, despite the very obvious differences, in cultures, languages, and foods, than to a neighbour from your own region. During my early visits, my hosts, out of misplaced consideration for me, would take pains to point out the nonvegetarian sections of the menu at a restaurant; a dear friend regretted she could not introduce me to some Muslim friends who happened to have left town; another friend, as dear, pointed out a Muslim club I could join. A Gujarati woman asked me how I learned my Gujarati. At my mother's breast, I replied impatiently.

Partition had sharpened the separation; and Muslims, it seemed to me, instead of asserting their essential and primary Indian-ness, shouting it from the rooftops and from their guts, had fallen into the trap of allowing themselves to be seen as a minority and as outsiders, accepting a primary identity defined by faith, in a unity (called the "umma") that crosses political, cultural, and ethnic boundaries. But such an identity is often abstract and culturally rootless. How dangerous such a self-affirmation can become for young people we have witnessed in our own times—for example in the July 7, 2005, bombings in London—when in their frustrations about the plight of their "brothers" across the world, they run amok attempting to destroy the very societies that have nurtured them.

On the other hand, I come across Muslim sympathizers—in India as well as Toronto—who need their Muslims as the distinct Other, the antagonist to pit against the "majority" society they consider unjust, to which of course they implicitly and comfortably belong. To tell people that politically and culturally you don't subscribe to this gulf among the same people, and that in matters of faith you were brought up in a very local Indian tradition that was a blend of the two faiths, is to appear naive or quixotic. It is to meet a blank stare, it is to end a conversation.

I come from simple Indian village and town folk who happened to follow a line of Muslim mystical singer-preachers, the first of whom, per legend, arrived from the Near East nine hundred years ago and was welcomed in the capital, Patan, of the Gujarat kingdom. He was, to mainstream Islam, a heretic. How could we possibly identify with the conquering Afghan and Turkish hosts, who professed to be Muslim in a very traditional, orthodox sense? For me the Afghan-Turkish, and later Mughal, dynasties and their cast of characters are fascinating because of their sheer alienness and their distance in time, and because of the manner in which they influenced the history and culture of the subcontinent. Their achievements have been remarkable, and they present us with the paradox that while producing works of sublime beauty they were capable of the utmost physical cruelty. History brings them down to us as real and intriguing personalities that make us ponder about our own humanity and times.

✑

There was an African who came to Delhi seven centuries ago; even before I read of his journey to India, the retroflex music of his name,

Battuta, had thrilled me as a child, for he had also visited my part of Africa and written about it. He did not use his observations to flaunt his literary skill, as Khusrau did; nor was he sanctimonious, like Barni. He simply travelled and travelled, and at the end he wrote what he recalled, when no sultan could look over his shoulder.

In 1334, from a crossing at the banks of the river Indus in the northwest, the intelligence service sent a report to Delhi's sultan, who ruled almost the whole of the territory of India, that a North African traveller had arrived by way of Kabul, on his way to the capital. He was a respectable man, accompanied by an entourage of forty; he was well travelled and had visited the holy cities and performed the hajj, and he appeared well versed in Islamic jurisprudence. This intelligence would have taken about five days, by relayed courier, to reach the sultan. The traveller waited two months in Multan before the reply came, bidding him and the other visitors waiting with him to come to Delhi. But he had to sign a statement that he had come with the intention of settling permanently in India, otherwise he would have been turned back. Delhi needed qualified Muslim immigrants.

The visitor was Ibn Battuta (1304–1368), perhaps the greatest traveller of the medieval world. In 1325, at the age of twenty-one, saying goodbye to his sorrowful mother and father, he had set off east from his native Tangier with the aim of visiting the holy cities of Mecca and Medina; but the urge to travel proved insatiable, and by the time he returned home to settle, he had spent twenty-nine years on the road, his journeys having taken him across varied lands and seas all the way to China. In the interim he had time to make a sea voyage down the Indian Ocean to the coast of East Africa, up to Mombasa and Kilwa. His last voyage, when he was well on in years, was across the Sahara to the Mali kingdom of West Africa. Back finally in Morocco, in Fez, he prepared a memoir of his travels with the aid of a young secretary. He was not a man of letters, and this was his only book. Its great appeal today is precisely that it is a memoir: intimate, expansive, unpretentious. Ibn Battuta had to be a survivor, too; his journeys were often hazardous, and he came across rulers who rewarded him and gave him positions in their lands, but who also made him tremble and could have had his head cut off and stuck on a rampart for all to see. Alberuni, the great eleventh-century Persian scholar-traveller, after spending ten years in India learning all he could, produced an invaluable record, but he does not reveal himself so openly. Ibn Battuta gives us the man on the road.

On the way down to Delhi from Multan, Ibn Battuta describes seeing sati processions in which "richly dressed" widows were carried to the cremation site to be immolated with their dead husbands. The Muslim sultans tolerated this practice, which was alien to them, and the traveller's reaction to the spectacle is only to tell us how happily the women embraced their dead husbands and burnt with them.

It had been eighteen years since Alauddin Khilji had died, and the Tughlaq dynasty was now in place. The sultan was Muhammad Tughlaq, son of Ghiyasuddin, the builder of Tughlaqabad, the third city. Muhammad, credited with arranging the death of his father (who died when a wooden shelter fell on him), had raised a fourth city, essentially comprising the two older Delhis, Alauddin's Siri and the older Qutb area, which together were enclosed within a protecting wall and given the grand name of Jahanpanah, "Asylum of the World." This was the city to which Ibn Battuta arrived.

Muhammad Tughlaq was one of the most enigmatic and controversial of India's rulers, brilliant, idealistic, pious on one hand, and extremely cruel and arbitrary on the other. He learned Arabic so he could read the religious literature first-hand, became adept at the art of calligraphy, and wrote Persian verse. He held learned discussions with Hindu ascetics and Jain scholars, not to mention those of his own faith, and has even been called a nonbeliever and a rationalist. At the same time his administrative and military achievements were significant and astute; he ruled over a vast empire and defended its borders. Yet to be close to him was to live on the edge. Some historians have called him mad. Ibn Battuta, who wrote in the comfort of his home in Morocco, describes him fearlessly.

> This king is of all men the fondest of making gifts and shedding blood. His gate is never without some poor man enriched or some living man executed, and stories are current amongst the people of his generosity and courage and of his cruelty and violence towards criminals.

Soon after his arrival, Ibn Battuta obtained an audience with the sultan. In the magnificent Hall of a Thousand Pillars, he came before the "Master of the World, a tall, robust, white-skinned man seated, his legs tucked beneath him, on a gold-plated throne." One imagines standing among the courtiers beside the sultan, the historian Barni (who would also write about this sultan) watching the nervous Moroccan's performance as he paid his respects. Writes Ibn Battuta,

> I approached the sultan, who took my hand and shook it, and continuing to hold it addressed me most affably, saying in Persian, "This is a blessing; your arrival is blessed; be at ease, I shall be compassionate to you and give you such favours that your fellow-countrymen will hear of it and come to join you." . . . Every time he said any encouraging word to me I kissed his hand, until I had kissed it seven times, and after he had given me a robe of honour I withdrew.

Craven, but otherwise he might not have lived to tell the tale. There is a charming transparency about him. The sultan appointed him a qadi, a judge, of Delhi on a lavish stipend. No wonder that he extols the sultan's "dominant quality" of generosity, even as he talks about his bloodiness.

Although Ibn Battuta describes Delhi as a magnificent city, he also says that it was empty and unpopulated when he arrived. It could not have been quite so, but the statement reflects the fact that this "second Baghdad," which had trembled under the siege of the Mongols yet staved them off successfully, had recently experienced a terrible upheaval at the hands of its own sultan.

As long as Delhiites did not run afoul of the sultan they could live their lives in peace; what blood was spilt was among the ruling elite. But around 1327 events took place in Delhi that completely shattered this peace. Muhammad Tughlaq decided to move his capital four hundred miles south to Daulatabad, in the Deccan, so it could be at the centre of his vast empire. But he did not merely move his government, he forced the entire upper class to pick up and go along as well, lock, stock, and barrel. These cosmopolitan elites were naturally reluctant to leave the splendour of their great capital—"Hazrat-i-Delhi," Khusrau had called it—to set up anew in a provincial town in a distant, alien region of the country. Anonymous and abusive letters were thrown into the sultan's audience hall in protest. The sultan responded with measures appropriate to his nature. Among those who resisted the move were the Sufis, for Delhi had become an important centre for them. Nizamuddin was dead, so a major battle of wills was averted. With the lesser of these men of God, the ruler had his brutal way. They were dragged out of their houses, pulled by their beards, tortured. The khanqahs, the Sufi centres, were emptied. "They walked with loud lamentations, like persons who are going to be buried alive," says Barni. There were women, children, and the elderly among the migrants, it was summer, and the ground was burning hot.

Within a few years Daulatabad was found unsuitable and the court returned to Delhi, which was, naturally, completely shaken up by these upheavals.

Ibn Battuta arrived in Delhi a few years after this experiment in forced migration was over, and what he writes is from hearsay and rumour, but it is perhaps also indicative of how bitterly the episode was remembered.

The sultan ordered a search to be made for any persons remaining in the town, and his slaves found two men in the streets, one a cripple and the other blind. They were brought before him and he gave orders that the cripple should be flung from a mangonel [a mechanical projectile thrower] and the blind man dragged from Delhi to Daulatabad, a distance of forty days' journey. He fell to pieces on the road and all of him that reached Daulatabad was his leg. When the sultan did this, every person left the town, abandoning furniture and possessions, and the city remained utterly deserted. A person in whom I have confidence told me that the sultan mounted one night to the roof of his palace and looked out over Delhi, where there was neither fire nor smoke nor lamp, and said, "Now my mind is tranquil and my wrath appeased."

In 1342, after seven years in Delhi, Ibn Battuta was dispatched by the sultan as his emissary to the powerful Mongol emperor of China. And he was away. He would die happily in his old age in his native Morocco.

><

And, when they see me march in black array,
With mournful streamers hanging down their heads,
Were in that city all the world contained,
Not one should 'scape, but perish by our swords.

CHRISTOPHER MARLOWE,
Tamburlaine the Great

The third sultan of the dynasty started by Ghiyasuddin Tughlaq was the gentle Firoz Shah, known as a great restorer, who repaired, among other sites, Aibak's tower, the Qutb Minar, and Alauddin's great water reservoir, Hauz Khas. Soon after his accession, he issued a statement prohibiting the use of torture by the state: " . . . there shall be no tortures, and . . . no human beings shall be mutilated." "Terroristic severities have been replaced by mildness, kindness, and affection." His new Delhi was considerably to the north, by several miles, and called Firoz Shah Kotla (now the site of Delhi's cricket ground). After Firoz Shah's death in 1388 there began a rule of ineffectual kings of the dynasty with short-lived reigns. Mongols continued to threaten in the north.

In 1398, the Mongol Timur (known in the west as Tamerlane or Tamburlaine) swept down upon northern India from his capital in Samarkand (in present-day Uzbekistan), leaving behind a trail of utter devastation. The Mongols, who had started out as "heathen" conquerors two centuries before, had become Muslims after their ravaging of Muslim lands. Timur's purpose in undertaking this current adventure, as he writes in his memoir, was to inflict punishment upon infidels and unbelievers, "for it had reached my ears that the slayer of infidels is a ghazi, and if he is slain he becomes a martyr." Timur of course had had no qualms thus far about slaying people of any creed, including his own. This time he could not decide whether to attack the infidels of India or China. He picked India. On December 17, after first putting to the sword one hundred thousand captives, by his own account, whose loyalty to him could not be certain, he met the Tughlaq army in what is the centre of the present city, and overpowered it. The Delhi sultan at first took refuge inside his fort, then in the night he fled into the mountains. Delhi surrendered, and Timur, after much entreaty, promised to spare its citizens. However, a street brawl between soldiers and citizens led to a bloodbath. Of this, Timur himself writes,

> The flames of strife were thus lighted and spread through the whole city. . . . The savage Turks fell to killing and plundering. The Hindus set fire to their houses with their own hands, burned their wives and children in them, and rushed into the fight and were killed. . . . On that day, Thursday, and all the night of Friday, nearly 15,000 Turks were engaged in slaying, plundering, and destroying. . . . The following day, Saturday the 17th . . . the spoil was so great that each man secured from fifty to a hundred prisoners, men, women, and children. . . . The other booty was immense. . . . Gold and silver ornaments of the Hindu women were obtained in such quantities as to exceed all account.

This cold-blooded account of a massacre itself makes us wonder how to respond. As Timur says, he said his prayers devoutly. The following day he departed. And the dazed remnants of a citizenry watched the blood-quenched army of the conqueror march away with booty and slaves.

Timur is the national hero of Uzbekistan, where his statues adorn the cities of Tashkent and Samarkand. When he left Delhi he took with him all the artisans, master craftsmen, builders, and stonemasons he could find. Uzbekistan, and especially Samarkand, therefore boasts some of the most beautiful medieval architecture.

Following the Tughlaqs came the Sayyids, and Delhi was by now a provincial city, shorn of its previous prestige and power, the rule of the sultan reduced to a few square miles. It was the dynasty of the Lodis, which came to power in 1451, that brought some of the former prestige back to Delhi. The second of these kings, Sikander, is buried in a magnificent tomb in the beautiful Lodi Gardens, a popular picnic ground and walking area behind the India International Centre. Sikander's son Ibrahim, however, had to face the Mongol Babur on the field of Panipat, forty miles from Delhi, in 1526, and was killed while deserting his troops. He is buried in Panipat. The Mughal (Mongol) dynasty of India thus began.

✕

With Babur's victory at the Battle of Panipat, the Mongols fulfilled their old dream of conquering the enigmatic subcontinent, from whose doors they had been beaten away numerous times over the previous two to three centuries. Babur was descended from both Chinghiz Khan, "the accursed," as the historians of the sultans had called him, and Timur. With Babur, now began the Mughal Empire ("Mongol" translates to "Mughal" in India), which at its zenith was the greatest in the world, spanning most of the subcontinent and parts of Afghanistan, with more than a hundred million people under its dominion.

The first several emperors of the dynasty are called the "great Mughals," their list of begats known to all Indian school children, at least in the past. I remember reading about them in the history books in Africa, their names associated with what now seem rather inane titles: Babur the Brave, Humayun the Kind, Akbar the Great. Babur, the first of them, went on to Agra after a stop in Delhi to pay his respects at the tombs of the sultans and the Sufis. He died in Agra and was buried in Kabul, according to his instructions. His son Humayun moved the court back to Delhi in 1530, and his capital was in the region of the Humayun tomb and Purana Qila (the Old Fort) in today's central Delhi. Humayun was chased out of the country by a Pathan rival called Sher Shah, whose brief dynasty ruled in Delhi between 1540 and 1555. Sher Shah is responsible for the Purana Qila and the grand buildings inside it, including the mosque. Humayun, however, returned triumphant, and the Mughal dynasty resumed. Following Humayun, Akbar (1556–1605) ruled briefly from Delhi before moving his capital to Agra and later to his new city a short distance away, called Fatehpur Sikri. Shah Jahan (1628–1658), Akbar's grandson, took the court back to Delhi. His new Delhi was called Shahjahanabad, which continues to this day as the present-day Old Delhi. The last of the great Mughals was the stern and bigoted Aurangzeb, who died in 1707 at the age of ninety-nine. After him began the slow disintegration of the Mughal empire, though the dynasty lasted until 1857.

Babur, whom paintings depict as an austere-looking man with high cheekbones and a flowing, light, pointed beard, wrote a memoir, the *Baburnama*, in which we get a glimpse of the man behind the conqueror's mask. Unlike his ancestors, of whom he was quite proud, he comes across as quite a charmer. He describes his father as fat, with a round beard and wearing a tight tunic, so that when he released his breath the ties would fall off. He makes a bawdy joke, quotes poems written by himself and others; characterizes people and observes nature's beauties; he reveals a conscience, as when he repents writing bawdy verse. We get a picture of a sensitive man. And yet, casually and without revealing inner conflict, he writes of a massacre. As soon as he arrived in Delhi, he went and paid respects to the tomb of the Sufi Nizamuddin, then to that of Alauddin Khilji, and finally he visited Tughlaqabad. But he did not like India, found the people and landscape alien; he describes two ways of eating the mango, and he disliked the jack-fruit intensely. And so one is thankful for his *Baburnama*, for its candidness, its confidences.

There are Mughal legends, of course, sweetened versions of history that live on in the imagination, aided in modern times by the movie industry: the justice of Akbar; the love of Shah Jahan for his wife; the love of Akbar's son Salim for a common girl, Anarkali.

The great Akbar would not tolerate the match for reasons of state and had the girl walled in for defying him, but he had promised a boon to her mother and so he had the prison left open at the back so she could walk away, a tragic heroine, singing, "The world belongs to one who's loved." Two films have been made of this love story; the songs are legend. Then there is the story of Babur the father walking in despair around the sickbed of his son Humayun, when there seemed no hope. Babur said to God, "Take me instead," and the Almighty complied. Babur died and Humayun lived.

Monuments tell a story, reflect a mindset: Aibak's tower of victory and his great mosque built over a Hindu temple; Alauddin's vain attempt at a bigger tower, his more practical Hauz Khas water reservoir for the people of Delhi, his fair-trade regulations; Akbar's new capital Fatehpur Sikri for his ideal of a unified India; Shah Jahan's incomparable Taj Mahal for his beloved dead queen, and his new city, Shahjahanabad. Each visitor must surely have a favourite among the monuments that transports him or her to a mood, a vision.

I have never been struck more by any monument than the relatively plain Safdarjung tomb, lying unobtrusively behind a drab wall along the bustling north-south Aurobindo Marg, roughly halfway between the old Delhis of the Qutb area and the more recent Delhis of the north. Hardly on the tourist trail, but a walking distance from the Lodi Gardens. Buses stop outside, and rickshaws; fruit and drink stands ply a steady trade; the ticket booth very occasionally collects a five-rupee entrance fee. The first-time visitor already in doubt if the trip will be worth the effort.

But as soon as I entered through the gates, I had stepped into another world. Not that the place, a central tomb surrounded by a walled garden, had been perfectly kept or reconstructed; the fountains were dry, the walls dirty, the tomb not preserved, though not a ruin either. And according to experts it is but a poor architectural cousin to Humayun's grand tomb, not far away. Yet one slowed one's pace, drew one's breath. Perhaps the stunning impact was due to the absence of tourists and cameras, and the quietude that suddenly met the eye and the ear. The old tomb was all there was to contemplate.

To this untrained eye there seemed such a perfection in balance, composure, to the place: the grounds not so large, with generous paths between fountains and gardens to walk on; the tomb construction neither overbearing nor insignificant; the fern, palm, mango, and other trees liberally planted and well spaced, offering shade to seek shelter in. And in these shades a few young lovers had got away from the clutter of public life of India to find the privacy in which to embrace, put a head against a shoulder.

The domed and arched building, its smooth lines, its red-brown and white were subdued, yet had a quietly imposing presence. The tomb itself invited one to go around it first, walk the verandah, take in the whole scene, the courting couples and the rows of trees and the defunct fountains from a height: it didn't draw one in vulgarly to look at the burial site and go away; for after all, who was Safdarjung? There was a spaciousness to the monument, a dignity, a presence, the predominance of an abstract that inspired awe and suggested mystery; what design or artifice there was—and there was much—was unobtrusive, as was everything else here, and symmetry and balance were paramount.

Throwing a glance from this raised tomb to the bustling, screeching street outside over the wall, I was forced to acknowledge that, yes, a truly different mind, an alien being, had contemplated this space.

Safdarjung was a Mughal minister at a time when the dynasty lay tottering and Delhi had seen its worst devastation in a long time, under Nadir Shah of Persia.

In March 1739 Nadir Shah entered triumphantly into Delhi, and following a riot of the citizenry against the Persian troops, a massacre ensued, continuing for five hours as the Persian ruler watched from the roof of the Sunehri Masjid (the Golden Mosque) in Chandni Chowk. Some 20,000 to 150,000 people are believed to have been killed in that bloody episode. Nadir Shah left behind a plundered Delhi beaten into a stupor. Wrote the poet Sauda, an inhabitant of the city, "How can I describe the desolation of Delhi? There is no house from where the jackal's cry cannot be heard. The mosques at evening are unlit and deserted, and only in one house in a hundred will you see a light burning." Another poet, Mir Taqi Mir, said it all in the words, "Alas! Alas!"

Nadir Shah took with him the "Peacock Throne" (as the jewel-studded Mughal throne was called), bullion, jewels, works of art, and arms. In the following decades Delhi saw years of peace, occupation, plunder, internal strife, assassinations of its emperors, and gradually it whittled away into a small kingdom. In 1785 the Marathas, a class of warrior people who had given much trouble to the Mughals, had been called to protect the emperor, and after 1788 the general Scindia ruled under the name of the emperor, until in 1803 the British defeated the Marathas at a point across the Jumna from Humayun's tomb and occupied the city. The old emperor Shah Alam received the British at the Red Fort and recognized British protection and authority.

A dizzying history, of which I try to make some order with the aid of a table:

Dynasty / Rule	Prominent Rulers	Prominent Places
Rajput (before 1192)	Prithviraj III	Qila Rai Pithora
Early Turkish sultans (1192–1290)	(Muhammad of Ghur) Qutbuddin Aibak, Iltutmish, Raziya	Qutb complex, Qutb Minar, Quwwatul Islam mosque
Khilji dynasty (1290–1320)	Jalaluddin, Alauddin	Siri; Hauz Khas; Alauddin's incomplete tower
Tughlaq dynasty (1320–1414)	Ghiyasuddin, Muhammad, Firoz Shah	Tughlaqabad, Jahanpanah, Firoz Shah Kotla
Sayyid dynasty, Lodi dynasty (1414–1526)	Bahlol, Sikander	Lodi Gardens
Mughal dynasty (1526–1857)	Babur, Humayun, Akbar, Shah Jahan, Aurangzeb . . . Bahadur Shah Zafar	Shahjahanabad (Old Delhi), Humayun's tomb, Purana Qila, Safdarjung tomb
East India Company (1615–1857), British Raj (1858–1947)	governors general, viceroys	Shahjahanabad, New Delhi

The City of the Poets: Old Delhi

O limpid waters of the Ganga
remember you the day
when our caravan stopped by your banks
and forever came to stay?

ALLAMA IQBAL

AT THE AGE OF FORTY-SEVEN, the fifth Mughal emperor, Shah Jahan, having built the Taj Mahal in memory of his beloved wife, Mumtaz, moved his capital from Agra to Delhi, where he built a new city far to the north of all the previous ones. In between lay scattered villages and settlements, including the buried ruins of ancient Indraprastha. Delhiites should perhaps be grateful to Shah Jahan, for without his city, India's capital might be elsewhere. Thousands of labourers and skilled craftsmen brought in from all parts of the kingdom worked on the project, which took nine years to complete. The result, in 1649, was a grand city of palaces, gardens, parks, and mosques. This was the newest Delhi, the Mughal Delhi, named Shahjahanabad after its founder, and now known simply as Old Delhi. It was laid out like a polygonal fortress, a wall running around it, the Red Fort at its base, and fourteen gates to leave or enter it. Only five of the original gates remain, the prominent one on the south side being Delhi Gate. The Red Fort lay on the eastern side, on the bank of the Jumna river, which has receded in the intervening centuries. It was at the Red Fort where the last Mughal emperor surrendered to the British, where the British lowered

99
–

their flag at India's independence, and where the prime minister of India raises the national tricolour every Independence Day.

To get to Old Delhi you can take an auto-rickshaw or a tempo (a similar vehicle, fitted for seating eight and squeezing in more) from Connaught Place, proceed through Delhi Gate and on to the market area of Darya Ganj, and get off at the corner of Chandni Chowk, the most exciting, throbbing street in the entire modern metropolis, for this visitor, at least. (Nowadays you can also take the subway, pride of modern Delhi, where it's forbidden to eat or drink, and get off at Chawri Bazar and walk or catch a bicycle rickshaw to Chandni Chowk.) Across the road from the Chowk is a vast ground, at the head of which stands the Lal Qila, the Red Fort. Chandni Chowk is a wide avenue that was once a promenade but today is so clogged with people and traffic you have to practically push your way through. On either side, shops and restaurants spill over into the sidewalk and street, hawkers thrust their wares and shout their prices, which are negotiable, fresh jelebis fry in woks, carts of stuff are pulled away along the road through the throngs. A man bounds across the road by quickly stepping upon a succession of rickshaws.

The Delhi companion of my recent visits is Mahesh, former Marxist, a writer and translator, who has also tried his hand at a couple of businesses, book publishing and an eco-friendly gift shop. He was born in today's Pakistan and grew up in Nehru's Delhi, a city of refugees then, and recalls it when it was a much smaller city and much of South Delhi was farmland and small settlements. He himself is intimate with it, possessive, more its gregarious storyteller than guide.

We reach the jewellery market, a cross street lit up with neon and gold and shimmering saris, crowded with middle-class women out to shop here from the suburbs, cell phones to the ear. This famous street is called Dariba Kalan, the word "dariba" derived from the Persian and meaning "incomparable." A man hails us from one of the shops. Mahesh replies and then explains to me that

Satish is a Hindi teacher at a local college who comes to the shop every afternoon to ply the family trade in costume jewellery. We go over and exchange greetings. The store is more of a stall, with an open window at which Satish sits cross-legged amidst the glitter of bangles and anklets, elaborate necklaces, rings and hairpins, all displayed in the showcase before him and on the wall behind. His eyes all the time dart upon the busy street. I am told that both Mahesh and Satish taught at the same college as young graduates, before Mahesh left for a doctorate and a university post. They banter about their youth. Satish, post-Partition, supported right-wing parties, and Mahesh of course was the Marxist. That was a long time ago, the politics now are less intense, the old antagonists more mellow. Satish's family has had the business since 1917, renting the site originally from a Muslim who departed on the eve of Partition. The landlord now is the city. Relations in the neighbourhood were cordial once upon a time, Satish explains, and you could go from roof to roof from one end of the city to another, irrespective of whether the house you trod on belonged to a Hindu or a Muslim. The Muslims are mostly the craftspeople, the Hindus the traders. Tea is brought for us as we stand outside, and samosas, in spite of our demurrals (we know we have no choice), the tumult of Old Delhi brushing at our backs. It is acknowledged with a smile that business is booming, property values have multiplied, what with the new subway stop close by. But a neighbour has now laid a claim to the site where the stall is located and the case is in court. Two of Satish's children are in the United States. So many people I meet in Delhi have relations, especially children, overseas that I wonder if this phenomenon is the undying resonance of Partition, the restless refugees never completely at home. We depart, and Mahesh explains to me how time has whittled away the old joint families, in many cases a single branch remaining to run the business or simply to hold on to the family property. Disputes are legendary, ruthless, and Dickensian.

From Dariba Kalan we turn into Kinari (Border) Bazar, dedicated to all sorts of multicoloured decorations for festivals and borders for clothing.

Pre-modern Delhi was a grand place once; here, the aristocracy lived and mingled and came to shop; splendid parades were held.

Travellers from Europe, and ambassadors and agents of its kings and queens, drawn by curiosity, business, or intrigue to the grand Mughal's capital, strolled its avenues. A waterway ran along the main avenue to provide the residents with water; the beauty of the moon's reflection upon it, so goes one story, confirmed by Satish, gave the area its name, *chand*, meaning "moon." Much blood was also shed here, when Nadir Shah the Persian swooped down upon Delhi and oversaw the massacre of its citizens and the plundering of Dariba Kalan, and during the "Mutiny" of 1857, when the last Mughal emperor was drawn into it and his forces lost against the British. Nowadays there is no distinction between the business and residential areas. Many of the wealthy houses used to be havelis, compounds entered through large gates on the street which opened into square courtyards, all around which were the quarters of an extended family. Some of these old havelis are in ruins, others have been converted into godowns, or warehouses, or divided into individual shops and residences.

><

Let's go find Ghalib's house, says Mahesh.

Ghalib's name is a household word in northern India; he occupies a place in Urdu letters somewhat akin to Pushkin in Russia. (The two were born within three years of each other.) Enthusiasts often compare Ghalib to Shakespeare, which is perhaps reasonable in terms of his exalted status, but he wrote only poetry and letters, and Urdu does not have the status of English. Ghalib tugs at men's hearts, he sings to the romantic in every Indian male. After all, the song part of the song-and-dance Bollywood until recently was nothing but pure Urdu poetry (many of the original songwriters were poets in that language), of which Ghalib is the acknowledged god.

He was born Mirza Asadullah Baig Khan in 1796 in Agra, to parents of Turkish ancestry. Ghalib was his pen name. He did not have family income, his father having died when he was young, and therefore he depended on a pension from the British and on other patronage. Money problems seem to have dogged him all his adult life. His career coincided with the tenure of the last Mughal emperor, Bahadur Shah, a great lover of poetry and no mean poet himself; therefore he was witness to the violence against the British during the so-called Mutiny, and the devastation of Delhi and its population at their hands when it was quelled. Ghalib loved mangoes, wine, and gambling, for the last of which sins he was once sent to prison. His sense of humour is legend, and there are many affectionate stories told about him, in the vein of the irreverence of genius. And so: When one night during the Mutiny he was confronted by British soldiers who asked him if he was a Muslim, Ghalib is said to have replied, Half a Muslim; I drink wine, but don't eat pork. He was married to a pious woman of his class, but in his younger days had had an affair with a courtesan called Chaudvin, who died quite young. Despite his sense of humour, his ghazals and his quite beautiful letters carry an undoubtedly distinctive tone of sadness. A picture of him, almost emblematic for its familiarity, shows a white-bearded elderly man in a tall black hat, an embroidered robe over a kurta.

Of his love affair he wrote late in his life, in a remarkably frank and moving letter, "It is forty years or more since it happened, and although I long ago abandoned such things and left the field once and for all, there are times even now when the memory of her charming ways comes back to me and I shall not forget her death as long as I live. . . . Fate poured into my cup too the poison of this pain, and as the bier of my beloved was borne along the road, the dust rose from the road of that fortitude which was my essence. In the brightness of broad day I sat on sack cloth and clad myself in black in mourning for my mistress, and in the black nights, in the solitude of sorrow, I was the moth that flew to the flame of her burnt-out candle. She was the partner of my bed, whom at the time of parting my jealous heart could not consign even to God's keeping."

What moviemaker could resist this scene of Old Delhi, the old poet recalling his love and its loss, against the backdrop of the Mughal court in its final days, where rival great poets still gathered to recite their poetry and the doomed emperor, too, joined in? Two Indian films have been made about him, in which the poetry is sung by the country's finest singers of ghazals. The sparse and clean streets in the films and the large almost empty houses couldn't provide more contrast to the reality of Old Delhi today.

Mahesh and I walk through a maze of gulleys—small narrow streets—in pursuit of Ghalib in this his neighbourhood. Mahesh knows it like his backyard, which it is, in a manner, for the former Marxist Party offices were here. As the evening hour approaches, congeals, the crowds around us thicken. In places, the old architecture still lingers, visible in the latticework balconies and screens, many now in tatters, and arched doorways, their original massive doors repainted; precarious and ugly vertical extensions rise up like scabs upon old single-storey structures. One alley contains a slaughterhouse, a few cows awaiting their fate patiently outside. There is a street where books are saddle-stitched, another has the paper market, shops selling fax and copying paper, old-style account books, cover stock, notebooks; a street of formerly copper, now mixed, ware. Here my companion stops abruptly and points to the backroom of a hardware store, to what looks like a medieval scene framed by the doorway: a man seated cross-legged on a floor covered in white linen, doing accounts on a book placed on a low table. He is the munim, leaning forward as he writes with painstaking care. Millions of rupees of business is conducted every day here, where walking carelessly, unaware of your wallet, can be a hazard. Once more the veiled women, then boys in handsome kurta-pyjamas and white caps walking to prayer.

But it's difficult to find Ghalib's house. People don't know it, we sound foolish simply asking about it: What kind of worthless layabouts on a busy day would go looking for the house of a poet long dead? Finally at some kind of educational stall with Urdu signs above the entrance, we are told to take a rickshaw to some street. Here, after a few more questions, we are directed to a perfumer's stall. The man sends a boy with us, past an entrance, then through a room, a courtyard, then another room, on one wall of which is a boarded-up window. Through broken slats we see brick and rubble outside. On the other side of the room is an arched doorway or window, it is difficult to determine which, that leads, we are told, to the room where Ghalib wrote his poetry. As we come out, the perfumer dabs us with a fragrant oil, tells us that the hotel down the road—a modern two-storey boxlike concrete structure—is where Ghalib's house once stood.

This, of the greatest and most revered poet in the Urdu language, and one of the great literary figures of the subcontinent. We walk back slowly with a strange feeling of emptiness.

Some years later I find out that the government of Delhi has purchased a site where Ghalib had lived, and put up a museum to him. I decide to pay it a visit. The place is indicated on a map as situated near a street called Balli Maran (Dead Cat) intersecting upper Chandni Chowk. Even with this information, it is not easy to find; my rickshaw driver has to stop twice to ask for Ghalib's haveli, the second time when we've just passed it. And now that I am here, it's impossible to tell which of the two places I previously saw, the rubble or the hotel, has become the museum. It is not very impressive. A narrow corridor leads to a medium-sized room divided into sections by mocked-up arched doorways. This apparently is a reconstructed portion of the haveli where Ghalib spent the latter years of his life. Built into two walls are showcases exhibiting a dummy of the poet sitting, some artifacts from his period, a few quotations from his poetry. A young couple have brought their boy to see the great poet's house, and as the father instructs him how to operate the camera, the mother sings from the poetry. A Pakistani woman has come with a porter bearing a large camera.

It seems to me that perhaps the rubble should have been preserved as a monument, not to the man but to his neglect. Is this all there is? I ask a man in a skullcap who now sits at the street entrance. He tilts his head to indicate, Just so.

I walk outside, sit down at a stall next door for tea. It is Sunday morning. Three boys evidently dressed up and recently bathed walk in, grinning, and take their seats. Confidently they order paya and parantha for their breakfast. Paya is a curry made of goat trotters; fatty but tasty, and a breakfast delicacy even in Toronto. I am reminded of childhood.

⤜⤛

On March 29, 1857, an Indian sepoy called Mangal Pandey shot his English adjutant in the parade ground at Barrackpore army camp, near Calcutta, with his musket and then slashed him with his sword. Lieutenant Baugh was not killed, but when the colonel ordered the guard to arrest Pandey, they refused. Pandey, however, at the point of finally being overpowered, shot himself, but was not killed, and within ten days was convicted and hanged in a hurry. This event is often regarded as the flashpoint of a widespread insurrection that followed, called the Indian Mutiny by the British. Indian nationalists prefer to call it the First War of

Independence. Whatever one calls it, it was provoked by a general sense of suspicion and resentment against the rule of the British East India Company that was already prevalent in much of the country, and especially within the army, where it was believed that the cartridges for the new Enfield rifles which had recently been brought into use came coated with beef or pork fat. This fuelled the rumour that the British were out to defile the religious purity of the Indian soldiers serving in their army, with the object ultimately of converting them to Christianity. Whether Mangal Pandey was a revolutionary hero, or a sepoy high on bhang at the time of his deed, is a question still debated. But while on his rampage he gave voice to the suspicion and hatred that many inside the army and outside it harboured towards the ruling race, and he became a symbol of Indian resistance to British rule. A few weeks after the incident at Barrackpore there was a mutiny at the army camp in Meerut, near Delhi, and in the violence, which spread to the bazaars, fifty-two European men, women, and children were killed. Some of the mutineers then headed for Delhi to enlist the Mughal emperor to lead their cause, and mutiny and violence erupted in other places as well.

The emperor was Bahadur Shah, a frail eighty-two-year-old resident of the Red Fort, a puppet whom the Company kept on the throne with a pension, but still beloved to his subjects. His father was a Sufi and his mother a Hindu Rajput. He is said to have likened his Muslim and Hindu subjects to his right and left eye, did not eat beef, and visited Hindu temples wearing a mark on his forehead. He liked animals and the arts, and was devoted to Urdu poetry. His own compositions are recited to this day by the aficionados. A weak, broken ruler at the sunset of Mughal rule in India, or a philosopher poet who knew his time and that of his ancestors was at last over?

But when a contingent of the rebels of Meerut arrived in Delhi and pleaded with Bahadur Shah to lead them in their war against the British, perhaps sensing a glimmer of hope for him and his dynasty, after saying first, "I did not call for you," he relented. He sat down on his throne and accepted their tribute. He appointed several princes to positions of command in the new army and wrote to neighbouring rajas to join forces with him.

"On May 11, 1857," Ghalib wrote memorably of that day in Delhi, "the disorders began here. On that same day I shut the doors and gave up going out. One cannot pass the days without something to do, and I began to write my experiences, appending also such news as I heard from time to time."

Ghalib had English friends, drew an English pension, and with his station in life did not have much sympathy for the rebels, who were not of his class and had only disrupted his life. He relates how they overran the city, and describes with remarkable empathy for the foreign, white victims how the rebels began killing men, women, and children, and burning down their houses:

> There were humble, quiet men, who passed their days drawing some modest sum from British bounty and eating their crust of bread. . . . No man among them knew an arrow from an axe. . . . In truth such men are made to people the lanes and by-lanes, not to gird up their loins and go out to battle. These men, when they saw that a dam of dust and straw cannot stem the fast-flowing flood, took to their only remedy, and every man of them went to his home and resigned himself to grief. I too am one of these grief-stricken men. I was in my home . . . but in the twinkling of an eye . . . every street and every lane was full of galloping horsemen, and the sound of marching men, coming wave upon wave, rose in the air. Then there was not so much as a handful of dust that was not red with the blood of men.

In contrast to this sympathy, which would have been shared by many upper-class Delhiites, many others embraced the incoming sepoys as liberators, the local Urdu paper going so far as to gloat over the murders of the English. Once the foreigners had been expelled or killed, the sepoys increasingly came to be seen as unruly and undisciplined, peasant warriors who seemed to have lost their zeal and spent their time creating disturbances at the tea houses and brothels. Still, with the imprimatur of the Mughal emperor, the insurgency continued to spread widely in the cities of the north, to become, as the historian William Dalrymple puts it in his detailed account of the events, "the single most serious armed challenge any Western empire would face, anywhere in the world, in the entire course of the nineteenth century."

The majority of the rebels were Hindus. Among many Muslims the revolt took on the tone of a jihad against kafirs (infidels), an attitude of hostility against Western dominance that in one form or another has lasted to this day.

Four months after the attack on Delhi, in September 1857 the British forces, with the help of Sikh soldiers, retook the city and quelled the uprising everywhere else, and the retribution that followed was savage.

History, as is so often the case, and not unlike reports of "rebellions" in other colonies or occupied countries, has given us a skewed, victors' look at the events. Indians did not record details as the British did. The British were few, each of them accounted for and written about, and their fates appear to us as personal tragedies or acts of heroism, illustrated sometimes by photographs; the Indians in the aftermath simply died or were hanged in their multitudes. Whereas the English showed themselves as arrogant, incompetent, brave, or pathetic, their descriptions making them live as individuals with faces, the sepoys were merely low-class fanatics and murderers.

Of the aftermath of the Mutiny in Delhi, its poet Ghalib would write:

Now every English soldier that bears arms
Is sovereign, and free to work his will.

Men dare not venture out into the street
And terror chills their hearts within them still.

Their homes enclose them as in prison walls
And in the Chauk [Chandni Chowk] the victors hang and kill.

The city is athirst with Muslim blood
And every grain of dust must drink its fill.

The emperor tried to escape but was captured at Humayun's tomb in the Nizamuddin area. His two sons and a grandson surrendered, after which they were stripped and shot dead by the officer in command outside the walls of Delhi, in the presence of a few thousand of their men who had been convinced to lay down their arms. Their corpses were taken by the Sikhs and displayed in front of the gurudwara, their temple, where 182 years before their Guru Tegh Bahadur had been executed by another Mughal, Aurangzeb. The officer, William Hodson, wrote that night, "I cannot help being pleased with the warm congratulations I received on all sides for my success in destroying the enemies of our race."

Bahadur Shah, the last Mughal emperor, after a trial whose outcome was no surprise, was exiled to Rangoon, Burma, with his wife and other family members, where he died three years later and is buried. He wrote an epitaph for himself, often quoted as a celebrated lament of exile. The last verse reads, "How unlucky is Zafar! For burial / Even two yards of land were not to be had, in the land of the beloved." A portrait of Bahadur Shah shows a wasted man with a long, quite handsome face and a white beard, in royal tunic and turban; a photograph in an English account of the Mutiny depicts a sickly old man in bed. We see what we want to see.

A film has been made, called *Mangal Pandey*, about the events that apparently triggered the Mutiny. It bears little resemblance to documented history, and with typical Bollywood illogic (Pandey forms a close friendship with his British commanding officer, who in turn rescues a widow from her husband's funeral pyre and falls in love with her) is an attempt to create a new legend for the gullible or patriotically romantic. The film ends with footage about Gandhi, thus grafting this new romance onto the real-life struggles for independence. *Mangal Pandey* is one of a spate of recent political films, including *Lagaan* and *1942: A Love Story*, all extremely popular, in which the English are portrayed mostly as boors and thugs. A remake of the classic *Umrao Jaan*, which is based on a novel set in the same period, about a young girl who is kidnapped and becomes a celebrated courtesan, has a lengthy scene depicting mounted British soldiers (no Sikhs) attacking Lucknow's citizens. A blood-soaked rapist is forgiven by his victim because he has taken up arms against the British. It is not the films so much as their provenance that is interesting, telling us that memories of British dominance go deep and continue to smart.

This was demonstrated in a remarkable fashion when a group of British historians and descendants of the fallen came to India recently to retrace the events of the insurrection on its hundred and fiftieth anniversary and commemorate the dead. In Meerut the group was barred from entering the cemetery by protestors bearing black flags, consisting of Indian nationalists and Muslim clerics according to reports, who saw the purpose of the visit as "an insult to Indian freedom fighters." In Lucknow the tourists were pelted with stones, cow shit, and other objects. The tour was aborted. "What sort of world is this?" said one of the visitors later. "People throwing muck at an eighty-two-year-old who can't even walk without help."

Old Delhi, fetid Delhi
alleys and little squares and mosques
like a stabbed body
like a buried garden

OCTAVIO PAZ

There is an organic quality to this old city of the Mughals, Shahja-hanabad, a thrilling wholeness consisting of a multitude of people and occupations jostling in a close space rich with history, and a pace of life you will find nowhere else in Delhi. Here, as in Manhattan—though the two places could not be more different—you do not tarry, are simply swept up by its life and pace and carried along.

On our way, busy meat shops; sweetmeats, salty namkeens frying; fresh-baked breads and cakes on display; a sidewalk book vendor eating meat curry with chappati opposite the Jama mosque; a

perfume seller calling out, rubbing samples on people's backs; boys playing alley cricket; cycle rickshaws, horses, mules, cows; burqa-covered women walking stiffly, proudly on the street; busy shopkeepers, idle shopkeepers, a bevy of women gathered around outside a shop to inspect a heap of material. I've never seen so many veiled women in India before.

But you don't see this Muslim presence outside the fabled gates. It seems as if they have barricaded themselves into this old city of the poets and kings where once their glory lay. What was life like for them here, before Partition, before the mass influx of the Punjabis and all the others who extended and transformed the city?

><

One of the most pithy, achingly nostalgic accounts of upper-class Muslim life in Old Delhi—Shahjahanabad—is contained in the novel *Twilight in Delhi*, by Ahmed Ali. Written in English and published first by Virginia and Leonard Woolf's Hogarth Press in 1940, most copies were destroyed in the London Blitz, and the book remained long out of print and mostly forgotten, until a new edition came out in 1966 in Bombay. It is now a recognized classic.

It is 1910 as the novel opens. Day begins in Mir Nihal's haveli with, as always, the sound of the dawn call to prayer from the great Jama mosque, the voice and identity of the muezzin, the caller, high in his tower, familiar to all in this Delhi community. Thence we witness in slow movements the final days and years of Mir Nihal, which coincide with the decline of the old Delhi as the British consolidate their hold over India. The tone of the novel is elegiac, its gaze ironic and tender upon this old lover, Delhi:

> Destruction is in its foundations and blood is in its soil. It has seen
> the fall of many a glorious kingdom, and listened to the groans of

birth. It is the symbol of Life and Death, and revenge is its nature.... But still it is the jewel of the eye of the world, still it is the centre of attraction.

Mir Nihal is a member of the old elite, his ancestors having arrived centuries before (this we surmise) from the Muslim lands of the north and west. He has an interest in a lace dealership, where he goes to work every day, but he also has property in his village and in the city. He has a young mistress, whom he supports and visits in the evening, a male indulgence; for his other leisure he flies pigeons, and he maintains an interest in alchemy and medicine. This is the Delhi in which suddenly someone in the midst of a conversation may break off into a line or two of Ghalib, say, or Saadi, or any of the beloved poets, including the former emperor Bahadur Shah; where your beggar at the door may be a desperate soul or a well-known mystic; where, sitting on a terrace in the balmy night, suddenly you hear a qawali recital in progress at a neighbour's house, the devotions addressed, the author informs us, to Allah, his Prophet, or an earthly lover; where in thanksgiving a family might go to pay respects at the grave of Shaikh Nizamuddin or some other saint. The women, behind the gates of the haveli, spend their time "eating, talking, cooking, sewing, or doing nothing"; or arranging marriages. And the muezzin at the Jama Masjid continues to give his call to prayer at the regular intervals.

So life passes, at its own beat; a life that has, one feels, maintained a thread of continuity from the Middle Ages in Isphahan, say, or Bukhara, or Balkh, to the present. But in reality the world has changed, continues unpityingly to change. On Chandni Chowk, the main thoroughfare, preparations have been underway for the upcoming coronation of King George, the foreign emperor; those old enough to remember, and Mir Nihal is one of them, recall bitterly the bloody British takeover of Delhi just over fifty years previously. And when Coronation Day arrives, they swallow the bitter pill and go and watch as the royal procession leaves the Red Fort and proceeds through their Chowk,

> one long unending line of generals and governors, the Tommies and the native chiefs with their retinues and soldiery. . . . In the background were the guns booming, threatening the subdued people of Hindustan. Right on the road, lining it on either side, and in the procession, were English soldiers, to show, as it seemed to Mir Nihal, that India had been conquered with the force of arms, and at the point of guns will she be retained.

As he watches, Mir Nihal recalls the former glory of Delhi under the Muslim sultans, Shah Jahan, Humayun, Firoz Shah, and even the Delhi of the *Mahabharata*. As the procession passes the Jama Masjid, "whose facade had been vulgarly decorated with a garland of golden writing containing alavish greetings from the Indian Mussalmans to the English King," he recalls how, in 1857, Delhi fell into the hands of the English, who contemplated the destruction of the mosque, or its conversion into a church; how the Muslims defended it, with swords against guns, and a bloodbath ensued.

To be fair, the sultans had also often retained Delhi by force of arms, though they were Indians now, their ancestors having arrived centuries ago and married locally, and there was no other land, no other flag, to which they owed allegiance. But Mir Nihal's world had to end, its time was over.

Soon after the Coronation, cruel changes are in store for this occupied city. Its ancient walls are proposed to be demolished; the row of peepal trees that forms the central boulevard on Chandni Chowk, giving it beauty and character, will be cut down. The seventh Delhi has fallen, and an eighth new Delhi is under construction beyond the walls; "strange people had started coming into the city, people from other provinces of India, especially Punjab." But, people predict, this new Delhi and its rulers too will one day fall, as the others had done. Already calls for freedom have begun, and there is word of a "Terrorist Movement."

Three years after the Coronation—Mir Nihal cannot know this—a bomb was thrown at the viceroy's procession in Chandni Chowk. The viceroy was splashed with blood and the man behind him was killed.

A woman's point of view, from a generation later, is presented in Attia Hosain's tenderly evocative novel *Sunlight on a Broken Column*. The setting here is Lucknow, another northern city celebrated for its courtly culture, its romance, its poets, and its architecture. Hosain describes the inevitability of change in the fortunes of the traditional Muslim feudal elite as the independence of India draws near. The story is told by a young woman called Laila, a devourer of books and curious about the world outside, and her refusal to accept her circumscribed, protected place within the family system and the role of a consort to a husband who will be selected for her. Not only does she question the absolute authority of the male elders of the family, abetted by the women, she also questions the privilege of her class over those whom they rule in their domain. Independence arrives, and Partition. Whatever country these Muslims opt for, India or Pakistan, their world is now utterly lost, their way of life, their privileges, erased. Those who choose to go to Pakistan lose their homeland, their beloved city; and those who stay have to accept a new, insecure, and often second-class existence.

If the pronouncement of Satish, the Hindi professor-jeweller I met on Dariba Kalan, on how Hindus and Muslims lived together sounds a bit too practised, the celebrated novelist Krishna Sobti evokes, in her *Dil-o-Danish* (*The Heart Has Its Reasons*), a relationship between a married Hindu lawyer and his Muslim mistress that is more textured. The time is the 1920s in Shahjahanabad, just about a decade after Ahmed Ali's Mir Nihal watches his world pass away in the wake of the Coronation procession. Kripanarayan, Sobti's character, is from the upper-class Punjabi Hindus who have benefited from the British takeover of the city. He is a romantic as well as a successful lawyer. At the end of the day he longs to spend his hours with Mehak, a passionate and beautiful woman "who ruled his heart" and by whom he has had two gifted children whom he wants to do well in life. But he is married to Kutumb, whom he has crowned "queen of hearth and home," and there are family and traditional obligations to which he is bonded. And so we find him helplessly strung between two worlds, two households, two relationships. This modern novel of Old Delhi, told in several voices and quite aware of the women's position in society, cannot help but also be elegiac as it reflects on the passage of time and the loss of poetry and romance, though in the fates of Mehak's two children it also looks to a future that seems more positive.

><

Mastering this old city, getting to know its narrow streets and gulleys, can also become an obsession . . . it seems just about achievable, perhaps one more visit will do it. During my more recent visits, Delhi Gate, the southernmost entrance, has become my geometric origin or reference point. Straight ahead (northwards) comes the Red Fort by the Jumna river; westwards from it runs Chandni Chowk. West from Delhi Gate runs Asaf Ali Road, presumably along the old wall of the city, on which are also the Turkman Gate and the Ajmeri Gate. Within these bounds, Old Delhi is yours to explore.

From Delhi Gate, the Bazar Chitli Qabar Marg goes its crooked way to the great mosque, the Jama Masjid, offering along its length sweetmeats, a Jain temple, jewellers, scrap metal, restaurants, pots and pans, clothes, money changers and Pakistan visa forms, flowers, peanuts, popcorn. If Mir Nihal's world is gone, his Delhi, though transformed, still thrives, as one pushes through the bhid—the crowds—without the space before you even to lift up the map in your hand. A motorbike arrogantly speeds through the crowd without a pause as people jump aside to escape with their lives; thus a metaphor comes alive, representing power and wealth. Otherwise the bicycle rickshaws patiently ply their trade, these alleys are made for them. They are the speediest conveyance in this bustling place. There can actually be a rickshaw traffic jam here: three alleys meet near a drain that is being opened, each of them jammed with rickshaws full of dainty-looking uniformed girls returning home from school and women in niqab; and the pedestrian has to jump over a rickshaw wheel to get through the knot.

The Jama Masjid, built by Shah Jahan and completed in 1656, is a glorious and commanding sight, pride of this old city and once its very heart. It is the largest mosque in India. Built on a hill, it stands ten yards above the level of the city, flights of steps leading up to its gates. As I arrive, a Japanese camera crew is at work at the southern gate. The vast courtyard can hold up to twenty-five thousand people, five hundred to a row. An arcade runs all around it, from which is visible a panoramic view of the city. There are three gates, and on the fourth, western, side, as in all mosques east of Mecca, is the roofed section which is the prayer hall, with its many pillars and eleven arched entrances from the courtyard, the central one larger and surmounted by a dome. Two smaller tapered domes are on either side, and two tall minarets. Visible from the eastern gate, in the near distance at the end of a wide promenade that must have been beautiful once, is the Red Fort; it is along the promenade and through the imposing eastern entrance that the emperor arrived, so it was also known as the Shahi Gate. Outside the northern gate, when the Mutiny had been quelled, the defenders of the mosque faced off an English officer called Thomas Metcalfe as he stood down on the street below with his men, ready to demolish the site. The imam of the mosque is a direct descendant of the man brought from Bukhara by the emperor Shah Jahan to inaugurate it and is an influential figure much courted by politicians and media, especially before elections.

❧

In the days not long gone, before globalization gained pace and "IT" opened the door to an Alibaba's cave of economic success and exuberant consumerism, you were told by friends before you left for Delhi where you should look for nonvegetarian food, should the craving come upon you, or, what was more likely, should the kids rebel, having had enough of mattar paneer, alu gobhi, and toor ki daal. There were the large tourist hotels, and one or two places in Connaught Place, and one or two at Khan Market, a five-minute walk from the India International Centre, which itself also served nonveg of a simple but consistent variety, but where you had to be a member or go with one. And finally, for the connoisseur and the committed carnivore, there was Karim's, capital of Mughal nonveg, tucked away in Shah Jahan's Delhi on Chitli Qabar Marg, a few yards down from his grand mosque. Nowadays nonveg has become so accessible and acceptable that many people don't remember the days when asking a friend how to get to Karim's could be an embarrassment, especially in the days of Hindu-Muslim tension following the destruction of Babur's mosque. In any case, in the mostly vegetarian Delhi of the time, here was meat galore, cooking on spits outside a rather drab-looking establishment. With its reputation now established internationally, and the Delhi-wallah with even a more modest vegetarian palate nibbling at chicken or fish (as my friend Krishan Chander now does, convinced after an angiogram that they are not a bad substitute for veg cooked in ghee), Karim's has branches outside the area, though people swear by the good old plain Karim's of the walled city. Any bystander will point out its small sign, and you say, Ah! and head towards it, as the owners of neighbouring establishments, their menus no different, peek out with looks of envy and wonder what could be so special about Karim's. The claim is that Haji Karimuddin's forefathers were employed in the royal kitchens of the Mughals; after the banishment to Burma of the last emperor, the Haji brought his culinary knowledge to the service of the common man and woman outside the walls of the Red Fort. Karim's opened in 1913.

You enter a short alley and are greeted by a large red board and a counter where curries are cooking in metal pots, and to your right kebabs are grilled on fires. There are three dining rooms around the small courtyard, which allows parking for a few motorbikes, and another dining room a floor up. It's all very informal, as you expect. Once seated on the bench seats, you can't decide what to order. Succulent mutton curries, various kebabs, biriyanis, assorted naans and rotis pass you by. The menu is diverse, at variance with the typical north Indian. I find the shammi kebabs, as starter, perfect in texture and taste; the seekh kebab is good; the mutton burra a little too dry. The brain curry cooked in garlic and spices comes under a layer of oil, so you have to forget health warnings for the day. The lamb stew and Shahjahani chicken curry are wonderfully spiced but drenched in oil, so that after the meal a good jog back to Lodi Road is worth contemplating. The biriyani is disappointing, it is what we called pilau at home, and no better: essentially rice cooked with garam masala and meat, in this case two rather bony pieces of lamb.

As you return from Karim's at night, Chitli Qabar Marg has lost little of its bustle from daytime and gained all the festive brilliance of neon and the aromas of foods grilled and frying. Even the children are about. But the woman with you is obviously from the suburbs—her clothes identify her—and even though her head has been covered for the occasion with a dupatta, the stares are discomforting and the crowds seem perhaps a little threatening—this she will not admit but you can sense—so a rickshaw is called for, though this in itself draws attention.

❤️

The Jama Masjid is surrounded by mechanical ugliness: stores selling used motor parts—tires, brakes, engines and their parts, fenders and doors, all spilling into the greasy sidewalk, customers inspecting, shop owners looking on, attendants attending; the odd Urdu bookstand.

Instead of taking Chitli Qabar Marg out of the city you could take Chawri Bazar from Jama Masjid; the two are roughly, crookedly, parallel, both ending at Asaf Ali Road, one at Delhi Gate, the other at Ajmeri Gate. First comes the paper market, carts and rickshaws carrying away cartons of papers and paper products. We reach an intersection where Nai Sarak—the textbook market—takes off, and where, from first-floor windows, courtesans once upon a time looked down upon the street. At this corner is an old mithai-wala shop, selling kachoris, samosas, etcetera, with lassi; a shack that has been busy since 1837, so says the elderly man who runs a paper business from an even smaller area partitioned off from the main shop, while his nephews run the old snack shop. The children are studying hotel management and catering, to carry on the family's food business. The paper merchant shows us greeting cards, wedding invitation cards, the latter always in demand. The conversation lingers on the subject of digital scanning and design copyright, and it is agreed that you can't stop the pirates but ultimately it is the reputation that counts. Anyone can make mattar kachori, says the irrepressible Mahesh, to illustrate the point, but there's nothing like the ones you sell here. The man is gratified, business cards are exchanged.

We push through the crowded sidewalks, Mahesh pointing out the various trades as the paper market gives way to hardware, plumbing, and plastic, calculating for me the millions of dollars of business transacted here every day—and pausing occasionally to answer his cell phone as he keeps track of his only living uncle's declining health. Mamu—his mother's brother—is only a few years older than Mahesh and more like his own brother; in the early days of Partition, still just a teenager, Mamu would fly kites with Mahesh in the neighbourhood and sold ice cream on Chandni Chowk to help his newly homeless family, refugees from what had become Pakistan. Banias—traders—by caste, they rebuilt themselves in Delhi, succeeding at a stationery business while living in the same house they were awarded by the city as compensation for what was lost, and Mamu is now at a private American-style hospital costing several hundred dollars a day, which would crush an ordinary Indian.

Chawri Bazar crosses Sitaram Bazar, then arrives at Ajmeri Gate. Across from the busy Asaf Ali Road is the Anglo Arabic School, founded as a madrassa in 1692 by a dignitary of the Mughal court named Ghaziuddin. It later became Delhi College, where in 1842 Ghalib came to be interviewed for a job; he declined it when he arrived on his palanquin and did not receive the welcome he expected from the English principal as the preeminent poet of Delhi. The college is the alma mater of several eminent Indians and Pakistanis, including Pakistan's first prime minister. The British introduced English, mathematics, and the sciences here, and today it is the local school for the inhabitants of the old city.

The shabby arched front entrance opens into a quite handsome quadrangle with a green at the centre; the walkways which cross it are of red sandstone, and the cloisters on three sides are arched and painted an off-white. There is a look of recent repairs, apparently undertaken by the city. On the fourth side, directly in front, is a grand mosque next to the tomb of Ghaziuddin. The quadrangle leads through a gate on the left into a run-down area where once Delhi College was located, where Mahesh finished his upper schooling. At the sight of the gate my friend runs through it gleefully, nostalgic, excited; he trots about with his camera, shows me the old library, the Hindi classroom—where he, the future Hindi translator, would make a point to miss his classes, answering the roll call while standing outside, chatting—the prep rooms, the girls' room, outside which the boys would perpetually hang around, and the wicket where they would pay their fees. Delhi College has since moved, and these rooms are used by the Anglo Arabic School.

At the steps of the open mosque a shaikh sits reading the Quran; a few other men sit inside. No one knows anything about the history of the place; but, says the shaikh, people do come around asking.

⟡

It's Saturday.

Asaf Ali Road, edging Old Delhi at its southern boundary, is moderately busy, its low office buildings effectively a containing wall, in place presumably of the original city wall. West of Delhi Gate on this road comes a quite remarkable sight: on the sidewalk outside a bank, a dozen or so men and a single woman are sitting on chairs at makeshift tables busily typing on old-style typewriters. They are law clerks, their clients waiting patiently around them for their documents to get typed. Further along the road comes the Turkman Gate. A few yards inside this gate appears the bead market, a row of stores selling loose and strung beads; further in, and the shop signs are no longer in Urdu script but in Devanagari. And suddenly there are no goats about. We are now in Sitaram Bazar, evidently Hindu in character. It's not that Muslims do not use Devanagari in modern India; and in the past educated Hindus, of course, read and wrote Urdu and even Persian. But here in the present, the sudden change is meaningful, denotes two peoples. My friend Mahesh calls this a recent phenomenon, reflecting the rise of Hindu communalism. The shops sell a variety of items, including circuit boards and Holi paraphernalia—heaps of coloured powder to dissolve in water and pumps for spraying it—for it is the eve of the festival of Holi, when people go about throwing or spraying colour at each other. Oranges, grapes, and bananas are also on display, occasionally guava, whose season, early in March, is ending.

There comes the Chaurasi Ganthi Mandir, the temple of the eighty-four bells, a cluster of which is visible from the street, hanging in the front hall. I have yet to find someone who can tell me what the bells signify, if there is a special story to this temple with such a lovely name. Otherwise it's a simple building, blending in with the business-residences which are its neighbours, right in the thick of the shopping. I walk inside, into a small dark hall, to discover that the cluster consists of numerous small bells hanging around a large iron ring; there are also individual bells hanging from the beams, and large bells at the front and back entrances, which are vigorously rung by worshippers. I can't help but raise my hand and follow suit. The shrine to the left, a brilliantly lit, colourful area in the otherwise dingy room, indicates by the icons present there that the temple is to the god Rama.

Almost next door in Sitaram Bazar is the building that's become famous as the childhood home of Pandit Nehru's wife, Indira Gandhi's mother, Kamala. This used to be an old-style haveli in a neighbourhood of Kashmiri Hindus, who are known to eat meat. It is here that young Nehru's barat, the wedding procession bearing the groom on a horse, would have come to take the bride away. Indira was the only child of that marriage, in which the husband and father was often away during the struggle for independence, canvassing or in prison. There is an outer gate with a massive door leading into a courtyard: cowpats on the ground; a communal water pump; an arched doorway leading into an interior; all around us the back sides of apartments. Obviously the old property has been greatly rearranged. Through the doorway we enter a corridor opening into the offices of an advocate and of a real-estate business that seem to belong to a single family. The corridor comes to an abrupt end at a wall, which could be of recent vintage. A man appears, understands our query, and shows us hooks hanging from the ceiling, from which apparently fans had once hung. He takes us to his office, offers us tea, but we decline. Evidently he is used to curious visitors. But there's nothing else to see. Kamala's haveli is oral history, her ghost haunting this location.

Outside, on the road, preparations are under way for the Holi celebrations tomorrow. At the crossroads, "holikas" have been constructed: piles of wood which will be burnt later, in the evening, to begin the celebrations. But this is also an occasion for spring cleaning, says Mahesh, with his knack for the little detail, pointing out how people have also heaped their junk—old furniture, baskets—on the firewood. Women and children come to stand worshipfully before the holikas.

This being Saturday, we pass a road shrine to the god Shani—Saturn—who's a minor deity but not to be ignored on that account, for he can be vengeful. The shrine is extremely modest, consisting of a low stool, about eighteen inches high, placed strategically at the edge of the road at a busy intersection. On the stool is a metal tray to collect offerings to the god: mustard oil, coins, iron nails. "Black" items, those containing iron, are not to be bought on Saturday, so as not to offend Shani; therefore many people will not buy cars, for example, on this day. Shani is a god to be feared and propitiated, for he is wilful and can bring bad luck, just like that, even though he is a very minor god in the hierarchy, nowhere close to Shiva or the Goddess. In particular, there is a special curse to be avoided, called the "Seven," that can beset you for seven years, causing havoc in your life. If you find yourself a victim of persistent bad luck, chances are you've been struck by Shani's Seven. There is no attendant in sight at the shrine now, for obviously who's going to steal from Shani? But Mahesh tells me there's probably a fellow somewhere who has put up all the Shani stalls in the area and periodically goes around—like a parking attendant (Mahesh's image)—collecting money from them, and the oil and coins and nails. Shani also has temples to his name, which many people visit. Mahesh tells me a colleague's wife, a university professor, had gone to pay her respects to Shani only yesterday, what with a grown daughter's marriage prospects to worry about. A Shani Seven in such a situation can be deadly; it's best to preempt it. Such belief in supernatural agencies can be quite casual among the educated. Consulting a horoscope, after all, is an essential part of the marriage process. A few years ago, many people had subscribed to the sensational stories of Ganesh statues, in various parts of India and abroad, imbibing real milk; some people even claimed to have seen the phenomenon.

A grand temple to Shani is situated just off Chandni Chowk. Above the entrance hangs a massive statue with seven horses. This is the sun god, but what is he doing in such a strategic spot outside Saturn's temple? Because, we are told when we inquire, the sun is the father and will keep naughty Saturn in check.

Ghantewala's sweet shop, a pre-Mutiny establishment, is close by on the Chowk. Equally old are the teeming parantha shops of the Paranthewali Gali, just further up, where you squeeze into benches at allocated tables and order from an assortment of paranthas available, stuffed with bhindi, karela, daal, carrot, or any of half a dozen more items. It's as well not to look too hard at the cloth used to wipe the table, and not to worry about the same hand being used to fry the parantha. Gloves are not the thing here.

Still on Chandni Chowk is the Sunehri Masjid—the Golden Mosque—from where Nadir Shah looked upon his troops' massacre of Delhi's citizens. The mosque, which has three domes, is not really golden. When I inquire in the neighbourhood, nobody really knows about it; someone even points me to the Sikh temple, which has golden domes. Having the temerity to inquire about the mosque at the temple, where a Sikh guru was martyred by a Mughal emperor, I am duly rewarded with a scowl.

⊱⊰

The only queen to occupy the Delhi throne was Raziya Sultana, who lived from 1205 to 1240.

Her tomb lies in the midst of a residential area, in a courtyard surrounded by the back sides of grimy old buildings. Local residents know about it, rickshaw drivers find it with difficulty. It lies tucked away within a maze of gulleys close to Sitaram Bazar. Passing dimly lit workshops from where busy young men and boys look out at us from their seats on the ground, hand-printing plastic bags, beading leather, and hand-decorating clock faces, we enter what is essentially a residential block, go through dingy corridors, climb some steps, and there below us is the burial compound of the queen, surrounded by a low brick wall. There are two ancient graves to look at, of Raziya and her sister, and, in a corner, two children's graves. There is a mihrab—a niche, which you face—for prayers, and a tap for ablutions. A man in modest traditional attire, presumably a caretaker, is readying himself for prayer. There's no sign to identify the site. But for seven hundred years the young queen has lain here, while all around her grave, houses have been built, demolished, rebuilt.

But there is a mystery here. This is still Shah Jahan's Delhi, so why is the Turkish queen from centuries before the Mughal's period buried here?

Raziya's story is a tangle of vaguely remembered historical intrigues; it is also one of a heroic and able female ruler in a male-dominated medieval world full of court machinations and treachery. She was named successor to the throne of Delhi by her intensely religious father, Iltutmish, the second sultan of Delhi, against the wishes of the mullahs and some of the Turkish nobility. After Iltutmish's death, the nobility, having first rejected Raziya's claim in favour of her weak brother, eventually installed her as queen. In order to take direct control of the affairs of state, she emerged from purdah and abandoned her female attire, appearing in public dressed in a cloak and hat. Delhiites would be amazed by the sight of her openly riding on the back of an elephant. Plots were soon hatching against her. She had elevated an Abyssinian slave called Yaqut to a high status, and it has been suggested that there was a love affair between the two, which historians have with surprising alacrity dismissed as baseless. Yaqut was ultimately murdered, and Raziya, after further misadventures, was finally killed in battle. Bollywood has made a film about her. And the next queen to rule in Delhi, so to speak, was Indira Gandhi, also killed, whose memorial lies not far away in the necropolis along the Jumna.

Punjabi Delhi

I know even after I am gone I will still wander the streets of Delhi....
The noisy racket of Delhi's people I will hear as one who listens to
music. Jamun, shahtut, phirni, chat-pakodi, bedmi kachori, rabri
khurchan. Ahh! Ghantewala's pista-lauj.

KRISHNA SOBTI, *The Heart Has its Reasons*

MANY OF THE DELHIITES I have met are Punjabi, having come as
children with their refugee parents from the part of Punjab that is
now in Pakistan, or having been born in Delhi of such refugees.
Punjabis form a majority in Delhi, and there seems a sense among
them of entitlement to the city. Where once Persian or Urdu might
have been heard on the streets, now it is Punjabi and Hindi, which
is essentially the same as Urdu (the national language of Pakistan)
but after Independence has become more Sanskritized. Attempts
were made to purge Hindi of its English and Persian loan words,
to render it more "national," but of course that proved impossible,
as it is impossible now to avoid Americanisms. My friends during
their lighter moments together often break into Punjabi, which
would be partially understandable to most north Indians, and I find
it rather close to Kutchi, so it is not quite foreign. Mahesh recalls a
train ride with his mother at the time of Partition, and her, pointing at smoke in the distance, saying, Look, Lahore is burning.
Lahore, the pride of Punjab, went to Pakistan. Right up to the time
of her death, she would refer to her birthplace as "Our Pakistan"—
not in the political sense that it belonged to India, but to indicate

where she came from. I've often seen Mahesh, a liberal-minded professor, get into confrontations with those among his colleagues whom he sees as Hindu chauvinists or nationalists. His interest is African literature, and he has translated several African authors into Hindi. I was introduced to him as an African Asian author outside a book fair when my first book was published in India. Over the years, I have seen him look progressively more stressed and harried, for Delhi life, for a man with several interests, who is also a father and a son in an extended family, demands much more than he thinks he can give. In India traditional obligations—of a parent, a wife, a son—which we from East Africa have learned to turn coldly away from, are not neglected even in the most dysfunctional families. But remove Mahesh from his sansara, the prison of worldly responsibilities, say to the bar of the International Centre or to the venerable United Coffee House in Connaught Place, and he is at his expansive best, a different man.

The coffee house is a den of the affluent. It being Saturday, both the main and the mezzanine floors are full, crowded with middle-class families and young couples, and, at the round table at which we sit, a rambunctious middle-aged group. The place is about seventy years old, the seats are plush, unlike the metal-and-plastic of the "cool" new establishments so favoured by the young. The food is north Indian—daals, sabzis, a variety of naans and chappatis.

Mahesh grew up in the Delhi of independent India, Nehru's child, if you will, and his memory and his narrative art are phenomenal. Eyes shining, wide smile on his bearded face, his voice loud and expressive, he lets forth. Even the waiters pause to listen. He tells us of the time when the well-to-do families of the city came to the United Coffee House so that a child could view a prospective spouse, and when the great merchants of the city would gather for their coffee in the morning and make their deals. He details the progress of a cricket match in Delhi way back in the sixties, when the West Indies were here to play India. Ah, the days of lost youth; this Delhi is as dear to him as Mir Nahal's was to him. He speaks of a secret meeting in the night with a minister when he was a leader of the powerful teachers' union. The next day, when the union leaders called off the strike, shoes were thrown at them and they escaped (perhaps) with their lives. He describes his travails as a tour coordinator when he led a group of uncouth fellow English teachers to a conference in East Germany. He describes the dramatic appearance of Indira Gandhi at an embassy function. And he tells us how one day he met Rajiv Gandhi at a bookstore next door.

Vegetables of all sorts are a passion. He will angle towards them at a market or a stall, and fondle a tomato or an eggplant to make you blush. Recently, to add to his demanding sansara that often keeps him on edge, he has bought a farm outside Delhi where he grows vegetables to his heart's content, and he is able to carry out lengthy knowledgeable discussions with the vendors he meets on the streets. Politics arouses him, though one suspects that he is now at the calmer stage in his life, and he detests the nationalist Bharatiya Janata Party (BJP), which created the electric climate in which the Babri (Mughal emperor Babur's) Mosque was destroyed by its fanatical supporters, leading to violent communal outbursts, and whose state branch oversaw the pogrom against Muslims in Gujarat. And yet curiously, I have always thought, he does not appear to have any close Muslim friends or any from the lower castes. This reflects more the divisions in Indian society than deliberate choice. And this is true of all the Punjabi Delhiites I know. I myself have not come to know any Muslims in Delhi; I hardly see them, except in Old Delhi or, in minuscule numbers, at a university class or at some function. Discrimination in housing against Muslims is quite common. It is, when one becomes aware of it, the oddest feeling, because everywhere in Delhi are signs of that historical Muslim presence. It is also a subject one never talks about; few people outside of

India, one imagines, are aware of these absences and silences. The writer Ramachandra Guha, however, recently published a very forthright piece in the *New York Times* about this aspect of living in post-Partition Delhi:

> Yet among my close friends in India there was not a single Muslim. The novelist Mukul Kesavan, a contemporary, has written that in his school in Delhi he never came across a Muslim name: "The only place you were sure of meeting Muslims was the movies." Some of the finest actors, singers, composers and directors in Bombay's film industry were Muslims. But in law, medicine, business and the upper echelons of public service, Hindus dominated. There were sprinklings of Christians and Sikhs, but very few Muslims.

But this is how my friend Mahesh came to meet Rajiv Gandhi in Connaught Place. He was on his way to pay an electric bill somewhere on this block when, to his great surprise, he saw the prime minister himself browsing outside a bookstore. A young man had just asked him for an autograph, and Rajiv looked around for a pen, then asked Mahesh if he could borrow his. Certainly, Mahesh replied. This was two days before the prime minister was killed by a suicide bomb down south, set off by a Sri Lankan Tamil separatist, his body shredded beyond recognition.

As we leave the coffee house, we pass the very bookstore, which is hardly more than a stall, with a rack of magazines at the doorway. Twenty years after Mahesh's meeting with Rajiv Gandhi, the same shopkeeper sits at a small table at the entrance. Yes, he confirms to my friend's enthusiastic reminder, two days before his assassination Rajiv had stopped by. Not a spark, a twinkle, in the eye, not a twitch in the face or a change in the voice to betray any emotion—as though prime ministers regularly stop by at his store before getting blown to bits.

—

Thus Mahesh, among a circle of friends, a bit of a showman. But at more private moments, when no one else is around, and because he has become a close friend, he reveals the soft core, tells me of the toll of Partition on the refugees who had to leave everything behind and start anew.

His parents, from a small town in northern Punjab, had been given a home in Sabzi Mandi, the vegetable market in the Old Delhi area; his mother's family—his nana and uncles—were first at a camp, a converted British jail that later became the Maulana Azad Medical College near the Delhi Gate, before moving in with his parents. Refugees were awaiting compensation for the homes and businesses left behind in now-Pakistan, and so while his younger uncle sold ice cream on the street, his proud nana, formerly a village moneylender, put to use an old skill, stringing cots to earn a modest income. More than twenty people were crammed into a two room apartment, until the in-laws were finally settled in Lajpat Nagar further to the south, now a bustling shopping market, their bitterness towards Muslims never abated. The young uncles flirted with the RSS, the right-wing Hindu communalist organization with its own paramilitary corps. His nana was awarded a stationery store that would go on to make a fortune. There must be thousands of Bania trader families in Delhi with similar stories. The number of refugees who arrived in India from Pakistan has been estimated in the millions.

But it is in the details of the new family dynamics—the scrounging for money, the extra jobs, the paying guests taken in to make ends meet, the straining marital relationships in a tradition where marriages are never broken, however tormenting—it is in these that the painful memories lie, that bring a shudder to the face and a tear to the eye as they are recalled.

His stories bring to mind the black-and-white Bollywood family dramas of the fifties and sixties, in which the protagonists are almost always poor, and the families, stressed to breaking point, always come through in the end. In my childhood the circumstances depicted in these films had seemed imaginable but distant; now, through Mahesh, they seem strangely close and real. There is one image that is etched clearly in his memory, as it is now in mine: his young mother with her young children returning home from her parents' house, taking a shortcut by walking along the railway tracks. His uncle, her younger brother, would accompany them part of the way.

It is the attitudes formed during those harsh refugee days, Mahesh affirms, all the insecurity, then the resultant greed, aggression, and self-centredness, that persist today in the relationships and attitudes of the modern Delhiites that outsiders often remark upon.

And so this is the newest Delhi: converted refugee camps and settlements—presently booming in the new globalized economy— interspersed among and over the old Delhis: the markets and housing colonies of Lajpat Nagar, Sarojini Nagar, Patel Nagar, Vasant Kunj, Hauz Khas . . . progressing ever southwards, towards the oldest Delhis and beyond.

We are sitting one day in a hotel room—we've been travelling in Kerala—and news has come over Mahesh's cell that the younger uncle is critically ill in hospital. (The older one is already dead.) Mahesh is the next oldest male in the family. And so this freest of spirits, one who would prefer to travel and explore, write and tell stories, is the family's crutch, for all to seek comfort and decisions from.

His daughter has recently got married. It is our mutual regret that I missed the ceremony and celebrations. They were lavish, he says. Drinks flowed freely and the food was both veg and nonveg. (He eats only veg.) The groom is also Punjabi, and a Canadian, in the business of developing condominiums in the satellite town of Noida.

We talk of caste. He would not have objected, he says, if his daughter had picked a man of a lower caste. How low? It is a difficult question to ask, and I do not ask it. He is quite liberal in this matter, he says, and I know.

And a Muslim?—I ask. What if she had picked a Muslim man?

The family would not have accepted that, he says. The memories are still bitter.

It's a deeply unsettling revelation. Sixty years after Partition, to hear this. But it's not sixty years, it's not Partition, I come gradually to realize; the prejudices go deeper, and they work both ways. Happily, the new generations in North America are kicking them off.

><

In November 1858, a year after the Mutiny and directly as its result, the East India Company, which in 1613 had been granted permission to open a trading post on the coast by the Mughal emperor Jehangir, and went on to dominate much of the country while representing British interests, was abolished, and India was placed under the direct rule of the British government. The governor general, Lord Canning, became the first British viceroy of India. A new era called "the British Raj" began.

In 1911, at the Royal Durbar in Delhi, held on the occasion of King George and Queen Mary's visit, the king announced that the capital of "the Empire" would move from Calcutta to Delhi. Shortly thereafter, Edwin Lutyens was commissioned to plan the new city in collaboration with Herbert Baker. Lutyens, a highly talented architect with connections in high places, had begun his career as a designer of elegant English country houses. Recently, however, he had designed the Johannesburg Art Gallery, with which project he began to think of a Classical architectural style suitable for the overseas possessions of an empire. For one thing, they had to project strength and stability.

Lutyens corresponded regularly with his wife, Lady Emily, and in his lengthy, candid letters we learn much about his attitudes and thoughts concerning the imperial capital he had been commissioned to lay out.

Lutyens arrived in India bearing a certain intellectual hauteur. He was arrogant and imperialistic, always conscious of the superiority of the West. India was the antithesis to his tastes and values, everything about it irked him. "It is all baffling, people and objects," he wrote. He was appalled at the lack of sanitation ("nil") and cleanliness. Of Indian architectural accomplishments he was utterly disdainful, and its historical ruins he found bad and lacking dignity.

> Architecture—there is practically nil. Veneered joinery in stone, concrete and marble on a gigantic scale there is lots of, but no real architecture and nothing is built to last. . . .

> Personally I do not believe there is any real Indian architecture or any great tradition. They are just spurts by various mushroom dynasties. . . . And then it is essentially the building style of children.

The Qutb Minar was an "uncouth and careless unknowing and unseeing shape."

How could he then design a city sympathetic with Indian lives and values? That was not his purpose; he had come to build a city that would be a symbol and an administrative centre of the Empire. Ironically, on his home front, Lady Emily had become a devotee of J. Krishnamurti, who according to the theosophists was the Maitreya (the successor of Buddha according to prophecy), causing Lutyens a great deal of unhappiness.

The location of the capital was much debated. The viceroy, Lord Hardinge, flip-flopped between three sites: North Ridge, beyond Old Delhi to the north; Malcha, on the South Ridge, to the far west and south of the old city; and Raisina, adjacent and to the south of the old city. Finally the last site was picked. Then there was the "Battle of the Rise." Lutyens preferred the secretariat buildings to be on a gentle rise along the Rajpath (then called the Kingsway) so that the Viceroy's House (now Rashtrapati Bhavan), to be designed by Lutyens, would be at the top and be visible along the whole way. Baker wanted the secretariat buildings, which he designed, to share the height with the Viceroy's House, which as a consequence would become blocked part of the way. Baker won and Lutyens was furious. In the matter of style, Lutyens naturally preferred Western Classical; the viceroy wanted Indo-Saracenic. In the end a compromise was achieved.

Between the old Shahjahanabad in the north and the deserted older cities to the south, New Delhi was laid out as a pattern of contiguous and overlapping hexagons and triangles of wide avenues, its central axis the Rajpath, which joins the Rashtrapati Bhavan—by far the grandest building in the new city—to the massive war memorial, called India Gate, beyond which lie the Purana Qila and the excavations of the ancient Indraprastha. The grandeurs of Persepolis, the Acropolis, the pleasure dome of Kubla Khan, and the Mughals—these were the visions in its architects' minds as they began to conceive their project. They produced a magnificent and beautiful city, but unfortunately more of a showcase capital, a monument to the arrogance of Empire, to demonstrate daily to the native its might and what it represented. It reminded one visitor of a "little Versailles" and another of a more pleasing Nuremberg. It is a city to take a pleasing drive through and admire the legacy of "the Britishers" en route to somewhere else; to come to for a picnic on a holiday at one of its lush green parks and play cards and watch the kids fly balloons and kites; to come to and watch a military parade on Republic Day from its broad sidewalks. But the commercial and the cultural hubs thrive elsewhere.

Twenty thousand Indian labourers were employed in the construction, Lutyens tells us. "The sandstone used was of the same strata as that used by Akbar and Shah Jahan. The stoneyard was one of the largest in the world, employing over 3500 men, who dressed over 3½ million cubic feet and about 350,000 cubic feet of marble. To the south of the city, 700 million bricks were made out of 27 kilns. . . . There were 84 miles of electric distribution cables and 130 miles of street lighting. 50 miles of roads and 30 miles of service roads."

><

From one of the contractor families that built New Delhi comes Khushwant Singh, the nonagenarian grand old man of the city, author of numerous books, including the classic Partition novel *Train to Pakistan* and a scholarly history of the Sikhs, and essayist par excellence, whose columns speak to millions every week in India and are circulated over the Internet. An institution. Born in a small town in the Punjabi part of what is now Pakistan, he attended Lahore College, the alma mater of a number of eminent men of the subcontinent, before practising law for a brief period in Lahore. He has been a government press attaché, a radio journalist, and editor of a number of newspapers and magazines. I met him briefly at a book party at the end of my first visit. Penguin India had published an edition of my first novel and he had written a very flattering column on it in a newspaper Sunday supplement. He gave me a warm embrace when I was introduced, and then identified the community I must come from, which figured fictitiously in the novel, and which not a single person outside of that community, in India or elsewhere, had been able to do. It was an embarrassing moment, for he was and is a presence much vaunted, and I did not know what to say; my spoken Hindi, too, was abominably halting.

He can get away with saying things sometimes in much the same way a naughty grand-uncle might, to the mild disapproval of the parents. Thus he writes about the "nauseating" habit of nose-picking, then with relish goes into details of the practice, using as his reference an American book that came his way. He hands out a lesson on sex: "Also, in monogamous marriages, the absence of variety (which is indeed the spice of life when it comes to sex) and monotony deprive both partners of the urge to engage in love-making." Often there will be the pithy observation on some aspect of Indian culture—the fast of Ramadan, the festival of Diwali, the significance of the river Ganges—a reminder, actually, for mutual understanding and tolerance, in this monolithic-looking nation teeming with differences. India has many holidays, he reminds his readers, because it is not monoreligious like its neighbours. He scorns politicians and journalists, and always decries bigots of any stripe. Politicians are crooked "windbags" and rabble-rousers. For the journalists he has a special term, "crawlers," because of their craven attitudes towards the politicians. Quoting a poem by the great Allama Iqbal, he chides the imam of Delhi's Jama Masjid for making inflammatory remarks to a crowd of followers on the Janpath, the grand avenue of the capital. To the previous home minister, L. K. Advani, he once said in full public hearing at a book launch, "You are a puritan. You do not drink, you do not smoke, you do not womanize. . . . Such men are dangerous." And he was incensed, as he reports to his readers, when "the crawlers" did not even mention his presence at the event, over which he had presided, no less.

He is therefore a humorous, arrogant, and yet modest encyclo-pedia of Indian life; and an old scold; and his readers, helpless about the state of their country's politics, love him because they agree, more or less, with what he says. He's been around, does not need to kowtow, and the list of people he has known is enviable—politicians, writers, film stars. He can tell many a historical anec-dote. There is one admittedly titillating account of the time when he was the press officer at the Indian High Commission in London. Pandit Nehru was attending the first Commonwealth Prime

Ministers Conference, and after an embarrassing incident reported in the London papers involving Prime Minister Nehru and Lady Edwina Mountbatten (the two had a relationship, long a subject of gossip and speculation), the high commissioner, Krishna Menon, advised young Khushwant to keep out of the prime minister's way, which he did. On the day of Nehru's departure, however, "many London papers carried pictures [of Nehru and Lady Edwina] taken in the cosy basement of the Greek cafe." Khushwant continues, these many years later,

> This time there was no escape. I was summoned to Claridges Hotel. As I entered Panditji's [Nehru's] room, he looked me up and down to ask me who I was. I had been with him for an entire week. "Sir, I am your press officer," I replied. "You have strange notions of publicity," he said in a withering tone. At the time, it did not occur to him or to me that the only person who could have tipped off the press was Krishna Menon. Menon had a mind like a corkscrew.

In two columns he bewails the Delhiites' lack of pride in their city's history, and the politicians' "strangling" of its heritage.

> Twenty years ago you could go from Safdarjang to Mehrauli, from the Qutub Minar to Tuglaqabad and Suraj Kund and get one uninterrupted view of ruins of ancient monuments. . . . They made a spectacular sight. Today you can't see any of them because housing colonies have come up around them and the monuments themselves are occupied by squatters. In mosque courtyards buffaloes are tethered, mausoleum walls are marked as wickets for boys playing cricket; where the Sultans of Delhi held court, chaiwalas ply their trade.

> The only minus point about the citizens of the capital is that the majority of them have not yet developed a sense of pride for belong-

ing to it. Most of them are refugees from Pakistan who have yet to put their roots in Delhi's soil.

Succinctly put; the kind of detail and honesty only rarely found elsewhere. Admittedly, the country and the city have been looking forward. "It is hard to believe that these acts of vandalism of our historic city took place in the regimes of our two most forward-looking prime ministers, Jawaharlal Nehru and Indira Gandhi." Here is a man looking back; but he is old. It should not be forgotten, though, that the politicians who have looked back in modern times have been those ardent nationalists who fomented a climate of intolerance and communal violence.

Khushwant Singh, of course, was witness to the partition of India. Of its place in history, he writes,

we Indians and Pakistanis have chosen to forget what we did to each other to gain our freedom. We have no museums, no memorials to commemorate what was undoubtedly one of the greatest tragedies in recorded history. The uprooting of ten million people from their homes, the loss of one million lives, rape and abduction of thousands of women have all been swept under the carpet of oblivion.

And like many others I have met, he affirms, "When we search our souls, we will be forced to admit that little or nothing of the Gandhi legacy remains with us."

Humorous and arrogant, yes; but also committed, passionate, and sad. He's seen wars, assassinations, horrific communal violence, and always calls for tolerance, humour his shield. When Indira Gandhi sent the Indian army into the Golden Temple, the holiest site of the Sikhs, Khushwant Singh returned his Padma Bhushan, one of the country's highest civilian decorations. He has recently received an even higher award.

Late in his life, now, he does not go out much but gives audiences between certain hours in the evening. He lives in an upscale apartment complex quite close to the Khan Market and within walking distance of the Purana Qila and Humayun's tomb. I paid him a visit one night in the company of my Indian editor with a bottle of wine, which he accepted with thanks; he was sunk into an armchair, a white kerchief over his head in place of a turban, a shawl around him. The place was as modestly furnished as many Indian homes I'd seen, but not cluttered. Three middle-aged women had come calling, one on either side of him, whinging somewhat. He loves the company of women, and they, his. The third one buttonholed me on a distant sofa and wouldn't let me go, invited me finally for a drink at the International Centre, which I declined, much annoyed, for I did not get a chance to get close to my host. His visiting hour was up and we had to leave. Since then, I was told discreetly that the lady in question had been banished (for a while) from the great man's presence. When I went again, two other women were present, and a man, and the meeting was more managed. Ever the raconteur, Khushwant still holds attention. But he is hard of hearing, and it was the women's higher pitch that more easily reached him. He told us wistfully of a time when he shared a room one night with a Finnish woman and didn't attempt to make a pass. The next morning the Finnish woman said, Let's go for a swim, and she did so, in the nude. He wondered now, with a twinkle in his eye, that perhaps his reserve and fear of receiving an indignant slap on the face the previous evening had been unfounded. He had just published a book of Urdu poetry in translation. One of the two women present was a columnist, the other was involved with women victims of the Gujarat violence of 2002. We talked about a recent incident involving the Bangladeshi writer Tasleema Nasreen, who was threatened with beheading by a Muslim member of the state assembly in Hyderabad. He had his one Scotch, didn't touch the hors d'oeuvres. Then it was time to leave.

The commercial heart of Lutyens's New Delhi—laid out like a wheel, its hub Connaught Circus in three concentric blocks, A, B, C, with wide avenues radiating out like spokes—invites you to walk and explore this city, unlock its wonderful geometries; and indeed the odd tourist may be seen on some ample sidewalk, map in hand, somewhat hopelessly attempting to do precisely that. New Delhi streets are not always marked for the convenience of walkers or those who do not quite know the city. It is not really a walker's city, there being few places to stroll into or otherwise engage with on the way; traffic runs in torrents beside you, and it looks terrifying simply to cross a road. But Connaught Circus: here you can indeed stroll around to your heart's content, albeit mostly in circles. The new and even newer suburbs and complexes of South Delhi, with their wealthy populations, may boast of their bustling markets, but the Circus, due to its former status, its striking circular plan, and its quaint colonial-era business names (Pearey Lal is my favourite) to give it a sense of historical gravitas, retains a somewhat mystical hold as the centre of New Delhi. This is a place to go (or come) to, for an expedition. The shopping is leisurely compared to the mad bustles of the markets elsewhere; it opens late and closes early in the evening. If you are seen walking about outside these hours (say at eleven in the morning), you are evidently a tourist and are treated as such by the hustlers. It has its memorable old haunts—the Volga and the United Coffee House, the Bookworm, the American Express office, less essential after the advent of the ATM, the Regal Cinema, the shoe stores, and Vedis of Rangoon, tailors. And there are the modern electronics stores offering the latest technology to the nouveau wealthy of India, and the new and cute—and very kitschy—metal-and-plastic-decor restaurants, like the PiccaDelhi with its London theme, to remind you of the West, and that India has arrived. The sidewalk vendors, as always, selling curios, magazines and newspapers, and pirated paperbacks wrapped in Cellophane. There used to be the tiny STD booths not long ago, for making calls to anywhere in the world, now made redundant by the ubiquitous cell phones. There seems one stuck to every head.

One of the radial roads out of Connaught Place is Sansad Marg, or Parliament Road, for obvious reasons, off which lie both the YWCA and YMCA hostels, convenient, economic places to stay. Roads are named after great people in this area; the more modest Tolstoy Marg takes you to the major radial Janpath, where the multi-storey Cottage Emporium dispenses an impressive range of pricey but high-quality Indiana for the tourist to take away, from carpets and clothes to gods' icons and jewellery. The book and CD section is a small treat. The atmosphere inside is rather hushed, perhaps due to the large space and the rich decor, and because those who come here are, essentially, all strangers. On Janpath one finds stores that sell the same goods as the Emporium (except for the books and music) but several times cheaper, if you know how to bargain, and quality control is up to the buyer. Further along Janpath are the state emporia, more goods for visitors to take away, each Indian state represented by its own store selling regional items.

Tolstoy Marg keeps going, changing character, getting busier as it crosses the other radial roads, then finally goes under a new bypass, where you turn into a residential area and the famous Bengali Market. We are not far from the Jumna and Old Delhi. The Bengali Market is a busy town square throbbing with commerce and dominated by two sweet shops, face to face. No one quite knows how the market received its name, but Bengal is known for its sweets. Perhaps there was an original sweet shop owned by Bengalis, perhaps not. The two on the scene today are owned by Punjabis. For decades these vegetarian havens have been places to take the family, or go with friends, or buy gift boxes wrapped in shiny paper, and I have received and bought many over the years. With the spread of the city and the growth of traffic, the market has lost some of its essentiality, for you can buy the same food items elsewhere, but the throngs here early in the afternoon are impressive. Inside is standing room only. The glass counter at the door, and the shelves behind, filled with dozens of sweets and farsaan (savouries), are an explosion of bright colours in the midst of people and noise.

Postscript: Night Thoughts, Delhi

September 1, 2007

YMCA AT 2 A.M. and dead stillness outside; then a bevy of dogs barking; silence again. The faintest trace of the muezzin's cry, the azaan—from a mosque in Shahjahanabad, perhaps, travelling across the unimpeded Delhi skyline. A lonely sound here, alien. The dogs again; a belch next door, someone's not digested their curry. Then quiet.

The joys of jet-lag: time to meditate; listen to vagrant dogs barking, the muezzin's cry, a belch.

The Samjhauta (meaning "understanding") Express, Delhi, India, to Lahore, Pakistan, was bombed the other day near Panipat—where Babur won his decisive battle and began the Mughal dynasty. Sixty-eight people, mostly Pakistanis, died; one man lost five family members. The devices were crude pipe bombs placed in suitcases, but with sophisticated detonators—two suitcases were recovered when a passenger in a stupor threw them out, earning for himself much publicity.

According to a recent poll, 80 per cent of young Delhiites said they would like to go overseas. Of course they could mean they wished to go at least once; and the poll could include wishful thinking by the poorer classes who would never make it in any case. Many of the wealthy classes do go in and out of India. But there are frustrations that make people leave for good.

Walking at Connaught Place, I was stopped by a young man who wanted my help. Apparently he had been admitted to a hotel school in Switzerland and wanted me to draft him a letter. It was to—of all people—his employer, asking for permission to leave for a year. The whole thing sounded bizarre—the boy could barely speak English. I dictated a letter, and he gratefully took off.

It was at about this time in the night that I had arrived—nervous, excited, in a daze—from the airport during my first visit, fourteen years ago, and was dropped off at the sister institution, the YWCA, a block away, by Krishan Chander. He had not done his homework and assumed I was a returning Indian, and had me find my way through the utter chaos of New Delhi railway station. I still wonder at how I found my train, my compartment and seat . . . and began an adventure that brings me back here, now, many years later. Then, those who became my friends travelled second class by train and economized. There would be blackouts in the city, and water shortages. Now they casually fly in planes, use credit cards and ATMs, buy the latest electronics, eat expensively, invest; they have two cars in the family; and they all look more and more frazzled, existing on roller skates, as it were. All have at least one child overseas.

India has changed. The country brims with confidence, a refreshing contrast to the images of my youth (*Life* magazine) of starving, dying India. Embarrassing India. Now, on this sixtieth anniversary of Independence, the *Times of India*'s headline is "60 and getting sexier"; tabloid language, unfortunately, is a marker of sophistication and coolness even in this Establishment newspaper. The media talk is endlessly of the economy and growth rates and "Chindia"—the superpowers on the threshold, China and India;

film celebrities, cricket, and America are the obsessions. America is to be emulated, competed against, bettered. Everything on television (if in English) gives the appearance of a studied mimicry of America. Cool India (the phrase itself lifted from Tony Blair's Cool Britannia) is to some degree Mimic India.

I love cricket. In Toronto I have sat up nights to watch it, as have others I know, from South Asia, South Africa, the West Indies. But here it is an obsession to dwarf all obsessions. Every series is analyzed in excruciating detail, as if a war, the Mahabharata, has been fought. A fallen wicket (an "out") in a national-level match is announced in a news flash on every channel. On the sixtieth anniversary of Independence, one of the two editorials in the *Times of India* is on the recent victory over England. On cricket hangs the lajja, the honour, of the country. It is an emblem that cannot tarnish, for it represents the success of the country. And victory over Pakistan, above all else, represents the worth of the nation. Once, on my way to Delhi airport to pick up my family, my taxi was suddenly stopped. A dark, scruffy face appeared through the window and handed me a few sticky grapes—a sweet offering, mitho modho, for India had just beaten Pakistan in a match. But a more recent series, when India played in Pakistan, and Indian visitors were treated magnanimously by their hosts, put a wrench into this hysterical competitiveness. It touched a lot of people.

The media corniness, the naïveté and runaway enthusiasm, reminds one rather of a new country. Indeed there exists a double vision of India. In terms of economic achievements and development, India is seen as a young sixty-year-old, a dazzling over-achiever, statistics and indices trotted out like school grades, the nearest competitor, China, the role model, America; and in discussions of its many problems ("a billion people, a million problems," someone memorably said in the papers) the nation is seen as a complex, ancient, and diverse culture that somehow always manages to stay on its feet.

This is India's turn finally, and its people—the privileged classes, at least—know that. The world needs it, the world is theirs. Dignitaries arrive to sing its praises, sometimes in undignified, silly ways. Everywhere restoration and construction proceeds apace; new highways connect the cities, connect neighbourhoods within cities; neighbourhoods get renewed. (I visited Tughlaqabad again after many years, and what was a blackened collapsed ruin when I first saw it is now under repair and looks rather pink.) The new vision of India is that of an emerging economic, military, and cultural superpower. The enthusiasm is boundless, the euphoria catchy and undoubtedly built on substance. Nothing seems impossible—there are few other countries in the world that could feel this way.

But everywhere there is also the underclass which has no part of this shining Indian dream. Its lustre does not reach the inner cities, the smaller towns, the crowded gulleys with open drains where the poor and mutilated cry out. The girl who touches your feet in desperation after begging (and you squirm); the woman in burqa who runs after you holding up her baby (you squirm); the peon who presses himself against the wall when you pass (your heart sinks); the family at a shrine earning twenty-four dollars a month; the roadside chaiwallah who sells at two rupees a cup and rarely leaves the neighbourhood. The desperate resort to suicide, by immolation, by hanging: the school student, the techie, the farmer, the army cadre. Life is a constant *battle*, someone said to me, with all the emphasis he could muster, and he was not a chaiwallah but a teacher. Statistics are often skewed, he said. A few may get astronomical salaries touted by the media as comparable to those of the West, but the rest will make do with a thousand rupees, about twenty-five dollars, or less a day and struggle. Then there is the corruption, the inertia. A good number of parliamentarians are currently fighting criminal charges, but the cases will drag on till doomsday, I am assured. And the rapes, the gang rapes, and murders, even of minors. Perhaps they were always there, someone says, they only get reported more.

And what of Gandhi in this new India, you want to ask, but don't, for you know that Gandhi has become an embarrassment.

Nevertheless, the progress is undeniable; India's self-belief has paid off. Creatively, the movies once ridiculed are now a worldwide glamorous presence, a magical, alternative, and indeed welcome new aesthetic; Indian English, once mocked cruelly in the mother country, is now the voice of some of the world's most admired writers. Intellectually, once possessing a glut of degreed people—in India, Ph.D.s sweep the roads, we used to hear as children—now its educated classes are the leaders of a new economy and technology. It is a military power to contend with, and there are plans to land an Indian on the moon. Once a Third World country, it is now exporting movies and software, teachers and doctors to its former colonial ruler. There is no stopping it. It's as if a spring, long coiled up, has been set loose.

And surely those of us "wogs" who suffered slights due to our Indian origins can feel gratified, if also remain a bit wary.

Shimla:
A Spell in the Mountains

I saw
the mountains of the sages
where the wind mangles eagles
(A girl and an old woman, skin and bones
carry bundles bigger than those peaks)

OCTAVIO PAZ, "Himachal Pradesh (1)"

The Sahibs' Resort in the Hills

"Look, Hajji, is yonder the city of Simla? Allah, what a city!"

"My father's brother . . . could recall when there were but two houses in it."

RUDYARD KIPLING, *Kim*

THE HOWRAH MAIL ARRIVES at the Old Delhi railway station late in the night, at about 11 p.m., from Calcutta, bound for Chandigarh and Kalka in the state of Haryana. This is a brief stopover, and inside the second-class carriages passengers stir in their bunks to cast wary eyes upon their luggage as we board and find our places by the dim overhead lights. There are four of us, two adults and two wilting children. The journey ahead is seven hours, roughly, and Kalka is the last stop on the plains, from where we'll catch an ongoing train for Shimla in the Himalayan foothills. The jolt and clang of the train stopping wakes us up in Kalka, a station vastly smaller than Delhi, and it's a short walk across the platform to the narrow-gauge tracks from where the famous "toy trains" depart for Shimla, formerly called Simla, the romantic hill town in the western Himalayas famous as the summer capital of the British Raj.

There follows (past a few construction eyesores), a slow, winding train ride through a succession of tunnels and hairpin bends with spectacular views of the mountains and valleys. Mysterious snow-covered peaks in the distance; little towns, a hut or two hugging the hills; an ascetic on the road; tall pine trees rising straight up from the valley depths just outside the window. This could be a dream. As children, we had heard of Simla, but only in the title of a famous Bombay film. How far, this pristine mountain beauty of the gods, from the tropical paradise of our childhood, the hills and plains, the wildlife, and the solitary snow-peaked mountain of Africa which also was a god. We pass cluttered little stations where passengers get on and off, where samosas and chai can be bought. The sun is bright and hard, and the mood inside the compartment is happy, even jubilant, for many of the travellers are tourist families escaped from the sweltering plains, crowded lives in crowded cities, monotonous landscapes. On the way we are treated to a dance number from the current Shahrukh Khan hit movie, performed by two schoolgirls and much to the delight of everyone. The men like to take turns to stand on the steps of the open doorways and face the bracing headwind and take in the sights in comparative solitude; in the tunnels the youths shout to hear themselves, and when the train bends on itself the young lean out to view its entire length while held onto tightly by a parent. Our little one is asleep.

Before the railway, access to Shimla was by a road; people went on foot or horse or mule, their luggage had to be carried on the backs of coolies or pulled up on carts. All the teak used for the prominent buildings of the town, all the furniture and all the needs of the residents were brought up this way. The narrow-gauge sixty-mile railway was completed only in 1903, its extra-duty rails going through about a hundred tunnels, bending sharply across the hills to make the climb, and running over high viaducts before reaching its final destination.

The first stop in Shimla is the small Summerhill station, the name indicative of the strong British presence here once upon a time, its memory kept alive decades later by the retention of quaint English place names as a tourist attraction. A steep climb leads up from the platform to the yellow blocks of the Himachal Pradesh University high above. After this brief pause the train hauls off to its final destination, the more substantial Shimla station hardly ten minutes ahead. It's a little past eleven in the morning as we draw in. As coolies crowd the doorways, a friendly face hastens forward, someone I had first met on the Puri Express to Bhubaneswar during my first Indian visit a few years before. How it opened up India to me, that train ride which might not have been, but for an airline strike. Now I am back, this time to spend four months at the Institute in the hills.

A short way up from the station lies the main Mall Road, at one end of which is Shimla's Institute, and at the other end its Mall. Coolies are already trotting up, bent-backed, carrying passengers' luggage to their destinations, for not all roads are accessible to motor vehicles. A car, however, awaits us and takes us directly uphill to our destination, past the wooden Gurkha Gate, the name so thrilling with associations.

Himachal Pradesh, long a part of Punjab, became a state of the Indian union in 1971. Bordering several territories, including

Kashmir and Tibet, it is mostly a rural place in the mountains, the land of the gods, as its residents like to call it, with many ancient temples and untainted folk traditions. There are no major cities in the state, the largest town is Shimla. Travelling can be arduous if not downright perilous on the roads; planes go to some places but flights often have to be cancelled due to weather.

A spur on the western Himalayas called the Ridge is the high point of the town, behind which is the Mall, the fashionable shopping strip not more than a quarter-mile long, further down from which the rest of Shimla lies spilled out on the lower ridges and slopes. Progressively, one hears, the town is getting crowded, with people, with cars and buses. But it started out very modestly.

Shimla is said to have been discovered by the British soon after the so-called Anglo-Gurkha War of 1814 to 1815 between the increasingly powerful and upstart Gurkhas of Nepal, who after their defeat at the hands of the Sikhs had started overrunning local kingdoms, and the British who wanted to control them. A treaty was signed between the two parties to end that war, and thereafter Gurkhas became the legendary elite soldiers of the British Indian Army. In 1817, two Scottish officers stopped at Shimla, describing it as "a middling sized village where a fakir is situated to give water to travellers," and "a name given to a few miserable cultivators' huts." One wishes they had been a little more curious or precise. What, after all, is a fakir—a yogi or a Sufi? Perhaps they only meant an old man.

In 1822, a certain Political Officer to the Hill States called Captain Charles Kennedy constructed in Shimla a two-storey summer house that came to be called the Kennedy House. The locale soon gained a reputation for its beauty—the pine-covered hills, the rhododendron forests, the oak and the fruit trees, the bracing mountain air—and European visitors began to arrive here to escape the punishing summer heat of the plains. By 1824, as the town's dedicated historian Raja Bhasin informs us,

European gentlemen, chiefly invalids from the plains, had, with the permission of [local] chiefs, established themselves in this locality, building houses on sites granted them rent-free, and with no other stipulation than that they should refrain from the slaughter of kine [cows] and from the felling of trees, unless with the previous permission of the proprietors of the land.

In 1830, the governor general of India, Lord Bentinck, formally acquired four thousand acres of the Shimla hill, purchasing it from two local rulers. A residence for the governor general was soon constructed, and it was called Bentinck Castle. The following three governors general, however, were housed in a residence called Auckland House.

In a mere few years since the arrival of Captain Kennedy, so established had Shimla become as a little English town that in 1831 a French naturalist passing through described it as "the resort of the rich, the idle and the invalid." Shimla air was considered good for the liver and good for the soul, it cleared the plains dust out of the brain. For the English, life in Shimla was even more ideal than the typical one of a sahib, for it reminded them so much of England, including the dampness and the rains, though the monsoons were of shorter duration than in the plains and therefore more endurable. There were of course numerous servants to take care of them, and liveried coolies took them up and down hills in hand-pulled rickshaws. Wild strawberries and raspberries grew beside the paths, deer strolled in the nearby woods, and there were leopards, bears, and golden eagles for the men to shoot at. We read of pony rides and parties, gardens and fancy fairs, dancing and fireworks, daily promenades on the Jakhoo road. In 1839, Emily Eden, sister of the governor general, would write,

Twenty years ago no European had ever been here, and there we were, with the band playing the "Puritani" and "Masaniello," and eating salmon from Scotland and sardines from the Mediterranean, and observing that St. Cloup's *potage à la Julienne* was perhaps better than his other soups, and that some of the ladies' sleeves were too tight.

And, Miss Eden said, "I have felt nothing like it, I mean nothing so English, since I was on the terrace at Eastcombe, except perhaps the week we were at the Cape." Her letters provide some of the most detailed and enthusiastic descriptions of English life in Shimla during its early days.

In the British Raj (as the British presence in India was called after 1858, with a viceroy replacing the governor general), Shimla became the "summer capital of the Supreme Government [of India], of the Punjab Government and of the army headquarters." Every summer, officials of the Raj arrived to run the country from these misty heights. The viceregal residence initially was a place called Peterhoff, perhaps half a mile up the road from the Kennedy House. Further up, a short distance away on Observatory Hill, construction began on a new, larger, made-to-order Viceregal Lodge, into which the viceroy and vicereine of the time, Lord and Lady Dufferin, moved in 1888. All three great houses lay on a single road along a ridge, ending at the Mall.

A young reporter called Rudyard Kipling would show up in the summers of 1883 to 1888, to report on the "Season"—the goings-on at this summer capital and resort of the colonial elite—for Lahore's *Civil and Military Gazette.* "That in itself is fairly lively work," he wrote in a letter, " . . . [and] entails as much riding, waltzing, dining out and concerts in a week as I should get at home in a lifetime." He published *Kim* in 1901. The railway had not yet been built, and the journey young Kim makes from Kalka to Shimla with the horse trader and British secret agent, the Pathan Mahbub Ali, is on horseback. But the landscape Kim sees on the way, breathtaking to any mortal visitor from the plains, gets rather short shrift.

Kipling's interest is characters, and some of them are wonderfully drawn, or caricatured. Shimla's Lower Bazar, consisting of a series of parallel crowded streets that go winding down the slope from the Mall and are reachable from it via steep steps, gets a few quick but colourful strokes.

> He led the horses below the main road into the lower Simla bazar—the crowded rabbit-warren that climbs up from the valley to the Town Hall at an angle of forty-five. A man who knows his way there can defy all the police of India's summer capital, so cunningly does veranda communicate with veranda, alley-way with alley-way, and bolt-hole with bolt-hole. Here live those who minister to the wants of a glad city—jhampanis who pull the pretty ladies' 'rickshaws by night and gamble till the dawn; grocers, oil-sellers, curio-vendors, firewood-dealers, priests, pickpockets, and native employees of the Government. . , . Here, too, Mahbub Ali rented a room.

The Lower Bazar is where much of the local shopping for essentials still gets done.

After Independence, the Viceregal Lodge was taken over as the summer residence of the president of India, one of whom, S. Radhakrishnan, the well-known philosopher, handed it over for use by the Indian Institute of Advanced Study, which still occupies it. The fate of Peterhoff, outside the gates and down the hill, on the other hand, was to house the Punjab High Court, and it was here that the trial of Mahatma Gandhi's assassin, Nathu Ram Godse, took place in 1948 to 1949. It burnt to the ground in 1981, and in 1991 a luxury hotel was built in its place. Kennedy House, the last of the three great houses of yore, is the site of the state legislative assembly.

✂

We've been charmed suddenly into another world, both strange and beautiful, where everything suggests the small, the quaint, the different: different from the hectic India of the plains, from which we've literally been lifted up; and different from the tightly ordered, mechanical Toronto. Here the air is to breathe, the trees to touch, the ground to walk upon, the sky to gaze and marvel at. Time has slowed down. How has this privilege been possible?

I am here on a fellowship at Shimla's Indian Institute of Advanced Study, an extraordinarily generous offer to a foreigner. The Institute's one previous experience with a foreigner, I have been informed, was not positive. Yet here I am, where I will live and work, and gaze upon the gods' mountains to my heart's content; I am anonymous, for most people assume that I am from another part of India, this diverse subcontinent. I am as strange or familiar as anyone else.

We have been given the Postmaster Flat, a two-bedroom residence at the head of the long and steep winding driveway from the Gurkha Gate, and right above the defunct fire hall. This is presumably where the viceroy's postmaster lived; I imagine the variety of post that must have passed through his—or his workers'— hands, Christmas packages, books and magazines, preserves, detailed letters in longhand linking Britain to India, including those of the apparently good-natured Lady Emily Eden to which we have now become privy. We've arrived in March, the winter is over; mornings are cool but sunny and bright, the nights cold and clear, speckled impeccably with stars. The comforts of the viceroy's summer residence, however, are far from stately and barely adequate. Interiors are not well heated. The furniture is decidedly ancient, hailing from the Raj era or not much later, though some of the best antiques, we are told, were pilfered by previous residents—more well-placed ones, one supposes, than the poor scholars. The bathroom ceramic fixtures still bear the brand names of once extant British companies, the fireplaces everywhere are defunct, the carpets threadbare. But no sign of a threadbare budget can take away from the thrill of our escape.

Our flat opens at the back onto a paved path, beyond which is a small green lawn edged with flower beds and with a shady oak tree at its centre; across the lawn from us is the Guest House, a broad, plain, two-storey white building. The upper floor accommodates occasional guests and the lower floor consists of a kitchen and a dining room on one side and a clubby lounge and television room on the other, with heavy drapes and furnished in the English drawing-room style. In the dining room, whose French doors open into the lawn, the scholars, who have been accommodated in houses and flats in the surrounding area, and who hail from various parts of India, those from the south typically in the warmest clothes, come to have their meals at tables covered with neat white cloths. In the morning at breakfast, a warm sunlight bathes the tranquility outside.

The front door of our flat opens to a flight of wooden stairs descending to the driveway and the main building of the former

Viceregal Lodge—now the Institute—in its ample grounds. The Institute can also be approached directly from the Guest House by descending a steep flight of stone stairs at the far corner of the lawn.

The Viceregal Lodge is perhaps the most visited site in Shimla. It stands majestically alone, like a temple atop a hill, its beautiful gardens and lawns ideal for family or honeymoon photographs, an emblem of the Raj and historically linked to its conclusion. Indeed its prohibitive, almost alien, reserve gives it the distinctive look of a colonial object. Whatever the humiliations of the Raj, some of its reminders are treated fondly and proudly. Especially on weekends, a steady stream of tourist cars comes racing up the driveway spitting gravel, and foreign backpackers march all the way from the Mall to have a look around, sit in the sun, take a tour of the buildings.

The viceroy's residence was commissioned by Lord Dufferin, who had come to India having served previously as the governor general of Canada. The architect was Henry Irwin of the Public Works Department, though the overall conception seems to have been that of Lord Dufferin, who was obsessed with the construction, visiting the site regularly, often with bewildered visitors in tow, and always ready with suggestions. The design, with its Dutch gables, exterior ornamentation, mullioned windows, and cupola, has been described as "English Renaissance," though the stonework details and second-floor balconies might suggest the excessive and baroque. The grey stone for the exterior was carted all the way from Kalka. It would not measure up to the best of English country houses, and English visitors generally loved to condemn it, but in its setting and with its history it is a striking place, reminder of a Shangri-La that was.

The entrance faces the south and is reached from the driveway. Through the doors, to the right, a curving staircase goes up to the bedrooms on the second floor and the viceroy's, now the director's, office on the third. To the left is a seminar room and a corridor that leads past a gallery of photographs of eminent people to what once was the ballroom and drawing room and an adjoining dining room. These are now all parts of the library, one of the most extensive in the country, with the advantage that it's never crowded.

During the Raj, this was a bustling place in the Season, with a vigorous social and administrative life and hundreds of servants and officials. The population of the town apparently tripled in the summer, from a little over ten thousand in the colder season, and the English had a strict hierarchy of social status among themselves. Not everybody could be invited to a ball at the viceroy's residence. Housing the academic Institute now, it is a quiet place we have come to, ideal for some, a nightmare of loneliness to others, and surely an escape to those not used to so much personal space. The town, the Mall, actually, remains busy during the day but is a long walk away.

In this retreat we are not quite aware how the days and weeks pass; we simply allow ourselves to be. We take long walks out the Gurkha Gate to the Mall and, behind the Institute in the opposite direction, to the local market area and bus depot known as Boileau Ganj. Everywhere, we climb up and down the hills; during our very first outing, we realized that the baby stroller we've brought for our three-year-old is useless—the paths are not continuously smooth and often too steep. Sometimes we cook in the Postmaster's kitchen, other times we eat with the fellows in the Guest House dining room, whose phoolka, puffed-up chappatis, we find difficult to reproduce. Early in the morning every day, with a knock at our back door comes a tray of "wake-up tea." It's worth getting up just for that. Inevitably, too, we have made some friends: a Bengali couple who have a son in Virginia; a Hyderabadi couple, he having just edited a collection of Partition stories; Bhishm Sahni, a Hindi writer, and his wife; a young man in a blazer, a nostalgic Oxonian. We've travelled by taxi down to Amritsar in Punjab, which is my wife's father's birthplace, a memorable visit. And we've been to Chail, a charming resort higher up in the hills that boasts two clay tennis courts and a cricket ground, reputedly the world's highest, though it seemed that there were more monkeys than people in the town. My older son has taken to cricket, and hunting for a lost ball in the bushes with him has brought back memories of my own childhood; it's also given us rashes from poison ivy. Other times he catches up on school work. The three-year-old charms everyone, thriving on chappati and "rice pudding" (kheer), at the sight of which he'll push away his chappati. Inevitably he eats the family's entire ration of dessert. A thousand-piece jigsaw puzzle, occupying one half of the large, ancient dining table, is approaching completion, everyone in the family contributing.

Finally, however, they have to return to Toronto, and I am alone, and there are intensely lonely quiet periods and yet also rewarding ones, as I sit, read, and write, and contemplate the vistas before me, strangely content in my solitude.

The rains have come, and with it the scorpions. The spiders are immense but harmless. They scurry in and out with amazing speed from behind the door posts.

The wooden front stairs of the Postmaster Flat are old, a couple of steps worn out and yielding. One damp monsoon afternoon I come out the front door on my way to the Mall. A few steps down, I slip and fall heavily on my back. During one fateful instant, as my head snaps back and hits something hard, I think I'm about to die. But I survive, winded, my back savagely sore, and slowly climb the remaining steps down. The next morning I report this near demise to the residence office, not only for the sake of my safety in the days ahead but also the safety of future residents of the flat. I am reassured warmly that the matter will be taken care of, not to worry. Nothing happens. That's the reverse side to the warmth and easy informality, to all the namasté-ji and the flexibility to accommodate to your needs.

Sometimes, in the late afternoon, as a residual sunlight strains in through the western sky, I come to sit at the small outdoor café of dilapidated sticky furniture and numerous small flies, at the cliff edge in the lee of the Institute, under the windows of the library that was once the viceroys' ballroom. Watching the sunset from this vantage point becomes a game, one repeated frequently. There is nothing between me and the distant peaks of the Himalayas, the sun always behind them.

Down below, the green hills. Undulating hills, moving shadows at play with the angular glare, shades of green, textures and depths of pine foliage merging with the jet black of the western slopes. A thin haze hangs in the air. A road curves round some hills and departs the town; a train whistle blows close by, but the train, directly below at the bottom of the cliff, is not visible. Straight ahead again, light blue of the sky meets orange glow of the sun and forms a sharp line of transition, behind which the mountains peep like dim shadow-figures through the haze. Suddenly the air turns cold, the sun now a bright yellow and sharply delineated disk no bigger than a fat full moon, no harder on the eye. And the sky hued from blue through green, purple, and orange, all in soft tones. Are there clouds in the west, way in the distance? As if to answer, a wisp appears in front of the setting sun, attains sharper and sharper focus as it moves down, like a mountain range viewed through a telescope. A cold wind blows. The disk, covered it seems by a wave of alternating orange and yellow, suddenly enters a swath of cloud, sinks deeper into it until a thin crescent, more an arc, peeps out at the top, and yes, a similar curve at the bottom, grey in between. The clouds have been made visible only because the sun must go behind them, behind everything. Then, having teased, the sun, smiling now, oblate to the eye, reappears and then ever so slowly, majestically, just perceptibly, plunges between two peaks, never for a moment in a hurry, even when it's become a small red point in the horizon.

Sometimes a pale silver moon appears from the opposite direction even as the red disk of the sun still watches, and there is the spectacle of the source and its reflection vying for attention at once.

Nights are cool and, on clear days of spring or the few days of summer, crisp; the moon when full is so large and low as to appear to have been simply hung there by the friendly, mischievous gods, and bathed in its thin white light the crowns of the oaks acquire a glowing cover; on moonless nights the stars are sharp, and the Milky Way is observable from the unlighted corners of the lawn, running like a strip of gossamer veil way up above, across the darkness and the beyond. Across the valley, the lights of the town like bright points conglomerate in a section of the darkness, an entire small galaxy viewed from up close; elsewhere on the valleys and the hills, isolated pinpricks of habitation. During the rains a thick swirling fog may overhang the area, its effects enhanced by the white and yellow lamps on posts; and with the grey gothic building in the background the entire place acquires a certain macabreness. If one lingered a little in this night, did not turn away quickly into the embrace of a hearth, then that shadowy figure in the near distance who is barely visible might just respond to the call: "Heathcliff!"

And yes, they say there are ghosts here, of British folks long dead and gone.

Once, a professor of a particularly rational and scientific bent of mind, I was told, when on a visit to the Institute was given a rather posh set of rooms in the former viceroy's residence. Every day during his stay, he noticed his bottle of hair oil had been somewhat roughly treated, even thrown about, and he would place it back neatly where it belonged. One morning he said somewhat irritably to the attendant who had been assigned to the room, "Why do you people throw around my things?" To which the attendant replied, "Lady Curzon does not like the smell of your hair oil." The guest room had belonged once to her. Bad history but good story, said my informer: The lady is believed to have been poisoned with arsenic; her lord might even have had a hand in her death. "Did she die here, then?" I asked. No, she died in England.

England still haunts the place, from a distance. Blue blazers are popular among the select; and there's nothing better than a degree from Oxford. Harvard has not arrived here, but give it time.

Unlike the time of the viceroys, there is little social life at Observatory Hill, or indeed in the town, at night. For one thing, it is not easy to get around. A simple dinner party, at the director's or another scholar's residence, for example, requires strenuous climbing on the hilly paths and up and down steep steps with wobbly banisters, at times in pitch darkness with the help of only a flashlight. Even then, the threat of a cheetah or hyena lurking in the woods, real or imagined, can make night sojourns a little unsettling. No wonder then, the alternative settled for by most: an austere regimen of early-to-bed, followed perhaps by a long walk in the beautiful, quiet dawn, when there's little sign of life but for another solitary walker or, in the terraced gardens, someone practising yoga, or calisthenics, or voice.

><

I've revelled in my precious mountain solitude, and I've sat through dreadful loneliness, nights so dark and still outside my dimly lit rooms that I could be in a capsule at the edge of the universe. This state of alternate highs and lows is alleviated briefly by the arrival of two friends from Delhi, one of whom is Mahesh. Sometimes, tiring of the monotony of the fare at the Guest House, daal-and-subzi, rice-and-chappati, day in and day out, we take the long walk to the Mall in the late afternoon in search of the simple pleasures of diet and drink that in the pristine air of this roof of the world almost bear the aura of sin or debauchery. A steep winding climb down from the main building, past the Gurkha Gate, brings us to the halfway point of Chaura Maidan. Here is a post office facing a statue of Baba Ambedkar—the hero of the low-caste and "Untouchables" and a key architect of the Indian constitution—past which is an old, defunct hotel, called the Cecil, being renovated, and a modest shopping strip: a boy frying jelebis outside a sweet vendor's; two grocery stores with long-distance STD phone booths which are always in use; a large cow, not always the same one, eyeing mournfully a sack of potatoes or onions; and a tall, old bearded man in cap who sells flaccid fruit one just can't make oneself buy, even out of sympathy. Past this modest strip comes an area we distinguish by its belligerent monkeys, and then the long climb up to the Mall, on which motor traffic is prohibited. By the roadside sit hawkers of apricots, apples, pears, and plums, whose prices we carefully mark for later bargaining, and roasted-corn sellers who supply our first indulgence of the day. A little further along we arrive at our second stop, the Indian Coffee House, a venerable old place with perhaps the only authentic fresh coffee in these foothills.

The Mall proper begins at the statue of Lala Lajpat Rai, a hero of the independence struggle, who died from his wounds after beatings by police, famously saying upon his death, "Let every blow that falls upon me beat a nail on the coffin of British rule." Perhaps an appropriate place for his memorial, this little capital of the Raj, this England away from home. The Upper Mall is where the British themselves shopped and was inaccessible to Indians not properly attired; an ill-dressed wog was simply pushed down the steps towards the Lower Bazar. Now locals come for strolls in the evenings or weekends and noisy tourists pack it in the summer. Sometimes Bollywood comes to shoot the exotic locale. The location of the statue is known as Scandal Point, which, mentioned the right way, I am told, is enough to bring a blush upon the cheeks of a damsel, which is the only way to describe some of the women here, fair and high cheekboned, hair braided down to the hip, a large red bindi on the forehead. It was here apparently that the Maharaja of Patiala once teased an English woman, whereupon he was refused the privilege of access to the Mall.

One branch of the Upper Mall goes up to the ridge, which looks upon an uninhibited vista of mountains and valleys, as far as the eye can see; vendors sell snacks and ice creams and balloons and soap-bubble rings, the children are given horse rides, young couples rent colourful mountain costumes and have their photos taken. There are two ugly statues here, of two Gandhis, the Mahatma and Indira, commissioned by the government, it is said partly in jest, from the lowest bidders; from a high bandstand above the Mahatma a band sometimes gives a bravura performance. The most eminent building here is the yellow Christ Church at the far end of the ridge, with its square tower and clock, its Tudor porch and stained-glass windows, visible even from Observatory Hill, from where we've just come. It was designed by one Colonel Boileau, after whom was named the area of Boileau Ganj (pronounced "Baalu gunj" locally).

The lower branch of the Upper Mall is where the fancy shopping takes place, for Western-style clothes, English books, liquor, cakes, brown breads, and processed cheese, unfortunately the only kind available. At regular intervals along this street, steep steps go down to the several levels of the Lower Bazar, crowded with local shoppers and knowing visitors. Here, you find the hardware store, the halwais, the fruit sellers, the gold- and silversmiths, the grocers, the stationer, the ironmongers, the tailors, the cobblers, and the chemist, and the temple and the mosque. Right at the bottom is the Cart Road, which heads out of town. Originally called the Grand Hindostan and Tibet Road, it was completed in 1856.

In the Lower Bazar—which meets the Upper Mall at a hairpin bend marked by the dhaba called Sher-e-Punjab—opposite the fruiters, is one tempting stop: the boy outside the halwai making reputedly the best jelebis in town, or anywhere: not too thick but crisp, just out from the hot oil and dipped in syrup, rich yellow and dripping, sticky whorls of sweet. We might have the jelebis first or head for a meal at Aunty's, up ahead above the mosque. There is nobody who could be an aunty at this small, single-room restaurant always packed during dinner time, but there apparently had been one. Now it is run by a young Chinese man, proprietor and chef, and his one waiter. No possible request is refused, the food is cooked to order, Chinese and Indian, veg and nonveg. And after Aunty's or jelebis or both, we walk back to the Institute, speculating like young escapees what malicious concoction from the Guest House cooks we have dodged today. Ah, but there is one more stop. Chaura Maidan, with its cow and its halwai, where we stop for a last tea before making the long climb up. By this time the road back is dark, and the grounds of the Viceregal Lodge, though lighted by lamp posts, are suffused in an eerie stillness, and it seems just possible that a cheetah might be lurking somewhere. Mahesh, partly in jest, has his umbrella at the ready. From here the lights of the town we've left behind shine like distant stars.

Even the Delhi papers have something to say about our monkeys. Until recently, monkey catchers used to come routinely; business was lucrative, on a per-monkey basis, when large numbers were sent to North American laboratories for experimentation. But that export has been prohibited recently, and the monkeys are proliferating.

There are two types of monkeys here. The langurs, grey with black face, slim and taut-bodied, handsome and quite strong; they can be seen on tree branches or in bushes feeding on vegetation, babies sometimes clutching at their fronts. Early in the mornings they will land with a crash upon my corrugated-metal roof, startling me awake. But otherwise they are the silent type, and timid; and so they get pelted with stones from children and cruel tourist youth. It is the other monkeys, "the monkeys," which are always the subject of discussion. No Curious George, but ugly and hairy, always dishevelled, the females with fiery red daubed on their behinds, babies clutched underneath as they prowl on all fours, or sitting before them as they contemplate the passersby, waiting for a chance to mug someone.

Stories about monkeys, I realize, are like those about backaches; once you've been afflicted, all manner of incidents are revealed to you. My local friend, silent on the subject so far, confesses finally to an incident in which, when she was a girl, a large female monkey jumped on her shoulder and she screamed for dear life. And so it is not only the visitor or the tourist who gets victimized, or walks nervously past a group of these simian cousins, but the locals also; and like many predators, they prefer to victimize women and children.

The monkeys on the way to Jakhoo Temple, dedicated to the monkey god Hanuman, are considered by the locals to be the most aggressive. This small slander has come about perhaps because the Mall road to the Institute is not as well travelled. In my experience, the most odious of these creatures are the monkeys of Chaura Maidan on the way to the Mall. A group of women come down the road eating ears of roasted corn, a monkey lithely climbs down a parapet, tries to swipe one out of a hand; before the woman can be scratched she yields up her snack. A man gaily walks along swinging a polythene bag of mangoes he's just purchased; along comes one of the creatures from behind, snatches the bag and makes a dash for it. As two women walk by with bags in their hands, two monkeys from behind a parked truck appraise them, get under the truck to begin their surprise attack; the women notice, clutch their bags close, and the monkeys change their minds. A group of boys just out from school with their backpacks walk nervously through a monkey gauntlet.

At other places they can expect to feed off leftovers or get into garbage or help themselves to temple offerings; but the monkeys of Chaura Maidan have mean, grumpy, restless looks as they prowl up and down and jealously guard their offspring, humourlessly though diligently pursuing their nefarious occupation, resentful at having been reduced this way to the role of scavengers, beggars, and robbers of their neighbours on the evolutionary ladder. When you see a group of monkeys, said a companion to me, you have to walk like a newly wed bride, looking down and clutching your things close to you.

To be sure, there are cute moments; like the time there's not a monkey in sight, and then, when you look up the hillside, you see a row of them, ten or more in number, taking turns intently grooming each other, presumably before they all hit the road like the Forty Thieves as the tourists arrive on their strolls. And of course there are monkey legends. The monkeys of the temple area had so bothered an Englishman who lived in the neighbourhood that he one day packed up his bags to leave. But a priest from Jakhoo Temple advised him, Hold on, no need for this extreme step; he called together all the monkeys of the area and gave them a good talking to in, presumably, Pahadi, the local mountain dialect. The Englishman was left alone after that.

It is easy to imagine a Valmiki, author of the Sanskrit epic the *Ramayana*, sitting under a tree or outside a hut and invoking these creatures in a story; it was they who made a bridge across to Lanka, defeated the demon Ravana, and set the island aflame.

Rudyard Kipling even composed a poem to the Shimla monkey ("bandar" in Hindi), which begins:

> It was an artless Bandar and he danced upon a pine,
> And much I wondered how he lived and where the beast might dine.

And many other things, till o'er my morning smoke,
I slept the sleep of idleness and dreamt that Bandar spoke.

✒

The Jakhoo specimens of the bandar turn out not as aggressive as advertised. My companion on my visit to the temple, a devout worshipper but also the author of a scholarly book on the female mystics of south India, is nervous all the way, clutching her bag in front of her; on a previous occasion her camera had been stolen by a monkey, but a group of locals entreated the thief, who had climbed up a cliff and realized it couldn't be eaten. Finally, she relinquished it. The path, cut through a forest of cedar and rhododendron, is paved and the incline steep, and all the way we are stared at but untouched by these creatures of Hanuman; we could have bought a walking stick (in effect a monkey fending stick), but our umbrellas do the job. Right outside the temple, the monkeys seem somehow tamer; or perhaps it is the people here who have been tamed. At a water tap, humans wash their hands before entering to worship, and monkeys come to drink. The ancient temple, a small, evidently rebuilt, red-brick structure with a tiled roof and a front porch supported on decorated pillars, is situated on the highest hill of the region. Apparently the monkey-god Hanuman had stopped here to look for the sanjivini plant, a herb he needed to cure Lakshman, brother of the eponymous hero of the *Ramayana*, who lay wounded after a battle on the island of Lanka.

Having visited the temple, my companion is a transformed person, her anxiety gone, and beaming she proceeds to distribute the prasad—the offering of sugar balls blessed by the temple priest—to the monkeys. A large one goes to her and waits patiently for the sugar; to a little one, somewhat impatient for his share, she says tenderly, "Wait, son, your turn will come." Meanwhile, a monkey steals a bag of unblessed prasad from the woman vendor; another is biting a dog; yet another one steals a large bread pakoda through the window of the canteen and runs away and, the attendant distracted by the thief, a fourth one snatches another pakoda and makes a dash through the door. "He gives and he also scares us," my companion says pithily to the prasad lady, making a reference, evidently, to the god Hanuman.

Another temple, and this time with two other companions, one of them Mahesh of Delhi. This visit is to the Tara Devi Temple, outside the town, on the road to Kalka. We have come out in a joyous, even playful, mood this Sunday morning; high on mountain air, perhaps, we are teenagers again, out on a romp, though it's been raining and grey—the monsoon has arrived—and we descend down the back road from the Institute to Boileau Ganj, from where we take our bus. It deposits us on the highway at the bottom of a hill, where we gird our loins, so to speak, for the climb up to see the Goddess.

Rows of tall straight pines run down the valley on one side of us; close to the track, wildflowers, berries, drops of water clinging to the leaves after the most recent downpour. Somewhat foolishly we've left our umbrellas behind, having used them so far to ward off monkeys and, for Mahesh at least, to take comfort from the fear of the leopard or cheetah reportedly seen around Shimla. What a short umbrella can achieve against a leaping large cat has not been brought up with him. Mahesh regales us with his pilgrim's tales: how three crates of Alphonso mangoes were picked by a seller in Bombay to ripen exactly on the day—no, the very hour—of his arrival in Czechoslovakia some years ago; how his arrival in Dalhousie (a local town) once had been announced to his host on the local cinema screen; he recites the poems of the two mystics, Kabir and Rahim.

A clearing of trees beside the path, at a cliff edge, reveals a grand and beautiful vista—hills and valleys, the green in a variety of textures, shaded by clouds in motion overhead, their shapes friendly

or menacing. The trek is always upwards, until the halfway point after forty-five minutes, when it eases and at the same time a downpour begins. We take shelter among the trees but get drenched to the skin anyway. A pilgrim from Bihar pauses to spend a moment with us, discusses the virtues of this track and its facilities (none) compared with the temple of Vaishno Devi in Jammu. Having imparted this knowledge, he hurries along. In a sense, visiting different temples across India is like earning stars; there are major stars and minor ones, the temple we are visiting is an average one.

When the downpour diminishes, we walk, and when it surges again, we pause for shelter. It is a well-known adage among visitors to the hills that when a hill person tells you your destination is "right there," it could be fifteen minutes to an hour or more away. Several times we meet groups returning from the temple. "How far is it?" we ask. "Twenty minutes," they all say. One time a wife corrects her husband: "These are tourists—thirty minutes." Finally, after we are told, "You are right there," it takes us twenty more minutes to get to the temple.

The temple is on a ridge at the top of a hill. The odd sight of a woman working by herself cutting stones at the base prompts Mahesh to recite a beautiful poem in Hindi by Nirala, about stonecutters:

> A woman breaking stones—
> on a road in Allahabad I saw her
> breaking stones.
>
> No shade
> from the tree under which she sat.
> Her body black, her young breasts
> bound tight in the choli;
> eyes lowered,
> mind turned to her lover
> and acts of love.

Our subject is not as voluptuous as the one in the poem, and the sun is definitely not shining. It has taken us two hours and forty-five minutes to climb up to the temple; on a rainless day, it might have taken an hour less. The Goddess images in the temple are of clay and draped in coloured cloth. Hundreds of coloured chudis, glass bangles, have been left by local women for the Goddess, in the expectation of some blessing. The temple building itself is new but simple—a white structure with a verandah of arches, a red-tiled roof, and a front porch from which flies a red flag. There are adjoining quarters for the priests and caretakers. A sign outside informs the visitor that this is one of the fifty-one shrines to Devi.

A specialty of this temple is that it helps you obtain your driver's licence, therefore many men climb up the hill to pray for success in their driving tests. All of them pass, we are solemnly reassured; those who refuse to humble themselves before the

Goddess invariably fail, then finally make the journey and beg forgiveness.

It takes considerably less time to go down, and when we reach the road we are dry but hungry. It is 4 p.m., and the dhabas on the road don't sell food anymore. We have tea and catch a bus. Rain clouds prowl overhead. By the time the bus drops us off, it is pouring again, and we get drenched once more. Another dhaba, more tea, but again no food; then another steep climb, the incline almost forty-five degrees, before we arrive at Boileau Ganj, which has the feel now of a metropolis. Dripping, we walk into yet another dhaba, which serves us samosas, chana, jelebis off the fire, and tea. From here, after picking up some vegetables—Mahesh a compulsive buyer of them—we climb up to the Postmaster Flat, where there is a heater and a bottle of brandy.

It's taken us ten hours to go visit the Goddess. Some good should come of that, we tell ourselves.

><

If the viceroys' tribe loved gardens, so do the Indians. Fixtures might come off the walls, toilets stink, roofs leak, stairs have deadly unrepaired sections, rugs be coated with dirt and hair, doors be painted over so many times they jam, and window panes have streaks of dried paint running down them—such is the state of maintenance at public places crowded with workers—but public gardens, to put it simply, work. And they work wonderfully; they are tended with care and devotion, they are neat and colourful, and they proliferate.

A large, lush green lawn is the frontispiece to the Institute, at one side of which stand three Himalayan oaks, a tall, straight-trunked deodar or Himalayan cedar, and a slim tulip tree brought by the British—perhaps the only one in India, the director says, his voice glowing with pride. On the way to the greenhouse and nursery, a juniper and a holly. And everywhere else space permits, flowers: dahlias, gladioli, marigolds, daisies, football lilies, lilies of the valley, torch lilies, white lilies, roses, and irises, in pink, blue, and white, as tall as hedges. The greenhouse this day is a glowing, dizzying red with masses of geraniums stood in rows on stands, all bred and grown locally, among them the prizewinners of a recent flower show wearing their ribbons. A gardener comes up holding a flower. They are dropping, he informs the director, there's something in the soil. He uses a Hindi word, which the director interprets as "virus." A brief technical discussion ensues. Whatever level of formal schooling this gardener has received, he is a true horticulturalist.

At the back of the main building is a long terraced garden on four levels. There are two chinars here on the first level, a rare Japanese maple lower down, two Chinese elms, and the Himalayan variety of pine with drooping needles. And the most imposing one, outside the vicereine's bedroom window, a massive oak, reputedly six hundred years old, host to a dozen smaller plants growing on, climbing up its bark, basking in its shade on the ground. Two former outdoor tennis courts now make a wildflower nursery, behind which, at the farther end, in the midst of trees and bush, is an indoor tennis court, now used as a badminton court, its walls constructed of the same grey stone as the main building, with a wooden gallery at one end where once stood a billiard table and the sovereign's representative perhaps sat watching a game. This day a children's badminton game is in progress, part of the local welfare program. Other days, the Institute provides music lessons.

There is no more tennis in Shimla. On the way back a rather odd sight comes into view, a coat of arms fixed on the side of a parapet. These gardens were designed, apparently, by Lady Minto. As you climb the steps back to the main level there stands before you an imposing pedestal of brick or stone, on which is mounted a copper sundial; it is now broken, defaced by tourist scratchings. Also once mounted here, on the parapet, I am told, was a map of the horizon, etched on copper, so that standing looking in the distance and consulting the copper map at your elbow, you could identify the mountain peaks of the Himalayas. It was taken down some time ago.

An alien race had descended here for a time, so it seems from this vantage point, and then gone away, leaving behind all these amazing structures. Tourists leave behind cigarette packs, potato chip bags, polythene bags, all the indestructible refuse of economic liberalization and Western ways, which the director's staff picks up every day. Young visitors from abroad hike up all the way from the Mall to gaze at these grounds in silence and wonder was it truly their ancestors who had lived here once in such opulence.

The sunset today is a tremendous, loud, clanging surprise from the heavens. Initially, an orange slit perforates the clouds in the west, soon a faint cloud-veiled orange breaks loose and dips behind the mountains. That should have been the end of the day, but suddenly there's a tinge of faint red in the east, and you know it must come from the sun, but how? You look west again and the whole western sky is ablaze, a fiery red and orange, almost reaching overhead, so bright you can barely face it. The sun god Surya having a final laugh somewhere beyond the horizon. Across the valley, in the east again, the white buildings of the town are bathed in his glow.

The director, a native of Assam, is the local raja, driven up and down the hill every day to his large opulent home in a white Ambassador with DIRECTOR printed over the licence plate. He is in charge of everything, from funding to labour disputes; wherever he turns, hands join in namastés. He knows every bird call, they say, and can name everything that grows on the ground. But he was trained as a philosopher, in England. Even after sitting through the most jargon-filled seminar he will come up with a precise, plain-worded, incisive question reflecting a philosopher's clear mind at work.

But the kingdom rests on shaky ground. Every once in a while the government, which has been generous thus far, reminds the Institute that it is merely a tenant, and so a Damoclean sword hangs over the place. Only other pickings, one supposes, and distance, keep the bureaucrats and politicians at bay, but one fine day they could come and convert the place into a five-star tourist complex with a casino, or a conference centre resort for themselves. It is something too good to be left only to scholars and teachers; it invites takeover, pilferage. It is said that when the public works department replaced the eighty-year-old wooden beams of the greenhouse, material was used which began to rot in a year; meanwhile, the original wood, which was still good, went into private homes. The PWD has also built an ugly concrete apartment building on a green space outside an old Institute cottage, and a courtroom battle has ensued. A building at the gate has been occupied by the local university for a pittance, and the university refuses to budge. What belongs to the government is up for grabs. Fine antique furniture has disappeared and there is not much left of the original. Such are the travails of running the Institute. What amazes is the resignation, a touch of irony maybe, but nevertheless no outrage.

The Institute has a resident jinn, a flitting peddler to attend to your needs; when you walk to the Mall you see him hurrying the opposite way with his long strides, carrying something back in his jola; when you go to Boileau Ganj, he is there, too, making purchases; when you return, he is already on the grounds; when you visit someone at their office, he suddenly appears, bringing tea from the canteen outside. Square-faced, with a thin moustache, curly hair, chappals on his feet, walking at a slight backward tilt, his jola swinging about his shoulder, he has the manner of a village teacher. He is a presence easy to describe yet unknowable in his personality. For twenty years or more—and he doesn't look over forty-five—he's been the local peddler; if there were drugs on the scene he'd be a pusher, I imagine. No sooner do you run into him than he'll offer you something. He'll be the first to discover your cigarette habit and take it upon himself to keep you supplied. He'll corner you on the way to a seminar— "Sah'b you need a cigarette now, take it"—he'll even call you up to remind you of your habit. He'll offer to bring you your groceries: "Madam, can I bring you chicken?" Once, he badgered a scholar I was visiting into ordering tea. The reason, apparently, was that she'd got some clout, and he knew she always received a generous supply of milk, not all of which she would use. So after she'd finished preparing her tea, he would take the tray away and place it on a windowsill and drink up the remaining milk, presumably with the sugar. His name is Rampal and he's already built himself a house, it is said.

><

It is my friend Vijaya, the mystic scholar who took me to Jakhoo Temple, who shows me the little church she has discovered.

After breakfast on a Sunday we walk through the French doors at the rear of the Guest House, past the porch, to a settlement where some of the peons—the lowest-level servants—live with their families in their shacks. Some kids are running around, a young one or two play naked, a woman combs the hair of a girl who sits in front of her. A man smiles at us; he is the oldest of the dining room workers and finished serving us not long ago. A short distance ahead is the church, which Vijaya has already visited once. Although she had looked nervous that evening on the road to Jakhoo, I have discovered that she is an intrepid hiker and has been to all the temples in the area at least once. She assumes a peculiar gait during her walking expeditions, hanging forward as she takes her lengthy strides, her arms swinging forward and backward at an angle.

The church is an old rectangular red-brick building, its short side visible from a distance and distinguished by a large wheel-like attachment above the door under the pitched roof. As you draw closer, you see on the wheel a makeshift patch made of flattened tin containers, on top of which is a red Christian cross. A sign on the wall says, "ANGLICAN CHURCH, DIOCESE OF BOILEAU GANJ, REV PARDESI."

As we enter, a short dark man welcomes us fervently; he is finishing sweeping the floor, which is of dusty, crumbled concrete. There is a lectern at the far end, covered by a white cloth with a cross on it.

It is a completely dilapidated interior we have walked into, roughly twenty-five by a hundred feet. It's been stripped bare: apart from the draped lectern and three metal chairs, there is no other furniture. Old wood panelling covers the lower half of one side wall; the plaster above has peeled off in places, the uprights are rotten. The windowpanes are plain and simple; around their rectangular frames are the arched shadows of the presumably more elegant original windows. There are two lightbulbs, both turned on, hanging from the rafters. By way of added decor, about twenty potted plants have been brought to stand in a huddle on the opposite side of the panelled wall.

The reverend proceeds to lay out two rough, red carpets on the swept but still dusty floor; this first layer is covered by another, newer carpet on which goes a cloth spread. Beyond this covering he places the three chairs. Another rough piece of red carpet forms the runner to the lectern. He places seven pairs of hymn books on the covered floor, one in Hindi and English, the other in Hindi only. He gives a pair each to me and my companion, asks us to sit on two of the chairs, and gives us a black Bible, which is in English. Then he goes to the lectern and begins the service. There are only the two of us in the congregation, neither one born or brought up a Christian.

It is a sight at once pathetic as it is inspiring. What is the point of this performance? It must be that he believes in his truth and his calling, and he must carry on. What would he have done without our presence?

He sings a hymn in English, in not the best of voices, then reads the story of Cain and Abel from Genesis. "Am I my brother's keeper?" In another twist of irony, both of us, schooled in former British colonies, familiar with Western culture, can pick out the chapter and verses from the Bible.

In between Bible readings are sung hymns in Hindi—Christian bhajans—which he sings off-key, banging a tambourine in accompaniment.

Suddenly two girls of about eight arrive, with neat pigtails and wearing clean clothes, and sit on the clothed carpet in front of us. The reverend goes on, exhorting them to join him in singing, but they are too shy. Epistles of Paul and John follow, in Hindi. And then he begins a sermon, the subject being the treatment of our fellow beings: Cain was the murderer; Jesus says don't even call your brother a fool; and John says if you are angry, you are a murderer . . .

Towards the conclusion, two couples arrive, with a baby, parents it seems of the two girls. The women are better dressed than the men, who look like labourers. I wonder if they have arrived late because they don't have the patience for the reverend's full hour of service.

"Lord they love you, but bring them closer to you," says Reverend Pardesi, referring to us in the final prayer, and when it is over he comes to say goodbye at the door and tells us to return next Sunday.

As we depart, past the rubble, the stones, and the cowpats, I wonder, Surely the viceroy might have attended here sometimes?

Waning Days in the Hills:
Recalling Love, Art, and Politics

> This blemished light, this dawn by night half-devoured
> Is surely not the dawn for which we were waiting.
> This cannot be the dawn in quest of which, hoping
> To find it somewhere, friends, we all set out.
> FAIZ AHMED FAIZ, "The Dawn of Freedom"

"IT HASN'T COME OUT, HAS IT," she says regretfully.

No, she's not quite captured the previous evening's glorious sunset in her watercolour. Her husband, Bhishm-ji, comes into the living room which is also her studio and says he'll make the tea.

"I will," she offers.

"No, I'll do it." And he goes to the kitchen.

"I was good," she says to me. "I used to take lessons in Delhi, just after my wedding. I was eighteen."

This was before the Partition, her father was with the police and had been transferred to the capital for prosecution duty.

Bhishm-ji comes in with the tea and says something in Punjabi, which I take to be, "Did the painting come out all right?"

"No," she replies.

"Next time," he tells her, a sympathetic smile on his face.

Later he lights a cigarette and they share it.

"Tell me about Moscow," I tell him.

Once could not imagine one without the other, Bhishm-ji and Sheila-ji, Bhishm and Sheila Sahni. He nearing eighty, with shrunken frame and crumpled face; soft-spoken and gentle is the overall first impression. She with hip-length gold and white hair, a flushed clear face, somewhat squat from age now, though it is not hard to imagine the sprightly girl she must have been from all her talk about her youth. A venerable old couple, an institution during their two years in Shimla, humane light in an otherwise dry academic atmosphere, reservoirs of memory—of the decades of glorious idealism and expectations in Punjab before Independence, followed by that tragic divide of Partition, which displaced them both, and then the struggles of a literary life in place of a Congress idealism. They live here in what must once have been a lovely cottage belonging to the viceroy's bandmaster. There is a ramshackle wooden verandah in front, behind which are the large dining and living rooms, with high ceilings and large windows looking out to the yard and the trees; upstairs are two bedrooms with private baths, connected by a corridor. In the morning she paints watercolours, he writes.

Every day at lunchtime they set off together from their house, walk slowly up the rising driveway, to the dining room; she in her Punjabi shalwar-kameez, he in kurta-pyjamas and vest, in the rather drab pastels that often adorn the men in northern India. After lunch they come outside for their tea: sitting on the lawn under the solitary tree there, or on the steps between the two levels of the garden, they become the epicentre of our gathering, for we are all aware we are in the presence of two luminaries. When they depart from the Institute, their two years ending during my tenure, the monsoon has finally set in; they could have stayed longer, but the dampness has been a concern for his breathing. It is fitting that many of the other fellows leave at the same time, on holidays, on assignments, or permanently, for the place will no longer be the same.

He is one of the most renowned modern Hindi writers. While some of his contemporaries indulge in Western modernist story-telling, Sahni's stories and plays are concerned more with the reality of Indian life as experienced by simple, ordinary people. He examines the cynical brutality of rulers, the tragic consequences of bigotry, the plight of the lower classes and of women. His gentleness and humanity pervades his work; if one needed to find a fault, it is perhaps the lack of anger or passion in the writing, yet there is a dogged probing of human foibles, and a humour that persists in the face of tragedy. He has come to the Institute to write a play on Dara Shikoh, the liberal-minded brother of the puritanical Mughal Aurangzeb, who had his brother beheaded and the headless corpse paraded before the denizens of Delhi in Chandni Chowk; but he's discovered that he's more captivated by the loneliness he sees in Aurangzeb. His most famous work is the novel *Tamas*, which describes in relentless detail the unfolding of an episode of communal violence and is now a classic in the literature of the Partition. The first chapter of the novel, a masterpiece of humour and terror, introduces a low-caste Hindu man who is coerced into killing a pig and placing it near the entrance to a mosque. It is typical of Sahni to describe the plight of this lowly individual, who has a pregnant wife and an ailing mother, and who has no stake in the politics of the day as he goes about his humble business. He is both a victim and a pawn in the hands of the fanatics who foment violence to vent their hatred in the days before Partition.

I spend many hours with the Sahnis after my family's return to Toronto. Conversation with them is always touched with humour. He will talk, and she will augment; or she'll talk and he will remain silent, on his mouth a touch of an indulgent smile, as she reveals her frustrations, her regrets: his life a success, she the wife and companion who sacrificed.

But for a silk string, Bhishm-ji once says with that smile, he might have risen high in politics. Then we might have been something, Sheila-ji interjects, unable to hold back her regret. Ministers, rich! But would he have written?

He joined the Rawalpindi area branch of the Congress Party during the Quit India Movement around 1940. He was on the verge of a party nomination, but someone at a meeting noticed that the string of his pyjama was made of silk, not khadi, the homespun cotton which was the Congress dress code inspired by Gandhi. Sheila-ji apparently had threaded in the silk string, hoping nobody would notice. But it was noticed, and so his nomination was refused and he never made minister. But he was campaign manager for a Congress candidate, a Muslim, in the 1945 elections—the name of the candidate escapes him, but he recalls how reviled the candidate was in many Muslim areas, refused service in restaurants, entry into homes. Nevertheless his candidate lost only by the narrowest of margins, a few hundred votes, against a prominent opposition member.

The years of 1946 and 1947 were tense; communal riots sprang up in all the major cities, and in hundreds of villages. Since they lived in a Muslim area, he saw the dynamics of the violence from up close. Marauding gangs went about murdering, looting, raping, burning, but not in the areas they themselves came from, the gangs unable or unwilling to turn against their own neighbours and friends. He recalls a young man in his neighbourhood called Lateef who was friendly and even protective towards his Hindu friends, and yet up to all sorts of devilry in other areas. Bhishm-ji and his father would watch as the riot victims from the villages arrived, took trains for the south. "How foolish," his father would say. "So what if this becomes Pakistan? We'll stay."

He went to Delhi in August 1947 to witness the Independence Day ceremonies at the Red Fort as a Congress Party official. On the way, he saw Lahore burning—a sight many people, including my friend Mahesh, remember. He didn't know he would never return. When the train reached Meerut he realized that communication with areas in Pakistan had broken down. His wife and mother were in their family home in Kashmir, his father back in Rawalpindi, his brother Balraj in Bombay.

He recalls a disturbing incident from those days. It was discovered that in a Sikh village a number of women had jumped into a well to save themselves from attackers. During communal violence, it is commonplace even today that women and girls are brutally raped. After the attack was over, the deputy commissioner of the area had asked health officers to go and do the necessary. Bhishm-ji went along as observer, with some members of the Congress Party. When they arrived they saw a gruesome sight: the bloated bodies of the dead women had surfaced in the well. The husband of one of them came to Bhishm-ji and said, "My wife had a gold bangle on, can you help me retrieve it, it's mine." A callous thought, it might seem, but refugees needed all they could get to survive.

His father remained alone in Rawalpindi for a few months, before being smuggled out by some of the locals, wearing a red fez so as to appear a Muslim. He left for Kashmir, whence he flew to Delhi.

Following the afternoon seminars at the Institute, where we sit around a long oak table on plush upright chairs bequeathed by the viceroys, and tea is served individually with separate milk and sugar, and accompanied by biscuits and crackers, some of us repair to the outside cafeteria at the cliff edge, less for the extra tea than for the conversation. Further along the ledge where we sit on our flimsy plastic chairs, sometimes there will be an entire family of Tibetans or some mountain tribespeople crouched on the ground pounding stone to pieces for use in paving; other women and children walk by bearing bricks on their backs; men pass carrying heavier loads. A caste or tribe of people, coolies to a town.

Here Bhishm-ji and Sheila-ji one afternoon reveal a standing argument: Which brand of Punjabi, the variety of Sialkot, where she comes from, or the one from his native Rawalpindi, is the better? She admits that his is the softer, but hers, she says, is the more authentic; the difference apparently is in the gender allocations for certain nouns. And then she tells of the time when the poet Faiz, perhaps the greatest modern poet in the Urdu language, came to Delhi. There was shortage of water or electricity, problems Delhi was prone to, and it was blistering hot, and she apologized to him for the discomforts, at which he told her, Am I a foreigner? Faiz, too, was from Sialkot, but being a Muslim he remained and became a Pakistani, while these two became Indians and had to leave. Both Bhishm-ji and Faiz had been members of the influential Progressive Writers' Movement in their early years, a collective that believed that writers should serve the public interest. I remember seeing Faiz at a mushaira, a recital, in Toronto, where an adulating crowd of more than five hundred had gathered to hear him; the next day at a meeting with him I asked him some rather foolish questions about a writer's commitment.

The talk now turns to the subject of real people turning up on whom fictional characters have been based. Bhishm-ji says the eponymous character of one of his books used to live in his neighbourhood, and he hopes that she will never pick up the book. "If after seven or eight years I don't hear from anybody, then I know I'm safe." Once, though, he had got into a fix. The most unpleasant character in one of his novels was based on a man who had been flattered by the portrayal, and said to him, Please write another one about me. But a minor character turned out to offend family members and Bhishm-ji's brother Balraj flew in from Bombay to convince him to withdraw it. He didn't.

Balraj, whom they both recall very fondly, was the famous Bombay film actor Balraj Sahni, one of whose best roles was in the film *Garam Hawa*, based on a story by the Urdu writer Ismat Chugtai. Bhishm-ji himself is no mean actor, having appeared in several cameo roles.

It was while in Bombay that he was offered the chance to go to Moscow as a translator. He jumped at it. This was during the tenure of Premier Khrushchev. Bhishm-ji's first translation assignment was a difficult mining treatise, and he remembers also long translations of Khrushchev's speeches. He wishes he had translated Tolstoy instead. There were some wonderful times in Russia, and their attachment to Moscow has remained, but Bhishm-ji and Sheila-ji both concur that those seven years of their life were wasted. Sheila-ji alternates between describing the wonderful visits to the ballet, the grand parties they attended, the adventure of living in a foreign place, and calling that period a black hole in her youth.

Their son is a physicist who has been in Toronto, and it turns out that I might have run into the three of them in an elevator when I didn't know them. Their daughter is a professor of Russian.

In the early 1970s, after their return from Moscow, Bhishm-ji was in Bombay when communal riots erupted. Balraj was on his way by car to the distressed area, to observe and assist, and Bhishm-ji went along with him. What he saw brought back memories of what he had witnessed during the carnage of the Partition; it inspired him to write almost nonstop, and the result was the novel *Tamas*, which won the country's highest literary prize. The novel leaves no community free from blame, no community free of suffering. The role of the British commissioner is that of a cynic, impatient of the natives' barbarities, whose lives matter little: You want us out, so solve the problems yourselves. The cynicism of the British rulers then, Bhishm-ji believes, is matched by that of India's current politicians, which subject he has explored in other works.

When *Tamas* was serialized for television, opposition to it mounted from the Hindu nationalist organizations, such as the VHP and RSS, the identification of the latter with the khaki-clad fascists of the film rather obvious and accurate in many eyes. Effigies of the author and director were burnt in public demonstrations.

And what of the writer's wife? Favourite daughter of a police inspector, trained in painting and classical singing, top of her Master's class in philosophy. She cannot but divulge her disappointments, the opportunities she missed being an Indian wife, and a socialist writer's one at that. She couldn't take up singing after marriage, had to follow him with two kids to Moscow in his quest to see socialism first-hand. She had had a job as a news reader at All India Radio; after Moscow, she got the job back but then lost it on account of her husband being branded a communist. Obviously she has sacrificed her opportunities for his career, her marriage. She says as much: "Just any mother could have raised children." Now she's started painting again, doing watercolours, having taken instructions from a young professional. She works at them every morning in the living room, where several of them stand displayed on easels. It is frustrating; she so much wants to be better at it.

She's complained about her sacrifices so many times to him, she cannot control herself even before a guest. No writer whose career has been aided by his family, even just by their diminished demands upon him, could fail to appreciate the situation. But she loves him. He's too good, she will say, meaning he is too nice to one and all. And she is a stalwart defender and promoter of his work: Read such and such, it's wonderful. He's a wonderful translator; I was a translator too.

One thing they disagree on is the reservation system for so-called scheduled castes and backward tribes, India's affirmative action, a hotly debated topic among the middle classes during my time in Shimla. "Some form of reservation is necessary," he affirms one afternoon, true to his natural sympathies, and she clams up, picks up a book. A subject that has come up many times before, apparently.

There is bitter anger among the upper classes with regard to reservations of government jobs and university positions for the lower and "backward" classes. The resentment, liberal middle-class

Indians take pains to point out, is against the cynical politics behind the ways in which the reservations are implemented.

In 1979, the Indian government set up the Mandal Commission to "identify the socially or educationally backward" classes among the population and consider the question of reservations, or quotas, for them in the educational and government sectors. The commission took into consideration social, economic, and educational criteria to determine "backwardness," and in its report, released in 1980, recommended an increase in the number of reservations that were already in place for these classes, which included the lowest castes among Hindus, the "tribals," and others. The report was implemented in 1990 amidst great controversy and led to the fall of the government. The percentage of reservations for the backward classes was increased, and the upper castes found the number of university places and government jobs for their children drastically reduced. In some areas, protesting students went so far as to commit suicide by setting themselves on fire. The Supreme Court of India, in its ruling on the issue, while admitting that the number of reservations allocated to the backward castes was large, put a ceiling of 50 per cent on them. For the court to allow even this number of reservations in a bid to right past wrongs was a strong admission that Indian society had a long way to go to be rid of systemic inequalities. For it even to consider the question is a triumph of India's democracy, whatever its practical and historical problems.

At public functions that I have attended, in the representations of India at home and abroad through books and columns, and in Bollywood films, which project images of India all across the globe, the almost complete predominance of upper-caste Hindus is truly remarkable. India's story, it would seem, is their story. Of course, this lower-caste submergence has to do with their traditional occupations and poverty. The lowest castes traditionally did the lowliest jobs, associated with dirt and pollution, such as sweeping streets, cleaning toilets, and tending to corpses, and in the past they could not even approach the upper castes. In my own childhood, not as much exposed to the caste system, the derogatory epithets "chudo," "neech," and "bhang," all indicating the lowest castes, were common, though I was not aware of their meaning. They were even used for the Africans, who did most of these jobs, but we had our shoemakers and potmakers who were visibly of the lower castes.

And yet, here in India, even among the most liberal, especially those with children, resentment of the reservations is common. The policy rewards mediocrity in the name of equality, runs the familiar argument. Or, economic status should be the criterion, not caste. It is pointed out that a beneficiary of the present system can rise up to wealth and privilege yet continue to receive further benefits for his children, depriving others less privileged. And the so-called backward classes constitute well over half the population in many areas. The system can be further abused in almost comical ways: castes competing as to which is the more backward.

There is a deep yearning among some intellectuals for an essential Indian-ness, to do away with these ancient divisions, the messiness of India. The nostalgic Oxonian at the Institute blithely speaks of the Hindu mind, comparing it with the Jewish mind. This is silly, if not dangerous, for it only enhances exclusivity and division. What of the Christians, the Muslims, the Buddhists, the Jains, all as ethnically Indian? Is a Tamil "mind" the same as a Bengali "mind"? A visiting professor says, of the nationalist policies of the BJP, the right-wing political party that recently fomented the communal tension in the country, "Even if it's Hindu nationalism, it's nationalism. Is it my fault that I was born a Brahmin?" One might ask, Would you have liked to be born an Untouchable, one whose ancestors dared not raise their heads to exchange a look with a high-caste person?

One of the ironies of the upsurge of middle-class Hindu nationalism is that this same class of privileged Indians is instrumental in shaping the new concepts of citizenship in Canada, Britain, and the United States, by their immigration to these countries and their largely successful struggles for equal rights even as small cultural, racial, and religious minorities. Their Western host countries, of course, no longer see themselves in racial or nationalist terms— which is not to say that such consciousness, especially in discus- sions of culture, do not exist. But it is always contested, and not the least by people of Indian origin. Affirmative action continues to be used successfully to redress a racist past, and systemic non-representation. In a reverse irony, many of the Indian middle classes, assured of their rights in their new, multicultural homes, turn around to support financially and promote militant national-ism in the native country. Many of them would wish for a Hindu India but not a Christian or Euro America or Canada.

><

Shimla, this peaceful little town where the only threat appears to be the rumour of a cheetah and perhaps a monkey-thief on the road, is intimately connected with the last days of the Raj and the parti-tion of India. This is well known, but walking along an isolated path in the woods, or in the paradisaical garden of the Institute, the reminder nevertheless manages to hit one with a jolt.

In June 1945, the viceroy, Lord Wavell, invited Jawaharlal Nehru, Muhammad Ali Jinnah, Mahatma Gandhi, Tara Singh, and other Indian leaders to the so-called Simla Conference to decide on the future of India; specifically, what form self-government should take with respect to the representation of India's minori-ties. Nehru, of the Indian National Congress, arrived straight from jail, where he had done time for civil disobedience. Jinnah, for-merly of Congress, now represented the Muslim League, which was at loggerheads with Congress regarding the representation of Muslims in independent India. An astute lawyer, he was not very much liked by the British; the viceroy's ADC, Peter Coats, privately called him "the Muslim in the woodpile." The conference was a failure, for the Muslim League and the Indian National Congress could not agree.

Wrote the *Atlantic Monthly* a few months later,

> The most powerful figure in Indian politics today is not the Viceroy, nor Mahatma Gandhi, nor Jawaharlal Nehru. It is a lean, gray-haired, impeccably dressed Karachi lawyer, Mohammed Ali Jinnah, the leader of the All-India Moslem League. Upon his attitude depends the success or failure of the present attempt to solve the Indian problem.

An arguable assessment, conforming to the portrayal of Jinnah in Richard Attenborough's film *Gandhi*, which in its turn outraged the Pakistanis, who revere Jinnah as much as Indians do Gandhi, perhaps more. (A 1998 film on Jinnah's life, with Christopher Lee playing the lead role, could not obtain distribution and came out as a DVD.) The partition of India, which had to be agreed upon after Simla, is debated to this date, the subject fraught with accusations and regrets. It was him; it was them; if only. History and historical interpretation, too, suffered division, and belong to two separate worlds.

Not all Indian Muslims followed Jinnah; one of the delegates representing Congress at the Simla Conference had been Maulana Azad, who spoke Persian to Freya Stark, the well-known advisor to the British Empire. The irony was that it was Azad who was the practising Muslim, and not the "snappy dresser" Jinnah, who got his clothes from London's Savile Row, did not speak Urdu, let alone Persian, and reportedly drank wine. There is a belief, therefore, corroborated by some of Jinnah's later speeches, that it was a secular state for a Muslim majority that he had in mind, not anything like the current Islamic state with a gun-toting Taliban on the rampage. Perhaps he did not know his constituency well enough.

Ayesha Jalal, a well-known Pakistani scholar in the United States, has even put forward the argument that Jinnah did not want a separate Muslim homeland at all, but merely used the threat as a bargaining chip to win safeguards for India's Muslim minority.

In 1947 arrived the last viceroy of India, Lord Mountbatten, to oversee the division and independence of India. A Boundary Commission was established, which put up in Shimla at the Cecil Hotel in Chaura Maidan, to draw the boundary between independent India and the new state of Pakistan. The boundary was drawn, and the transfer of populations, which took place in the northwest and the northeast, was accompanied by scenes of gruesome violence in which half a million lives were lost. The figure is quite readily trotted out, as I have just done; but when one pauses to think about it, it is, quite literally, stunning.

In what remained of India, in Gujarat, Kerala, and Tamil Nadu, for example, substantial Muslim populations continued to live alongside a Hindu majority. But the acrimony and suspicion of Partition would remain, the Muslims of India for long left to wonder if they had made the right decision to stay, always wary, especially during the wars between the two countries, of being seen as a fifth column or rooting for the enemy. Taunts would be suffered, and Muslim areas of India dubbed "Pakistan" to this day. Countless bloody riots would take place. Today there are roughly one hundred and fifty million Muslims in India. The problem of Kashmir remains unsolved. The two countries face each other with nuclear weapons. And today's Pakistan would surely be Jinnah's nightmare.

Raja Bhasin, the Shimla historian, wonders if the bloodbath of Partition could have been averted had there been no summer capital and had the government thus been more in contact with the people. He quotes Gandhi: "I can no more effectively deliver my message to millions by travelling first class than the Viceroy can rule over the hearts of India's millions from his unapproachable Simla heights."

After Partition, most Muslims of Shimla left; Mahbub Ali's Pathan ilk disappeared.

><

It is fitting, then, that in this palace which hosted the Simla Conference to decide the fate of independent India, where Nehru and Gandhi and Jinnah and others came to wrangle, and ultimately where the line was drawn to divide the country, there takes place a seminar to commemorate the author Manto, whose stories are the most savage indictment of the insanity that prevailed at Partition.

Saadat Hasan Manto is one of the greatest story writers the country (if one forgets for a while the political boundary that so incensed him) has produced. While Tagore has the lofty grace, the wisdom, the aesthetic quality, the diversity, Manto is the story writer, pure and raw, and his narratives about Partition are like a kick in the gut; they will never become simply quaint, simply great, simply admired; they will continue to shock and probe and haunt each generation as it grapples with the incomprehensible violence that accompanied the partition of the subcontinent and continues periodically to erupt.

It is of course particularly satisfying for someone such as I—to whom the concept of the Partition comes as an offence on the self, because it asks me to choose, and it invites others to put a label on me—that this conference takes place on Indian soil, with visitors also from Pakistan (albeit via the United States). But most of these Manto fans are Hindus, if one wants to put a label on them; and they delight in Manto tales, just as they delight in stories about Faiz, another great secular writer who wound up on the other side, ultimately to be exiled. At this conference translations of Manto stories are read and debated over; themes therein are discussed; a three-volume collection of Partition stories is launched, compiled by the scholar Alok Bhalla, who travelled to Pakistan to collect some of them. And finally the film of Bhishm Sahni's Partition novel *Tamas* is shown.

But this seems too much dwelling on the tragic as the academic and the aesthetic. Tragedy becomes career. I decline to see the film on this occasion, after which the audience will undoubtedly meet for tea and cookies. The subject is still too raw for me; only three years before, there was the massive communal violence in Bombay and Gujarat that shocked me to the core. Still, this is intellectual life at the Institute, the former Viceregal Lodge, at its best. At another time, however, a professor of astrology comes to explain his theory of how the entire world received its civilization from India. The new nationalism is not far beneath the surface of this exposition. But the director, with all his philosophic composure, treats the astrologer with due respect, with a pointed and polite question at the end.

><

After the food, when everyone is sitting around, she says to him, "Come on, sing." And she announces, "Bhishm-ji will sing."

This is at the Sahnis' farewell party at the director's house.

"No," he says, in that gentle tone. "I don't remember the words. Next time," he promises, "we'll come having practised."

But finally, after exhortations, the two of them sing a song from a film in which his brother Balraj had acted. Bhishm-ji's voice is low, hers high; there are some false starts, words sometimes forgotten. The voices crack, but the melody is there.

And once again I marvel at the presence of song in Indian life, the spontaneity, the love with which people in a circle will begin to sing. For now there are others among us who take their turn. London for some reason reminds someone of a ghazal of the last Mughal emperor Bahadur Shah Zafar. It is the one he wrote before his death in Burma, in which he says there's not even six feet of his beloved Indian homeland to be buried in. Does anyone know it? someone asks. Bhishm-ji and Sheila-ji sing: and the wonder for me is that there is help from everyone present, especially the Punjabis, who suffered some of the worst traumas of the Partition, some of whom were born on the other side. It is, after all, a ghazal by a Mughal emperor that they are reciting with such devotion.

"I'll sing an IPTA song," Bhishm-ji then says. By this time a round or two of Scotch has been poured. "The words are not so great," he smiles, "there's hardly a tune, but I'll sing it anyway, because it is an IPTA song."

And gently, unwaveringly, he sings.

Excursion to the Plains:
The Old House in Amritsar

The year I do not remember, but there was great revolutionary fervour in Amritsar. . . .

I would spend the entire day at Jallianwala Bagh. Sitting under a tree, I would watch the windows of the houses bordering the park and dream about the girls who lived behind them. I was sure one of these days, one of them would fall in love with me.

SAADAT HASAN MANTO, "The Price of Freedom"

MY WIFE NURJEHAN'S FATHER is a Punjabi from Amritsar. In Dar es Salaam, where we were both brought up, she was a minority among Gujarati and Kutchi Indians. And so even she, speaking Kutchi and Hindustani (the pre-Partition cosmopolitan form of Hindi and Urdu), did not quite know how much of a Partition child she was. Those of our generation hadn't even heard the word. Her father and mother moved to Tanganyika in 1946, just before the Partition. At Partition, the rest of the family made their escape in the night, leaving almost everything behind them, and headed for Bombay by train, whence they dispersed to Africa, England, Pakistan, Canada, and the United States. My father-in-law has returned to India many times, never to Amritsar. But he did send us to look at the place of his birth. I wonder at the knot of feelings he must carry inside him, which he has never revealed.

Bhishm Sahni has a poignant story called "Amritsar Has Arrived," which he read to us around the viceroys' long oak table in the seminar room at Shimla one afternoon. In the story, during the tumult of Partition, a train leaves Lahore, bound south. Into a compartment get a tall Pathan of typical arrogant bearing and a mild-mannered, small Bania, from the trader caste, considered cowardly but cunning. The Bania withers before the Pathan's belligerent boorishness, constantly deferring to him. Suddenly, however, the train stops, and the familiar clamour of a railway station is heard. Coolies get in. Amritsar has arrived! goes the cry. This city is now Hindu and Sikh, cleansed of its Muslims. (As Lahore, correspondingly, has been cleansed of its Hindus and Sikhs; one must always balance the narrative on this prickly subject.) The little Bania discovers a sudden ferociousness awakening in him, and it is the Pathan who begins to cower, and is ultimately murdered.

We leave Shimla by taxi, go down to Kalka, and from there westwards on the Grand Trunk Road, which was not only the main setting but also a character in Kipling's *Kim*. We pass Ambala—where Kim gave his coded message to the Colonel in his bungalow about an uprising in the north—Ludhiana, and Jalandhar, pass two of the great rivers of Punjab, the Sutlej and the Beas. On both sides are the fertile fields of the green revolution, growing wheat this season. The GT Road, built by the emperor Sher Shah Suri in the sixteenth century, begins at Peshawar in the northwest of Pakistan, passes through India, and ends beyond Calcutta in Bangladesh, spanning a distance of one thousand five hundred miles. We don't see the throbbing pedestrian life that Kipling described on the road, but there are trucks and buses, and roadside dhabas with bare string cots spread out for travellers to rest and have their samosas, teas, paranthas, and the oiliest vegetable curries that go burning down your throat like acid.

This trip is going to be short; there is a three-year-old to cater to, who is particular about where he pees. If he doesn't approve of where you take him, he simply says, "Doesn't want to," and holds it in. The adults have had malaria in Africa and know their mosquitoes, they think; it is the two kids they need to worry about. The GT Road enters Amritsar in a street that is bizarrely lined with numerous bicycle shops. We find our accommodation, a guest house at the Guru Nanak Dev University, a splendidly spread-out green campus, and then, leaving a message for one Balwinder Singh, who is to show us the old family house, we head for the Golden Temple, where in 1984, in an operation called Blue Star, Indira Gandhi sent in troops against extremists fighting for a Sikh homeland, thus giving cause to her assassination.

The Golden Temple is usually known as Harmandir Sahib (God's Temple) and Darbar Sahib. It was built in the time of Guru Arjan Dev, the fifth of the Sikh Gurus, on a sacred pool called Amritsar ("pool of immortality"), which had been dug by the fourth Guru. It was this pool that gave the name to the city that grew around it. The foundation stone of the temple was laid in 1588 by a great Sufi from nearby Lahore, Hazrat Mian Mir. It was completed in 1601 and incorporates both Hindu and Muslim elements in its design. Situated on a platform in the pool, with a walkway bridging it to the gateway on the land, it houses the original Adi Granth, the sacred book of the Sikhs, which contains the sayings of the Gurus and also some of the compositions of Muslim and Hindu saints. In a reverse tribute, in one of the ginans—songs— recited in the prayer house of my childhood, Nanak, the first Guru and founder of Sikhism, is listed among the great souls along with other mystics.

The Sikh religion is a blend of Islam and Hinduism. Khushwant Singh, in his book on his people, calls it "a Hindu renaissance produced by Islam," and "an edifice built as it were with Hindu bricks and Muslim mortar." Belief in the one God and the paramountcy of the Book are reminiscent of Islam; the devotion of this God in the form of songs is akin to the devotions to Krishna and Rama of Hindu bhaktiism, devotional mysticism. Guru Nanak (1469–1539), the founder of Sikhism, is believed to have been influenced both by Kabir (died 1398), a disciple of the great south Indian mystic Ramanand, and the Sufi Baba Farid of Lahore, who was also the master of Shaikh Nizamuddin of Delhi. This network of mystical influences spreading out across northern India is reflected in the common language of the songs, commonly called bhajans, of the mystical devotees, which are appreciated by masses of Indians to this day and celebrated even by Bollywood. It is said that when a young Guru Nanak reappeared after a mystical experience which lasted three days, during which he saw God, the first words he uttered were, "There is no Hindu and there is no Muslim." Sikhism also did away completely with caste. It is even believed by some devotees of Guru Nanak that he made a visit to Mecca, where he performed some wondrous feats. All this was forgotten in the Hindu-Muslim-Sikh butchery and mutual cleansing of the Partition.

Sikhs from across the world come to pay homage to the Darbar Sahib; yet it is a peaceful, orderly place and remarkably clean. Sikh bhajans are sung at the entrance, and as you leave you are given a prasad, which is sooji halwa—much to our excitement, identical to the prasad received at our khano, where it is called sukhreet, from the Sanskrit *sukrita,* meaning "well made."

Important for us, now that we are in Amritsar, is the family story: Nurjehan's family had lived in the metal market area, Loha Mandi, behind the Golden Temple, two silver doors of which bear the handiwork of her grandfather or his father.

In 1984, Indira Gandhi, then prime minister, sent the Indian army into the temple to capture ("flush out") Jarnail Singh Bhindranwale, one of the leaders of the extremist movement, and other armed militants who were operating from within its confines. The military operation, called Blue Star, has since become infamous in Sikh and Golden Temple history. In the confrontation, Bhindranwale was shot dead among hundreds of others, many of them simply caught in the crossfire. The Akal Takht, the sacred seat of the Sikhs, a beautiful white building with a golden dome, was damaged. Directly as a result of this sacrilege of the holy place, the prime minister was assassinated by her two Sikh bodyguards, and the head of the army was also killed. There followed in retaliation a massacre of Sikhs in Delhi, conducted by mobs, in which a few thousand people were killed, sometimes in the most gruesome manner. Seen among the mobs carrying out the violence were members of the ruling Congress party in their whites and police officers in their khakis.

Operation Blue Star of independent India is an ironic reminder of another Amritsar bloodbath, the Jallianwala Bagh Massacre, which took place under British rule in 1919. To most Indians, there couldn't be a greater difference between the two confrontations, though in the minds of many Sikhs, Operation Blue Star looms even larger. It is to Jallianwala Bagh, a short walk away, that we go directly from the temple.

The scene is as it has been shown in the movies: a narrow corridor leads into an enclosed park. The corridor was blocked as General Dyer (who had been a student at the Bishop Cotton School in Shimla) brought his troops at a run into the Bagh. At the general's orders, they took aim with their rifles, and on his command they fired on more than a thousand unarmed men, women, and children who had gathered for a protest.

There is the well near the centre, into which people jumped to escape the bullets. On the boundary walls of the Bagh are the bullet holes. Plaques describe details of the incident. Our eleven-year-old is much taken with this story. Unprompted, he will describe it for his school project; and he will buy a book on the Indian Mutiny. This grandson of Partition refugees will return with a Sikh friend some years later and spend a night at the guest house of the Darbar Sahib.

Upon receiving news of the Jallianwala Bagh Massacre, Nobel laureate Rabindranath Tagore in protest handed in his knighthood to the British government. And after Operation Blue Star, the celebrated writer Khushwant Singh, hardly a separatist, handed in his Indian decoration, the Padma Bhushan.

In the middle of the night, in our room at the university guest house, the air-conditioning—the surest way to keep mosquitoes at bay—goes off; in the morning our three-year-old is covered in red spots. Fortunately he will not catch malaria; the recommended quinine tablets, which have been administered hidden deep inside laddoos, must have done their work.

And at breakfast, who should come and greet us but Professor Balwinder Singh. We had just about given up hope. He is of medium height and reserved manner, wears a red turban. He has been in communication with Nurjehan's father, having met him once in Vancouver, and knows exactly where the family lived. And so off we go to Loha Mandi, in the walled city.

Parking the car near the Golden Temple, we walk into the warren of streets of the old city and finally arrive at a street devoted to copper and silverware. At one such store, which has a wide entrance, an elderly man acknowledges our guide. Tall and close shaved, a mild smile on his face and reserved in his nature, he is introduced to us as Mr. Chaddha. This is not an everyday event for him; we are reminders of the past, we are memory emerged from the sidewalk. Ghosts. Yes, he says, and points, that one is the old shop. We turn to look across the narrow street at a dilapidated two-storey structure, padlocked. The building next to it, the Sindhi Club, has been demolished.

The story is that the reluctant family had been convinced to leave after a day during which the rioters had prowled around; the family asked Mr. Chaddha's father to lock them inside their shop and keep the keys, so that when the thugs came around he could tell them, "They are gone, the Muslims." It was April 1947; Amritsar was under curfew, the British were nominally in charge, trying to control the violence. The family finally decided to leave on one of the crowded trains departing for Bombay, with a bag in the older boy's hand and perhaps a few smaller belongings. There were the two parents, the three sons, and three daughters. On the way, someone took the bag from the boy. It was never seen again. The family arrived in Bombay with almost nothing.

We are shown the Chaddhas' home, see the courtyard, the upper floor with a balcony overlooking the courtyard, the stone carvings decorating the walls . . . surely the abandoned home across the street would have been similar. We climb up to the roof terrace, observe the street. There is some nervousness about taking photos from here; some of the properties must still be under dispute, I understand later. It is hard not to imagine the happy life of a child in such a neighbourhood. My father-in-law has some sweet and delightful tales about his boyhood here.

Back in the shop Mr. Chaddha, now warmed to us, tells Nurjehan, Why don't you call my sister Madhu? She was a friend of your aunt Sheru. A phone call is made from the shop. Past the greeting and How are you, I am so-and-so's daughter, the conversation gets emotional, Nurjehan weeps and we can tell that on the other side Madhu is doing the same. Madhu and Sheru had known each other since they were toddlers, had been inseparable friends. Madhu had never heard again from her friend, didn't quite know where she had gone. If it was India, they would have communicated, so she must have been in Pakistan, whose border was some ten miles away. Lahore, once the great city of all Punjab, is less than thirty miles away. Pakistan TV can be received and is watched here, as we saw people doing at our guest house. Now it is the niece who brings the two childhood friends together.

On our way back we take a detour to pass by a small warehouse from where sacks are being carried out. This, says Balwinder Singh, was the old khano, the prayer house, where Nurjehan's grandfather was mukhi, the presiding headman.

In the afternoon we visit Madhu and her husband at their apartment in a suburb. We have tea with them. The city cricket ground is next door, and from their balcony you can watch the matches being played. The previous week one of the World Cup games was played here. Madhu and her husband have two children, a boy and girl, both in the United States. She giggles when told that her friend produced twelve children. Finally we exchange addresses and depart.

What happened to the family exiled from a city where they had lived for centuries? To support the family the older son traded between Hyderabad, a Muslim princely state still, but not for long, and Bombay, prone to communal violence. Finally they caught the last ship to Karachi, Pakistan. The three sons and the parents did not last long there, they turned up in East Africa, from where the young men dispersed. Ultimately two of Nurjehan's uncles ended up in London, one to become a business tycoon, his daughter to marry the son of a Scottish baron. The third uncle, Sherali, ended up a hotelier in Nairobi and is now in Vancouver and runs a hotel in Seattle. Two aunts married in Pakistan, one in Muscat, one in Africa; their numerous children are in Pakistan, the Middle East, and the United States, more or less successful. Thus, one Partition family's fate. Successful, but scattered across the globe.

Back in Toronto one Sunday morning, having sent a holiday greeting card to Madhu and her husband, we receive a friendly phone call from her daughter in Los Angeles. Madhu is visiting her. Subsequently we inform Nurjehan's father and uncle in Vancouver about her; perhaps they should give her a call. Uncle Sherali, we learn later, took a flight to Los Angeles to meet her, whom he had not seen in more than fifty years. He took extra care with his dressing that day, his wife says. How exactly the meeting went we never find out.

It seems morbid, impolite, to ask about the Pakistan border—just a few miles away on the Grand Trunk Road—the creation of which was a cause of so much killing, and which over the years has come to symbolize pain, hatred, and suspicion. Three wars have already been fought between the two neighbours. Newspapers go on about Pakistani infiltrators and agents; Bollywood superheroes perform marvellous feats against them in defence of India's honour and safety. Both countries have tested nuclear weapons. Mutual threats are uttered. But when we ask about the border, to our great surprise we are told, Go see it, it's not far, lots of visitors go. There's a parade every day at six. The border, at a place called Wagah, is apparently a tourist attraction.

When we arrive at Wagah, it is crowded with parked cars; vendors come to sell snacks and tea, but there is no milk for the tea. The air is almost festive, though there's a strange, expectant quietude around all the same. We follow others on foot, come to a halt some ten feet from the gate. The area is farming country, a pair of barbed wire fences cutting through it, dividing the two nations. Along this route, from the other side, came the Turks, the Afghans, the Mughals.

As I look at the border, a story by Manto comes to mind. In the story—comic and tragic at the same time, for in Manto rage finds form in the bizarrely comic—at the time of Partition a transport of non-Muslim lunatics is to take place from the new Pakistan to India. Among them is one Sikh fellow, called Bishan Singh, who wants to return only to his village, called Toba Tek Singh, but nobody knows whether it has been allocated to India or to Pakistan. The last scene of the story takes place at the Wagah border where we now stand. The Pakistani guards have given up attempts to push Bishan Singh to the Indian side, and allow the old man to stand where he is, frozen to one spot in between, where after a full night he gives a scream and collapses to the ground:

There, behind barbed wire, on one side, lay India and behind more barbed wire, on the other side, lay Pakistan. In between, on a bit of earth which had no name, lay Toba Tek Singh.

I am reminded also of two men I worked with some years ago in Ontario, one an experimental physicist, the other a theoretical physicist. They had been born in the same town, but one had come from India, the other from Pakistan. This fence has cut deep.

Meanwhile a show is about to begin. We are kept at bay by a handsome soldier, tall and starched, in a plumed hat and smiling. He chats with the people, allows the kids to stand with him and be photographed.

Suddenly he steps aside, and our crowd rushes forward and abruptly stops. Before us on our right to our great surprise there are bleachers packed with more people, craning their necks to see; in front of us are the Indian soldiers. Before we know it, there is heard a series of commands, loud and crisp, each followed by the thumping of feet as soldiers, one by one, go marching forward towards the Indian tricolour at an open gate, perform a salute and return to their positions. Each impressive soldierly performance is followed by applause from the crowd. And to our amazement, an identical, almost mirror-image display is taking place on the other side of the gate, impressive-looking Pakistani soldiers in darker uniforms and plumed hats marching, thumping their feet in exact synchrony with the Indians. Each side approaching its flag, the two flags within a foot or two of each other. Finally the last pair approach the flags and, facing away from each other, lower them exactly together, fold them, turn, and smartly bring them back to their sides. The crowd cheers.

There's more.

The gates are closed, but the people are now free to go, and they rush forward to the gates on cither side to get a look at, stare at, drink in, each other's faces. What has come between us? I try to imagine what they might feel; surely not hatred. They all, *we* all, look so ordinary. A Gujarati man waves, is told by a soldier to behave. The rest seem to be Punjabis on both sides, similar to each other in features—if there is Turkish blood, it's hard to say on which side it predominates.

In Amritsar the temperature has been over a hundred degrees. In Shimla, when we get back, hail has fallen, the ground is white. It is night and desolately silent. We put on our sweaters, turn on the heaters. Cards, jigsaw puzzle, books to entertain us.

Bombay Getaway:
The Distant Uncle and the Bohra Rebel

And when they know what old books tell,
And that no better can be had,
Know why an old man should be mad.

w. b. yeats, "Why Should Not Old Men Be Mad?"

Yes, my father-in law confirms in a letter, the famous writer Mulk Raj Anand is a cousin of his. I should try and see him, Nurjehan suggests. I am skeptical. How real and how strong is this connection? There are cousins and cousins. My father-in-law's name is Hakim Abu Aly. A cousin to Mulk Raj Anand? But the possibility is intriguing—it's exciting—for it promises to cast a light on a past that some of us in modern times would rather forget, or suppress if necessary.

Without much of a social life in the beautiful high aloofness of the Institute, the family back in Toronto, my friends back in Delhi, it seems a reasonable idea to find an excuse to travel out of station. And so I write a letter to Anand about the possible family connection and ask him if I could come to Bombay to talk to him. The reply comes quicker than I expected, inviting me to come and have my chat. He gives me the address and the time.

The Himalayan Queen from Shimla stops at New Delhi railway station; I proceed to the university guest house, where a reservation has been made for me. It is a dingy place whose redeeming features are the cheap, decent meals and its closeness to Connaught Place. Otherwise, the bathroom is wet, a tap dripping constantly, the light is bad, mosquitoes are many and eager. The following afternoon I go to the New Delhi station to catch the fast Rajdhani Express to Bombay. There is something about train names, which

are known to all Indians, that makes every railway journey special; the train has a name, and you have a seat on it. But it is the monsoon season and my Bombay Rajdhani is late. Night has fallen, no one can tell me when the train will leave, beyond "early next morning." The platform clearly is not the place to spend the night, you become an easy target. Already touts hover around me like vultures. Somewhat hesitantly I call up Pabby, Krishan Chander's troubleshooter, who has helped me before, and put my quandary to him. Immediately he takes off with his wife in the Delhi traffic to come to my rescue. It is one of those instances of extraordinary kindness that makes you bewail the formality we have assumed after moving to the West, where time has become so precious it has to be hoarded. It turns out that the railway station has its own guest house, where Pabby finds me a room, decent and private. They'll come and call you when the train is ready to depart, he says. Which is what they do.

The Rajdhani duly leaves for Bombay; there are delays on the way, and it appears that we will arrive late in the night. A reservation has been made for me at a Parsi club, but now I learn from my fellow passengers that there is a taxi strike in Bombay. Will there be rickshaws? Not really. It seems that this trip has been jinxed from the start. How will I get to the club? My fellow passengers have made their own plans, no one offers help, a ride to my destination, for example. I am told something will come up. But what?

Nervously I walk out from the station when the train arrives, watch the other privileged passengers of Second AC, Rajdhani Express, being met and disappearing into the night. How dependent one is on the simple conveniences, the habits, of city life. A simple taxi strike, and here I am, stranded in big bad Bombay in the middle of the night. As I prepare to walk back to the station, suddenly a man walks up to me and asks furtively where I want to go. It turns out he's a scab, runs a private taxi operation, and he looks as nervous as I feel. My fellow passengers must have known about the likes of him: Something will turn up, they said, and it has. There are a few others he's collected, including a woman, which is reassuring, and we pack into his small car, parked some distance away. He does not quite know the place I am headed for, but drops me off in the vicinity, from where I make my way to the club, wake up the caretaker, and am taken to my room.

Mulk Raj Anand is one of the most renowned Indian writers of the twentieth century. He was born in 1905 in Peshawar, now in Pakistan. Although the family trade was in copper and silver smithing, his father was in the Dogra Regiment and Mulk was educated at cantonment schools. He did his B.A. in Amritsar, and after earning the wrath of his family for participating in Gandhi's civil disobedience campaign as a teenager, for which he was jailed briefly, and later for falling in love with a Muslim girl, he left for England in 1925, where he attended Cambridge and completed a Ph.D. in philosophy in London. He returned some twenty years later to an India on the brink of independence. He started writing in London, and his first novel, *Untouchable*, was rejected by nineteen publishers before being published in 1935 after E. M. Forster, whom he met while working at T. S. Eliot's *The Criterion*, agreed to write an introduction. It is now considered a classic. He himself comes from an upper caste, and although the biographies and novels published more recently by writers from the "Untouchable" castes are more powerfully immediate and visceral, Anand's novel made a large impact when it came out, for it held up a mirror to Indian society to reveal perhaps its worst evil. The caste system was a subject not discussed in polite society, and it is still a subject best avoided. Even now, *Untouchable* remains one of the very few well-known novels on the subject. And obviously, the subject of untouchability has hardly been embraced by Bollywood, that exotic fairy-tale mirror of Indian society. Anand's second novel was *Coolie* (1936), which depicts the desperate life of a coolie called Munoo. These two novels are, in the words of a critic, "India seen third-class," without the romanticism. In total, Mulk Raj Anand has published dozens of books, of art, criticism, and fiction, and he is actively involved with social causes.

In *Coolie*, Munoo leaves his home in the Kangra hills to seek a better life in a city in the plains, whence he continues to Bombay, where he becomes one of the faceless millions of toilers in the factories:

> Shivering, weak, bleary, with twisted, ugly faces, black, filthy, gutless, spineless, they stole along with unconscious, vacant looks; idiots, looking at the smoky heavens, as they sighed or murmured "Ram, Ram" and the other names of God, in greeting to each other and in thanksgiving for the gifts of the Almighty. The boy recalled how his patron Prabha in Daulatpur used to say that everything was the blessing of God, even Ganpat's ill-treatment, the beating the police had given him, and the fever of which he nearly died.

Finally Munoo is taken back to the hills, to Shimla, by a kindly English memsahib. There, he enthusiastically takes her around in a rickshaw, along the Mall, on the Jakhoo road, to Christ Church, everywhere the English socialized in their summer capital, all the places that the tourists now delight to visit. One Friday evening he takes her to the Hotel Cecil on Chaura Maidan for dinner, after which he races up the hill along with dozens of other coolies to drop her off at the ball at the viceroy's residence. Amidst the strains of exotic Western dance music, as the sahibs, the memsahibs, and the occasional Indian maharaja and princess waltz around on the polished oak floors of the ballroom of the Viceregal Lodge, Munoo collapses and dies on the steps outside, awaiting his mem.

By a curious coincidence, it is from the former Viceregal Lodge that I have come to meet Munoo's creator in Bombay.

I am a little wary about meeting a writer with such a reputation. He knows nothing about me, and my knowledge of him is superficial. My only interest at this point is to take a look at him, and to confirm the family connection, hopefully find out more about that.

He lives in an elegant white building on Cuffe Parade, a wealthy area, in a ground-floor apartment; the entrance is from the side. A woman opens the door, asks me what I want, then lets me in. I find him in the large front room, apparently a study: books on shelves, and more books, magazines, papers, in piles on the floor. He is a short, somewhat stooping man, not thin; bald, white hair at the sides, wearing a white kurta-pyjama, sitting on a chair looking abstracted, lonely.

What does a writer do at this stage of life, his energies spent, his vogue diminished?

He takes up an aggressive posture at the start: What does writing a novel (as I have told him I am doing) have to do with the Institute of Advanced Study? He has spent time at the Institute and perhaps feels that I do not quite qualify to be there. I tell him defensively that I am also conducting research for a book about "returning to India." What's so special about returning to India? he asks. He should know, he returned having missed a crucial part of its history, but I keep quiet. He calms down. He's quite deaf, so it's easier to let him talk, and he has much to say that he's most likely said many times but I have not heard before. He talks about Nehru, Muhammad Iqbal, Gandhi. But his life in London, where he fraternized with the literati of the time, including the Bloomsbury group, he remembers with pride, speaks of with confidence. It's the favourite soundtrack. Virginia and Leonard Woolf, T. S. Eliot,

Malraux, Forster, Orwell—he's known them all. And this to my great surprise: he fought on the Republican side in the Spanish Civil War. Clearly he was one of those young Indians who set out to conquer the world: writers, scientists, at least one mathematician.

Yes, he then says, his family had been Agakhanis, the term Indians sometimes use for Indian Ismailis, for they were followers of the Aga Khans, the first of whom came to India from Iran in the mid-nineteenth century. What they were before the Aga Khans came is obscure and somewhat contentious today, but they were Indians holding a syncretistic belief combining elements of Iranian Ismailism and Indian Vaishnavism, Vishnu worship. The term "Ismaili" itself is a relatively recent import to India. (The Khojas of Gujarat have also adopted this description in modern times.) Anand says his grandfather or great-grandfather was a mukhi, an Ismaili headman; and his mother used to have a photo of the third Aga Khan as well as statues and prints of the regular gods. The family quit this path when the third Aga Khan, Sultan Muhammad, went to Europe and married a French woman, as Anand puts it. He remembers another woman in his family besides his mother who was always a follower of the Aga Khan. The Arya Samajis, a modern Hindu group, proselytized among them in the early twentieth century, and according to his estimate some two-thirds of the copper and silver workers of Amritsar reconverted to Hinduism. He feels negatively about the third Aga Khan for his pro-British and pro-Pakistani positions. He advises me to write a book about the Aga Khans, an exposé of sorts.

I am, of course, extremely curious to know more about this duality of beliefs in the family; the syncretism, what it was like, and what the family history was before the Aga Khans came from Iran in the 1800s. Nurjehan's grandmother had at one time been called Durga, and her grandfather Panna Lal, whose first wife had been a Sikh. What to make of this? The family belief is that they were "hidden" (gupti) Ismailis, which sounds to me like a revisionist idea, adopted after the split. But this is the kind of information that gets obscured as people move on to the more rigid identities of modern times. What can this old man tell me?

But Mulk, my witness, is deaf, and his interest is focused on something else, his own life, about which he goes relentlessly on.

He recalls that Annie Besant, the famous theosophist, came to Amritsar and recited the creation hymn from the Rig Veda, both in Sanskrit and in English, and he had been rather moved. She had also come to look at Jallianwala Bagh, the place of the massacre. The principal of his college was transferred and there had been riots on campus. Although a career in the army had been planned for him, he did not want that. He went to see the philosopher and poet Muhammad Iqbal in Lahore, and Iqbal advised him to go abroad and wrote letters for him and from what I understand, gave him some money. And so he went to Europe.

His knowledge about fiction is encyclopedic, though distorted by the occasional time warp. His *Coolie* and *Untouchable* have been translated into numerous languages, he reminds me repeatedly, but not into his native Punjabi, and not into many Indian languages. I wonder if it is because his books don't have the immediacy of caste experience that a native Indian reader might demand. I don't say this to him, of course; this is not a discussion but a one-way discourse. Recent politics have vindicated these two novels, he says. And he has no complaints about "Mandalism," the recommendations of the Mandal Commission regarding reservations for the lower or backward classes, which has the middle classes up in arms. The ruling upper classes, he says, consist of 20 per cent of the population and control the media, academia, business.

At the end, he is unstoppable. Tea is offered me, and he turns on the fan; he introduces me to his wife, the woman who let me in, and calls me progressive; and he goes on. Write a biography of Aly Khan, he says. I tell him one already exists, he doesn't understand.

He has used his money to start two charitable foundations, one in Bombay, the other in Delhi, gives me their addresses. I ask him about Rafiq Zakaria, a man who has written on Muhammad Iqbal, and on Muslims in India. It turns out that Zakaria is a neighbour and a friend. Anand calls him up, and I speak to him, set up an appointment for the following day.

I leave Mulk Raj Anand pottering about his front-room study a lonely old man comforted by his memories of relevance and glory.

When I call up Rafiq Zakaria the next day, it turns out that there has been a misunderstanding. One of us has got the time of our interview wrong; it has passed. He is extremely annoyed, gives me a talking to, calling me a typical Indian who cannot be punctual. He will not listen to my explanation, sounds very much like one of those Indians who will tell you openly he is not like the others in their slack habits. And so I miss the interview, but with no regrets.

Mulk Raj Anand comes to see me when I return to Bombay a few years later and give a reading there. He is friendly and introduces a young man whom he wants me to help in Canada. I am rather touched by his having made the effort in his condition, for he needs support moving about. Before he leaves, he presents me a book of his, inscribed, "A small gift to you on your visit home!! Let us keep in touch. Warm regards, Uncle Mulk."

When he dies in Bombay in September 2004, at the age of ninety-eight, the obituary in *The Guardian* calls him a founding father of the Indo English novel.

><

Bombay seems refreshingly different from Delhi; it's coherent, connected; taxis and rickshaws (not just the latter) ply its roads, will take you anywhere; it invites walking, from neighbourhood to neighbourhood, each self-contained in its own way. There is the sea to walk to and walk along. And there is the train, so convenient. It's an orderly city, it's been called Western in its organization. I have not come to know it as I know Delhi. But I recall, too, that I had to miss Bombay on my first visit to India because Bombay was burning, as they said, in the grip of vicious riots. From my plane, which had flown low over the city, the streets looked deserted, the billowing smoke visible in some places terrible indication of the violence. These thoughts cross my mind as I make my way by train to the suburb of Santa Cruz. The stench as we pass a slum area is overpowering. A man slips his feet out of his shoes and stands in his socks on the grimy floor for no obvious reason; a little boy sweeps the floor of this first-class compartment—same as second class, as far as I can tell, but for more breathing space—and holds out his hand to the passengers for money, beating his stomach to indicate hunger; a young man responds to his beeper.

The Santa Cruz station has a bus stand outside it; red single- and double-decker buses depart and arrive. I pass fruit stands, their products resplendently ripe, grocery, hardware, and hair places, dispensary, bank, on my way towards where I have been directed over the phone, the institute of Asghar Ali Engineer.

Engineer is a prominent Muslim spokesman who heads the Institute of Islamic Studies and the Centre for Study of Society and Secularism. He is known for his comments on the moderate message of Islam and on the communal violence in India. He belongs to the Dawoodi Bohra community, a closely knit Gujarati Shia sect which has its origins in twelfth-century Egypt and Yemen. Due to the persecution of the sect in Yemen, its leadership moved to Gujarat, where they were welcomed by the raja and thrived. The sultans were not always kind to them. In Delhi, in Alauddin's time, they were accused of incest and some of them sawn into two as punishment. Most of the Dawoodi Bohras of Gujarat are the descendants of converts from Hinduism. Their leader is a supreme lord, the Sayedna, to whom absolute allegiance is due. Engineer, whose father was a priest in the community, is a reformist and progressive Bohra, representing a group that strongly criticizes the leadership for its corruption and retrograde thinking. As a result he has faced ostracism and even physical attacks.

Engineer's institute consists of two rooms on the second floor of an apartment building. There are several people about as I enter, behind and between desks, and the impression is one of clutter and computers. I meet Engineer in the inside office. He is somewhat paunchy, bald, with a tuft of hair at the chin, and speaks with a soft voice. I had expected a younger, slicker person. On the wall above his desk is an honorary doctor of letters citation from the University of Calcutta, from 1993.

He is a believer in the Quran, which he finds completely compatible with modern thinking, especially civil rights and the rights of women. In some detail, he draws an example from the Hadith: how a woman went to the Prophet to ask for a divorce from her husband, who loved her but was not good looking. She got her divorce, and the man wept until his beard was wet. The story illustrates that Islam actually looks out for women even to the disadvantage of men. It is Islamic leadership that is backward and misguided. He comes to the notorious Shah Bano case of the early 1990s, which brought a lot of antagonism towards Muslims. Shah Bano was a sixty-two-year-old divorced Muslim woman with five children and no adequate means of support. The Indian Supreme Court, ruling in her favour, required her former husband to pay her maintenance. This, says Engineer, is perfectly in accordance with the Quran, which requires that a woman be provided with support upon divorce. And yet orthodox Muslim leaders protested that the courts had interfered with Islamic law, upon which the Congress government of Rajiv Gandhi during an election year overturned the court's decision, giving the appearance of appeasing the Muslims for their votes.

Engineer says the Partition dealt a blow to India's Muslims. The wealthy and the educated left, leaving behind for the most part the underclass. He doesn't deny his Indian heritage. The Bohras used to start their new year with Diwali, like the Hindus. The Khojas, my people, until Partition would keep a photo of the god Ganesh in their shops.

What of his position in his community? He has been ostracized, he tells me. I recall that in the 1960s the Bohra leader had been denied entry into socialist Tanzania, because of the widespread belief that he collected large sums of money from his followers and took it out of the country. A reform movement had begun in Dar es Salaam among the Bohras, as well as a conservative trend, in which their women began wearing the veil. I recall returning from a party one night in Dar es Salaam in the 1990s. An African friend had given me a ride along with a Bohra woman visiting from the United States. She was wearing jeans and a shirt, was very pretty. When we reached her street, making a sly remark she took out a black veil from a bag and put it on, then said goodbye, opened the car door, and departed.

Time was, Engineer says, when if he happened to pass through a Bohra neighbourhood, the women in the flats would spit from their balconies and say, There goes Satan. By and large now the orthodox Bohras leave him alone, but the effects of the ostracism are harsh. An ostracized member is denied marriage into the community as well as burial rites and a place in the cemetery. This applies also to those who go against the sanction and associate with the outcast, as well as to their families. Engineer says he can't meet his mother or sisters, except in secret. This is a tight community, with a centuries-old tradition, and the charismatic hold of their leader on them is immense. Many reformists leave their city before the leader visits, so as not to cause offence.

For all his liberal beliefs and his courage, Engineer is essentially a fundamentalist—not in the sense of being an extremist, he is far from that, but in the sense that for him the Quran has fundamental authority; he will derive modern, moderate, and tolerant interpretations from it, and he will not impose it on others. But for any personal meaning in life he has to resort to the Book, to seek guidance, to understand, to justify. And so I can only listen to him. There is no common ground.

✂

After a week of heat and sunshine it is time to return to the retreat in the cool hills. The visit to Mulk Raj Anand has been worthwhile, having given me a thoughtful link to the murky, obfuscated past of my people.

The Bombay-Delhi trip is uneventful. I arrive in the morning at the New Delhi station, from which I had left. The trip out to Shimla is at night, from the city's other station, the Old Delhi station. As soon as I reach here, having put up for the day at the university guest house I used previously, I am greeted by a crowd of touts and coolies who inform me with great relish that the Howrah Mail to Kalka has been delayed, due to the monsoons. It is about ten in the night. The locals, those who have ways to find out when the train will arrive, have departed, and it seems I am alone; I and the touts and porters who try desperately, in my own interest they tell me as I sit alone in a dingy waiting room, to go stay in "the hostel." I have no intention of leaving the station and putting myself at risk. I can also not impose once more on Pabby. I stay put.

I don't know how, but some porter finally convinces me— perhaps because he is the least aggressive, perhaps, too, because I need to use a bathroom—that the hostel he has in mind is right here at the station; I can go with him and talk to an official. Which I do, and before I know it I am shown a dormitory somewhere upstairs, with the understanding that I will be called when the train arrives.

The yellow-painted hall contains about twenty beds in two rows, all occupied by young travellers, who have their luggage chained and padlocked to the legs of their beds. Some sit, some lie down and read, all strangers to each other, all silent. I have no chain and lock for my bag, which could easily be carried off by a passing thief. Or by any of these fellows. Feeling silly, though not earning even a passing stare, I carry my bag with me to the toilet. Soon after, a matron arrives, a broad woman in uniform with the look and manner of a warden, who asks us about our trains and announces that she will lock the door from outside. Suppose my train comes in the middle of the night?—I ask in a panic. You'll be woken up. You'll unlock the door? Yes. I can hardly believe this; but the door clangs shut, the key turns in the padlock. As I lie down in bed, my bag for my pillow, I am quite resigned to the possibility that I will miss the Howrah Mail. In the far distance, in the bathroom area from which I have recently emerged, I can now see two rats, as large as cats. One of my roommates turns off the lights, and I fall instantly asleep, for it has been a long day. The next thing I know, there is a loud sound at the door. At the now open door, to my utter disbelief, stands the silhouette of the same matron who locked me in, now jangling her keys. The train has arrived, and off I go to Kalka, from where I take the winding train to Shimla. I know the place well enough that, arriving in the evening, I can walk back to my flat in the Institute and partake of a meal at the dining hall. Daal and sabzi, rice and chappati just off the pan.

And so, as many times before in my journeys in India, it has all marvellously worked out. Years later, I relate this adventure to my friends in the comforts of the International Centre bar in Delhi. I feel rather proud of myself, having recently made it to Shimla despite another mishap (my Kalka-Shimla ticket was for the previous day, and there was apparently no room on the train) and to Dharamsala during a day of landslides. But to a man and woman, my friends shake their heads and tell me I should have stayed put that night at Old Delhi, not gone off with a coolie to the hostel or anywhere else.

What could have happened—some Thugs among my roommates might have strangled me with a knotted kerchief?

Postscript: Shimla Revisited

I NEXT MEET THE SAHNIS in Delhi a couple of years later, at the India International Centre, where we have tea together. He is sick and breathless, but otherwise at his best; he quotes a sonnet by Chesterton about the evening of life; and two couplets in Urdu, one of which goes, approximately, After a night of tumult, saqi, the dawn draws near, now remember your God. There is a sense of premonition here. And he tells me about a quarrel he's become entangled in, between two well-known women writers, in which he's been accused of taking sides. And oh yes, I check this: he did translate Tolstoy into Hindi, some long stories, including *The Kreutzer Sonata* and *Resurrection*. Of Premier Khrushchev he remembers a very limp handshake.

And this I overhear from her, when she doesn't know I am listening: "He's such a good Muslim!"

That pricks. I always thought of her simply as Sheila-ji.

A few years later I hear that Sheila-ji died. Shortly afterwards, Bhishm-ji died.

And then I see him resurrected in Toronto, in the excellent film *Mr. and Mrs. Iyer*, in which he plays an elderly passenger in an intercity bus who meets a brutal end at the hands of ruffians. Typical Bhishm-ji.

During a more recent visit to Shimla I stay at the Institute Guest House. It's August, monsoon season, pleasantly cool after the crushing summer heat of Delhi. Early mornings are wet, a light drizzle falls; outside the window, across the lawn, the low grey brick building that is the Postmaster Flat squats like a cat, partly veiled in a thick mist. I could shout with joy at this familiar, now beloved, sight. It's still here! By now I have put the Gujarati narrator of my India novel here, where he writes in seclusion.

There is evidence of recent renovation. The floors are new, of a pine veneer, and so are the doors; there's a TV in my room, and I suppose in every other room, and new furniture. The bathroom floors have been tiled, and there is no bathtub now, only a shower; but the ceramic sink is from the viceroys' time, as are the electric switches on the wall. The mantelpiece is also new, and the fireplace is boarded up.

My friend who picked me up at the railway station brought along the umbrella I had left behind, and I take it now and set off to explore the old haunts.

The Sahnis' bungalow has been partly renovated but looks as dilapidated as before, and so strangely familiar. Here, she stood before her easels, painting; this was the kitchen; here, Bhishm-ji and I would sit on a sofa while she worked. The Institute library looks as distinguished as I've remembered it, hushed, spacious, and solidly furnished, its precious hoard of publications for the use of a favoured few. I introduce myself and sit at a table to read up on medieval Delhi history, later walk outside to the old chai shop at the cliff edge from where I would watch the sunsets. Mist covers the distant peaks. The tables are wet, but I have my cup of tea and samosa anyway, for old times' sake. Afterwards, beyond the lawn, along the way down to the local market of Boileau Ganj,

I notice that the hill of refuse which had begun to rise and stink during the last days of my stay has disappeared.

On the way to the Mall, I see that the century-old Cecil Hotel at Chaura Maidan, where the Partition lines were drawn, and which had been undergoing renovation during my fellowship, is up and running now. Recent roadside signs prohibit littering and even smoking, and they seem to be obeyed. Prominent buildings are posted with their former names and brief histories where available. The town now knows on which side its bread is buttered: its English heritage. My first stop as I enter the Mall area is the Indian Coffee House, which looks exactly the same, and as always with hardly a place to sit. Further on are some of the old eating places, the three bookstores, Fook Cho's shoe store, and some new additions—two Chinese fast food restaurants, Dominos Pizza, Citibank, a coffee franchise, which by its ambience and loud music is more a hangout for rich Indian teenagers than anything else. Nonveg food is served freely now on the Mall; before, there was not a single place here that did so. And now they no longer call this shopping promenade the "Mal" in the English and Hindi way, but "Mall" as in North America, the land of shopping malls. The Lower Mall looks unchanged.

But do the climbs seem steeper now, ten years later, or do I imagine it?

At the Guest House, the staff is new, but the menu and food— the daal and sabzi, the rice and chappati, the rice pudding and the morning porridge—have not altered in the slightest. Here I meet two scholars from a college in Uttar Pradesh. One of them speaks irately and unprovoked about the "diaspora" (a current academic buzz word meaning Indians abroad), and some strain develops at our table, which over the breakfasts I share with them during the next few days is happily overcome. They speak about the bleakness beneath the globalization veneer, the plights of the colleges and teachers in the smaller cities, the corruption. The phrase "Neolithic syllabuses and teaching methods" sticks in the mind.

I ask an attendant called Emmanuel about the church I had visited at the back of the Guest House. It's very much there, he says, giving an appreciative smile, then adds that it is closed for now. Apparently the reverend had laid claim to the property and lost.

Later I take a walk to have a look. There's been some construction in the area, the church appears hemmed in by new dwellings, and it's not so easy to reach the entrance. The sign board on the door is missing, as is the cross.

Gujarat:
Down Ancestral Roads, Fearfully

Small of body, big of mind . . .
the lover is a Gujarati

AVINASH VYAS, song

I see phantoms of hatred and of the heart's fullness and of
the coming emptiness

W. B. YEATS, "Meditations in Time of Civil War"

These Moon-faced Ones

> It is not hidden from knowing, intelligent men . . . that the king-
> dom of Gujarat is one of the greatest provinces of Hindustan
> whose ruling planet is Jupiter in the second clime. . . . Its inhabi-
> tants, male and female . . . are handsome and delicate who rob per-
> sons of life with a sight and bestow upon them by talk. How nicely
> it has been said
>
> *What can one say about these rose-faced Gujaratis*
> *That comely beauty is God given to these moon-faced ones.*
> ALI MUHAMMAD KHAN, *Mirat-i-ahmadi* (Persian history of
> Gujarat, c. 1756–61)

THE IMAGE OF GUJARATIS that I grew up with was that of essentially a mercantile people, soft, yet adventurous, ready to pick up
and set up business elsewhere. All they required was to be left
alone. Clannish, yes, but you would expect such people to be, by
and large, tolerant. Perhaps ethically slack, for business practices
require shortcuts. But brave, for in East Africa—Kenya, Uganda,
Tanganyika, and Zanzibar—they would set up shop in the remotest
places, in small numbers, sometimes singly or with just their family with them, so that they became indispensable to colonial expan-
sion and administration. My grandparents were among these
entreprencurs of the nineteenth and early twentieth centuries.
European explorers depended on them for supplies, and indeed
took credit from them, and when they returned home—as I learned

when I read their accounts—ungratefully turned around and wrote about them in the most unflattering terms as unscrupulous Shylocks. You would not think of them as a violent people; in East Africa, when confronted with violence as a community or individually, they were more likely to make a run for it or hide behind closed doors. Bollywood, thriving on stereotypes, enjoys casting the Gujarati man in comic roles, with his funny, infected Hindi and slightly effeminate manner. Mahatma Gandhi of the Banya (merchant) caste epitomized the Gujarati character: the nonviolence, shrewdness, self-effaciveness (or at least a show of it), and sense of humour. He came from the same place as my maternal grandfather, the port town of Porbandar.

And yet, in recent times, the bloodiest communal violence, with the most hideous attacks on the human person, especially on women and children, has taken place with some regularity in this ancestral homeland, among these people I thought I knew, whom I have called—culturally, ancestrally—my people. For me to come to this realization has been profoundly shocking. If anything makes me feel alien here, it is my utter incomprehension of such violence, my inability to shrug it off. My generalization of Gujarat, too, was naive, I realize; but there it is, in tatters.

Mira Kamdar, American author of the book *Motiba's Tattoos*, which explores her Gujarati heritage on her father's side, writes in a paper for the World Policy Institute, "My father, who loved Martin Luther King, hates Muslims. He hates them blindly, viscerally, categorically." She adds, "My immigrant Gujarati father is both a liberal democrat and a supporter of Hindu fascism."

One could argue that the homesick expatriate exhibits a more extreme form of nationalist passion and zealotry. But that is not the case; the violence unleashed in Gujarat during the so-called communal riots is so giddyingly intense and horrific that the country simply shakes its head and watches and waits for it to spend itself and subside like some natural disaster. But natural disaster it is not, for it is inspired and fuelled regularly and systematically by the politics of hateful bigotry.

Kamdar goes on to quote in her paper a well-known pledge distributed by the communalist Vishwa Hindu Parishad (World Hindu Council):

I will not buy anything from any Muslim shopkeeper
I will not use those traitors' hotels or their garages
Boycott movies casting Muslim heroes and heroines
Never work in Muslims' offices and do not employ Muslims

During my first visit to India, bloody riots were in progress in parts of Gujarat, following the destruction of the Babri Mosque in the northern state of Uttar Pradesh. In Bhubaneswar, Orissa, receiving solicitous advice to take care of myself during my travels, I had joked that with a turban I could easily pass as a Sikh. In the jocular atmosphere of that precious moment, our Sikh friend duly removed his headgear and placed it ceremoniously upon my head, and it was affirmed by all present that I could indeed pass as a Sikh, and a photo was taken as proof. Since then, it was always with a little sadness and a tangible nervousness that I would travel in Gujarat, with nightmarish visions of rampaging mobs drunk on violence, of getting caught in a train by such a mob and being asked to prove physically my communal affiliation. And yet, I have always felt a sense of wonderful elation while travelling in India. It has helped that I remain, and indeed feel, communally anonymous and ambiguous, identifiable only by that cipher of my very Gujarati last name.

To introduce Gujarat this way is painful. Its language I speak, its food I eat, its dances I danced as a child. I could start with the romance, the exotic: the colours of the saris, the sweets, the fields, the arrival of the rains. The galloping new economy. The lavish, colourful weddings. All these would make my account more palatable. But this current reality seems to overshadow every other: two cultures, two peoples so close to each other, yet so apart; and I, by my traditions and history, straddling the two.

After my first Indian visit, I would be asked, back in Toronto, why I let the violence bother me. I did not live there after all, had never lived there, and I was safely here, anyway. I could have said that surely all violence anywhere should affect us; what came to mind instead was that I could not accept India's embrace and turn away from the violence. It must in some way be a part of me.

Two necessary disclaimers.

I have already said that I find the labels "Hindu" and "Muslim" discomforting, because they are so exclusive. They have not defined people for me in Africa (where we were simply called "Wahindi," Indians), in the United States (where I lived for some years), or in Canada. I refuse to use them this way, perhaps naively and definitely against a tide; but I am not alone. I use the distinction of "Hindu" or "Muslim" only in context, and especially when it has been used by people for themselves or others, as in the Gujarat violence.

So deep is the suspicion when one talks of conflict, that one has to state over and over that to describe the murder of a Muslim here is not to deny, let alone justify, the murder of a Hindu elsewhere, that a fanatic group does not represent an entire people, and there is no entire people, Hindu or Muslim, anyway. Attempts to create them, of course, have always been there.

Gujarat lies in the northwest of India, bordering that part of the Indian Ocean called the Arabian Sea, a region where the Indus Valley pre-Aryan civilization once prevailed, four thousand years ago. Many of its towns and cities are of ancient provenance, their silent ruins witnesses to the rise and fall of kingdoms, the clash of immense armies on elephant, horse, and foot. Shrines casually litter its landscapes, memorials to its holy men great and small, comfort to the needy. According to legend, Krishna, the dark sage-god and the charioteer in the *Gita*, ruled in the region of Dwarka in peninsular Gujarat (known as Kathiawar or Saurashtra). The temple at Dwarka at Kathiawar's northwestern tip beside the Arabian Sea is today one of the great Indian pilgrimage sites. The Maurya empire in the time of Asoka, who ruled from 263 to 222 BC, extended all the way west to Kathiawar, where one of Asoka's rock inscriptions—upon which are etched his principles of Buddhist dharma, or right moral conduct—is displayed at the outskirts of what is now the city of Junagadh. Asoka, remorseful at the suffering caused by his bloody conquest of the Kalinga kingdom in the east, in what is now Orissa, had become a follower of the path of the Buddha. Eight centuries after Asoka, the celebrated Chinese Buddhist traveller Hiuen Tsang would describe the city of Vallabhipur in Gujarat as containing more than a hundred Buddhist monasteries and a few thousand monks. Buddhism disappeared soon afterwards from this region and from much of India. Various other peoples ruled here, including Greeks and Gujjars, a northern people of Eurasian origin, who gave the area its name. A race of rulers of Central Asian origin known as the Kshatrapas ruled parts of Gujarat as the satraps of Persian kings roughly between the first and fourth centuries AD, minting their own coins with inscriptions in Greek, Brahmi, and Kharosthi scripts.

From about the ninth century onwards there came into prominence in north and west India, including Gujarat, a number of small kingdoms belonging to related clans going under the name Rajput (from the Sanskrit for "son of king"). Rajput origins too may lie, at least partly, in the north, a claim naturally dismissed by those of Rajput ancestry, for it would place them among the class of "foreign invaders." Whatever the truth, it was these Rajput kingdoms that bore the onslaught of the invading armies from present-day Afghanistan, which finally defeated them. Delhi's Tomar Rajput king Prithviraj was defeated by Muhammad of Ghur in 1192 in a battle that changed the face of India; from that strategic northern base invading armies of Delhi sultans overran the various Rajput kingdoms scattered throughout Rajasthan and northern Gujarat, including Kathiawar.

240
–

The Rajput kingdoms of India are renowned for their civilization and culture, their patronage of the arts and learning. They are also the subject of a great deal of legend and folklore describing the honour and courage displayed by their noble warriors who set off from their forts to do battle, especially in the tragic and climactic confrontations against the Muslim hordes from the north. It is said that when defeat was inevitable, the Rajput womenfolk, rather than face dishonour at the hands of the enemy, collectively immolated themselves in a fire, in a practice called jauhar, before their men set off to fight the enemy to the death. This practice, highly romanticized, not to say politicized in the Hindu-Muslim context, was not universal; and the Rajput kingdoms, of course, had been constantly at war against each other, and later allied themselves when necessary with Muslim armies. In present times, Rajput courage and honour, pitting good against evil in the setting of the beautiful Rajasthan desert, has become a staple of the Bollywood "masala western," though it also provides the stereotype of archaic and dogged old-fashionedness and male patriarchy.

Perhaps the most glorious Gujarati Rajput kingdom was that of the Solanki dynasty, from 942 to 1242, which ruled from Anhilvada (at present-day Patan, sixty-five miles northeast of Ahmedabad), and more precisely during the reigns of Jaisingh Siddhraj and his successor Kumara Pala, in the twelfth century. Much of the history of this period still comes down in the form of bardic lore, folk legends, and inscriptions. Two nineteenth-century British administrator-scholars, James Tod and Alexander Kinloch Forbes, trekked through the forests and byways of western Gujarat collecting stories and manuscripts, and describing and even rediscovering monuments and ancient ruins. Forbes, a reserved man who did not mix much with other Englishmen, produced a book called *Ras Mala* (translated as "garland of stories") which he published at his own expense, and he also founded the Gujarat Vernacular Society in Ahmedabad. It was Tod who in 1822 discovered Asoka's rock inscriptions at Junagadh (in the ancient Brahmi script, though he believed they were in Greek). He produced two tomes based on his travels, one of which is *Travels in Western India*. Despite the colour of their bias, the enthusiasm of these two Englishmen for Gujarati history and their achievements in recording it are remarkable. Their books are still in print and serve as valuable repositories of folkloric history.

Anhilvada, so Forbes tells us, basing his account on the poetic history *Ratna Mala* of Krishnaji, was founded in 746 by a forest foundling called Vanaraja ("forest king"), descendant of the kings of Vallabhipur, which city had converted from Buddhism to Jainism before being overrun—at the paid instigation of a vanity-wounded local Marwari businessman—by "barbarians." The so-called barbarians are presumed to have been Arabs from Sindh. (Jainism and Buddhism were both founded before 500 BC in reaction to Brahminism, the faith and practices associated with the Indo-Aryan Vedas that developed into present-day Hinduism.) Anhilvada during its heyday under Siddhraj and Kumara Pala was the capital of a large empire, a great centre of trade, learning, and culture. Jainism was a strong force at the court and competed fiercely with Brahminism. While the Rajput kings generally ate meat and partook of alcohol, the Jains forbade them. (Today, Gujaratis are by and large vegetarian, and alcohol is prohibited in the state, with the result that it is a much-appreciated gift.) Priests of both religions were in attendance at the court, including the great monk and scholar Hemachandra, whose *Dvyashraya* was composed to serve as much as a primer on Sanskrit as a history of the kings. Such was the esteem of scholarship in the kingdom that when the book was completed it was taken around the city in a procession on the back of an elephant. Learned debates were common. A famous one reportedly took place between the representatives of two Jain sects, the Svetambara, whose monks wore white garments, and the Digambara, whose monks were clothed by the atmosphere, that is, went about in the nude. In the contest, the Svetambaras (the home team, as it were) were led by Hemachandra and Dev Suri, and their opponents (the visitors) by the awesome Kumud Chandar of Karnat, reputed winner of eighty-four previous contests. The party of the nude monks was, however, defeated and, as was the custom for losers, had to leave the kingdom, their tails between their legs.

The tolerance of Jaisingh Siddhraj (1094–1143) is one of his many enduring legends. Arab traders (in contrast to the constantly threatening Afghans and Turks in the north, who had made several destructive forays into Gujarat) lived in the coastal towns, and there are reports of a Muslim embassy in Anhilvada. Once, there was a riot in the ancient port of Cambay involving the local Parsis, Hindus, and Muslims, in which the local mosque was destroyed. The mullah wrote a petition to Jaisingh, a patron of poetry, composed in the form of a poem, as a result of which the king gave funds to rebuild the mosque. According to the Khoja tradition, in which I was raised, an Ismaili mystic called Satgur Nur arrived at the court of Jaisingh from Egypt and was welcomed. Satgur Nur is a pir of the Khojas, and a has a divine status among several syncretistic (nominally Hindu) sects who worship him at his dargah in the southern city of Navsari. According to the tradition, Nur outwitted the king's magicians and priests with a display of his own powers, as a result of which the king became his follower. The Bohras, a Shia sect who escaped persecution and arrived from Yemen, also claim to have received hospitality from Jaisingh and converted him to their ways. And the Parsis, who escaped persecution in Persia, also lay claim to him.

Thus the liberality of Gujarat's greatest king. He endowed temples and reservoirs throughout his kingdom, and against his enemies fought like a lion. "O sea, make a swastika of pearls! O moon, shine in full splendour," wrote Hemachandra in praise once, "conquering the earth, Siddhraj arrives." He was slight in stature and fair, and enjoyed going about incognito in the night to mingle with his subjects (and no doubt hear good things about himself) and visit popular entertainments. He was indifferent to religion. Legend reprimands his lustiness and intrigues with Brahmin women. And due to a curse from a low-caste woman called Jasma, he could not have a son to succeed him.

A curious story was told to Forbes about Kumara Pala, who succeeded Jaisingh, and Hemachandra. According to this legend, the king and his priest scholar both became Muslims, through the wiles of a Muslim magician. A more mainstream tradition says that the monk Hemachandra and the monarch Kumara Pala once visited together the great temple of Somnath by the Arabian sea. While the two sat in the inner sanctum of the temple, through the power of the monk's meditation Shiva himself appeared and instructed the prostrate king to learn the true path from the monk. Thus Kumara Pala was converted to Jainism and forbade the slaughter of animals in his kingdom.

Hemachandra is an attractive, enigmatic character: a scholar, a poet, and an ascetic, as well as a trickster, and surely political? Having held influence in the courts of Gujarat's two great kings, at eighty-four years of age he prepared himself to die, and abstaining from food gave up his last breath.

But legend presents two quite delicious alternatives regarding his end.

The Jains had gained ascendancy in the kingdom, and there were already a hundred thousand of their monks in Anhilvada. There was much hatred between them and the Brahmins, who, having lost an argument (due to an illusion produced by Hemachandra), were preparing to leave the capital. However, just at this time the great Brahmin and pan-Indian ascetic Shankaracharya happened to be in the area and was asked to assist his coreligionists. In the morning, when Kumara Pala called the Brahmins and ordered them to leave the kingdom, Shankaracharya stepped forward. What's the need to expel anyone from the kingdom? he asked. At nine o'clock the ocean will rise from the west and swallow up the entire country. Hemachandra denied this could happen, for according to Jain doctrine the world had no beginning or end. When nine o'clock arrived, Kumara Pala, Hemachandra, and Shankaracharya climbed to an upper storey of the palace and looked out the western window and beheld the sea approaching in waves. On and on the waves came, until Anhilvada began to drown. The three climbed still higher, until they reached the seventh floor. Water had submerged everything in the capital, even its tallest spires and trees. Kumara Pala turned in terror to Shankaracharya and asked, Is there no escape? Is this the end? Shankaracharya told him, A boat will come this way from the west, whoever jumps into it will survive. Soon enough, a boat appeared, and came closer, and the three prepared to jump. But just when the time was right to leap, the wily Shankaracharya stayed the king with his hand and let Hemachandra go first. The ocean and the boat turned out to be illusions, and Hemachandra fell to his death on the pavement below.

Another story describes how Shankaracharya stirred with his little finger a glass of milk destined for the old Hemachandra. The Brahmin's fingernail, however, contained a poison. The monk died.

All communities have such folk histories. Delightful stories, they are also propaganda, repeated generation to generation, with variations. But as soon as you remove them from the realm of the imaginary, they become dangerous messengers of communal divisiveness.

The Solankis were followed by the Vaghela dynasty, whose rule came to an end in 1298, when the armies of Alauddin Khilji of Delhi conquered Anhilvada. The last of the Rajput kings of Anhilvada was Karan, known to posterity by the unfortunate title of Karan Ghelo, or Crazy Karan, who is said to have wrought his own tragedy.

The bards tell of how Karan had stolen the wife of one of his ministers, Madhav, and killed Madhav's brother, Keshav. Madhav, whose wife happened to be a Padmini Brahmin—that is, of the highest order—vowed that he would not touch food in Gujarat until he had avenged himself and brought back the "Turks" to destroy Karan's kingdom. Therefore he went to Alauddin in Delhi and enticed him with the prospect of Gujarat's conquest. There is no doubt, according to the historian S. C. Misra, disputing the counterclaims of modern revisionist historians who see in this bardic tale an aspersion on the Hindu character, that Madhav did collaborate with Alauddin. Madhav had been a powerful minister, second only to the king. Evidently, he must have been provoked. Karan abandoned his capital to the enemy, offering no resistance.

When Alauddin's generals Nusrat Khan and Ulugh Khan took Anhilvada, "the treasures, elephants, and women-folk of Raja Karna [Karan] fell into the hands of the army of Islam," according to the contemporary Delhi historian Zia Barni. Karan's queen, Kanvala Devi, was taken to Delhi and joined Alauddin's harem. She became his favourite queen. A few years later, instigated by Kanvala Devi, the sultan asked Karan, who was back in Anhilvada, to send Kanvala's daughter Deval Devi to be a wife of the heir apparent, Khizr Khan. Karan seems to have agreed joyfully but perhaps had treachery in mind, for when Alauddin sent his army under the former slave "thousand-dinar" Malik Kafur (later to earn infamy for his dark treachery at the Delhi court) to Gujarat, Karan had fled. The Delhi army found the young Deval Devi on the road among a party fleeing Anhilvada. Disguised as a young man, she was almost killed by the soldiers before her identity was discovered. She was taken to Delhi posthaste and married to Khizr Khan.

The passion of Khizr Khan for Deval Devi moved Amir Khusrau of Delhi, a friend of Khizr, to depict it in an epic poem written in 1316 in Persian, which he called *Ashiqa*, "The Lovers."

The story is controversial.

For many, even to this day, the thirteenth-century story of Rajput defeat and humiliation festers in the mind, writ large as a chapter in the continuing saga of Hindu-Muslim enmity, and as one more invasion that Mother India had to endure in the travail that has been her history. A Rajput-Turk war becomes one pitting Hinduism against Islam. In this tragic nationalist scenario, the Gujarati kingdom at Anhilvada becomes a Camelot where wise kings ruled harmoniously over their people, and culture and learning prevailed. There was no crime to speak of: the lower castes lived as good neighbours next to the upper castes and not out of sight, and presumably the rajas fought each other in the best traditions of chivalry. A historian writes, "Amir Khusrau seems to have been suffering from a delusion that the Hindus had no sense of honour and their women no sense of chastity." By such history is extreme nationalism backed. Even the existence of Kanvala Devi and Deval Devi has been doubted. S. C. Misra, on the other hand, after considering claims and counterclaims, has little doubt about the basic authenticity of the story of Deval Devi and Khizr Khan. Khusrau was not only a poet but also an able historian.

Getting on with the story, the young Gujarati princess's ultimate fate in Delhi, in a court teeming with ugly intrigues, was a tragic one.

Having had Alauddin's queen put in prison, Malik Kafur, the evil schemer of the palace, had Khizr Khan imprisoned and blinded, his only solace his beloved Deval. The ailing Alauddin himself was possibly poisoned by Malik. He was succeeded by

Qutbudin Mubarak, another of his sons, who had Khizr Khan executed. In this bloody dungeon scene the devoted Deval, clinging to her husband, had both her hands cut off by the murderers and was wounded in the face. An alternative ending has Deval Devi ending up in the harem of Qutbudin, who was subsequently murdered by his favourite companion, a Hindu convert, who for a short time ruled as Nasirudin and took Deval Devi into his harem.

One shudders.

Amir Khusrau claims to have been told the story by his friend Prince Khizr Khan: "My head was exalted by the honour of my selection, and I retired with the narrative in my hand." He was not beyond embroidery, of course.

Timur's (Tamerlane's) sacking of Delhi at the end of the fourteenth century considerably weakened the Delhi sultanate, whereupon in 1407 Gujarat's governor, Zafar Khan Muzaffar, asserted his independence and began a local dynasty of Muslim kings. Zafar Khan was himself a Hindu of the Tank caste who had converted to Islam—such are the wonderful ironies that India throws up. The portion of Gujarat actually ruled from Delhi and later independently from Anhilvada, increasingly called Patan in the accounts, was a strip stretching from Patan south via Baroda, including the wealthy ancient ports of Cambay and Broach. To the east, west, and the north lay independent or semi-independent Rajput kingdoms and military garrisons of the sultanate. There were frequent rebellions and acts of defiance, the Rajputs and the Muslim generals often at war against each other, or in alliance with each other against the king in Patan. Also to the east was Malwa, another province of Delhi, whose governor often became involved in plotting against his rival in Patan. Much of the sultan's energy was therefore taken up marching across the land subduing rebellions or extending his conquest. Understandably, some of the dispossessed Rajputs had taken to banditry or guerilla warfare. Palace intrigues continued, here as in

Delhi. It would appear from the histories that more rulers died by poison than any other means. Zafar Khan received his cup of poison from his grandson Ahmed Shah, for allegedly having put to death (by poison) Ahmed's father, Tatar Khan. Ahmed Shah (1411–1442), on his way back from campaigns to the south, established Ahmedabad as the new capital. Anhilvada receded into insignificance and is now no more than the small regional town of Patan, known more for the exclusive weave of cloth made there than for its early history.

The Mughals had arrived in India with Babur and were extending their reach south from Delhi. In 1573, Akbar, the third Mughal, wrested Gujarat from its sultan and annexed it to the Mughal empire, of which it remained a province for two hundred years. It was during this period of Mughal ascendancy that the future masters of India took their first steps on the subcontinent, in 1608, when an English ship arrived at the wealthy Gujarati port of Surat under Captain Hawkins, envoy of King James I. Jehangir was the emperor. Shortly thereafter, by a treaty of 1613, signed in Agra, the English were given permission to trade and open factories in Surat, Gogha, Cambay, and Ahmedabad. Surat became the most important port of Gujarat.

Akbar, whose memory is beloved to Indians of all backgrounds, began a period of Mughal rule that was tolerant, and in his own time indeed benevolent, towards religious differences. He was a great conqueror, a stern and just ruler, and a pious worshipper of the Sufis, whose wives were from the Christian, Muslim, and Hindu faiths. He attempted to found a universal Indian religion, and in his new capital of Fatehpur Sikri, outside Agra, he had three prayer rooms for his wives of three faiths. His great-grandson, the stern, bigoted Aurangzeb, however, repressed both Hindus and nonorthodox Muslims. Aurangzeb ruled for almost fifty years, during which time he carried out lengthy campaigns across India. After his death in 1707, the Mughal empire lay exhausted and in a state of centrifugal decline. The Marathas, a group of Marathi-speaking warrior clans from Maharashtra, after a few decades of battling against and sharing power and alliances with Mughal remnants, finally, by about 1760, established themselves in parts of eastern and central Gujarat, including Ahmedabad. The rest of what we know as Gujarat broke up into local kingdoms.

With Mughal decline and Maratha ascendancy, the British began to exert a greater influence and gradually took control, first of Surat, and later, defeating the Marathas, of most of Gujarat. Five districts were ruled directly by the British, the remaining areas made up of princely states ruled under supervision of British Residents. This was the political situation that prevailed at Independence in 1947.

In the City of Sandalwood

[Its air] is healthy, and the earth picturesque; the vineyards bring
forth blue grapes twice a year, and the strength of the soil is such that
the cotton plants spread their branches like willows and plane trees
. . . and besides Cambay, the most celebrated of the cities of Hind
in population and wealth, there are 70,000 towns and villages, all
populous, and the people abounding in wealth and luxuries.

(A 1300 AD description of Gujarat)

BARODA, OR VADODARA, is the first city in Gujarat that I visited.
It is not my ancestral place, but I had made friends here, Raj
Kumar and Mohamed and others, on my first visit and was invited
back, and therefore it became the base from which I could explore
other parts of the state. Baroda is a small city in central Gujarat; its
ancient name was Chandanavati, "city of sandalwood," and it
formed one of the districts of Delhi's medieval Gujarat province,
mentioned in the histories as a junction on the way from Patan to
go down south to the port of Broach, or to get to Champaner in
the east. In 1590, a writer described the highway from Patan to
Baroda, one hundred and fifty miles, as lined on both sides with
mango trees, the fields bound by hedges, and the countryside so
abundant in fruit trees as to look like a garden. That road is now
paved, of course, with toll booths along the way and lined with
factories and dhabas, trucks and buses trundling along its route. In
itself it could not have been very important, and even today it can
claim not much more than a modest status. While parts of the modern city bear the clamour of any urban centre in India, here one

can still find green spaces and drive through quiet avenues, and no place is really too far.

Baroda was captured from the remaining vestiges of the Mughal empire by the Marathas in 1734 and ruled thenceforth by the Maratha Gaekwad dynasty, directly at first, then later under British protection as the capital of the princely state of the same name, until Indian Independence in 1947. In modern times it long held a reputation for its high culture, an aura of which it still carries to some degree, especially due to the presence of its major English-language university, but its greater importance currently lies in its industrial sector.

Baroda's prestige can be traced to a single name, that of its remarkable prince Maharaja Sayajirao III (1863–1939). His predecessor Khande Rao had left no male issue and was succeeded by his younger brother Malhar Rao, who was quickly declared unsuitable and deposed. Malhar Rao's sins were many. For one thing he had been accused of instigating an uprising against the British during the 1857 Mutiny; he had also been accused of trying to murder his elder brother by sorcery or poison. And later, after his succession, he tried to poison the British Resident. There was more. He was exiled to Madras, and Khande Rao's widow was asked by the British Government to adopt a son. A poor thirteen-year-old relation was found in a village in Maharashtra, duly adopted, and given the name Sayajirao. His education was entrusted to an English administrator, Mr. F. A. H. Elliot.

Perhaps due to this background, Sayajirao had a passion for reform that makes him look modern even today. Among his innovations was the endowment of public libraries and a major college (Baroda College, later upgraded to a university), and making primary education compulsory in his domain, even for girls and those of the lower castes. He passed legislation to allow Hindu widows to remarry and to prevent infant marriages. He provided scholarships for the "Untouchables" to study in India and abroad. One such beneficiary was B. R. Ambedkar, who went on to attend Columbia University in New York, and upon his return as a scholar and reformer he fought for the human rights of low-caste Indians, becoming finally one of the architects of the Indian constitution. Sayajirao was also an art collector and brought great painters and musicians to his court. The singer Fayaz Khan, it is said, would sit atop one of the gates of the old city early in the morning to perform. The great south Indian painter Ravi Varma spent many years at the court. His magnificent portraits of the royal family are collected in the small but charming Fateh Singh Museum, founded by the family, along with paintings inspired by classical Indian mythology. Since some of them inevitably remind one of Western paintings of classical motifs, his reputation waned somewhat before reviving. Sayajirao's second wife was given the name Chimnabai II (1871–1958). Educated after her marriage, she "imbibed from the Maharaja a passion for reform," according to the description beside her Varma portrait. She renounced purdah (not coming out in

public, as befitted a noblewoman by tradition) by one day sitting beside the maharaja during a prize-giving ceremony at the Nyaya Mandir, the Palace of Justice. And she co-authored a book, *The Position of Women in Indian Life*, in 1911.

Surely there must be more to explain this remarkable prince than his humble background. One imagines long informal chats with his teacher that served as avenues to discovery; there were the travels abroad to open his eyes to the backwardness of Indian society. And there were of course other modern Indians of the time, inspired by their travels abroad and imbued with the spirit of liberalism and change: Gandhi, Tagore, the Nehrus, Sarojini Naidu, Muhammad Iqbal, and many others.

The maharaja's university, called the Maharaja Sayajirao (or MS) University, boasts some elegant early-twentieth-century buildings of red brick, set off with domes, medallions, decorative arches, and verandahs in an example of what is known as Indo-Saracenic architecture. Alongside these are the more recent blank-faced box extensions, their occupants the unfortunate humanities departments, connected by unpaved paths, next to an area that appears blotted by the clustered mass of hundreds of students' parked motorbikes, which are the most convenient form of commuting in Baroda, used by both men and women. A ninja-like figure speeding along the road would be a girl in shalwar-kameez with a scarf covering all of her face except the eyes: as protection against dust and smoke, she would say; to keep her skin pretty and fair, say the cynics among the men.

I have often put up at the university guest house. It is a large, old-fashioned building in quiet grounds dotted with large trees, with the sedate look, from the outside, of a country club. Inside, it is refreshingly dark and high-ceilinged, providing a cool respite from the bright sun and the heat; the rooms are large, though the bathrooms are wet, the drain holes not covered, threatening rodent or reptile invasions, the mosquito net old, bloodstained, and punctured, the light not enough to read by. But cheap, secure, and convenient. To sleep, you simply pinch the net at the larger holes hoping to close them, light a couple of mosquito coils next to the bed, put up with the smoke and hope for the best. The last time I stayed there I was given a super deluxe room, which was new and large, but except for the bed and a chair it was empty, with the smell still fresh of cement and paint. With so many dark empty corners, a haven for mosquitoes. If Indian houses are so cluttered, how can a super deluxe room be so empty? Guests at this modest abode range from the country's top academics, to the lowly lecturer hunting for a job, to the foreign visitor putting on a brave face for the sake of his hosts who have kindly put him up here. The central hall is large, spread out with tables laid with plastic sheets, and tea can be had at almost any time, brought in from the dark, spare kitchen inside, with puris if you wish. But after two days of my super deluxe room, despite the anytime tea and puris, I decided that over the years I had paid my dues to modesty and politeness, and acting spoiled, took a room in a simple, quiet hotel across the road. Productivity increased.

The Lakshmi Vilas Palace was built by Maharaja Sayajirao as his residence, using the same British architects who designed the university, but where the latter has an elegant simplicity, the palace has a baroque, somewhat gaudy opulence both inside and outside. Stones from various places in India and marble from Italy were used in the construction, which took twelve years. Like other Indian princes of the time, Sayajirao was much taken with the culture of Europe, where he travelled extensively and bought art, good and bad, judging by the exhibits on display. In the palace grounds, next to a golf course, is a medieval step-well, still in use, with an Arabic inscription still in place. The maharaja's family occupies a part of the residence.

Baroda, therefore, has all the feel of an eminent university town, a small former princedom with ancient beginnings. Its attractions are modest but solid—its few historical buildings, its annual Navratri garba dances, its cricket team (the cricket club is next to the palace), its renowned university and diversity of students. But for all its cultural pride, it is also a site of frequent communal violence, small and large. As I write this, I read of an outbreak of violence due to the razing of a two-hundred-year-old Muslim shrine by the civic authorities, the stated purpose being the easing of traffic in the congested old city; a few people were shot dead by the police. During an earlier visit, my host, seeing my alarm at his mention of the threat of a riot in the city, tried to reassure me. Don't worry, it only takes place out there, he told me, naming an area, it won't reach here. To me that knowing calmness—and he was no exception among his class, I was certain—was astonishing. That was ten years ago. And now it's impossible to go anywhere in Gujarat and not be aware of the violence of 2002. Two years after its occurrence, it was still on the mind, very much in the air. The Best Bakery case has become celebrated. Located in a settlement on the outskirts of town, the bakery was set ablaze with more than a dozen people inside, who all burnt to death. Neighbours watched.

Communal violence is set off sometimes in the simplest of ways: some fellows drive a pig into a Muslim area; some others slaughter a cow and dump the remains in a Hindu neighbourhood. At other times, events play into the hands of more malign and organized forces lying in wait. This happened when Indira Gandhi was assassinated by her Sikh bodyguards in 1984; it happened when the Babri Mosque was demolished in Uttar Pradesh State in 1992; and it happened in 2002 in Gujarat when a train compartment caught fire, killing all the people inside.

✂

On February 27, 2002, a compartment of the Sabarmati Express, a train bound from Ayodhya, in Uttar Pradesh, to Gujarat, was apparently set on fire outside the station of Godhra. The compartment contained Hindu activists returning from the site of the Babri Mosque in Ayodhya, and they all burnt to death, some sixty men, women, and children. The fire was believed to have been set by Muslims of the town—Godhra has old Muslim communities not known to be docile, indeed the town has been prone to communal violence, Muslims having lived in the area at least since the time of Mahmud Begada the conqueror, who has not been forgotten—but no charges have been laid so far, and there are those who claim that the fire started inside the compartment. Whatever the case, the horrors of these deaths cannot be minimized.

The Babri Mosque was built by the first Mughal emperor, Babur, in the sixteenth century on a site at Ayodhya that many Hindus believe is the birthplace of the god Rama. Whatever the birth of the god means, "Ayodhya" of Indian mythology is a venerated city; in my childhood we sang a verse in which it was called Ajodha Nagari. The issue is therefore extremely contentious— mythology, legend, and devotion intersecting with premodern history, not an unknown configuration in our world—and the fate of the site is still with the courts. Many Muslims I have heard or read have no problems with the mosque being turned into a temple; after all, in the past, mosques had been converted or built from temples, and Hindu temples had displaced Buddhist temples in still older times. Many others, of course, will not hear of it. In December 1992, however, supporters of right-wing organizations, including the Bharatiya Janata Party (BJP), destroyed the mosque and set up a Hindu shrine at the site. In the riots that followed, several hundred people were killed and tens of thousands became homeless.

What followed the Godhra train incident, ten years later, was a statewide orgy of violence perpetrated upon any Muslim in sight by fanatical Hindu mobs goaded on by members of the right-wing Gujarat government. Claims have been made that this was a planned uprising, with weapons and bomb-making materials ready in advance, and mobs arriving with electoral rolls to ascertain the identities of their victims. According to the national, English-language, print media, the police looked away, in a few cases even fired at escaping Muslims; in one famously reported instance, the police informed the victims, "We have no orders to defend you." Not surprisingly, incidents were not recorded by police, or were recorded improperly so that charges could not later be laid. The response of the populist Gujarat chief minister, Narendra Modi, to the conflagration was to blithely quote Newton's law, that to any action there is an equal and opposite reaction. But the scale of the violence became a national embarrassment, for it was reported widely abroad, and a political football. On the basis of an Indian human rights report and pressure from American groups, the United States government a few years later refused Modi a visitor's visa. More recently, in an irate moment, in response to calls by the opposition BJP for his resignation, India's prime minister is reported to have referred to "the holocaust in Gujarat" as having occurred under its watch; most obviously not to be taken literally, but indicative nevertheless of the gravity of the violence that took place.

As many as two thousand people died in the violence, and more than a hundred thousand were rendered homeless, their houses or shanties—a large number of them were slum-dwellers—destroyed. What was truly horrifying was the quality of violence perpetrated, especially on the women, which cannot be quantified, unlike the numbers of the dead. Not surprisingly the middle classes, the moderates, shudder and look away. It is as if a horrifying wind, a natural, uncontrollable disaster is passing. It's happened again, it always happens elsewhere. A man burnt to death; a woman horribly violated; a child's head smashed.

Baroda, 4:30 a.m., jet-lagged and looking out from a hotel balcony
It's pleasantly cool and the dark is illumined by the odd bits of dim light scattered all around. Life begins early here. A few auto-rickshaws, a few motorbikes, the occasional car horn, engine sounds; at the foot of the lighted, fenced Sardar Patel statue in the centre of the raised roundabout below me, lie four homeless people, two within the fence, two outside. One wonders what territorial dynamics are at work. The two outside the fence are covered head to toe, each in a blanket, like corpses. Sardar Patel, a Gujarat hero, one of the leaders of the Independence struggle; in Attenborough's *Gandhi* he was played with panache by Saeed Jaffrey.

A few teenage boys come sauntering along and get into a parked bus—some kind of school trip must be under way. A cleaner of sorts goes around the area selectively putting things into the large bag on his back; later it appears that he is picking up plastic bags and containers. Ganesh Tea Stall, a sidewalk booth, opens. It makes good tea, cheap, and I usually have two cups of "special." Two old men sit on the edge of the roundabout, taking a break from their walk. Street dogs already trotting about, busy with whatever it is they do.

On weekend evenings, boys arrive at the statue on their motorbikes, park all around the circle, chat with their buddies for hours on end. Very few girls with them.

This cultured city was ruled once by a visionary Hindu maharaja among whose master musicians were Muslims; the grave of one of them is a small shrine that was recently desecrated during the communal violence. I cannot help recalling the giant Shiva statue on the Sursagar lake, a public space; it shouldn't offend, surely, Shiva is an Indian symbol. If anything, it's gaudy. And yet its presence is provocative in a secular country.

But what is secularism, this much-touted word? It is not atheism, says the philosopher S. Radhakrishnan, but a belief in "the universality of spiritual values. It is spiritual consciousness." This in his foreword to the excellent *The National Culture of India* by Abid Hussain, a brave book that looks at a single Indian culture in its diversity, and dismissing the silly notions of non-Muslims as infidels and non-Hindus as foreigners.

I've been told repeatedly of housing segregation in the city, both for reasons of safety and because of plain prejudice. There is safety in numbers, you live among your own kind, move out of mixed neighbourhoods to do so. The Mughal-wada area is an old neighbourhood, a warren of narrow streets through which cars, motorbikes, people, and goats negotiate. It is not quite poor but feels claustrophobic; one might grow up with tender and colourful memories of this place, but one gets out. It used to be a mixed neighbourhood, says a denizen, but after the riots of 1969 it became progressively Muslim. And he bewails that fact. He himself is a Gandhian and runs an ashram outside the city. The Tandelja area is another Muslim neighbourhood, with newer, wealthier houses.

My friend Mohammad, a professor of literature, speaks of traditional patterns of public and private spaces that I find familiar from the neighbourhoods of Dar es Salaam and Nairobi in which I grew up. People of all the communities would mingle in the public or market space, Mohammad says, but they went home to their communal spaces where they did their own thing. This was mutual segregation based on the idea of comfort zones; not unlike the idea of neighbourhoods in Western cities. In his town, my friend says, there was friendly interaction at festivals and celebrations. His father, when he set off for hajj, was bid farewell and given presents by all communities. But nowadays in the cities the segregation is of a different sort, enforced by fear and hatred. He has built a new house in the Tandelja area, though he still lives in a mixed university neighbourhood. If he wanted a house in the same area as his Hindu colleagues, he would never be able to find one.

Yet he is married to a Hindu woman; his only child, a daughter, was brought up as a Hindu and recently got married to a Hindu boy. His only demand on the suitor was that he come and formally ask for the girl's hand, in the old-fashioned way; which of course the young man readily did. Both are studying medicine in the United States. It's a good thing they got away, Mohammad says. I do not ask him, but I wonder if Mohammad belongs here anymore. A product of an English-style private school, he talks in such a rapid manner he can wear out anyone, and not only the time-wearied traveller; and he can become abrasive without thinking. His manner reflects, I have long ago concluded, a large but frustrated intelligence. Immediately after I first met him, thirteen years ago in Bhubaneswar, we had started speaking in Kutchi, and this is how we've gotten along. The last time I saw him he had been working with resettling victims of the violence of 2002. I ask him about this. He's given it up, partly because he got depressions from hearing their horror stories; and partly because he became frustrated with the favouritism and corruption and fanaticism that he came across. He does not want to move into his large modern house in Muslim Tandelja because he does not think he would belong there. His wife certainly would not. Recently he's taken to translating modern Gujarati poets into English.

>⚬<

"Out there," where the riots take place, is where my host, Raj Kumar, takes me one day. We go on his motorbike, not the Czech Java he once had, but a new and lighter Indian Bajaj. It's a nerve-wracking experience, in the noise and heat and dense traffic, with its law of push and go through if you can, the driver in his helmet, of course, the passenger, I, without one.

At the Sursagar lake, with its large gaudy Shiva statue in the centre, we park opposite the elegant nineteenth-century Nyaya

Mandir, the Palace of Justice, another of the enlightened maharaja's gifts to the city, and walk through the Lehripura Gate, with shrines set up in its carved wall niches, a ladder indicating that the flowers and bright sandalpaste are recent. Just outside the gate is the elegant Khajuri Mosque, newly painted green and white with, for some strange reason, a prominent panel in front depicting palm trees. An Arabian oasis? A modest stall outside sells small spicy chicken samosas and lamb pakodas, which Raj Kumar as usual cannot resist; I am wary due to a queasy stomach, but they don't sell vegetarian here. The street, MG Road, is closely packed with shops; there is an old, perhaps ancient, quite beautiful and recently painted small Jain temple, with a modern iron gate, squeezed in between businesses. A crowd of decrepit, wobbly old structures, with trellised broken balconies and prominent uprights, desperately holding on to each other for support. Clothes, utensils, hardware, motor parts. Shopkeepers hopeful at the doors. Narrow streets lead off into neighbourhoods, known as pols, which in olden times would be guarded by their residents.

A newly painted white clock tower is the centre of the old city. From here are visible, with some straining, the four city gates: the Lehripura Gate, the Pani Gate, the Gendi Gate, and the Champaner Gate. We choose to walk towards the last one, which recently gained some notoriety. On the way comes an old two-storey structure, a wide building with corrugated roof, which is the Central Library, founded by the maharaja. The more one learns of him the more impressive he seems.

Outside the library, on the lower of two verandahs, behind an iron railing, a few men read the daily papers on ancient wooden stands. Everything about this library suggests a bygone era. The assistant librarian, who escorts us after we introduce ourselves, says the holdings number three hundred thousand. There are indeed a lot of shelves assembled on the two floors. The library, inaugurated in the early twentieth century, moved into the present location in the thirties. Its construction received the enlightened maharaja's personal attention. The inside is metal and glass throughout to render it fireproof, the numerous windows and skylights ensured illumination at a time when electricity was scarce, and the ceilings are high to keep the place cool. The shelves were brought all the way from Belgium and suspended from the ceiling as a precaution against earthquakes. Finally, an American called Mr. Borden was convinced by the maharaja to come all the way to Baroda to be his first librarian, and his cataloguing system is still in place. A framed portrait of him shows a lean bearded man in collar and tie; beside him is a portrait of the maharaja, in a tight, buttoned-up tunic and a turban, somewhat full in the face. Except for the staff of three and the two of us, there is not a soul in sight; the old holdings, tight on their shelves, are dusty. But the books are in six languages, including English. The assistant librarian takes us to the absent chief librarian's office (where there is a desk and a bed) and shows us a cabinet containing miniature books, a set of which apparently is the complete works of Shakespeare; a few other miniatures are dictionaries. There is a small bust upon the cabinet which the librarian says is of Shakespeare, but it looks like Byron. All these were gifts received by the maharaja when he toured abroad. In the maharaja's vision was a school for every village and a library for every school; it was to a large degree implemented. The man who implemented this policy was one Motibhai Amin, who I am told would go around the public park nearby carrying a bag of shoes and a bag full of magazines. To anyone without shoes, he would hand a pair; to others he would hand out magazines and tell them, Read.

The librarian invites us to have tea and we sit down with him. Three small glasses of tea soon appear. He is a slim white-haired man of medium height, with some front teeth missing. His father had been a Sanskrit professor and, he says with a laugh, gave him such an odd first name that he couldn't find it in a book of first names. Apparently there are government grants to renovate and modernize the library. Plans include a children's and a ladies' section. One wonders if the shopping, travelled classes of Alka Puri will make it all the way to here.

We come out onto MG Road and keep going. Just inside Champaner Gate, two blue police vans are parked on the contentious spot where the grave of a Muslim saint was razed by local authorities, which led to a riot and shooting, in which a few men were killed. We turn at the gate, come upon a segment of one of the ancient city walls, of red brick; in a cavity inside the broken end of the wall is a rudimentary shoe stall. Across from that we pause for soft drinks. The sight of a police van driving by suddenly brings forth the choicest invective from a couple of contorted angry faces nearby, and one sees a glimmer of how a riot can erupt. We walk back in the direction of the Lehripura Gate from which we entered the old city. Along the site of the ancient wall runs the colourful clothing market street called the Nawa Bazar, displaying fabric and clothing of all kinds, hung like banners in stall after stall.

As we head for the parked motorbike, Raj Kumar says that the call he received on his cell a while ago was from his wife; a disturbance had begun in some area outside the city, and she had warned him to be careful in case something erupted here.

Fear, she says at one point, and I am not sure if I'm hearing right.

Priya is from a high Brahmin family, and unlike most Gujaratis of the area her colouring is extremely fair. Her people had fled the ravages of the sultan Mahmud Begada a long time ago and gone to settle in a neighbouring kingdom. And so Gujarati, her ancestral language, was not her first language, though she's caught up with it. During my first visit to Baroda, when I said to a seminar that I had expected to take back sweets from this ancestral homeland, not be close to such atrocities as had recently occurred, she had taken me to buy sweetmeats, and I had also bought some embroidered hangings. One of them, depicting Krishna playing the flute, adorns a wall in our house.

On our way to her home, driving along Old Padra Road, we pass the locality of Alka Puri, where the wealthy live and shop. It was once a suburb of elegant residences, on the sites of many of which now stand condominium buildings, new but cramped office spaces, and a compact modern shopping mall having the look and feel of a discount, claustrophobic version of its North American prototypes. I detect a touch of regret in my host as she drives me here, points out the newer buildings, in this neighbourhood that was in the near past more intimate and simple. Malls are very much the trend now, providing places for family outings and air-conditioned respite from the intense summer heat. During weekends they are jammed. Teenagers haunt the coffee shops and multiplex cinemas. As we park underground, take an elevator, and stroll around past stacks of displays, Priya wonders where people get the money to shop. They tend to overspend, she says, looking anxious, buy what they don't need.

The food court sells familiar fast food in plastic ware; this is a place to feel Western-cool, after all. Can we eat bhajias? I ask. We look around, but there is no place that sells bhajias. I'll make you some at home, she says.

As I sit in her living room and she potters around in the kitchen, a motorbike parks on the verandah outside; a girl arrives in shalwar-kameez. She must be one of the ninjas on the road; she too is fair, with strikingly delicate features and the gait of a dancer. The language the mother and daughter exchange is refined and musical, a far cry from the coarse vernacular of the streets.

It is when we sit down later, after the bhajias, and the daughter is upstairs in her room that the word comes up: Fear. I cannot tell the context, and she does not elaborate. But gradually, as she talks, it clarifies.

She shows me an article in *Outlook* about a Hindu extremist called Babu Bajrangi. How can unelected people wield so much power? she asks. According to the article, Bajrangi "bullies, coerces and terrifies citizens into doing his bidding." He "steered" a massacre in Ahmedabad that left eighty-nine people dead. The man's current mission is to "save" Hindu girls: "There is a ticking bomb in every home," he is quoted as saying. "It can explode any time. The live bombs are our girls. . . . Girls spawn our next generation. Saving her from marauding Muslims is our prime religious duty. Saving one girl from going astray is equivalent to saving 100 cows." So far, he says, he has saved 918 girls, "seventy percent . . . from the clutches of Muslims and Christians who had enticed them, spoilt them, even married them." The method of saving is simple, says the author of the article: "The girl is kidnapped while the boy is thrashed and forced to sign divorce papers." The slightly bemused tone of the article is somewhat alarming.

It's the first time since I've known Priya that she's opened up like this; except for her academic interests, she is a family woman, hardly a radical, and she would rather talk about her children, her elderly mother who prefers to live by herself, the pressures of her husband's job, their last visit to the United States. But this time a dam has burst, she has a need to speak about what we've never discussed before. At the university, she says, the local government has imposed compulsory Gujarati; students from other states and foreign countries will stop coming. The university's intellectual tradition is at stake, and the dissenting faculty is too cowed to say anything. And so, fear.

In the gated colony where she lives, a notice was circulated recently by the management saying that it should be informed about intended sales of houses. At a residents' meeting, someone explicated: We don't want those other communities. The implication was clear, Muslims were not wanted. During the 2002 violence, she says, fear was whipped up in the colony, vigils kept in the night to guard against Muslim mobs. But after several nights of vigil, her husband came to the conclusion that the neighbours were simply taking the time to enjoy themselves, have bhajias and tea and gossip. He saw no cause for fear and refused to participate, said he had work the next day. Relations became strained. I recall that when I came to see Priya the previous year, I had arrived in a taxi, and when I asked the next-door neighbour where Priya's house was, she claimed not to know.

And so the fear is of ostracism, intimidation, victimization. Recently, Babu Bajrangi's extremists have made impossible the showing of the film *Parzania*, about the 2002 violence, in Gujarat cinemas; video stores don't keep it; people are afraid to see it even in their homes.

I ask her how many of her social circle are Muslims, and she says if they were close by, that would be possible. I ask her about the Shiva statue on the Sursagar lake, a public place. She replies: The will of the majority.

How cosmopolitan Delhi feels.

She says that except among the university faculty the feeling is that Muslims should not be allowed to "come up"; that is, advance. But then, curiously, she adds she has heard that since Muslims have so many more children, within some years they will start to dominate.

I don't know how to respond. I do recall that in Kenya, an MP had raised a similar fear soon after independence, that the Indians with their birth rate would dominate and soon there would be an Indian president in Kenya.

She walks me past lines of houses to the rickshaw stand outside the gate, instructs the driver to take a straight route, not go through the back areas—she waves towards Muslim Tandelja. This for my safety.

I realize that whatever community you come from, the fear of being found in the wrong place at the wrong time is too palpable.

✂

The Jama Masjid, the city's main mosque in the centre of the town, attained prominence recently because the son of the muezzin—the man who gives the call to prayer five times daily—became a cricket bowling sensation when he captured the lion's share of wickets during India's tour of Australia. The young man is tall, curly-haired Irfan Pathan, with a trademark grin that bursts upon his face as he celebrates a fallen wicket.

In East Africa when I was growing up, cricket was the major sport among Indians. In Dar es Salaam there were more than half a dozen teams competing, in addition to the school teams. In every alley, every open space, in our neighbourhoods, there would be a game being played. When I went to North America, there was a virtual absence of the game. Gradually this has begun to change. In Toronto there are now about half a million South Asians, and even the major dailies report on the great cricket matches worldwide. And there is of course the Internet. So Irfan Pathan's name is well known.

Raj Kumar and I enter the mosque, ask to see the muezzin, Mehmood Khan Pathan, and to our surprise, without blinking an eye, a man directs us to the right wing of the establishment. In front of us is a courtyard, on the left a tank for ritual washing. We walk up a flight of stairs to the family apartments. We are told to have seats on the wide verandah, which looks down on the courtyard. Some women are about, extended family members, it appears, from the way they are addressed and the easy manner in which they go in and out of the inner rooms; an event is in progress. A young man comes and joins us, tells us not to worry or feel embarrassed—for indeed we have begun to look foolish to ourselves, having come to take a voyeuristic peek at where the great new cricketer grew up. The young man is from Ahmedabad, he tells us. The talk turns to the 2002 violence, or the "toofan," storm, as he calls it. He says that where he lives there is no conflict; people respect each other, who wants violence and curfew? Only the government benefited from it. The Babri Mosque event of 1992 was a frying pan it had kept warm, then it had turned on the heat when it was politically expedient. He himself is an Ayurvedic, an Indian traditional doctor, by profession.

Mr. Khan finally comes, a heavy-set man with a red hennaed beard, a deep-orange cap, and a long-sleeved long shirt over his trousers. He shakes hands, sits down.

It is God's grace, he says, that has brought his son this success, the way he took out Australia. Irfan and his brother Yusuf used to play down below in the courtyard as children, and also on the street. Later they played in the city grounds, and then someone from a cricket academy took them in without charge. Irfan is nineteen, Yusuf a year older; there is no rivalry between them. In fact, when Irfan was in Australia, he would take tips from his brother over the phone. I can sense how the father wishes the older son were as successful. He prays that Irfan will bring glory to India in the coming series against Pakistan. The boy will have to postpone taking his final exam at the local Gujarati school in order to play. Mehmood Khan's grandfather came to Baroda from near Peshawar, now in Pakistan, and worked as a muezzin for a pittance. So did his father. He himself earns about fifteen hundred rupees a month and supplements that income by selling attar. And indeed the apartment looks modest. The large family is close and they have returned from a big luncheon to celebrate the recent glory of their son. Halvah is brought for us; there are children about, young men, girls, women, all going in and out of the apartment.

As we shake hands to leave, Mehmood Khan says, quite suddenly, Let me show you something you've never seen before. He's taken a liking to us. We take off our shoes, go through a door and climb a flight of dark inner stairs, arrive inside a medium-sized room. In front of us is a large glass cabinet. It contains an immense copy of the Quran, roughly six feet by four. It was copied here, I am told, some two hundred years ago. The main text, in large Arabic script, is black; between the lines, in small red script, are words that Mehmood Khan says are Persian translations; in the margins is more Persian. The pages have a gold border.

This book is only one part of the whole Quran, I understand. Other giant-sized volumes lie closed on the shelves. To read this Quran, the books have to be stood up and two people are required to turn the pages.

We go down, shake hands with Yusuf Pathan, and leave, after a look at two chests of attar at the entranceway.

A modest family hit by the lightning of good fortune. Yusuf still awaits his moment of glory. In a recent match, he took his league team to victory, scoring a number of fours and sixes.

When Irfan plays for India against Pakistan, some months later, I read that Mr. Khan and his wife have flown to watch him in Lahore. It feels I am living a dream, he says to a reporter. It is the first time the couple have flown in an airplane; they go to visit, of course, the ancestral homeland next door in Afghanistan. Mrs. Khan appears in a photograph completely covered in a burqa.

Later still, a newspaper reports that Mehmood Khan has been asked to vacate the mosque apartment for allegedly damaging the old copy of the Quran. He has moved to the better Muslim neighbourhood of Tandelja by now, but has filed a suit nevertheless against the mosque committee.

And finally, during my most recent visit to India, I read that Yusuf Pathan has been selected for the Indian 20–20 team along with Irfan, to play a world series in South Africa. Their father, Mehmood Khan Pathan, is elated. "Team India gets a pair of Pathans," says the *Times of India* proudly.

⋙

A woman reporter called Manju, a former student of Priya, meets us to show us the site of a Jewish cemetery, which had apparently been "encroached." A committee consisting of a local Jew and his family had sold off the property, claiming to have permission to do so, using forged signatures. The man had then emigrated to Israel. Manju, a young, petite woman from the south and a recent graduate of the MS University, works for the *Times of India.* She and a few others had heard about the cemetery's plight and agitated to have it declared protected.

The site is at a busy intersection and the graves are dated starting 1950 or thereabouts. A few of them belong to children. The ground is used by a local family as a grazing site for their bullocks, though there is hardly any grass left. The family goes by the name Vaghela, a royal name, far above their occupation and caste. There isn't a Jewish community left in Baroda, but Manju gives us a few phone numbers to call in Ahmedabad, where there is a synagogue and a small number of Jews still reside.

The Road to Champaner

In Samvat fifteen hundred and forty-one,
in the month of Posh, on the third day,
the day of the sun, six rajas perished . . .
When Mahmud Shah, the great king, took Pavagadh.

"THE BARDS," quoted by Alexander Forbes

FROM A STOREFRONT at the busy Baroda bus station, beside a barber shop where a client is receiving a haircut and a head massage, we hire our taxi to take us to Champaner, a historical area that's been in the news recently. Our driver is a thin young lad barely out of his teens. His is a lankiness that seems to be an example of the long-legged look of a new generation of Indians. Although he is reluctant to talk about his family, it turns out that his brother is a barber, and he himself plans to join his maternal uncle in Dar es Salaam, where he will drive a taxi. He of course does not know I come from that city, and so this is quite a coincidence, but only the first of several that await me this day. I recall that my barber in Dar es Salaam, when I was young, had returned to Gujarat; and during a recent visit back, I had noticed taxi drivers of Indian origin, when traditionally the occupation was that of Africans.

Less than an hour northeast of Baroda on the Godhra road, through an almost blinding haze appears a significant protrusion in an otherwise flat, scrubby landscape. This is the Pavagadh hill, which appears as a series of rising plateaus, on the highest of which is a knobby protuberance, beyond which the hill falls down steeply. Further along the highway, beyond the bustling, open little town of Halol and closer to the base of the hill, we come to an arched gate in a fragment of a massive ancient brick wall. It is the outer wall of the fifteenth-century city of Champaner. Past the gate, to our left, appears a more solid, more massive wall of cut stone, which must have enclosed the inner fort. Two arched gates lead inside, one following the other, the inner of which is almost intact and decorated with circular floral motifs of the Indian style and Arabic calligraphy. On one side past the entrance lies a deserted old mosque, the Shehr-ki Masjid, behind an ample green garden enclosed by a fence. Across the road is a small well-tended temple with the date 1946 upon it, very much in use; within its gate, in the yard, a woman draws water from a pump. Further along the road lies the modern village of Champaner, with a population of some hundreds—a typical rundown place of a few dirt roads, with ramshackle houses and a few shops, one of which has a long-distance telephone service.

The importance of this location is the ancient Kalika Mata (or Kali) temple atop Pavagadh hill, which can draw thousands on important occasions or even on a weekend, and the remains of the medieval city of a Muslim conqueror. Therefore a place of contention. In spite of its small size, it's been in the news recently.

In March 1483, Mahmud Begada, the grandson of Ahmed Shah, founder of Ahmedabad, arrived by way of Baroda with half a million men according to legend and laid a long siege to the area, at that time under the domain of Chauhan Rajputs. Two previous sultans had marched against Champaner not long before; in the second case, the siege of Pavagadh, where the Chauhans had their fort, had been lifted when the raja sought help from the sultan of Malwa, a neighbouring region to the east and an opponent of the Ahmedabad rulers. This time, however, Malwa's current ruler fretted before Mahmud's might and withheld assistance. After a twenty-month siege, on November 17, 1484, Mahmud's army gained access to the fort. In the ensuing battle, says Alexander Forbes, "a Muslim shell—emblem of Kali's anger—fell upon the palace of its sovereign." The goddess had been angered, for the king of Champaner, during a Navratri celebration, had cast lustful eyes upon her as she appeared in the form of a beautiful maiden. He had even laid hold of her headscarf. But the Rajputs fought valiantly. In the end, in an act of jauhar, a funeral pyre was raised, upon which went the women and children and the wealth of the Rajputs. When the raging fire had consumed its human sacrifice, the warriors, bathed and dressed in saffron, came out to fight. A few of them survived, including the king and one of his ministers. Refusing to embrace Islam, they were both executed.

There are many stories about Mahmud, considered the greatest of the Muslim rulers of Gujarat. His rule lasted fifty-three years and his military campaigns were many and impressive, including a naval defeat of the Portuguese on the west coast of India, near the present city of Diu, with the assistance of the sultan of Turkey. His nickname "Begada" was due, some say, to his conquest of two (in Gujarati, *be*) prominent and well protected mountain forts (*ghad*), so he was Mahmud Two-Forts. He had immense moustaches, long and twisted like the horns of a cow (*bighad*), which he liked to twirl; this is the second explanation for the nickname. He came to the throne at the age of fourteen and immediately and with patient cunning thwarted a palace coup, meting out punishment according to the standards of the day. (One of the rebels was crushed under the foot of an elephant.) He had an immense appetite, his daily serving of food approximating forty pounds. Poisons had no effect on him—in fact, it has been said that he fed daily on them, so that if a fly happened to alight on his skin it would immediately die, and if he spat a scornful spray of paan juice on a prisoner, it was enough to produce death.

Mahmud, who had already constructed a mosque during the long siege of the Pavagadh fort, decided to build a new capital at the base of the hill, which he called Mahmudabad. It was an opulent city, much of it now buried under and around the present-day squalid village of Champaner. Some impressive and intriguing structures remain. Through the efforts of an architect at the MS University in Baroda and a local trust, the area has been declared a UNESCO World Heritage site, creating some local excitement at the prospects of increased tourism, though not everyone is happy with the idea.

The Shehr-ki Masjid near the town entrance is a low, wide building without the traditional mosque courtyard. There are five arched entrances on the east side, corresponding to the five round domes, and two tall minarets flanking the centre doorway. No one else can be seen as we enter the site, except a very shy courting couple, whom we've disturbed. The mosque is an example of Indo-Saracenic architecture, a combination of traditional Indian and Islamic—or, as some would put it, Hindu and Muslim—styles. (The Indian style is indicated by detailed, especially floral, patterns; the Islamic style is starker. The arches in the two traditions are also different, the Islamic arch representing the "true" arch which has come down from Roman times.) All old mosques hit the unwary visitor by the profusion, indeed a forest, of stone pillars inside the prayer hall, emphasizing from the beginning a geometrical aesthetic. There are five mihrabs, niches, in the western wall, the direction of Mecca. Though the pillars are square and plain, the mihrabs, each situated between two pillars, are intricately adorned with carvings, the Indian contribution to the aesthetic. Above each niche is a carved pattern with a shape that could be the head of a cobra.

This was the people's mosque, and once upon a time how it must have thronged with worshippers; after the prayers they would have flowed outside to the street with the well-being of those who had gone to remember their God. What confidence must have

exuded here, and hubris, at this site now silent like so many others the triumphant sultans built.

On the far side of the town comes another city gate, which opens at a road crossing the main highway. Here stands the magnificent Jama Masjid, the main and largest mosque of the old city, with two tall minarets at the entrance and one at each corner. Here, every Friday, the grand khutba would have been delivered by the chief mullah, praising Mahmud, linking his name to God. There are seven mihrabs, and the high central dome rises above succeeding layers of pillars. Here, too, we come upon a couple courting. Our driver jokes that in the countryside they seem bolder than in the cities. All around us is a vast and dry brown plain, remnants of the old city wall visible, with mounds that could be sites for future archaeological diggings. Further up the road comes a talav, a small artificial lake beside which is a pavilion—the spot where apparently the ladies of the court came to bathe. Across the lake is where, my companion Raj Kumar tells me, the army could have camped. The pavilion is a ruin, partly excavated, the road rather thoughtlessly passing right through it. Next to the lake is a cube-shaped red-brick structure, across the road is the ruin of something more elaborate. Pieces of marble revealed by excavations indicate some sort of courtyard. A path leads up from here to the Khajuri Mosque, only a forest of pillars standing, and one elaborately carved column that could be the base of a minaret.

The modern village of Champaner itself contains a number of ruins, some of which evidently belong to mosques. There are also a few modern Hindu temples, and a Jain centre and dharamshala, guest house, for pilgrims who come to go up the Pavagadh hill, which has Jain temples along the way.

Champaner lies in the Panchmahal district of Gujarat, where the bloodiest incidents of the 2002 violence took place. Some Muslims lived here, but they were driven away during the violence and fled to nearby Halol. One of the town's well-known residents is an extreme Hindu communalist, Prahlad Shastri by name. In a fiery speech, recorded on video, that he gave to a large public gathering after the Godhra train incident, eerie by its hateful tone and incitement, he calls upon the young men, calling them lions, to take "action."

"They set a train compartment on fire. Why did they set it on fire? Because someone did not pay two rupees for tea. What is the price of fifty-eight Hindus' lives? Two rupees! . . . I beg you, Hindu youth, the nation needs you! Your nation is your mother, and your mother is being raped every day. Rush to defend your mother if there is a drop of blood left in you. Many of you think you will get into trouble if you do all this. Well, you are already in trouble!" He proudly declares, "There are no Muslims in Pavagadh . . . all purged! [laughter and applause] When the collector asked me to let the Muslims resettle, I told him, 'Go to Kashmir first! Let my twenty-three thousand Hindus of Kashmir first be allowed back. . . . Just try! [laughter and applause] 'Hindus have beaten the Muslims, Hindus have beaten the Muslims,

Hindus have beaten the Muslims . . . ' After fifty years we have our turn to bat. [laughter and applause]"

Mother India evidently does not embrace Muslims. Nor Sonia Gandhi, for if she wants to be a Christian, he adds, she has no right to live in this country.

And so we decide to pay Prahlad Shastri a visit. His house is a modest one, with a verandah in front; as we step into the front room we see a very tan, tight-bodied man in his late thirties, perhaps, attired in a saffron dhoti with a white shirt on top. He has a thin face and protruding ears, short-cropped hair, and an earnest look. There are two young men with him, in dhotis but bare-chested, and the room exudes a distinct and sweet perfume. On the front wall are prominently displayed photographs of Indian nationalist heroes: Vivekananda, Subhaschandra Bose, Bhagat Singh; no Gandhi. On other walls are photos of Shastri himself on the stage at various functions, or shaking hands with notables. Apparently a vain man, for as we sit on a mat against bolsters, he passes around an album of other similar pictures of himself. There is a TV in the room, and a display of electronics—tape recorder, phones.

Our excuse for wanting to see him is to ask his opinion about the recent "disturbances."

Prahlad Shastri, in this private setting, comes across as an earnest, soft-spoken man, with an intense look in his eyes, reminding me of a student activist. He opens his mouth to reveal a rather crooked set of crowded teeth. He speaks about the goodness of all religions, and modesty in behaviour, condemns Western influence and politicians. He is worried about Champaner being declared a World Heritage site for what it would do to the livelihood and morality of the place. People come here, he says, to visit the pilgrimage site at the Kali temple of Pavagadh, not to see the medieval ruins and the mosque. And tourists come with their dubious morality, wearing immodest clothes. Muslims never lived here, in his memory, he says, which contradicts flatly what we have just been told by some of the townspeople, and what has been caught on video. But somewhat hesitantly, with a gleam in his eye, he suggests, Let's assume they were not here and not talk about it.

There is an unmistakeable sense of homoeroticism in the perfumed air, the two handsome youths in dhoti hovering about their master.

And the recent violence?

Hindus are killed in Godhra, he says, their train compartment set on fire, and Muslims celebrate. It rains in Pakistan and they hold up umbrellas here; when their hearts are elsewhere, you can't be surprised if some people are induced to commit acts of violence.

The idea of the beleaguered Muslim minority celebrating at such an atrocity is outlandish; but it is the familiar blood libel.

Prahlad Shastri is finally provoked when the issue comes to caste. All our discussion so far has been conducted with the most formal politeness. At his mention of Muslims we have not blinked. We are aware of the possibility of danger, are in the lion's den, so to speak; all he has to do is accuse us of something, call a mob together.

Social interactions across caste lines are fine, he says, and they do happen. But intermarriage is wrong; castes should remain distinct, caste purity and identity are essential. That is our heritage. It is a sin to call the reformed Hindus who live in the West Hindus. Then, oblivious of the contradiction, he adds, In twenty years the world will come to the Hindu way of life.

I must confess to a sense of voyeurism on my part at having desired such a meeting, to see what a real extreme communalist, who calmly explains mass murder, looks and speaks like. The man we have met is a picture of reasonableness, until you pay attention to his words, until you watch the video in which, in the heat of a public meeting, he lifts that mask—and what he reveals is frightening.

When I return to Baroda a year later, I discover that Prahlad Shastri hanged himself some months before from a tree near a Hanuman temple in Champaner.

The walk up Pavagadh to the Kalika Mata temple is a long one, of three miles. There used to exist a rope lift here, called Udan Khatola, to carry the pilgrims up in a few minutes, but it was broken in a recent accident. (According to newspaper reports, several people died in the mishap, for which the lift company conveniently blamed "outside agitators" but has been charged nevertheless with negligence.) The Bollywood classic *Udan Khatola* was filmed here, among the ruins, starring the legendary heartthrob Dilip Kumar. The hill is the only raised land mass for miles around. As we walk up we pass ruins of the old Chauhan Rajput fort. The path is well paved, and a festive atmosphere prevails: vendors on both sides aggressively calling out, selling coconuts to take up to the temple, as well as samosas, bhajias, gathias, tea, and soft drinks, and toys, music, and videos. Bhajans play loudly on the way, videos depict beautiful lissome girls dancing the garba to the accompaniment of folk songs, the movements evidently modulated by Bollywood and frankly erotic. Smaller shrines appear intermittently, offering extra blessing in advance of the main one awaiting at the top. An ancient granary is used as a urinal on the way by the men.

At one turn in the path we are trapped by a charismatic young sadhu seated at a stall, asking for merely a rupee to give us blessings. This is a well-rehearsed act, and we know it, yet foolishly we relent, if only out of curiosity. He is bearded, lean, and muscular, with the most intense, glistening eyes I have ever seen, and he sits erect, wearing only a white loin cloth. I want nothing from you, I have nothing, he says, but out of respect for the women folk, I would not possess even this (his loin cloth). He has us mesmerized. When he sings his incantations to Devi, "Jai Mata!" obediently we repeat after him. He takes our willing hands one by one, places limp flowers in them. Takes the flowers in his own hand, crushes them, then opens his palms and pours out red "sindoor" powder. Magic. He displays an empty hand, closes it into a fist: drops of water come trickling out.

"Jai Mata!" I have nothing, I need nothing—but we are constructing an ashram nearby, we need ghee and other things. He snatches five hundred rupees from me, having seen it as I opened my wallet to search for suitable, smaller currency to give him.

The ruins we pass, witnesses of so much history, are of little interest to the pilgrims, who pass them by without as much as a pause; many of these worshippers are familiar with the route, having been here many times before, and the goal is the Mother at the top, who will provide blessings. The climb gets progressively steeper.

It takes one and a half hours of steady climbing before we reach a sheer rock, egg shaped, up which we climb via steep steps. The crowds are thicker now, people paused for rest on the way. We begin to get breathless. All around us is an open panorama, the falling hills, the open flat land for miles around. From here the Rajputs would have seen the massive army of Mahmud laying siege to them, realized there was no hope. At one of the sites here their royal women and children would have walked into the fire, before the men went down to fight their last battle. Among us, couples, kids, entire families, old folk, cripples. A couple pauses at each step to paint on it the auspicious swastika with red paste, and drop a few flower petals on it. All the way to the top. Giving thanks for what relief, or bringing what pain to be assuaged? I recall being told how my mother performed a similar act to give thanks for the birth of my sister, seven years after her wedding; she went up the steps of the prayer house, placing a coin at each step.

Finally we arrive at a place where the shoe stalls begin, at the base of what appears to be a rectangular stone block, with some construction on top. The climb here is the steepest; the crowd is even thicker now; and gets thicker still, until the way is so close-packed you have to push and are pushed. You find a toehold and push your way up to the next step. If you fail to close the space before you, someone else is there. One begins to understand vaguely why Indians don't like to queue, or don't believe in queuing; the idea is to push, push, push. There is total individuality here, there's you and the Goddess at the top. No offence is taken by anyone. Push, push, push. But gently. Squeeze past someone, find the next toehold. A young woman, sixteen, maybe, tries to hold her purse behind her to prevent her bottom from getting touched, and she's given the inch of space she needs, this is sacred space, after all. We are all barefoot, the steps are of stone, and wet, and one can imagine the stampedes that take place at shrines, where many lives are lost. If a rush were to begin now, a panic, there would be no hope of escape. There are iron railings at the sides of the steps to hold the crowd in and provide support, but there are those who climb up even these to get ahead of the rest.

And so what is the worship for? For gain, surely, or relief, which is also gain. Not for renunciation or selflessness. But not an unhappy or angry face is here in this crush. A visit to the temple is a joyous occasion.

To climb up about sixty steps takes us an hour.

And then we are at the door of a modest white building that is the Kalika Mata temple; we touch the icon at the lintel, ring the bell at the entrance, give twenty rupees to the priest inside, say Jai Mata! as asked. And leave.

There is a Sufi shrine atop the temple, and there are steps at the side leading up, a thin but steady stream of people choosing to take them. The Sufi's name was Sadan Shah. When we get upstairs, however, we find a small domed structure that, an usher tells us, is a shrine to the Goddess, and someone tries to sell us Goddess charms called tawiz. It seems that the famous Sufi shrine was replaced during the recent violence.

When we reach ground level we inquire at the village about information regarding the Kalika temple and are directed to a local information office run by a volunteer who was previously a teacher. He is away on his motorbike fetching his granddaughter from school, but his son gives us a small booklet and tells us there was never a Sufi shrine on top of the Kalika temple. He tells a garbled story. The little structure on top was simply put there by the conquering sultan, Mahmud, to indicate his supremacy after he had been advised—beseeched—by a Muslim holy man—who might actually have been a Hindu—not to destroy the temple.

A proposal for the development of this World Heritage site produced by the Heritage Trust of Baroda suggests turning it into a recreational theme park following the American model, with facilities for hiking, yoga clubs, and the like. Essentially, putting it onto the world tourist map. Fast food would follow, one presumes. And so while the glory of the sultan's city would receive world attention, the local colour and isolation of the pilgrimage site—a distinction of all such sites located across India on top of hills far away from the busyness of daily life, making the effort of the climb to see the Goddess part of the supplicant's pleasure and satisfaction—would certainly be lost. And so, to be fair, the fears of Prahlad Shastri, it seems to me, were not entirely unfounded.

On the other hand, the *Times of India* recently reported that a stampede on the steps of the Kalika Mata temple on Pavagadh caused eleven deaths.

As we stroll back through the double gates of Champaner to the highway, juice, food, and tea stalls ply their trade by the roadside, buses drop off passengers. It is time to rest. We sit on rickety chairs provided for us at a tea stall, and a sadhu seated nearby accepts a treat from us. A small dark man with an amused look on his face, he is dressed in a white dhoti and has a long white beard. He is a Punjabi, he says, who stopped here some twenty years ago and decided to settle. He lives close by in the woods and does not accept disciples, he tells us, twice. We have no intention of applying anyway. He lectures us on psychology (his word); that is, the concept that there is no limit to what a mind can do, and there is no understanding of it. Sages of the past could accomplish feats that seem impossible today. He illustrates his point with an example. Recently he was at the Kumbh Mela—the annual pilgrimage where millions gather on the banks of the Ganges—and there he had occasion to see the famous Electric Bawa, who from two wires emerging from his mouth can produce an electric current to light a bulb. Electricity simply from the body. That is the power of the trained mind. But the Bawa has been demonstrating these electrical feats for a long time, and his energy must be running out, the sadhu says. Raj Kumar, a university professor, agrees, though I can't tell how seriously. We ask the sadhu about Prahlad Shastri and he flashes an enigmatic smile and says nothing.

We get up and Raj Kumar tells me there is a small shrine nearby that I must see. Must I, really? After the climb up Pavagadh and back, in all this blazing heat and dust? I have had enough, feel saturated with history and phenomena, the newness. All I want is to escape in order to reflect and write somewhere in a shady room with a drink at hand. Having already declined a visit to see a spiral step-well from Mahmud Begada's time, apparently quite unique, I relent, only because the shrine Raj proposes to visit—a dargah, burial place of a holy man—might be of special interest to me. He knows my background, of course.

⤞⤝

The shrine is called Sahaji Sawai no Dero, and it lies in Champaner behind Mahmud's Shehr-ki Masjid.

As you approach along a dirt road, you come across a gate, in front of which is a very unusual sign warning that there are dogs. Such signs are found outside the gates of wealthy fenced houses in the large cities, not in a village. We see no dogs, and it would appear that it is not robbers but other intrusions that are feared. The shrine is in fact a communal one, though open to the public. A well-dressed man waits outside the gate, with a well-dressed boy; a little further away, in the shade of a tree, sits a woman in burqa, the wife and mother. The man says that he is an auto-rickshaw driver; his father died recently, and on his deathbed he asked the son to visit the dargah of Sahaji Sawai. The man's wife suffers depressions and the family cannot make ends meet.

Inside is a large open compound, paved, and since we have had to remove our shoes and socks, burning hot to our feet, so we have to take rapid steps as we walk. There is a storage area at the far end and a guest house, for the community's own pilgrims, which is empty. To the right is the entrance to the shrine. It turns out, and this my companion had roughly guessed, that Sahaji Sawai was a descendant of Pir Imamshah, a member of the saintly pantheon whose teachings and songs I was brought up with. I had not heard of Sahaji Sawai. It turns out that the sultan, Mahmud Begada, had been a disciple of Sahaji Sawai and married a woman from his family.

There is an inner chamber in the shrine that contains the grave of the holy man. A corridor, a sort of verandah, runs between the inner chamber and the outside wall, and on the walls of the corridor are framed paintings of the ten avatars of the god Vishnu. The faith represented here is therefore akin to the one I was brought up in, based on the worship of the ten avatars, the first one of which is a fish and the final one a man. Also on the walls are verses handwritten in Gujarati; and I don't know whether to find this astonishing or not, but I can not only read them but also derive meaning from them, because they are in the language and form of the ginans of my childhood. A few verses I can even recognize.

One speaks of a devotee woman who breaks her necklace so that in picking up the pieces she can secretly bow to her lord who is passing by.

This shrine leads into an adjoining inner courtyard, which is the residential section, where the caretaker lives. There are three rooms to one side, and a kitchen and prayer hall to another. In the kitchen area there are some women on their haunches, attending to chores. The prayer hall is empty but contains a paat, or seat of the pir, where there are two trays of food offerings, an arrangement similar to one we had in our prayer hall, which we called the khano. There is an entrance out from this courtyard where there is a tap for washing.

I emerge quite shaken. What I have seen, evidently, and by accident, is a shrine and prayer hall of a group related to my own. And what had seemed a distant history of medieval sultans and rajas has been connected back to me through the sultan's relationship to the saint buried here, a descendant of the pir whose songs I sang. To see such immediacy with one's ancestral and spiritual past in this place where a holy man, a mystic, lies buried and is worshipped, begins to give me an understanding of the dynamics by which my own community of the Khojas might most probably have evolved.

✁

We depart towards Dabhoi, another ancient town. The road is straight and narrow, one lane each way, cultivations on either side. On the way, the odd motor vehicle, a tractor patiently chugging along, bearing passengers, all women, another bearing bales of cotton. Two women rise up from a small roadside shrine, a grave. There are countless small shrines in India: a little temple, a stand, or a grave at the roadside, in a village, or in a cultivated field. They fascinate me, for in East Africa we hardly had any, though a portion of our prayer house often functioned as a shrine of the temple variety. On an impulse we stop to inquire what kind of shrine this one is and who tends to it, but the women hurry away. Just then a scooter with two men comes by, and when we repeat our inquiry, they tell us to ask at the nearby town, called Jambu Ghoda.

The town is essentially one street. We are guided to a shop, where a rather thin middle-aged man with no front teeth greets us from behind a table that is his desk. He dismisses the men sitting on the chairs in front of him and asks us to sit. He is an estate agent, he says, his name is Mehrally Bhai. He tells us the story of the shrine, which is not very old. Someone in the town had a dream that at that location there was something mysterious; people went and dug there and found a grave. According to an old resident of the area, a fakir—a holy man—had sat at the place. He had never gone hungry, presumably because his needs were miraculously met. The villagers decided to build a shrine there, but a Public Works official was against it and would put all sorts of obstacles in the way; there was no way he would allow a shrine at the spot. One day, however, while driving on the road, a snake crossed his path; the man veered and ran into an oncoming truck and was killed. The shrine got built.

Yes, says Mehrally Bhai, when asked about the violence; there were disturbances here in 2002, and in nearby towns. He was not affected, but he points to one of the men he had been talking to and tells us he lost all his property. The modus operandi of these attacks seems to have been that the Muslims would be frightened into leaving their property, which then in their absence was destroyed using explosives (gas tanks for cooking) and fire. He acknowledges that the Adivasis, aboriginal people, were used to perpetrate the violence. The Adivasis, the so-called tribals, live close to forests and traditionally had animistic forms of worship outside the Hindu system. There are many in this region, which is thickly forested and a conservation reserve, and elements among them seem to have been incited with drinks and bribes, and by being convinced that the Muslims were their competitors, to attack them. It was not necessarily a case of neighbours turning against neighbours; but of course they had to look the other way, or else come to help.

I ask Mehrally Bhai if he is a Sunni Muslim. I don't know why I do this, but, no, he tells me, he is a Khoja. He is from Kutch, and we begin to speak Kutchi. This is not a Khoja area, though they do travel all over for business purposes. They went all the way to Africa for this reason, and he knows about where I hail from. There is now a bond between the two of us, and we converse like brethren, his language, his manner of speech, so familiar. We are given drinks, and he tells me about Khojas who suffered losses in the area, including his sister. There is a town nearby called Bodeli, where there is a khano and a small community, he says. You should go there.

What I find remarkable about this accidental meeting and others like it is the easy camaraderie, the trust. Why should Mehrally Bhai want to speak to a snoopy foreigner who's stepped off the road? I could be a spy. But he's judged that I'm not a foreigner, my snooping is justified interest.

As we enter Bodeli, a small but noisy wedding procession is under way in the heat of the afternoon, led by a small decorated flatbed truck carrying a few young men and the sound system. Behind it rides a rather cowed-looking groom on horseback, wearing a suit, his face uncovered, the white horse draped on the face and flanks, and all around on the road are more young men, some playing on drums and tambourines. We ask, as instructed by Mehrally Bhai, for the shop of one Firoz, and somewhat curiously are pointed to a shop across the street. There is a reticence about visitors in the area, it having been deluged by the media after the violence.

The shop is an all-purpose convenience store: an open window, some feet from the ground and almost the entire breadth of the shop, from which the proprietor supplies daily needs such as matches, packets of tea, soap, oil; a few items hang from the top of the frame. Firoz's father stands inside, attending to a customer on the sidewalk. The mandatory weighing scale of such establishments sits before him on the counter. And again, it is amazing how simple queries, using the right key words, establishes instant trust even in these suspicious and tense times. He is a quiet man, looks around nervously before replying; his shy smile, which could imply anything, reveals bad and missing teeth. The family is originally from Kathiawar in the peninsula. No, he says, they did not suffer harm in the recent riot. People in outlying areas did. There were a few Khoja shops up the hill on Pavagadh, but they had been driven away and not allowed back.

Firoz himself arrives on a motorbike and joins in the conversation. His little daughter, perhaps six, is with him. Soon afterwards he gets back on his bike, his daughter sits in front of him, and—as if this were the most normal thing in the world—he tells me to get on behind him. And away we go, up the hectic street to take her to a private school. The school has been set up by some Patels from overseas. As we drop the girl off, Firoz places a cell phone in her hand.

The khano is round the corner in a side street, and I go to take a look at it. It is a green, modern box with stucco exterior, solidly locked, carrying no identifying sign.

Go see the mukhi, Firoz and his father tell me, and off we go by car and motorbike to the mukhi's house, perhaps a mile away.

The mukhi runs a pipe factory at his property, which stands by itself, bordered by a wall. In front of the house are rows of concrete irrigation pipes, about a foot in diameter. The family is disappointed that the mukhi has missed us; he is away at a meeting. Perhaps we can stay longer, perhaps we could spend the night? Unfortunately that's not possible. There is the mukhiani—the mukhi's wife—their two sons, one daughter-in-law (these three seem to be in their twenties), a little girl, and the mukhi's brother's widow, the latter silently tending to the kid and perhaps with a lower status.

They were attacked, yes. A mob of a few hundred approached the property, but their Hindu neighbours saved them; someone fired a gun.

Were you scared? I ask, more to gauge the reaction.

Of course we were, the mukhiani exclaims in surprise. What could we do but pray?

One Holy Man . . . Three Contending Shrines

He puts ashes on himself
He plays the flute to tame your ear
But knows not the meaning of jog

IMAMSHAH

WHEN I WAS A BOY in colonial Africa, history began and ended with
the arrival in Zanzibar and Mombasa of my grandparents or great-
grandparents from Gujarat. Beyond that, nothing else mattered, all
was myth, and there was only the present. After a few years in North
America, I came upon the realization that that ever-present, which
had been mine, my story, had itself begun to drift away towards the
neglected and spurned stories of my forebears, and I stood at the
threshold of becoming a man without history, rootless. And so origins
and history became an obsession, both a curse and a thrilling call.

When I first came to India I did not know my family's precise
origins, what places they came from. These I've gradually discovered and intend to visit. There is also another origin, and that is the
history of my community of people, the Khojas—how they began.
The physical link to that origin, I've discovered, are a few shrines,
where are buried our holy men, called pirs, whom my Kathiawari
Gujarati ancestors followed.

I was brought up in an Indian mystical, or bhakti, tradition. Every
day, we went to a prayer house, called the khano, where we sat on

mats and sang at least two hymns, called ginans, in an archaic language that was mostly an old Gujarati, but sometimes Sindhi. We did not always completely understand these ginans, but we knew they were beautiful; they defined our spiritual life and sensibilities. Many of them were about personal salvation of a mystical sort, or about Krishna-devotion, similar in content to the bhajans of the more famous Mira or Kabir, or those of any number of India's devotional saints. We had two formal recitations of a prayer in the evening that was (until the 1950s) in Kutchi and so difficult to learn that students who recited it in the khano always received a gift. There was also a ritual ginan that was often sung, called the "Das Avatar," about the ten avatars of Vishnu, one of the three gods of the Indian trinity.

The ginans, according to their signature lines and according to tradition, were written for their followers by a line of pirs, whose ancestry was Persian Ismaili but who, except for the first one or two, were all born in India. The most prominent and prolific of these pirs, Sadardeen, also went by the name Guru Sahdev and Satguru. He is said to have lived in the fifteenth century and visited Benares. An antecedent of Sadardeen, an Ismaili called Nur Satgur, is said to have arrived in the twelfth century, from Fatimid Cairo, in the liberal and learned court of the Rajput king Jaisingh Siddhraj and made him a disciple. One of Sadardeen's grandsons was the famous Imamshah, one of whose descendants was Sahaji Sawai, whose grave I had visited in the remains of Mahmud Begada's capital Champaner, and who may have been related to that sultan.

Were we Hindu or Muslim? I believe both; some would say neither. But from the late nineteenth century onwards, we had identified ourselves as Ismaili Muslims, followers of the Aga Khans, the first of whom arrived from Persia in that period and declared himself the Ismaili Imam.

In Gujarat we have been traditionally called the Khojas. Our family names—ending typically with the sound *ani*—indicate our origins in the Lohana and Bhatia castes of western Gujarat and Kutch. The first names used by our people right up to my grandfathers' generation were purely Indian, in contrast to the Persian- and Arabic-origin names of typical Muslims, and indeed shared with Hindu communities. Older people among the Hindu Lohanas and even among the Khojas know of the ancestral unity of the two groups. According to the stories told by the Lohanas, their ancestors come from a Kshatriya group who had lived in the north, in the areas occupied by modern Afghanistan and northern Pakistan, and had migrated to the south in the eleventh or twelfth centuries during the period of massive unrest there. Mythologically, the Lohanas, like other Indian groups, trace their ancestry to a personality from the epics, in their case to Rama through his son Luv.

The history of the Khojas, except for this connection, is murky, much of it myth and legend. There were no written records until recent times; the earliest handwritten ginan manuscript dates only to the eighteenth century and is of the canonical "Das Avatar." There has been all the room, therefore, for manoeuvring a history and identity for modern times: forgetting, eliding, rewriting.

><

A different process of revisionism is very much in evidence when I visit the shrine of Imamshah, a grandson of Sadardeen, in central Gujarat some ten miles out of Ahmedabad. The context is very much political, in the climate of the day. The BJP is in power in Delhi and, at least according to that party's politicians and their euphoric pre-election slogans, India is shining.

Down a paved though narrow and rough road off the Baroda–Ahmedabad highway, after a couple of factories, past extensive wheat fields, comes the village of Giramtha. It is, essentially, about a quarter-mile of road; a sign outside the village put up by the communalist VHP welcomes you if you are a Hindu. Beyond that we see a clock tower, yellow in colour, and soon we have arrived at an elaborate, massive gate, flanked on either side by a life-sized stone statue of a guard wearing a traditional uniform standing beside a lion. This is Pirana, the shrine to Imamshah, grandson of Sadardeen. I was here nine years before but cannot recall the site being so heavily built up. Past the gate, we walk into an unpaved parking area of sorts, though there are no vehicles around, and thence enter the compound of a two-storey hostel-like building. A fair number of people are going in and out. A woman usher in white sari greets us and directs us down a corridor, at the end of which is a heap of removed footwear. We enter a paved compound containing a number of graves of various sizes, some of them large and prominent, in front of a square white building with a dome, which is the mausoleum of Imamshah. The place is active with worshippers, the atmosphere calm, almost torpid; a group of Muslim men, kerchiefs over their heads, stands around one of the larger graves, placing the traditional offering of a chaddar, a coloured cotton sheet, and flowers over it; then, palms open in front of them in the conventional gesture, they whisper their prayers, in Arabic, I presume.

The mausoleum has the structure of any number of dargahs, burial places of Muslim holy men. A few steps lead up to the verandah, which goes all around an inner chamber containing the grave. As in all dargahs, women cannot go inside. On the floor at the top of the steps, on either side of the doorway leading inside, sit two functionaries in white overshirts and trousers, white pandit caps on the head, and before them come to sit the supplicants. I walk past them through to the inner room, removing my socks (my shoes already removed), and come upon three graves overhung with intricately carved and painted canopies supported on silvered wooden posts. An odour of incense and perfume hangs in the air. Behind the graves, in the centre, burns an old wick lamp. Imamshah's grave is the middle one, on his left is that of one of his sons, and to his right that of his wife. All three graves are heaped with flowers and chaddars, and at the heads of the two men's graves have been placed crowns wrought of a dark metal, most likely silver.

What do I feel here, at this shrine of a holy man, a pir, whose ginans I can quote? Whose wanderings I had only imagined before, with all the distant reality of the comic book "classics" of a child? At any dargah, a shrine of this kind, and even at a temple before a priest, I cannot help but allow in me a solemn feeling, some respect and humility, for I stand alongside others in a symbolic place that in some manner reflects human existence and frailty, our smallness and exaltedness, and our striving for understanding. I cannot beg for a favour, as others do, as I might have done in another life that is long gone. Here stands a rational, a rationalized being who is acquainted with spiritual longing but cannot yield to it.

But this place is particularly special, because it connects me historically; I stand before a physical memento, a memorial over the buried remains of a personality who influenced and preserved the lives of my ancestors for generations in this part of the world. In some strange manner I feel I have a claim to the place that I have not felt elsewhere. My bearing, the quick confidence in my step, says so, and I am surprised at myself.

I come out and ask one of the two functionaries at the steps if they could tell me about Imamshah. Certainly, he says, call your friends. Like the other one, he is clean-shaven and fair. He looks a little uncomfortable. I sit down cross-legged on the floor before him, and my friends—who don't know this tradition and are somewhat hesitant—join us and do likewise, but we have to wait for the second functionary to finish hearing out the petition of a Sikh boy, who looks about sixteen and has come with his mother (a Hindu, we learn, though get no explanation). The functionary, as if to make sure the pir in his burial chamber is paying heed to the full details of the boy's pleas, leans forward and turns his head searchingly towards the open doorway and even occasionally repeats after the boy: " . . . help me get to Australia . . . Imamshah Bawa, help me with my studies . . . help me find a good job . . . and I will give you half of my first month's salary." The boy's mother

places a thick wad of hundred-rupee notes in the functionary's hand, then mother and son get up.

The functionaries now explain to us that Imamshah was born in Uch, Multan (now in Pakistani Punjab), his sons were so-and-so, etcetera. He narrates a miracle by which the lamp that burns inside the mausoleum was lit. When Imamshah was ready to depart the world, he sat on his seat, still preserved at this site, and instructed his followers to place a lamp some distance away. As he breathed his last, the lamp lighted up. It has continued to burn since then without input of any oil. I ask about Imamshah's ancestry. They say, somewhat uncomfortably, that it is not known and give me two pamphlets.

A woman comes and supplicates on behalf of her son-in-law; they tell her, rather brusquely, that he has to come himself, and can he afford to pay?

In the distance, the Sikh boy has put on a pair of anklets so that his legs are cuffed to each other. The functionaries explain to me that if the anklets on the boy come apart as he hobbles forward, his wishes will be fulfilled. The sooner his legs are released the sooner the fulfillment. As it happens, the anklets come apart in two or three hobbles. The boy is lucky, he should get to Australia soon.

This blatant monetary theme is unsettling. To my understanding, the message of the pirs is spiritual. It is about the soul's release from the bonds of the material world. I do not recall functionaries being present the previous time I was here, nor do I remember crowds this large. There are Om signs painted in various places, but then there are the Muslims who come to pray, and the graves with Arabic script on them. There is a policeman on the premises.

The woman with the Sikh boy tells me that she and her husband are Hindus and come once every few months to the shrine because they believe in Imamshah; the boy says fervently that he will continue to come even if his wishes are not fulfilled, because he finds something inspiring here. We do not ask why the parents of a Sikh boy are Hindu. Whatever else may be going on here, this liberality of attitude, this spiritual laissez-faire is one of the joyful aspects of India that one hopes will prevail over the rabid antics and murderous forays of the fanatics who seek purity.

I ask one of the ushers if I may see the Kaka, the head of the shrine, half expecting the request to be denied. To my surprise I am told to climb some stairs to where the Kaka is sitting. Perhaps my garb—walking shoes, short-sleeved shirt, khakis—and manner have given me away as someone from abroad, a potential donor of dollars.

The Kaka sits with a few men at the far end of a long anteroom upstairs, a row of high-backed red-upholstered chairs on either side of him. He wears a white robe, with a saffron sash around his neck, his head is bare, his hair sparse; he is fair in colouring, has baggy eyes and seems to be in his sixties. There is a benign look to him. His name is Nanji Bhai, or Nanakdas. He had been preceded by Karsandas. There are framed photos of the previous Kakas on the walls.

I go forward hesitantly and greet the Kaka the way one would a Khoja mukhi, a headman, in our khano, with a pranam and a shake of the hands. He gives me a blessing. He tells someone to show me the kursi, the "seat," inside. I am taken by the attendant to an adjoining room and shown a seat consisting of an embroidered white silk cushion, which will be the throne of the tenth avatar of Vishnu, called the Nishkalanki ("spotless") avatar when he comes. Beside it is a seat of worked metal, perhaps silver, given to the Kaka upon his recognition as a mahant, a major guru, at a great meeting of Hindu priests.

I nod appreciatively at these exhibits, don't quite grasp when the grand meeting of gurus took place, and return to the front room and sit down with the Kaka. One of his companions, dressed all in white with close-cropped hair, does most of the talking.

He says this Imamshah centre serves numerous communities without discrimination. There are centres worldwide and more than a million followers. People come with their problems or wishes, concerning a business venture, for example, or standing for election for the BJP. Imamshah was born in Uch, Multan, of Brahmin parents; they died when he was young and he was brought up by neighbours, a Muslim family, descendants of the Prophet. In the space of a week, before he was ten, he had learned the Vedas, the Upanishads, the shastras; he performed miracles—made the blind see, the sick well, and so on—and was recognized as a great soul.

The man says he is from the United States, sometimes comes to Toronto. My companions ask to film the scene and are granted permission. The Kaka for the occasion calls for his turban and puts it on, then speaks to the camera.

Before we leave, I cannot resist telling the Kaka that I am a Khoja. Yes, he says, Khojas do come here.

Could I be mistaken in thinking what I saw here some nine years ago was a much older-looking place? There had been only a minor attendant then, who had shown me a board on which the genealogy of the pir had been written down, including the name of his father (Hassan Kabirdeen) and grandfather (Sadardeen), so well known to me. The ginans of both of them were on my tongue, having been heard daily and drummed further into our heads by a certain Karim Master, who made us recite them in religion class at school. Hasan Kabirdeen sang the most beautiful, plangent devotional verses in the persona of a woman, and Sadardeen, besides the mystical verses also left behind cosmological and theological verses, one of them a life of the Buddha. Imamshah had performed a miracle at this site and converted some pilgrims of the Lohana caste to his teachings. Closing their eyes and without moving, they had completed their pilgrimage to Kashi (Benares).

It seems that a complete usurpation has been made, a clean takeover, with a new origin and new stories, new rites, new look, a lot of money, all to convert it into a Hindu site. Back on the main floor there is a ritual room, empty but for some paraphernalia to one side. On the walls are newly painted pictorial depictions of the life of Imamshah that we just heard.

This is still not a Hindu site, not that it matters what you call it. The tradition has been syncretistic, anyway, and to some degree it still is. One wonders what changes await. The Arabic inscriptions in places, the graves themselves, depicting Muslim burials, must be disconcerting to some.

On the way out, I buy a few mementos at a gift shop: three cassettes of ginans (CDs are out of stock), a book of ginans, and a small photo of the Kaka mounted inside a clear plastic stand. I also pick up a pamphlet, which reproduces a painting of Imamshah. He is depicted sitting on a cushion on a tiled floor, wearing white pyjamas and tunic, over which is an open white jacket with gold piping; he has a white and gold turban on his head, a black beard, and a tilak on his forehead. His right hand is raised in a blessing, the palm facing outwards, the fingers tight. The caption underneath says, "Sadguru Shri Imamshah Maharaj." The term "pir" is not used, but the biography inside refers to him as a Sufi saint who was born in 1440.

The police on the premises are an indication that a conflict is in progress. Next door to this shrine, beyond a barbed wire fence, we see an old mosque. The fence must have a tale to tell. We resolve to visit the other side. The only way is to go outside and around.

It is not easy to find the entrance. People stare at us, give vague answers to our queries; evidently there is much animosity around. One person points to a door that is very obviously closed permanently and says that's it. As we walk on, we realize to our surprise that a man is following us on a motorbike. We persist, walking up the road in a dilapidated section of the town, then turning to the right, until we finally arrive at a gate in a wall, with a sign. We enter through the gate and immediately a man appears dressed in ordinary shirt and pants. He says he is a sayyid, Imamshah's progeny and descendant of the Prophet. This place looks familiar to me, it was a part of Pirana when I last came here. The mosque is old but seems well tended, with a large open shed next to it. The man speaks slowly and gives me the genealogy of Imamshah I am familiar with, at least up to a few generations back. He says he had seen us on the other side; he himself goes there every day to pay respects to the grave of the pir and other holy men. He invites us to his home, a well-built though modest single-storey house, with a small living room in front where we sit on low sofas. We have water, then tea, we use his washroom. I ask him about the etched slab of wood or stone I had seen before, on which Imamshah's lineage had been inscribed. He tells me that it and several other items had been removed or destroyed. Literature as well. I am not oblivious to the fact that he has his own interests to promote, yet there seems to be some truth to what he says.

He brings out a chart that traces his family back to Muhammad and includes, of course, Sadardeen, Hassan Kabirdeen, and Imamshah.

He has sued the Kaka's group and the case is in court. But he does not expect an early resolution. I ask him about other Imamshah descendants, surely they must be around? He is vague about them—there are many, he says. His brother lives next door. His son is a manager of a communications company in Ahmedabad. And he confirms the story that one of Imamshah's progeny married a daughter of Sultan Mahmud Begada.

The next day, standing outside the Imamshah centre, observing. It is Thursday, one of the "big" days. A woman with her family walks in, the mother carrying a baby completely draped in gunny cloth. A grimness to her look. People bring their problems here, their dearest wishes. How close was my own upbringing to worshippers of this kind: my mother asked to be blessed so she could have children, was given an apple to eat, and conceived; my unmarried aunt would stand on one foot daily, praying fervently, and finally got married, but the man turned out to be a drunkard. I, too, was taught to pray for benefits. No longer do I hold such belief, though I cannot help but empathize with those who arrive here, so openly bearing their desperation.

An SUV passes by us slowly, inside is the Kaka's companion from the United States who gave us the story of Imamshah's Brahmin origins. He waves briefly and formally from the air-conditioned interior. He must know by now that we have been to see the Muslim contender next door and are, at best, curious busybodies.

There is a certain naïveté about this renovated shrine and its refurbished story, a certain hubris, perhaps due to the nationalist rise in the country; there are BJP posters around the village. The fact that the heirs to a syncretistic, mystical tradition uniting Hindu and Muslim elements would seek comfort from such politics is perturbing. Surely past visitors have written about Pirana and recorded the previous character of the shrine?

And so while my people, the Khojas, have been cleansing their heritage of Indian, so-called Hindu, elements, here at Pirana essentially the same heritage is in the process of being cleansed of its Islamic connections and history. But such cleansings cannot be complete, there is always evidence left behind, questions that remain.

One thorn in the flesh for the Pirana site is the mosque next door and the Muslim claim to the identity and heritage of Imamshah. We soon discover another.

As we prepare to depart from this town, someone asks us if we know about a stone that moves when you make a wish. This sounds intriguing in the extreme, and in spite of time constraints we decide to go and have a look.

Behold, then, a new spiritual wonderland.

We walk into an unpaved alley leading from the main road into what looks like a separate community: women at the doorways of their shacks, seated on the ground, working at some kitchen task, children playing about. We reach a gate with a sign announcing the Bakarshah Bawa Mandir—a temple, as the name indicates, to a Muslim saint. The people who worship here are another distinct Imamshah group. A modest but more spacious, open site; no new constructions here, no gift shop selling religious memorabilia. There are rooms at the sides along a wall for pilgrims to sleep in. The compound is paved, and roughly in the centre of it is an oblong-shaped black stone on the ground, about a foot long, some five hundred years old, we are told. A priest sits next to the stone, and a few other men are also about. The ritual is that you make a wish, then crouch upon the stone; if it turns, taking you with it, the wish will be fulfilled. A young man's wish has just been promised ful-fillment as we arrive, and he gleefully gets up. One of my compan-ions takes his turn; the stone turns for him, too.

I enter the main building, which houses the graves. Next to the entrance, on a board mounted on the wall, is a rather colourful and elaborate chart written in Gujarati. It lists the avatars of Vishnu, starting with the fish, but there are eleven of them here instead of the usual ten. The tenth avatar, according to this list, is "Muhammad dur rasoolilah," the Islamic prophet. The eleventh avatar is named as Nishkalanki, the Pure One, who was number ten for the other Imamshah group, as he has been for the Khojas. According to the story told here, he had been born but then disappeared. He is Bakarshah Bawa, the thirteenth descendant of Imamshah, and he died at the age of one. His body is believed to have turned into flowers, and he is the avatar to come.

There is a small child's grave, belonging to Bakarshah Bawa, to one side.

This is a complete fusion of Hindu and Muslim beliefs. Moreover, it identifies the Muslim origins of Imamshah, which is the genealogy as I learned it, contradicting the one described at the big shrine across the road. How will these two shrines continue to coexist side by side in the future?

In a small room at the far end of the grounds, facing the main building, is a gallery of painted illustrations. Here are bright paintings of the Prophet Muhammad, their creator oblivious to injunctions in the Islamic world; the Imam Ali; Fatima, his wife, daughter of the Prophet; the grandsons Hassan and Hussein. There are also portraits of Bakarshah and of a few other Bawas and their wives who, I am told, look like beautiful Brahmin ladies.

And so, a simple, modest place—no sophistication, no special garb, nothing fancy. A forty-rupee contribution is considered generous. The jemadar, caretaker, who is not a priest, is a volunteer, a retired railway civil servant. He comes six days a week, has a very simple room on the premises, with hardly anything but a rolled mattress and some personal items. He takes Sundays off.

∝

5:25 a.m., in my hotel room in Ahmedabad.

I wake up to an azaan from a mosque, a beautiful clear sound, high and always rising . . .

And then, a little later, the silence is broken again, this time by a sound that couldn't be more different: a bhajan from a nearby temple, almost like a ginan from childhood. I try and grapple with one from my memory that I think comes close to it, at least in a musical phrase.

Finally, the sounds of morning and a warm light suffuses the room.

Uneasy City: Ahmedabad

There is not in a manner any nation, nor any merchandise in all Asia, which may not be had at Ahmedabad, where particularly there are made abundance of silks and cotton stuffs.

JOHN ALBERT DE MANDELSLO (1638)

I had a predilection for Ahmedabad. Being a Gujarati I thought I should be able to render the greatest service to the country through the Gujarati language.

M. K. GANDHI, *Autobiography* (1927)

IT IS SAID THAT IN 1411, when the sultan of Gujarat, Ahmed Shah, was returning to the capital, Patan, from a campaign, having chased a rebellious cousin (who was the governor of Baroda) and subdued him in Bharuch (Broach), he happened to camp close to a town called Asawal by the Sabarmati river, where a hare was seen to attack the royal dogs. This act of rabbity bravery very much impressed the king, and he decided that such a location was a worthy place to build a new capital. He was also influenced in this decision by his spiritual advisor, the Sufi Shaikh Ahmed Khattu Ganjbaksh. The area was ruled by a chieftain called Asa Bhil, who had to be subdued first, before the city could be built. The sultan perhaps also fell in love with the chieftain's daughter. Thus the legendary and part-historical tale of the founding of Ahmedabad, Gujarat's premier city. It would be said later that when a hare dares a dog, then a city gets built; meaning, by an extension, that fortune favours the brave.

Ahmedabad is older than the present Old Delhi, Shah-jahanabad. (Shah Jahan had in fact spent some time here in his youth.) It grew over the centuries to become one of the great commercial cities of India. In recent times it has been called the Manchester of India; Erik H. Erikson, in his study of Gandhi, calls it the Pittsburgh of India. These comparisons hardly do justice to a city with a rich, complex history and magnificent architecture, much of it now, unfortunately, utterly neglected. It was here that Gandhi began his Satyagraha movement after his return from South Africa in 1915, founding the Sabarmati Ashram later that year. In 1918 he took up the cause of the textile workers of the city, going on a fast to win their cause. And it was from here that he began his famous Salt March, in March of 1930, which led to his arrest and mobilized hundreds of thousands throughout India.

The population of Ahmedabad has always been diverse, consisting of the great merchant houses, the middle classes, and the working classes, divided along caste and faith lines, caste often demarcating division of labour. Long renowned for its hand-woven textiles, the city's more recent wealth came from the mechanization of its textile mills, increasing its working class and migrant population. With so many different communities existing side by side, the potential for conflict always existed. It only got enhanced by the categories used by the British administration in their regular censuses for all India, which, though fascinating for the information collected every ten years, also divided the communities along strict religious lines, Hindu, Muslim, Sikh, Christian, Jew, with no space in between for ambiguity to soften differences or celebrate multiplicity within a unity. Folk traditions among "Muslim" communities were regarded by the census-takers, for example, not as indigenous and valid, which is what they were, but as adulterations to the pure and Quranic faith of Muhammad, which would have been alien to them. This clean division became even sharper and more hostile as the question of Indian self-government and identity came up in the early decades of the twentieth century. Frantic attempts were made to proselytize, counter-proselytize, purify, and organize among the Muslims and Hindus. Literature appeared dividing history into pre-Muslim and Muslim eras. As Independence loomed, conflicts broke out more frequently. In recent times, after the partition of India, the violence has become progressively horrific.

In 2002, Ahmedabad suffered yet another of these orgies of violence.

The old city of Ahmedabad, situated west of Sabarmati river and connected by bridges to the newer developments, is a sharp contrast to Old Delhi, Shahjahanabad. The latter still has a medieval feel to it; regardless of anything else, there remains some continuity, history still abides in its narrow streets and alleys presided over by the fort and the grand mosque. People are aware of the past. Not so Ahmedabad, uneasy with time and history. No one built a New Ahmedabad, and so the old one has had to simply make do, patching, adapting, resoling. Streets have been widened, gates destroyed, prosaic structures squeezed in to replace the old. If history seemed ignored to my eyes when I first went to Delhi, here it seems to have been beaten on the head. Not surprisingly, Ahmedabad is not a tourist destination. Searching the catalogues of three major libraries, I could not find a book in English describing the city; I'm not sure one exists.

Still, this is an historic city, there must be a story to every stone here. You just have to scratch for it. But it is a city to keep returning to; it bewitches you the more you discover of it. We have put up at a modest hotel on Relief Road, in the Teen Darwaza area, close to the river. The owner is from Siddhpur, an ancient city north of here. You should go there, he says. We plan to. Outside, the day is a blur: hot, sunny, dusty, traffic pouring along the street

as if from a spout, the wonder of life throbbing in all its variety and colour all around. At such moments, even with the heat bearing down, it seems a privilege to have got away from life's mundane chores, to be out on a quest, at large in this intriguing, frustrating city. A quest for what? We are not sure, but we hit the footpaths.

Walking along Relief Road, we turn right into a small street to head towards the famous great mosque of the city—built by Ahmed Shah, the founder of the city, what better place to start from?—when suddenly we find ourselves at the entrance to a shrine. It's called the Pir Mohamed Shah Dargah, and doesn't look very exciting, but on a whim we stroll in. A few people are about, tending to the place. There is a mosque to one side, and a tank in the middle of the compound for ablutions. Across from the mosque is the mausoleum of the pir, a modest structure with four small domes and a verandah with many arches. Inside is the grave, covered with a red and green chaddar. At the far end of the compound are guest rooms, presumably for pilgrims. What's striking here is the dark, cool shade of the interiors, away from the glaring sun beating down outside and all around. We are told we should see the library. What kind of library could there possibly be here? It's easy to be skeptical and turn out looking foolish, and this is one such moment. As directed, we climb up a flight of stone stairs situated near the entrance, walk along a corridor and come upon an amazing sight: beyond the entrance lie three rooms, leading one from another, people sitting behind desks, bookshelves along the walls, a catalogue system chart posted on a board. A research library.

We are asked who we are, then a guide is assigned to us, a retired man who volunteers. There are several hundred manuscripts here, he says, as he shows us the contents of a glass display case containing about a dozen examples. Handwritten Qurans, a manuscript of a work by the great traveller and scientist Alberuni, another with the seal of Ahmed Shah, the founder of this city, upon it. There is no way of telling, of course, how true these attributions are, but the specimens look old and are evidently much prized. There is a manuscript strip several feet long with a verse written on it; within each character are inscribed, microscopically, parts of the Quran so that the whole of the Book is contained in the verse.

With all this treasure, the library looks unprotected against fire, riot, theft. Against fire, the man tells us, they have extinguishers; and then there is God. It is the kind of place that, with its naive fragility, could suddenly cease to exist one day. My companion is the irrepressible Mahesh from Delhi, and as we sit and drink the tea offered to us, he gives the man a long lecture on the importance of preserving all the treasure that is housed here and making sure that there are copies. The library receives a government subsidy, the man says, and the department responsible has restrictions on the making of copies, in case the originals get damaged. A discussion ensues on methods of preservation.

—

Outside, we are back on a short but busy street; old, once-elegant balconied houses jostle against each other, barely upright. This is a street of shoe stores, from which lead off smoky residential alleys. Further on, a poorer section—a butcher crouched on the ground chopping meat for customers, cots outside houses, children playing (and staring). We come upon the main Gandhi Road, and find more shoe stores, lock and hardware stores, twine stores; in front of them, sidewalk vendors selling juice, fruit and vegetables, handkerchiefs and underwear, slippers, jewellery, luggage, one after another, so that it can be hard to get through into the street. It is the colour and the names on the signs that gives each place its character and distinction, stand in for architecture. Intermittently, bicycles piled like flies upon a piece of meat. Bright billboards shading the balconies. And then the mosque.

The Jama Masjid of Ahmed Shah was completed in 1423. Its majesty is marred by the fact that its minarets are absent, having been destroyed by an earthquake in 1819, and its front facade is lined with stalls, leaving only the entrance visible. There is a man who sits on the steps to look after the shoes, but we take ours in our hands, as we see others do, and proceed up to a vast square courtyard contained on three sides by walls carved with inscriptions in tall Arabic characters, presumably from the Quran. The fourth side has the prayer hall. There is a large covered pool in the centre where a few people do their ablutions before proceeding to the hall. The roofed section of the mosque is supported by a thick forest of pillars, about three hundred in number. A magnificent central archway constitutes the main entrance into the hall, flanked by lesser arched accesses. The entranceway is intricately carved, an example of the Indo-Saracenic style. Very few people are about, and they sit quietly and privately in prayer, away from each other. Two girls in blue and yellow chaddars at the entrance add a sudden dash of exotic colour to the old red sandstone background. They must be tourists. The electrical cables strung about among the pillars, the speakers attached to the ancient walls, the tube lights, the electric fans, the cheap clock, and the scaffolding are ugly reminders of today. The exigencies of daily life, the importance of prayer, leave no time for the appreciation of architecture, the contemplation of history. In the distance, above the walls, loom the drab modern buildings we left behind to enter here.

As I turn to go, waiting for my companion, who potters around near the entrance to frame just the right photograph to add to the multitude of Indian images he has captured in his lifetime, I experience a certain sense of bleak wonder. This vast, plain prayer ground, in the middle of it now a slight young man in white robe and white cap knelt in prayer, how empty it looks, and forlorn; how different this space from the enclosing, intimate, and perhaps oppressive space of even a large cathedral, or a temple clamouring with carvings and statues. How different are the senses of God represented in them. I imagine for this young man a distant, patriarchal, and even haughty Allah; but then he goes to a dargah to seek assistance from a pir, a man who could grapple with that distant patriarch.

On the opposite side of the prayer hall, at the eastern end, is a gateway that leads outside to the tomb of Ahmed Shah. The area is dirty and neglected, and endowed with a faint odour of urine. The path is littered; there is a goat or two running around, an overturned trash can, dysfunctional push carts, a parked scooter, a discarded mattress. Two kids ask us for pens, then chocolates, finally rupees. A man carving a red block of stone tells us it is for repairs to the mosque. Further on we reach the royal tomb, a rectangular stone building with a verandah and three rooms, the central one of which is the dingiest and contains the grave of Ahmed Shah, shrouded in a cloth of green with red borders, as well as those of a son and a grandson, who followed him as sultans. On the walls, badly framed pictures of the Kaaba, a mosque, and Quranic sayings. Elsewhere, an oil lamp, a money chest for donations, two threadbare carpets, gaudy fixtures. Everything is makeshift, a hand-me-down; there is an air, here, of neglect, ignorance, and poverty. People come to pray in this place, I don't know why—perhaps there are families that trace their roots to the sultan. The two other rooms also contain graves. The place has been looked after by the same family for nine gen-erations, I am told by a woman, who now has the job with her epileptic son, who has two front teeth missing. They earn nine hun-dred rupees (twenty-three dollars approximately) a month, paid by a committee, and she earns money part time by constructing paper flowers and such for sale in the bazaar. There is another son who works in the city.

Thus, the founder of Ahmedabad. The site is protected by the Archaeological Survey of India; but just outside the monument lie four carved stones broken away and perhaps destined for the mar-ket. Nearby, a goat rooting among the garbage, a chai shop selling excellent tea at a mere two and a half rupees a cup. There are no other customers about.

In the British Raj, musicians would sit at the entrance of the mausoleum with their instruments, singing verses three times a day. An urs festival was held once a year in honour of the dead sultan. And khichdi, poor people's fare consisting of boiled rice and daal, was distributed daily from this site. The expenses for all that were paid from the government treasury.

Past this site, after two cups of tea each, we enter the Manek Chowk market, which begins with a line of stores selling printed cloth, the owners or their assistants sitting in the wide doorways inviting you in as you pass. The one we patronize is world-renowned, belying its modest appearance. A narrow staircase leads to a second floor, a riot of colours and a whiff of cotton dust. The cloth is printed in Kutch and, while you sit on the proffered bench to inspect it, the owner, in impeccable white kurta-pyjamas, will spend as much time as required, spreading out his samples on the floor, from the more modest to the most exquisite, to suit your needs. The price is non-negotiable. After this uplifting experience we arrive at a bustling outdoor market, its stalls makeshift or permanent, displaying spices, cassettes, CDs and DVDs, decorations, dried and fresh fruits, worship paraphernalia, candies and paan masala, gift cards with coins attached to add auspiciousness, all in such a brilliant display of colour as to dazzle the eye. Behind these stalls, more clothing merchants. Then, right beside this section of the market, comes a shabby, quieter section, in the midst of which we have been told is the Rani no Hajiro—the Mausoleum of the Queens, where lie buried the queens of Ahmed Shah. We walk through a short, narrow, crowded street and finally find it, behind a row of stalls. How do we go in? we ask a hawker. Go round the corner, ask the aunty for the key, he tells us; it's self-service. We turn the corner, find the aunty, an impressive-looking woman with a white dupatta around her hennaed hair, her mouth red with paan, sitting with two other women on a metal charpai surrounded by junk. Behind her, steps lead up to a verandah and the tombs. There's the key, she says, it's hanging from a nail on a board. We climb up the steps of the mausoleum to a gritty verandah covered with charpais, bundles of merchandise, trunks, furniture, and more junk. A teenage girl sits on the floor playing with a toddler. And silent, muted witnesses humbled by time: ancient columns, fragments of wall carvings, delicate latticework, all covered in grime. The door is blue, oil painted; we open the padlock, step in. There, in an unswept, neglected, broken courtyard open to the weather, lie three queens in their graves, draped in old chaddars: Mugalibibi, Mirakibibi, and Hazaribibi. We stare a couple of minutes, then close and lock the door, greet the girl and toddler, and leave. As we depart, after thanking the aunty, the stall-keepers grumble about how the government doesn't preserve this precious heritage. They could do with some tourist business, obviously.

Ahmedabad, indeed Gujarat, is full of such neglected historical sites and architectural wonders. Perhaps there is simply too much of the past to cope with, written and rewritten, fragmentary and disputed; all of it seems to relate to sultans and rajas. If there is glory to remember, someone's victory is someone else's defeat, and memories are long, they are convenient. If history is taught in comic-book versions of us-versus-them, it's better that history itself has such a low premium. Better to keep your eyes on the future; on the stock markets and cricket scores; on globalization and the GDP; on America and China. And history can be revisited when it's less personal and wounding.

The market, Manek Chowk, is named after a fabled saint called Maneknath Godaria who—legend tells us—when the walls of Ahmed·Shah's new city were going up, would every evening unravel the threads of a quilt he was weaving, whereupon the day's construction would all come tumbling down. The sultan was understandably annoyed and sent for the holy man. He asked him what other wonders he could perform, and Maneknath replied that he could enter a badna, a teapot-like vessel, and emerge from its spout. Show me, the sultan said. Maneknath entered the vessel, whereupon the sultan quickly closed off the spout with his finger, thus smothering the saint.

A short walk from the tomb of queens, right in the midst of the market, is an exceedingly modest temple dedicated to Maneknath, who it seems was a very real figure, magician or not. We are met there by a woman and her son, the caretakers, who give us a very confusing account of Maneknath's sect. There is an inner room, with the shrine, and an outer room, which has a fridge with a variety of soft drinks for sale. We buy our Limcas, make a modest donation, and leave.

Further on, in the vicinity of the rather elegant old stock-market building—where in the Share Mania of the 1860s numerous people lost their fortunes—comes the jewellery market, the shopkeepers all looking out hopefully, there being not much business at this hour. A villager with a stiff, upright bearing, in the typical rustic white dhoti, white overshirt, and a high folded white turban, walks into a goldsmith's store and sits down on the floor. We wonder what this patriarch will come out with, perhaps there's a wedding in the village, but he takes his time. Walking further on, we pass the utensils market, gleaming with brass and aluminum ware—a brass bell catches my eye, reminds me of the one we had in my high school, which surely must have been cast in Gujarat—and come to a vegetable market with fresh produce and more than a dozen kinds of vegetables: long purple wormlike moghra, the tenderest okra, small green peppers, guar, green bananas, baingan (eggplants) of all shapes and sizes, to name a few. Mahesh is like a kid in a candy store. We buy what in my childhood we used to call English imli, a tender, mild version of the tamarind, which here is the red, rather than white, variety. Its seeds Mahesh hopes to plant back at his farm.

And finally on to Gandhi Road. Back in the hotel we have imli and watermelon for lunch.

At Fernandes Bridge is the Chopda Bazar, the paper and book market: stalls piled upon stalls in a narrow maze of alleys, selling paper, notebooks, envelopes, and books, mostly school and college texts, on shelves and piled on the floor. In some cases it's impossible even to push through inside to browse; you stand at the door and make your request, and a book makes its way to you from somewhere inside, or magically appears behind you, or it is recommended you inquire elsewhere. But ask for a book in English on Gujarati history, and you get a look that says, Are you kidding? The last such book, a very good one, was published in the 1930s by a Parsi with the intriguing name of Commissariat, and then nothing else appeared until a recent exhaustive survey by Yagnik and Sheth. But this one touches on the politics of communalism and therefore has met with dead silence in the state. I find it in Delhi.

For Gujaratis, business is of overriding importance. I did not have to be told this in Baroda or Ahmedabad, this knowledge was part of my growing up, it was in the blood, so to speak. And so the pride of modern Ahmedabad, across the river, where we wander off briefly, is the prestigious Indian Institute of Management. A degree from here can land a graduate, it is said with envy and wonder, a salary on an American scale. Everyone from this area of the city, you can be sure, has someone in America. Some Gujaratis even call their state the fifty-first state. We pass an American pizza store with the Stars and Stripes proudly displayed, and next to it a not-insignificant Statue of Liberty outside a storefront. We pass a mile-long strip of jewellery stores before heading back to the old city, where vendors run after us desperate to sell cotton kurta-pyjama suits for any price, starting at two hundred rupees, or four dollars, and coming down finally to a ludicrous fifty. With my proverbial Gujarati acumen, I cannot help but wonder, at that price, how much the cloth cost, how much the tailor, the presser, the vendor would make.

There is a story about Ahmedabad's legendary prosperity. One evening, Lakshmi, the goddess of wealth, came to the gate of the old city intending to leave it. The guard informed her he had to ask the sultan's permission to allow her to go. Certainly, the goddess told him, I'll wait. But the guard did not see the sultan, who surely could not have denied the goddess; instead, on the way, he cut off his own head. And so Lakshmi was left permanently to tarry in the city awaiting the guard's return.

This story is told to us by a half-mute man outside a dilapidated shrine which, he informs us, belongs to the guard who made Lakshmi wait. It seems odd for that hero of Ahmedabad to receive such shabby treatment. The shrine sits next to the imposing Bhadra Fort of the sultans, now in ruins. Stalls cling to its side like parasites, and it contains a government bookstore. The famous Lal Darwaja, the Red Gate, is a part of the fort, and not far is the sultans' private mosque. This is an exquisite structure, some of its pillars beautifully carved and others not. The beauty is marred by electric cables, ceiling fans, the ubiquitous ugly clock.

The cell phone is a sign of modernization, obviously, but it's also keeping families together over long distances—the ties, the obligations, the formalities—and therefore serves a function very Indian and traditional. Mahesh, speaking to me about something across the table in a restaurant, on impulse interrupts himself to call up his daughter in London, to greet her for the Holi festival, his voice rising several decibels, everyone staring at his English admixed with Hindi and the unabashed endearments. And later, Holi greetings come in from all over India by text message. Happy Holi!

What an afternoon.

The mosque of the shaking minarets is called Sidi Bashir's Mosque. If you shake one of the minarets, presumably at the top, the other one will shake too, while the intervening structure remains undisturbed. A civil servant called Colonel Monier Williams, who conducted an almost microscopic topographical survey of Gujarat, reports in 1809 this same phenomenon regarding the two minarets of the Jama Masjid, which were destroyed ten years later. Monier Williams lay down on the roof halfway between the minarets and observed that, when one minaret "communicated" its motion to the other, he could not feel anything where he was. Of the original Sidi Bashir's Mosque, only the two tall, carved minarets remain, with the gate in between. According to one legend, the mosque was commissioned by one of Ahmed Shah's slaves, Sidi Bashir. According to our rickshaw driver, Amir Khan, Sidi Bashir was from Africa; in Gujarat, "Sidi" refers to a member of the people who came from Africa. After the earthquake of 2001, climbing up to the top of the minarets was prohibited, the stairs having been closed off, and so there is not much else to see. The British had removed a brick from the structure, informs Amir Khan, and sent it to England to check it for hidden springs or other evidence of a mechanism that might make the minarets shake. The same way they stole the Kohinoor diamond, he adds.

As we leave the shaking minarets, we see rising from behind the buildings two similar tall brick minarets. According to local legend (that is, Amir Khan), these are the original minarets of the Jama Masjid, carried to the railway station by magic one night. We stop at a dargah close by, where is buried a saint called Kalu Sayad Pir. The place is right behind the station, and across from it are railway offices. It dates back to ancient times, according to a simple-looking old shaikh who meets us. The original stone structure has been covered with tile, but still manages to peer out in places. According to the shaikh, the visible structure is only part of the site, the rest is underground and sealed off now by the government for security reasons, for there are passageways extending a couple of miles right beneath railway property.

The man is soft-spoken and unassuming, and his presence has managed to create a lingering impression on us. He is short and scrawny, barefoot, with a long scraggly beard on a longish face; he wears a cap, a long white shirt over a green dhoti, and a checkered red and white cloth thrown around the shoulder like a shawl. He says the pir has no family member looking after his shrine; he himself is a volunteer and has been serving here for fifteen years.

What did you do before? asks Mahesh.

With a thin, diffident smile, the man turns stiff and answers in perfect monotone English, Please don't ask me this question.

We are astonished. Mahesh is thoroughly embarrassed, holds his ears in the traditional demonstration of shame, apologizes profusely. We should not have presumed. Forgive us. My friend does tend to dramatize, but he is sincere in his apology.

But the shaikh is forgiving, asks us to sit down on the stone bench next to the wall of the verandah outside the burial room. When we tell him why we are so shamelessly inquisitive, he bends his reserve and says softly that he worked for many years with the *Times of India*, in several cities. He was a special correspondent with his own byline. His name is Rahim.

He orders tea, sits between us. In his soft voice he tells us, to our further astonishment, that he was born in London, where he was partly brought up. His father was a doctor, a graduate of Bombay University, and was sent to England by the British government. What stories lie buried in this simple biography. What complexity in this simple-looking, humble man who humbles us in turn. One day he simply decided to give everything up and serve this ancient grave and its mosque. Perhaps some calamity befell him. He is not going to say. And we are not going to ask. But this truism keeps playing on my mind, as it has many times before: This country that I've come so brazenly to rediscover goes as deep as it is vast and diverse. It's only oneself one ever discovers.

According to Rahim, there was once a Marwari woman who was possessed. Every day, leaving her child to the mercy of the blazing sun, she would perform her antics before the Kalu Sayad dargah, leaping and somersaulting from early in the morning till three in the afternoon. One day, the child died of exposure, but the woman paid no heed to it; the people and the police finally got the woman to realize that the child was dead and that if it was not disposed off, the dogs and crows would eat the body. That broke her trance, and she began to grieve. She picked up the child's body and flung it towards Kalu Sayad's grave, shouting, "You called me, and I came. What wrong did my child do?" At this point the child began to cry, very much alive.

The somewhat Bollywood logic of the story eludes me, but obviously it means a lot to Rahim and to the people who have gathered here as we are finishing our tea. It is late afternoon, and the men and women have come to pay respects to the pir in his inner room, and Rahim, the former *Times of India* correspondent and son of a wealthy doctor, gets up to cut open a coconut and hand the two halves to a devotee, who will offer it to the pir.

There are actually two inner rooms, one an anteroom, the other the burial room. The former has niches in the walls and the grilles at the windows are stuffed with coloured cloth fragments left by devotees, especially the women. The burial room has a dome built on a typical octagonal structure and lavishly decorated on the inside. The dargah has evidently received some handsome donations from its worshippers.

Outside the shrine a few men have gathered to sit on their haunches and chat. They wave us over, tell us to go see the shaking minarets. A short distance from them, sitting on the ground against a wall, is a dark woman with a pathetic, beseeching look on her face, apparently begging, a disconcerting reminder of the Marwari woman of Rahim's story. There is no child.

Making inquiries of the men, we head off towards the main road on foot and find the entrance to the station. A train is about to depart from the nearest track, and an announcement is coming over the loudspeaker, but the crowd is not too heavy. Across from the train in an enclosed compound next to an office, two tall brick minarets rise in isolation directly from the ground. It's an uncanny sight, and it seems as if the rickshaw driver's story is correct, that the towers of the ancient Jama Masjid had flown through the air by magic and landed at this place. But short fragments of wall attached to either minaret reveal the obvious fact that they were part of the entrance to a mosque that existed right here. And indeed the entrance can be seen to have faced east-west, as required.

From here, Amir Khan takes us past a dead industrial area full of defunct cotton mills (the industry died with the advent of synthetics) to the Asarwa area to look at a vav, or step-well, a deep stone construction of several storeys in which you go down a series of steps to the level of the water. It and the mosque beside it are under the protection of the Archaeological Survey of India but carry no description and are in utter neglect. At the entrance to the well, on facing walls are two inscriptions, one in Arabic, the other in a Nagari script. Outside, boys, some of them actually young men, enthusiastically play cricket.

The sun has set, the street lights are on, and we sit like two vagrants on a sidewalk at a busy intersection in the Astodia area, hundreds of autos and motorcycles passing us by the minute, spewing thick, choking exhaust into the air. At times such traffic reminds me of a rushing torrent, at other times of a buffalo charge. You cross at your peril. There are other intersections, here, where in the evening the signals are off, and the traffic simply, miraculously, proceeds in all four directions simultaneously.

We are waiting for one Johnny Jacob to return from work and talk to us. He looks after the Ahmedabad synagogue across the road.

The Magen Abraham synagogue of the Bene Israel Jews is a tall, solid structure that stands out from its neighbours by its size and its typical, though modest, temple architecture. It was built in 1934. Its main entrance, kept closed, is on a narrow street, across from a Parsi agiary, or prayer house, and settlement. The facade is adorned on the left and right with Jewish motifs and panelled windows, a tall front arch in the centre embraces the entrance, leading between two columns on either side into the recessed porch and the door. According to my reading there are four thousand members of the community in India, though a few decades ago there were as many as thirty thousand.

Further up the street from us is the entrance to the busy market for vegetables and fruits, where people of all backgrounds mingle. Mr. Jacob's apartment is on the main road, behind an open unpaved space that seems to have become a parking area for autorickshaws, though there is a solitary bench in the middle. An old man wearing a kippa, at the behest of Mrs. Jacob, had earlier opened the side door of the synagogue for us, assuming, we soon realized, that we were from Israel. Past this entrance, in the corridor leading inside to the prayer hall, we saw plaques commemorating donations, including one from an association of Indian Jews in Israel. On the notice board were announcements for a Jewish camp in Israel, a book launch, and a film series with *Fiddler on the Roof* and *Samson and Delilah* on the program.

Mr. Jacob has still not arrived. Behind us where we sit is a makeshift road shrine, now preparing to close. A board with some announcement on it is taken inside, the floors are washed. It's a simple shrine, a small room. We take a rickshaw back to our hotel.

India has had four prominent Jewish groups, the Bene Israel, the Cochin, the Sephardic (European), and the Baghdadi (from the Near East). There is also a fifth group from the east, called the Manipuri Jews, whose Jewishness has been disputed by some rabbis. The Bene Israel claim to be descended from the tribes of Israel, their ancestors having been shipwrecked off the Konkan coast of Maharashtra more than two thousand years ago. According to the tradition, exactly seven couples survived and swam to the village of Navgaon, where they settled. From here the community spread to other places. They worked as oil-pressers, and because they did not work on the Sabbath they came to be called Shaniwari Telis, or Saturday Oilmen. Thus they fitted readily into the Indian caste system. They speak Marathi and have Marathi surnames. Many have emigrated to Israel in recent times, where apparently they were not initially readily accepted as Jews, until the rabbis decreed them as authentic.

We meet Mr. Jacob the next day at 3 p.m. He is waiting for us on his scooter outside the apartment building in front of the synagogue side entrance. His wife, whom we had seen last evening on her balcony, is fair, but he is darker, and small. His family has lived in the Ahmedabad area for a hundred years, he says. They still speak Marathi at home. This is the only synagogue in Gujarat. In Maharashtra, even villages had synagogues in the past. There are some 150 Jews in Ahmedabad, whereas there had been as many as 650. He lets slip that "Israel is our home," though he also quickly adds that he feels completely at home in India. Obviously, he could do better, materially. He runs a canteen in a school and goes to another job after that. He has a son and a daughter and is a vegetarian, though his family eats kosher meat. There is a local Jewish man who slaughters for them. One problem the community faces is that the only person who can do circumcision is an office worker in Bombay, who has to be brought in for the occasion. Jacob himself tried to learn the procedure when he was in Israel, but he was there only six weeks and the course lasted a full year. He can recite Hebrew prayers and read Torah, but he doesn't know the language. If they get ten people, a minyan, on Friday, they can say their prayers. They don't mind converting people to Judaism for the sake of marriage.

The above history of the Bene Israel is perhaps too easy, too clean. The oral tradition seems sparse, and one wonders about the written tradition, in any language. Two thousand years ago, India was a very different place. In the first millennium, many groups migrated into India, integrating into its cultures and evolving with them; few if any carry memories of the migration, let alone admit to it. Buddhism was robust; it has almost vanished. Islam arrived over several centuries in a major way. The languages and cultures of today have evolved through long processes from those of the past. In what manner did the Bene Israel evolve, if they did arrive that long ago? How old are the earliest synagogues? Was this community of Saturday oilmen ever nominally Hindu?

Still, there is a range of theories as to who the Bene Israel, or the original immigrants, were.

An interesting story from the tradition of these Jews is the arrival of a scholar called David Rehabi sometime between the eleventh and fifteenth centuries. Rehabi is believed to be the great Jewish philosopher Moses Maimonides. He picked three men from the Bene Israel and taught them about Judaism; thus the revivification of this community as Jews began. The three men were called kajis, from the Arabic *qadi*, meaning a judge and scholar. Maimonides (1138–1204), as is well known, lived much of his life in Fatimid Egypt. By the nineteenth century, the Cochin Jews and the Baghdadi Jews had begun to interact with the Bene Israel and provided religious teachers for them. Christian missionaries also reinforced their Jewish identity and brought them into their English schools.

The Bene Israel have produced two well-known Indian writers: Nissim Ezekiel (1924–2004), one of India's major poets in English, and Esther David, who has written a lyrically evocative novel, *The Walled City*, about a Jewish girl growing up in old Ahmedabad.

David's novel brings vividly to life the area of Relief Road, Delhi Darwaza, and Khamasa in an impressionistic, finely detailed account of a Jewish girl coming of age in her extended family in a neighbourhood full of Hindus and Muslims as neighbours, domestics, and vendors. So closely does it stay to the lived experience that, remarkably, there is no awareness in it of the larger political movements of the nation or the state. It is not even dated, though the period it covers seems to be the 1950s and onwards. The children of the family go to convent schools—England and English ways, the legacy of colonial rule and patronage, are preferred—yet among members of the family there is also a yearning to belong and be like the others. The narrator, who is unnamed, wishes she were born a Hindu like her friend Subhadra: "I dread to tell him [her uncle Menachem] that I find the colourful and noisy Hindu temple an easier place to pray in." When she falls in love with Raphael, without actually speaking to him, instead of the Hebrew prayer, she murmurs a song to Krishna under her breath, as his lover Radha had done. Raphael is from the community of Baghdadi Jews, who are supposedly superior to the Indian, Marathi-speaking Bene Israel. There is a scarcity of Jewish partners and a fear of marrying cousins lest it lead to genetic defects in the offspring. There are the family oddballs, the family secrets. And the call of Israel plays constantly in the background. Throughout the novel there exists an underlying sense of hopelessness, as the community dwindles through death and departure. At the end of the novel, of the extended family two girls remain, now women, looking after their old folks. *The Walled City* observes not only the Jewish family, but also the larger community in the Ahmedabad it is set in. One of its most poignant moments occurs as Mandakini, a Jain girl whom Cousin Samuel loves, is taken away dressed like a bride, in a silver chariot pulled by white horses, in a procession led by musicians, to a place where her hair will be shorn and she will become a barefoot homeless nun.

Constantly in the novel there are hints of a certain lurking danger. Yet when that danger, a riot, materializes, four times to my counting, Esther David's reference to it is oblique, almost reluctant. They are simply bewildering events, the murders and rapes carried out by mysterious strangers: "I think Ahmedabad is . . . always throbbing with a sense of danger. . . . Swords are drawn. The creepers and flowers in the stone carving are dying. The walled city is under curfew. There are guns and rifles. Outsiders, say the newspapers, are creating the disturbances. . . . Doors locked. What is your religion? Who are you? From where do you come? We are burning in the fires of hell." No more.

Uncle Menachem decides to move to a housing colony with Parsis and Christians as neighbours. And then, some unspecified amount of time later: "The riots have erupted again and the poison creepers grow like huge fishing nets in the rivers and in lakes, devouring the last of the dying fish."

Emmanbaba, a relation, is found dead on a street, stabbed in the stomach.

Is the reticence about details simply a weariness of stating the obvious; or a fear of speaking out and becoming a target? *The Walled City* seems to have been a painful book to write, for more than one reason. When I called David, who still lives in Ahmedabad, to ask to speak to her about the novel and the neighbourhood in which it is set, she told me, There is nothing there. And she gave me the name of another person to call, who in turn directed me to Johnny Jacob.

⨾

In the vicinity of the synagogue, at a busy, hectic intersection on Sardar Patel Road, comes the small and elegant Rani Sipri mosque.

This is an old neighbourhood of buildings of two and three storeys packed together, many showing signs of reconstruction or extension, some abandoned, others falling apart. Gates lead off into enclosed areas, the famous Ahmedabad pols, residential "micro" neighbourhoods of the poor variety. Traditionally, however, the pols provided security during riots to a community linked by caste, faith, or profession.

A small iron gate opens into the mosque site, which consists of a water tank in front, behind which, up some steps on a raised platform, are the mosque, on the left, and across the yard from it, the mausoleum of the queen, Rani Sipri. Both buildings are of red stone. The mosque, commissioned by Rani Sipri, widow of Mahmud Begada, was built in 1514 and is called "masjid-e-nagirna," jewel of a mosque, for its beauty, very much evident in the fine tracery on the outer walls and minarets, the intricate see-through latticework of the windows, and its proportions. The mosque is a shallow space, with three domes, three doors, two minarets. The mausoleum is padlocked, opening only at certain hours. From outside, looking into the dark shade of the room, lighted only by the rays filtering through the latticework, we see the single raised tomb of the queen, covered with a large red and a smaller green chaddar. The queen's burial chamber serves also as a storage space; there is a pile of mattresses on the floor, rolled mats, and metal kitchen and eating ware for communal meals.

Outside on the road, the traffic streams by, but the sound hardly intrudes here on the raised level of the mosque. A handful of people are about, a few walk in from the street past the small wrought-iron gate. It's close to prayer time. The azaan pierces the air; two cats go chasing after a chipmunk who runs up the tracery of the mausoleum wall. The Arabic cadences of the call to prayer linger high above us, but the voice is of a young man standing a few feet away, in clean and pressed white kurta-pyjamas and cap, a hand to his ear, reciting into an ancient microphone fixed to a pillar. On the next pillar, a sign in Gujarati asks, Did you switch off your mobile?

As we walk out, more people trickle in from the street. A woman sits on the steps begging.

A little further up the road an odd sight meets the eye: two round ancient-looking domes perched over otherwise quite ordinary squat, drab buildings. Between the two domes is a stone gateway, from which a narrow road leads into a pol. From one side of the gate a flight of stairs leads up to what I presume is a lookout post from bygone times, because there is a window at the top. The road branches inside into two narrow cluttered streets, the odd man sitting outside, women hanging out clothes or cleaning grain, resting on cots or stretched out on the ground. Boys and girls of various young ages run around happily, playing cricket with a bat no more than a foot long and a plastic ball. They pause in their play, watch us, big smiles on their faces. The adults look up curiously. We ask them what the domes signify, had there been a temple or a mosque here? No one has an answer. We walk back towards the gate.

One of the domed buildings opens onto the main road and is used as a tire shop. The other one does not open to the front; behind it, however, is a modest residence, with a little verandah with a cot, and on the wall above it small coloured prints of Ganesh and two other deities. At the end of the verandah, and opening presumably into the inside of the dome, is a shut door, on which is stuck a small printed symbol, an open palm. There comes a nonplussed look on Mahesh's face. Wait, I tell him, with a mysterious smile. I have been here before, and it was to show him this place with the domes that I dragged him all the way from Rani Sipri mosque, promising him a surprise.

The door opens after some minutes, and a man in his sixties appears, a wiry fellow with a bristly white beard all over the face. He is wearing a Muslim cap, and a long shirt and trousers, all white. He comes out with twinkling eyes and smiling. Greeting us, he says he's been saying the namaz, the Muslim prayer. He is a follower of Imamshah. He takes us inside to his room. What I see there stuns me.

Two years ago, the door had been similarly closed, and just as today, the man had come out and bade me come in. There was at that time in this room a small personal shrine to Imamshah in the corner just behind the door, consisting of a picture of the Imamshah shrine in Pirana, a lamp, an Imamshah symbol—the open palm—and other items. It was decorated with a series of multi-coloured festival lights. The man told me he had two names, Mohan and Akbar, that he was a Thakur by caste and a Parmar, descended from the kings of Gujarat. The room was quite dark and dingy, as it is now.

It was uncanny, this experience. Imamshah was hardly a major character known to all, like Kabir, Mira Bai, and Sufis like Nizamuddin of Delhi. I had no doubt that, were I to inquire, there would not be a soul walking outside on the road who would know the name. What was the probability that in this great bustling city, of all the roadside shrines here, I would walk into one I could directly relate to? Was this man a Hindu or a Muslim? He did not have to be exclusively one or the other, as his two names vouched, and according to the original Imamshah tradition. But for me, here was an example of how a holy man of the past could be reinvented and assimilated, how a tradition could be modified into a personal faith in total disregard to the orthodoxies that dictated to and bullied the masses. How contradictory and mysterious India could be.

And now, with Mahesh beside me? The shrine I had seen then is still here, but on the ground before it is something new: a small—a mini—grave covered with a green chaddar. On top of it are small stuffed animals looking like donkeys or horses.

Akbar-Mohan now says his two names are Akbar and Madhav—the latter of course is a form of Mohan, both are names of Krishna.

He tells us that he visits the Rani Sipri mosque to pray and he has a guru in Pirana who is a sayyid, a descendant of the Prophet. So is the man a Muslim now? Worshipping stuffed animals is as un-Islamic as you can be. And there are the two names. Is it a coincidence that Akbar is also the name of the Mughal emperor who conceived of a universal Indian religion? But scruffy-looking Akbar-Mohan-Madhav does not seem to be a man of lofty or regal thoughts.

We sit outside on the verandah, where Akbar-Mohan-Madhav offers us tea, which we are served in saucers. People come to his shrine, he informs us, bringing physical and mental ailments, and through "his" (I presume Imamshah's) mercy they get cured. A grandson lies quietly beside us on a traditional baby hammock, a ghodio. Akbar-Mohan-Madhav has two sons, who have decent jobs, he says. When he wanted his daughter to get married—he does not say when—money for expenses had appeared for him through "his" miracle.

And so this little branch shrine too has a commercial angle it did not have the previous time. And there's yet another angle.

The pol is entirely Hindu. This bit of information Mahesh, always the political animal, extracts from the man. No sane Muslim would live in an exclusively Hindu area in today's Ahmedabad. But this follower of Imamshah admits that the two domes could have had graves in them; one of them, the tire store, could well have been a mausoleum. In fact, he goes on, the area had been a Muslim graveyard before.

How did an ancient Muslim graveyard with a mausoleum turn into a Hindu residential area? The pol has a name, an attribute of Krishna that I will not reveal, written—as Mahesh shows me as we come back into the street—on a BJP poster, with the names of its patrons, well-known right-wing politicians, prominently upon it.

With politics part of the picture, this little shrine makes no coherent sense. The idea of a down-and-out Ahmedabadi inspired by the mystic Imamshah is wonderful, especially with his several names and mixed faith, even if he is also a rascal playing the money game. Mahesh, however, is convinced of the perfidiousness of Akbar-Mohan-Madhav; he must be an informer against the local Muslims, Mahesh says, in these times when every Muslim is considered a potential terrorist.

I tell my friend I prefer the unresolved enigma.

✐

After a long, hot day spent mostly on our feet, a treat seems to be in order. We decide to eat at the nearby upscale Agashiye, a vegetarian restaurant in the Teen Darwaza area, on the roof (as the name suggests) of a traditional home converted into a heritage hotel. As soon as you step off the elevator, you are invited first to sit inside a covered receiving room, a mandap of sorts, on low seats with bolsters for the back. In this formal ambience, with little time wasted, the starters are brought—a delicate sherbet of fudina and kothmir, with dhoklis and daal bhajias accompanied by exquisite imli and fudina chutney—after which you are taken to the open terrace for the main meal. Our longing for a cold beer on this hot night soon disappears as the food and accompanying drinks are consumed. There is the chaas with jeera, delicate, and endless; spicy hot daal for drinking; kadhi for drinking and to top the khichdi with; gobi muttar, tori patra that tastes like bhindi, pakri (rice bread), chila, gajar halwa. Nothing is overspiced, too sweet, or coarse; the courses are endless, but discreetly so. The servers come like Gandhis, wearing dhotis under long white shirts and white pandit caps. To conclude the meal, badam-pista ice cream, paan, and chai. A convincing answer to those who maintain that vegetarian fare is boring, plebeian, or at best merely homely. The night is clear, an almost full moon is in the sky. Other tables are occupied by noisy middle-class families. The talk is of business, and my academic Punjabi companion grumbles good-naturedly; business talk is one of those stereotypical Gujarati characteristics, the others being that they eat well, like sweets, and are miserly.

✂

Across the bridge from the old city, on Ashram Road, which runs beside the Sabarmati river, is the site of Gandhi's first ashram, named after the river. The road is a mix of residences and businesses, which stop a little way before the ashram, now the Gandhi Museum, opened in 1963 by Nehru, who planted an ashok tree at the gate. A couple of kiosks outside are the only signs of business in the area. The place is quiet and shady, has the feel of a university campus on a summer's day. There are a couple of rooms with somewhat patronizing tutorial-style questions and answers about Gandhi's philosophy displayed on the walls. The questions are posed in three languages, and below each one is its answer, a saying of Gandhi. The quotations are pithy, of course; and some of them are shown in enlarged specimens of Gandhi's handwriting. A room contains almost life-sized and vivid paintings depicting important episodes from Gandhi's life, for example the Salt March to Dandi, which gives the impression that Richard Attenborough and Ben Kingsley might have spent some time doing research here for their epic film on the Mahatma. The exhibition, and the film, spend little time on the personal side of Gandhi's life; this messier and personally painful aspect is depicted in a more recent and quite gripping Indian film, *Gandhi, My Father*, about the tragedy of his eldest son, Harilal, who started out by ably assisting his father in the South African struggles. A gift shop sells a few books and kitschy Gandhiana; for example, a pen with Gandhi's head at the top.

The residences from Gandhi's time, including his own with his few possessions, including his spinning wheel, have been preserved close to the river. The houses, of a red brick coated with white plaster, the wood all red, look plainly handsome and sturdy. Ashok trees proliferate, with some palm and peepal. Langurs sit quietly in the shade.

There are only a few people about, this weekday. A Japanese girl sits in the Mahatma's verandah learning to use a spinning wheel.

An altogether simple but necessary experience, and a moving one.

The well-known sweetmeat shop Kandoi's has been in operation since the 1840s, and now you can also order over the Internet. My companion has a new obsession—his in-laws, now that his daughter is marrying, and he has to bring back something for them. We had sweetmeat shops in East Africa, of course, and our mothers also somehow found the time to make all variety of sweets, when not tending to shops, teaching, or cooking meals. But the display here is bigger than anything I've seen, and there are specialty items, too; churma laddoo, for example, which I had not expected to see again in my lifetime. Mahoob and I taste the samples placed without question or hassle before us and make our selections, and we emerge with more than two pounds of goodies, in beautiful gift boxes wrapped up in silver paper.

Road to Road: The Places We Came From

Have I come back in truth to my home island?
HOMER, *The Odyssey XXIII*

A FEW PLACES IN GUJARAT were sometimes mentioned in my childhood, and I knew they were the places where my people came from. They included the city names Jamnagar and Junagadh, and Mandvi and Mundra. For some reason the names of the latter two cities were often twinned with the region in which they belonged. Thus: Kutch-Mundra, and Kutch-Mandvi. The other two were in nearby Kathiawar. Kutch and Kathiawar make up the elephant-ear-shaped peninsula in western Gujarat, and are separated by the narrow Gulf of Kutch. Kutchis and Kathiawaris did not intermarry, my mother would say, a taboo which was gradually lifting in my time; their languages were related but different, though some families, including mine, were bilingual. Bombay, in addition, was always a presence in our imaginative lives; it was the city of the movies. For the Africans, Bombay was the metonym for India. For the Indians, it was the port you left from and to which you returned, if you ever did. Many did, on "home leave," the long periodic vacation that was an entitlement when in government service. Any further details would have slipped my child's mind, which looked to the future and away from both the colonial present and the Indian past. But these names carried the ring of ancestry and origins, just enough to live by, in the embrace of East African small towns and cities that allowed us, and other Indians, to retain wholesome but not static identities. From the seashore of Dar es Salaam, I could look northeastwards to India without wishing to live there.

During my initial visits to India, it was enough for me to say that my ancestry was Indian, or Gujarati; the precise locations carried no importance or urgency. There were no relations I knew of, so what would I look for? And where exactly? I had a community, the Khojas, but how would I relate to them in India? I made one very brief exploratory visit to Jamnagar, when I did not yet know Gujarat outside Baroda. And, as I have said, what I did know of modern Gujarat since my first Indian visit made me nervous, so I always looked elsewhere, where I felt comfortable and had formed close friendships.

A tour of Kathiawar remained pending, until I was ready for it.

This time I come armed with a more precise knowledge of ancestral coordinates, gleaned from an accidentally discovered second cousin and from my mother. From the cousin I have learned the name of the village near Junagadh from where our great-grandfather came; and my mother has told me the name of a small town near Jamnagar from where her own mother came. I have two companions with me. They come with cameras, which can be intrusive; but they can also open up possibilities, for in my experience Indians (unlike the Masai of my youth) do not suspect the camera of robbing them of their personalities but rather love it, sometimes to the point of stealing into the frame. Perhaps that is the influence of Bollywood.

But before we head westwards for ancestral places in the peninsula, there is a detour to make, to another city I would hear of in childhood, in a few of the ginans we sang. It was called Patan. To those willing to listen to the meanings of those songs, Patan was the city where the king lived. One such monarch was the famous

Jaisingh Siddhraj. Patan's other ancient name was Anhilvada, I read much later, along with all its history and legends.

From the bus depot in Baroda we hire our taxi.

><

The glory of Anhilvada reached its zenith during the reign of the Solanki dynasty (942–1242), and especially in the reign of its greatest king, the legendary Siddhraj (1094–1143).

Of Anhilvada at its height, Alexander Forbes quotes the *Kumarapala Charitra*:

> Unhilpoor [Anhilvada] was twelve coss in circuit, within which were many temples and colleges; eighty-four squares; eighty-four market-places with mints for gold and silver coin. . . . There was one market-place for money changers; one for perfumes and unguents; one for physicians; one for artisans; one for goldsmiths and another for silversmiths; there were distinct quarters for navigators, for bards, and for genealogists. The eighteen wurun [varna, or castes] inhabited the city; all were happy together. The palace groaned with a multitude of separate buildings—for the armoury, for the elephants, for horses and chariots, for the public accountants and officers of state. Each kind of goods had its own custom-house, where the duties of export, import, and sale were collected—as for spices, fruits, drugs, camphors, metals, and everything costly of home or foreign growth. It is a place of universal commerce. . . .The population delights to saunter amidst the groves of champas, palms, rose-apples, sandal trees, mangoes, etc, with variegated creeper, and fountains whose waters are umrut [amrat, or ambrosia]. Here discussions take place on the Veds, carrying instruction to the listener. There is no want of Jain priests, or of merchants true to their word and skilled in commerce; and there are many schools for teaching grammar. Unhilwara is a sea of human beings.

This great city was conquered by the army of Alauddin Khilji of Delhi in 1297; Anhilvada remained the capital of Gujarat for another hundred years, though shorn of its prestige, before the capital moved to Ahmedabad.

Alexander Forbes, having described the glory of Anhilvada in his nineteenth-century *Ras Mala*, relates thus the state in which he saw it:

> Of all this splendour, it is melancholy to relate, hardly a vestige remains. The relics of Anhilvada lie in a flat country within and around the walls of the modern city of Patan . . . six centuries and the fury of the Mohammedans have done their work. . . . [A]nd the poor cold ashes of Anhilvada are sold for a pitiful gain by her vulgar Maratha lords, ignorant as they are alike of her glory and of their own dishonour.

Now Patan is a small, dusty market town in a flat, arid landscape. The once-famed Sahasralinga Talav, the water tank with a thousand Shiva lingams, is a forlorn rectangular basin amidst a grove of small trees, with a few structures outside, a few inside. There is not another visitor in sight as we walk about its edges, our driver waiting impatiently for us, having given only a cursory glance at the object of our interest. The tank was built by Jaisingh Siddhraj. The king is said to have become enamoured of a beautiful woman of the low-caste Oduns who had excavated the tank, and when he pursued her as she tried to escape, she plunged a dagger into her belly, putting a curse on his tank. The tank dried up, and the curse was lifted only upon the sacrifice of an outcaste Dhed. The Rani ni Vav is another ancient ruin here, but more intact. It is a step-well of several storeys and elaborate structure, so intricately carved that there's not an inch that is not a piece of art. Some of the carved female figures are also preserved, the sense of perfect beauty embodied in them—the curvaceous body, the round, tight breasts, the long, sharp nose, the wide-drawn eyes, and the provocation in the mouth—truly awesome. There are a few city gates left from ancient times, but not a trace of the royal palace, the houses of the nobles, the fortresses. To see what these might have looked like, Forbes advises us to look at the few ruins in some of the other cities.

The town is perhaps better known now for the hand-operated looms that make the famous weave called Patan Patola, using silk threads and natural dyes derived from plants, minerals, and insects. These enterprises are run by a few old families, known as the Salvis, brought from south India centuries before. A line I was taught to sing, to say that the body may break but the devotion of the faithful will not yield—"*Paadi, paadi patole bhaat-re, teto faate parn-re fite nahi, ho-ji*" ("The patola will tear, but its print will not fade")—is also, I see to my great surprise, pasted on a board in the factory which we visit. It is a modest enterprise, one or two looms operating, the dyes or raw materials kept in small bottles. The Patola saris, with their intricate designs, often using a lot of red and black, take days to finish, and the clientele of this humble-looking establishment is worldwide. You could not give a bride— or bring home for your wife—a better present than a Patola sari.

Thus Patan, which I had been craving to visit. Only scraps to see. A sobering discovery. There is nothing else to keep us here. We head west, towards Jamnagar on the Gulf of Kutch, in the Arabian Sea.

><

The land is hot and dry, with little cultivation on the way; trees sometimes shading the quiet road; camels, cows, trucks. Often on such journeys, between places, there comes a numbness in the mind, for the places we have visited cannot but leave their echoes behind. Inevitably there are questions, regrets—perhaps we should have tarried. But there is not enough time. We are pinned by our reservations, on trains, on planes. There is never enough time.

A short distance west of Patan we stop at the Sun Temple of Modhera, built by the Solanki king Bhimdev in the early eleventh century, before the reign of Siddhraj, and akin to the Sun Temple at Konark in Orissa. The Modhera complex consists of a rectangular water reservoir called the Surya Kund, which leads up to an unattached mandap, directly before the temple, all three built of red sandstone and aligned with one another. The domes of the temple and mandap are missing, though the rest of the buildings stand almost intact, solid on the ground and exquisitely carved. The steps of the surya kund, along all its four sides, are relieved with small shrines placed along them at regular intervals, and aligned so as to form a checkered pattern, and in addition to these, larger, spired shrines stand at the centres of three sides.

This site is used to hold festivals, but all is quiet as we walk around.

Further on our way we stop at a place called Becharaji, known for its famous Kali temple. Praying to the goddess (in the form of Bechar Mata) at this temple is believed to cure ailments. Numerous people are about, the road in leads through a gauntlet of stalls, the atmosphere as festive as that of a country fair, loud religious music playing over the loudspeakers. Vendors converge upon us, holding out little aluminum squares impressed with the shapes of human body parts; you pick the one that represents the diseased or aching part of your body to take as your offering to the temple. I will learn later that this tradition is relatively modern and may even have been imported from overseas. Ever the agnostic, I cannot resist participating in ritual, and buy an impression of two legs for the sake of my knees.

Outside the temple, in a large covered mandap, some priests conduct a ritual over a havan, a holy fire, blessing a harvest. The temple itself is multicoloured in oil paint, with an imposing porched entrance, and does not look ancient. It was in fact built—presumably on an older site—by Sayajirao, the maharaja of Baroda, in whose domain this region, Mehsana, was located. Inside the temple, we find Bechar Mata, plump, surrounded by flowers, sitting on the back of an elephant.

An interesting story is told regarding this temple. When the sultan of Delhi, Alauddin Khilji, attacked the area in the thirteenth century, informers told him about the wealthy temple of Kali at Becharaji. He dispatched there a contingent of his army, presumably to loot and destroy. Some of his soldiers, seeing the goddess's chickens in the grounds, summarily slaughtered and ate them. At night, however, these chickens tore at the bellies of the slumbering soldiers and emerged alive and clucking. Alauddin's commander was duly impressed, and he departed, leaving the temple unharmed.

Alauddin Khilji himself never came to Gujarat, of course. But his name as the conqueror is still remembered seven hundred years on.

I come out of the temple hoping the best for my knees.

There is another small temple to Kali at the side of the main one. It is sacred to everyone, of course, but especially to the pavayas, the eunuchs. There are three of them about, calling to us, one of them slim, long-faced, and pretty, wearing a black dress patterned with yellow flowers and a stud in the nose; he seems about thirty. Of the other two, one seems fifty or thereabouts, says he came here forty-five years ago; and the third one is old and wrinkled, silent. If you give them money, they bless you to produce boys. These pavayas were presented to Kali, or the temple, as young boys, when the "call" came for them. The pretty one had no parents when called. Perhaps the boys are consecrated when they arrive, perhaps abused. They brazenly ask us for money, of course—it seems to be expected of them—in their typical teasing, mischievous manner. Give us some American or Japanese coins, the pretty one says, moving his head from side to side, flashing a smile, eyes atwinkle. This is their public life, a performance—calling out to the people, clapping hands sharply in the characteristic manner of their kind.

What usually gives pavayas away is the slightly overdressed and overmade-up look to them, the false jewellery. The younger one is dressed this way, but if I did not already know otherwise I would swear the older two were just ordinary women.

The story about this little temple (which is essentially a stall), through which an ancient tree grows, is that once in ancient times two local kings took vows that their expected children would be married to each other. Unfortunately both children were born girls. One of the kings decided to mislead the other and ever since her birth dressed his child as a boy. The wedding day approached. Someone discovered the groom's secret and reported it to the bride's father, whose wedding party then demanded that the purported boy be seen undressed before the ceremonies proceeded. Meanwhile the child, upon passing the site of the temple, where there was a spring at the time, saw a bitch bathe in it and emerge a dog; a female horse similarly turned into a male one. And so the princess took a dip in the spring and came out a prince and was happily married.

Bhajans of the Kathiawari style blare out from speakers in the long line of stalls outside the temple gate; the food stalls display colourful mounds of gathias, jelebis, bhajias freshly removed from the fryers. We buy gathias for some children and an old woman and sit down and have our own meal. Then we depart, one Ashok Goswami blaring out of our tape deck.

The dhabas on the way are simple shacks with charpais in front to sit on, or sticky tables and wobbly chairs and benches inside. Outside, a standpipe sometimes for a wash, a car or truck parked. Tea is instantly made fresh on smoky stoves, with minimal tea and plenty of sugar. The fare consists of rich paranthas, vegetable curries, and here in Kathiawar, the specialty, looking so homely—the bajra (millet) roti, a thick, grey, and granular version of the usual refined wheat roti that only a Gujarati can consume. When I was young bajra roti (called rotlo, perhaps because of its masculine coarseness) was the poor man's bread, which you had with a simple curry or even just yogurt. You could make a laddoo with it, after mixing it with green garlic and ghee, to have with yogurt. We did not like it. My mother would say that when she was little the wheatflour white roti was so exceptional a treat in her home in Mombasa that the children, and they were plentiful, would cry out in joy when it was available. Now the grey, unwieldy bajra roti is a delicacy. The children still don't like it. Here the dhaba serves it with an oily, spicy curry of a simple vegetable, eggplant or squash perhaps, and the local kadhi, the tangy curry made with mustard seed and yogurt, thickened with chickpea flour, which is drinkable and quite different from the dumpling-filled thick Punjabi karhi of the north.

As we approach Jamnagar we see devout-looking Muslim young men walking beside the road outside some of the towns, dressed in long white robes and caps, bearded, and holding Qurans or readers in their hands. I recall having been to a Khoja village outside Jamnagar some years before, and so we stop and ask some of these men if there are any Khojas in the area. We are outside a village called Dhroll, and the young men, returning from a Muslim school, a Dar-ul-ulum, tell us, yes, there are some Khojas here.

We turn in to Dhroll, a rather drab-looking place with broken dirt roads, garbage heaps, and very modest shops and houses. What do people do in such a place? They perhaps go to the city to work, or sell things from handcarts on the road; and they service local needs. We ask around about the Khojas and are pointed to a small paan stall. Again the simple trust, the familiarity. The young man behind the window treats us each to a paan at once and directs us up the busy street. People stop to gape at us. Finally we arrive at a small but busy shop selling small grocery items through the open front. We sit or stand outside and chat with the Khoja owner sitting on the ground at the doorway, who tells us there are some hundred people in the community here. Presently a man comes strolling by, having heard we are in the town. He is the local kamadia, the assistant Khoja headman, and he walks us to his home, which is reached through a small alley.

The front yard of the house is strewn with metal junk, car parts and the like, attended to by a young Muslim in a beard. Some substantial business evidently goes on here, explaining the high local status of the head of the house. But the house, a suite of rooms side by side, is modest and dark and cluttered. There are a few women about and a man. I am told that all the Khojas in the town are of the Somani clan. I recall that the name comes from the Sanskrit, referring to the soma juice and also to the moon. A girl has recently got married, will soon be off to Kinshasa with her husband. Kinshasa, despite the bloody situation in the Congo, seems to be the new Eldorado, the frontier; people have also gone to Maputo, in Mozambique, and Kampala. All these places in Africa were recently devastated and are in need of small entrepreneurs. When I was in Nairobi once, I was told about such entrepreneurs, who were introducing simple items like soap in Uganda after the ravages of Idi Amin. A hundred years ago, Zanzibar was the Eldorado for enterprising Gujaratis from the peninsula escaping a dreadful famine; they went also to Mombasa, Bagamoyo, Dar es Salaam. One of the women here is on a visit from the village of Khoja Gaum, which I now recognize as the town I had visited nine years before. It is on the other side of Jamnagar.

I am taken now inside a room to meet a hundred-year-old woman. The exact number of her years is perhaps not to be taken too seriously. She lies in her bed against a wall, a shrivelled little woman with a deeply worked small face, extremely fair. Ma's brother died four months and a few days ago, I am told. Much to my astonishment, I am also informed she has been to Dar es Salaam, was in Zanzibar during the war, though she can't tell me which one, and no one else knows. She returned here after her husband died. My hosts ask me to say something in the African language of "there," to humour her, and to their delight I say, "*Jambo, Ma*," a simple "How are you?" in Swahili. "Ma, did you hear him? Say something in reply," the kamadia says. Remarkably, she's heard me and answers faintly, with a surprised look on her face, "*Jambo*," and explains to the others what it means. It's made their day. After all the stories of Africa she must have told them, now an authentication, walked in from the blue—or the dust, as it were.

We depart for Jamnagar, walking through an ancient stone gate on the way that, we are told, partly crumbled in the earthquake of 2001.

A couple of years later I read in a history of Gujarat that this obscure little town of the Somanis was where in 1592 the last independent sultan of Gujarat, as a captive of the Mughals following a campaign of resistance, alighted from his horse, went behind a tree, and slit his own throat.

><

If Jamnagar was the Indian city name I heard most often as a child (besides Bombay) this is hardly surprising when I see it. Parts of it bear an uncanny resemblance to the Indian section of·downtown Dar es Salaam when I was growing up. The low buildings, the tiled roofs on the older ones, the casement windows, the oil-painted green shutters and frames, the assorted shops—paan, snacks, tires, newspapers, a barber, a shoemaker. The names on the shops— Lakhani Shoes, Lalji Virji, Bhatia Stores, Rawji Jetha. And the easy pace of life in a city by the sea. All this is enough to make me nostalgic, imagine a boyhood here, traipsing off to school early in the morning, like the kids I now see on the sidewalks, or to khano in the evening. The only visible difference would be that I'd be swinging a satchel in my hand, while these kids carry backpacks. In Dar es Salaam, the buildings have been mostly torn down or reconstructed to produce ugly structures; streets are chaotic during the day and quiet at night. Here, before me, there is the typical Indian touch: bicycle and scooter, horse-drawn cart, Ambassador car, old bus, all in a row on the road. And in the manner of Indian cities, the streets are more chaotic at dusk, and brightly lit, when people come out to shop for groceries and other essentials.

The city was founded following a family feud in the royal house of Kutch, the region across the narrow strait from it. In 1535, Jam Rawal ("jam" meaning prince or king), having murdered an elder of the ruling clan, rather than fight his nephew (or cousin) who had sought assistance from the Mughal viceroy in Ahmedabad, crossed the strait into Kathiawar. This, according to a history of Kutch by James Burns, first published in 1839 and reissued in 2004. Five years after the crossing, the Jam founded the city of Navanagar, meaning "New City," which was renamed Jamnagar in the early twentieth century. The Jam, descended according to Burns from Rajput Muslims, though he was a Hindu, brought with him many families. This would explain why many people from this area, including my family, are bilingual, easily switching between Kutchi and Gujarati. Among the places conquered by the Jam was the town of Dhroll, which we visited on our way.

One of the greatest players ever of cricket was Ranjitsinhji (1872–1933), called Ranji, from Jamnagar's royal house. Starting out as a student at Cambridge, he played for both England and Sussex, his career lasting from the late nineteenth to the early twentieth century. It has been said, and often quoted, somewhat vaguely, that "when he batted, a strange light was seen for the first time on English fields." The Ranji Trophy, much coveted in India, is named after him.

It turns out that the hotel owners where we are staying are Muslims whose family came over to Saurashtra, or Kathiawar, with the Jam, and they speak Kutchi at home. Not only that, they have run dhows between Gujarat and East Africa for many decades; the business is still in operation, though now they carry only cargo and use an engine as well as the usual sail.

The young man who speaks to us, together with his father in the office, is in his twenties and intelligent and eloquent. He offers to take us to look at an old dhow being repaired. After about half an hour's drive, at a rather quiet part of the coast, we are welcomed by a short, dark, muscular man, with the weathered, scruffy face of an old sea dog. The dhow is nearby, and not very large. Painted black and white, with a gold streak, it stands propped up with logs on a patch of shore from where the sea water has been drained.

We follow the captain up a wooden ladder to the deck of the ship, clamber down into the hold. As we sit on makeshift benches, the captain orders tea, which comes in a kettle and is served black. The ship's hull is in the process of being repaired with new wood. The front has been cut away, and the sides will be extended to lengthen the ship from roughly forty to sixty feet. Where we sit, the owner's son tells us, is where the passengers would have been quartered for the duration of the voyage in olden times. The ship hands all speak Kutchi.

In such a dhow my paternal great-grandfather, Nanji Lalji, went to Mombasa, then proceeded to the interior of what is now Kenya. He settled in a trading village called Kibwezi and became the local mukhi. My maternal grandparents went to Zanzibar some years later. The journey would have taken about two weeks, and as far as I know, as for most other migrants, it was a one-way trip—though some men did return to marry, and they returned in style, newly wealthy. The old dhows were carried back and forth by the trade winds. The young man's father told us that pot makers (the kumbhad) would depart with their clay pots in little boats and let the trade winds take them to the East African coast, where they would sell their wares and return to Gujarat when the winds reversed. But many of the kumbhad did emigrate, and in Dar es Salaam they had their own settlement, or wadi, where as children we would go and buy clay from them to make models for school projects. Some of their descendants are now mechanics.

There is a very large oil refinery in the area, and my two companions, with cameras, are understandably nervous about being questioned by police and taken for Pakistani spies.

On our way out from Jamnagar we meet a young man at a gas station (or "petrol pump"), a Khoja who peddles stuff from his motorbike. Yes, he knows where the khano is. He leads us past a Hindu then a Shia area, through ever-narrowing and seemingly numberless gulleys, to the local khano, an old and rather grand structure at the end of the maze, looking rather out of place in an extremely poor, stench-ridden area. A couple of little shops are open selling small items and vegetables, goats stand perched on the ledges outside the closed doors of the homes. In the courtyard of the khano we meet an old woman who says she has a relation in Paris. She has the same family name as my mother's father; yet how is one to tell if we are related? A wedding took place here last night and the cleanup is in progress, along with the dismantling of the stage and decorations. A board on a wall announces upcoming events. Our guide presses us to come to his home for a meal, but we are late and depart on the road to Junagadh.

><

The village of Khoja Gaum, along an unmarked, unpaved side road off the main highway, looks more prosperous than I recall from before, when I saw it during a drought. Close to the entrance is a temple, a few people sitting idly outside it. We ask about the Khoja area and they tell us to keep going. After a couple of turns ahead, on rather neat but still unpaved roads, some kids inform us we've found it. We get out of our car, greet a few curious people who begin to gather. Talk to the kamadia, someone says, pointing to a man approaching. The kamadia, who could be in his mid-thirties, after the customary greeting begins to walks with me. We stare at each other. You look familiar, he says, curiously. I've seen you before. I tell him, Nine years ago? Of course!

Early one morning, I was at the Jamnagar bus station, inquiring about buses to Khoja Gaum, when a young man came up to me and said, I am going there, I will take you. We left together, and on the way, Nizar, which was his name, told me Khoja Gaum was one of a group of nine villages. He kept a motor scooter in one of them and every day rode to a few to teach the kids. The Khoja Gaum that I recall was poor, suffering a drought, but I had been treated well. The women wore saris, the men shirts over pants; I had been served tea in saucers at several houses, shown family albums. There had been old framed photos on the porches of the houses as well; in them, the women wore the odhani, which we called the pachedi, over their heads or shoulders, and I was surprised that the villagers did not know the term "pachedi." Their knowledge of ginans, our traditional hymns, also seemed rudimentary to me, a tradition which we in East Africa had been able to nourish. There had been a religion teacher of sorts, who had complained about village squabbles; his teaching material had been a couple of tattered books. All in all, I had met a rather dejected, hopeless-looking people, and I came away with the bitter impression that my parents' generation, having done much better in Africa than their kinfolk in Gujarat, had turned their backs on them. Not once do I recall hearing from them about cousins, aunts or uncles, grandparents in India.

I recall sitting in Nizar's local classroom. The children, ranging in age roughly between six and twelve and including Khojas and other castes, had sat before us on the floor, mesmerized by the apparition that I was. I was touched to see them recite the national anthem and a song in praise of Gandhi, to start with. Then Nizar gave them a lecture about who I was, where I came from, why I was one of them.

Now the village looks more prosperous, and Nizar is the kamadia, assistant headman. He tells me that after the earthquake of 2001 they received some assistance. He has moved into the village, is married, and has a child. He proudly takes me to look at three computers sent from Calgary by a well-wisher with past connections to the village. They are kept in a special room where young people receive computer training. There is a new khano beside the old one, which I had visited before. Then we go to sit in the yard of Nizar's house, an almost idyllic-looking area shaded by trees. Several men sit with us, on charpais and chairs, and the women hover at the edge, participating at times in the conversation. The fact that I am visiting a second time gives me a certain status. The local woman whom I had seen in Dhroll has returned.

A wedding is to take place, and some relations are in town for the event. I ask them what they know of the village history, and they look lost. Apparently, the man who could have told us has left for Rajkot; his mind is like a computer, he knows a lot. His brother is here, called Kassam. He is a strongly built man in his fifties, and he is from Porbandar; he wishes we could go there. There are many ways of speaking Gujarati, of course; these people, like the Somanis from Dhroll, speak in a manner familiar. It is a bantering style, informal, suited for discussions just such as this one. You heard it in the chai shops, outside apartments, outside the khano, at family gatherings. You still hear it, in Dar es Salaam, in Toronto.

Gradually, in the friendly, fraternal atmosphere that has emerged with my acceptance as one of these people, they open up and recollect.

They tell me their ancestors had come from Kutch with the Jam, who had given them this village for services rendered and consented to the description "Khoja" in its name. They can all speak Kutchi, of course, as a private language, though Gujarati is the formal language.

I ask about the town of Jam Jodhpur, where my maternal grandmother hailed from. The town apparently had been a local centre for Khojas, they tell me, but in recent times it has almost completely been abandoned by them.

Why was it abandoned? There were conflicts with the local Patels, Kassam says. One day they came in a horde and asked to check out the khano. They were told they could come, but in small groups. Fighting broke out, Kassam says, with relish. He happened to be visiting the town and was young and hot-blooded. And so he was drawn in and managed to beat up a couple of people. He had to leave town that same night, the Patels in hot pursuit bearing swords. He slipped onto a train awaiting to depart for Porbandar, and that is where he is settled now. I gather that he cannot go back to his town, because he would be found out. And of course I wonder how much of the story is true. This is the kind of chai gup-chup where embellishment is a *sine qua non*.

Khoja Gaum and its neighbours had once been Khoja villages. This comes as hugely surprising. In Africa we had been town folk without land, and here, to be told that we had land, entire villages, of our own; to discover that there is a way of speaking and bantering that I share so easily with the people before me. An elder from the local Patel community is brought to meet me, for, after all, I am a symbol of Khoja success and possibility. He is the former headman, the sarpanch, of the village, and is dressed in traditional white dhoti and turban, unlike the Khojas in loose-fitting shirts and trousers. The man confirms, yes, this was a Khoja place, his ancestors had been "nabda"—weak, in straitened circumstances—when they arrived, and they had been welcomed and assisted.

How a Khoja village then came to be dominated by Patels must be a story in itself. I can imagine lack of unity and foresight, perhaps the politics of post-Partition India. I recall the previous time hearing of a land conflict over a grave site. The drought had been crushing, people were ready to sell their land; some had taken to hawking on the highway and working in brass factories in the city. Now only a few of the Khojas own land.

A remarkable thing now happens as we sit chatting. Kassam once, then again, refers to a Kul Devi, the family goddess. My ears prick up, I ask him who this Devi is. It turns out his family has a goddess they call Mata, Mother. There is a shrine to her, here in the village. Can we see it? Off we go, the lot of us, to a relation's house; a few of us take off our shoes to enter a small room that faces the yard. A large number of people have gathered outside to watch.

On a wall hangs a brightly painted picture of a pretty Indian woman in sari. Her face is fair and long, her bosom pointed and pronounced. She has some jewellery on. The portrait is roughly eighteen by twelve inches and a garland hangs around it. Below is a niche in the wall stuffed with colourful ornaments, including what looks like a paper garland. This is where the Kul Devi resides.

From somewhere one of the men brings out a faded little picture in a metal mount grey with age, about an inch by an inch and a half in size. It is the original, and looks like nothing more than a trinket, perhaps a token in a cereal box some decades back. It was while family members were digging at this site that they found the little picture, and were convinced that it was of their Kul Devi and began to worship her. Then one day, Kassam says, in his relishing manner, he took it to a portraitist, bargained hard, and commissioned the copy which hangs on the wall. He paid four hundred rupees for it. How good a reproduction it is I cannot tell, I can hardly make out the original.

However crudely superstitious this looks, for me it is a marvel to witness yet again the persistence of old indigenous Indian traditions away from the eyes of stern orthodoxy or divisive modern ideology.

We cannot accept the villagers' enthusiastic invitations to stay for the wedding the next day, promising me a night under the stars; time is pressing, and we head out for Jam Jodhpur.

Jam Jodhpur, my maternal grandmother's birthplace, is indeed a disappointment. It is a featureless town with a main street of low brick buildings and not much else besides. We have an excellent thali, however, at a "lodge" on the main street, in the front room of an apartment on the second floor of a building. The inner room has two or three charpais without mattresses, on which the owner and his son sit, perhaps waiting to take a nap after we leave, for it is a little late. There are one or two Khoja families around, and across from the lodge we meet one at their home; their business is selling peanuts at a stall. The house is a nice bungalow, however, and we are invited to sit in the front living room, an enclosed verandah looking out on the main street. They have four daughters, two of them married away; of the two remaining, the older one is a beautician practising from the home. It's hard making ends meet, they say. There is a distinct feeling of having been left behind, with no extended family around anywhere to rescue them from their plight.

We head for Junagadh.

>◁

It is impossible not to feel a sense of wonder and exhilaration, driving by the coast, skirting the blue Arabian Sea under a bright sun, our young driver in his baseball cap and dark shades having quietly turned off our bhajans to play something more appropriate to his age. He is being indulged. And truly, there is no disappointment, everything is experience. What did I expect at Jam Jodhpur? I couldn't say, I had to see it. Dhroll and Khoja Gaum were an unexpected treat.

The countryside here is farming, there is no heavy industry as in the south; traffic is moderate, even absent at times. Junagadh lies some distance inland, but we decide to continue further down the coast to the southwestern tip of the peninsula, to visit the famous temple of Somnath, the political and historical significance of which cuts through from the tenth century to ours. Its reigning deity is Shiva, Lord of Soma, "the moon."

Past the dreamy little coastal town, once the thriving ancient port, of Veraval, comes an almost fairytale-looking place, an ornate white building shimmering in the distance. This is Somnath, the temple. Outside its gates the atmosphere is that of a funfair, buses unloading people, stalls selling all manner of items, vendors hawking postcards and mementoes. Long lines of pilgrims have queued up on the paved walkway through the lush green lawns to get the darshana of the lingam in the temple, a sandstone structure designed meticulously in the medieval style. But the overriding impression here is that of the clean, the new, the beautiful; indeed, this is a memorial to a destroyed ancient temple. For me it lacks the immediacy, the excitement, of the messier, dirtier, timeless temples such as the one at Puri, in Orissa. The visit inside, after a long queue to get in, is brisk and formal. Behind the temple lies a beach where visitors stroll about and children are at play. It is a peaceful scene; the policeman in khaki at the entrance could be one of the worshippers, the guns behind the sandbags at the outer wall could be part of the temple decor.

But they are not. What, then, is the story?

In 1026, Mahmud of Ghazna, in what is now Afghanistan, descended into Western India with a large army and plundered the wealthy and powerful temple of Somnath. The sacred lingam is said to have been crushed to pieces, vast amounts of gold and silver were taken away, along with the gates. Somnath's status was due to its strategic location, close to the important port of Veraval, which traded with places as far away as China, Arabia, and Zanzibar. Its most lucrative trade was in horses, and it counted among its residents a thriving community of Hindu, Muslim, and Jain businessmen, as well as priests, sailors, and others. At various times after Mahmud's attack, the temple was successively rebuilt by the Hindus and destroyed by the sultans and their armies, including Alauddin Khilji of Delhi.

In recent times Somnath has become a symbol and a rallying cry for militant Hindu nationalism. It was from Somnath in 1990 that L. K. Advani, a leader of the right-wing nationalist BJP, began his infamous Rath Yatra, a chariot procession, to end at that other "Muslim" insult, the mosque in Ayodhya built by the Mughal emperor Babur on the site claimed to be the birthplace of the god Rama. One of the aims of such yatras involving Somnath has been to unite diverse Hindus, including the lower castes, into a "Hindutva," a Hindu-ness. This would make alien minorities of all the others, beleaguered under a shrill, belligerent, and highly organized nationalism calling for a Hindu state. But India is not simple, it has a million parts. Diversity, even to the point of tolerating the bizarre (as I write this, the wedding of two monkeys is being celebrated somewhere), is its nature, and democratic secularism its strength. In contrast, Pakistan, Iran, and Saudi Arabia are Islamic states, hardly to be emulated.

But Somnath irks the nationalists, who are only too ready to take on the onus of collective shame and retribution on behalf of Hinduness, to the point of encouraging their wilder adherents, who went on the killing and raping rampages in the violence of 2002.

K. M. Munshi, a littérateur and politician, wrote in 1951, "For a thousand years Mahmud's destruction of the shrine has been burnt into the collective sub-conscious of the [Hindu] race as an unforgettable national disaster." Calling Hindus a race is in itself wrongheaded, doing away with regional, linguistic, and cultural differences across India, and overlooking the fact that the Muslims are as Indian as anyone else, with a diversity reflecting India's own. It is as if the Catholics of England were to be called a different race, or foreigners. Munshi made it a lifelong project in his Gujarati histories and romances to evoke the glories of pre-Muslim Gujarat, as idealized in the reign of the Solankis of Anhilvada. It would surprise—and perhaps offend—him that I take as much pride in Gujarat's past glories as he did. It was Munshi who led the drive to rebuild the temple, which was completed in 1951. It was a brand-new temple, the existing medieval structure having been completely dismantled in the service of the reconstruction, an act that in itself was controversial.

Munshi's plot-driven romances are continuously reprinted, still popular a hundred years after their first publication. They paint a pink picture of the past, in which the protagonists are all of the high castes and extremely conscious of that fact; they are observant, chaste, intelligent, brave, and chivalrous; even their Hindu antagonists have the same qualities. It is the Muslims who are barbarians.

Romila Thapar, a highly respected—and therefore also much vilified—liberal historian, in contrast to Munshi, provides a complex picture of Somnath in its heyday, and examines at the same time many of the interpretations of Mahmud's attack in the millennium that followed. Making extensive use of Persian and Arabic sources, Sanskrit inscriptions, Jain biographies, folk traditions, and other sources, Thapar gives us a Somnath that was a prosperous trade and pilgrimage centre, and a mixed community where Jains competed with Brahmins for ascendancy and Muslims were already present, living as merchants, sailors, and artisans who worshipped in their mosques. There is evidence of coexistence and mutual respect in the mercantile society of the pilgrim port: the building of a mosque by a Jain merchant for his trading partners from the port of Hormuz in the Persian Gulf; the striking of bilingual Arabic-

Sanskrit coins, some bearing the image of Shiva's bull, Nandi; a coin carrying the Muslim kalima in colloquial Sanskrit, "*avyaktam ekam muhammada avatara nripati mahamuda*," "the unmanifest is one, Muhammad is his incarnation and Mahmud is the king." (A remarkable illustration, incidentally, of how the Islamic faith could get transformed in the Indian context.)

Moreover, the temple and its pilgrims at this wealthy centre were already subject to plunder by pirates from the sea and by neighbouring Indian rajas. The attack on Somnath by Mahmud, says Thapar, was one event among many, in a complex historical situation. Post-1026 Sanskrit inscriptions written at or about Somnath do not mention Mahmud at all, raising questions about the actual magnitude of Mahmud's assault and its importance.

According to Thapar, it was the British who instigated the idea of the eternal wound on the Hindu psyche caused by Mahmud's attack, and sought, in the words of a parliamentarian in a House of Commons debate of 1843, to "relieve that country, which had been overrun by the Mohammadan conqueror, from the painful feelings which had been rankling amongst the people for nearly a thousand years"; a thought that Munshi echoes to the point of mimicry in his 1951 statement. With much fanfare the British brought from Mahmud's tomb in Ghazna sandalwood gates purportedly plundered by him from Somnath, only to have it be discovered that they were Egyptian in origin and could not have been from Somnath at all. They were quietly put away in a storeroom in Agra Fort, where they presumably rotted.

How important Mahmud's attack was and what it meant, over the millennium since, depended on who was telling the story. Any understanding of the event, insists Thapar, "should be historically contextual, multi-faceted, and aware of the ideological structures implicit in the narratives."

Nevertheless, while acknowledging the manipulation and selectiveness of memory and history in the service of chauvinism, communalism, and colonialism, the devastation of Mahmud is surely undeniable. What evokes wonder is how potent its memory is kept today. And not only by the Hindu nationalists: the Pakistan army has named its short-range ballistic missile "Ghaznavi"; that is, Mahmud of Ghazna.

⤬

Shortly before Junagadh, there comes a side road leading into a town called Paneli. Small and neat, Paneli is the ancestral home of Muhammad Ali Jinnah, the founding father of Pakistan. The birthplace of that other great leader, Mohandas Gandhi, who was so much against the Partition, is less than a hundred miles away. I know that Jinnah was a Khoja, though not a practising one. I can see a Khoja calling for Hindu-Muslim unity, as Jinnah earlier did— he had been one of the party who welcomed Gandhi back from South Africa in 1915—but how a Khoja could lead a bitter campaign for a Muslim homeland has always mystified me. What he really desired, however, and what he believed, are matters of intense controversy. Speaking to Pakistan's constituent assembly in August 1947, he said, "You are free; you are free to go to your temples, you are free to go to your mosques, or to any other place of worship in this State of Pakistan. . . . You may belong to any religion or caste or creed—that has nothing to do with the business of the State." This statement hardly describes an Islamic nation. He died an enigma, in 1948, barely a year after Independence. His wife, a Parsi, and his daughter, their only child, did not accompany him to the new state.

Jinnah's father's name was Jinnahbhai Punja Meghji (or Meghani), a typical Khoja Kathiawari name (*megha* means "cloud" in Sanskrit). Of Jinnah's Khoja background, his biographer Stanley Wolpert says, "Khojas fled Persian persecution to Western India, among other regions, between the tenth and sixteenth centuries."

There is no evidence of any sort whatsoever, in fact, of Khojas having fled from anywhere to India; it is well known in Gujarat that
they are from the Lohana and Bhatia castes. This is what the
Lohanas say; it is what other Jinnah historians say; it is what is
told at Pirana to this day; and in my childhood, full of Khoja legends, I never heard of an Iranian origin. It is remarkable how a
prominent historian could accept without question such a cock-
and-bull story, evidently invented in Pakistan to give the country's
"Great Leader" a more prestigious—that is, Persian and Arabic—
Islamic heritage. Wolpert also seems to have been told that
"Mamad" was Jinnah's pet name at home, when in fact it is how all
Khojas, by the very nature of their language, pronounce
"Muhammad."

Our mistake upon entering the town of Paneli, of such historical
connections, is to stop and openly inquire of some people standing
around a tree where Jinnah's family house is. From the responses
we receive, it seems it might be right across from where we have
stopped. But while we are still conversing, and just as a finger points
us to a building, a policeman comes by on a motorbike. What
Jinnah? he shouts angrily. There is no Jinnah here! If his house
were here, we would have burnt it! Go! And he escorts us on his
bike right out of Paneli like a small-town sheriff in a movie.
Knowing the level of corruption of the police, this is Gujarat after
all, we believe we have had a narrow escape. We also surmise that
others must have come around over the years to look for Jinnah's
ancestral home. This Gujarati Gillespie takes us right back to the
highway before turning around.

End of the Road

> The sun soon began to warm, and at the same time to remind me
> that I had yet much to see; but it was not easy to resist the influence
> which enthralled the senses in such a scene. I pity the man who has
> never felt the luxurious languor of undisturbed cogitation, to which
> for a while I surrendered my entire energies. . . . But there must be
> an end to all things, and retracing my steps, I at length regained the
> temple of the more beautiful and more amiable "Universal Mother."
>
> JAMES TOD, *Travels in Western India* (1839)

JUNAGADH, OLD FORT, lies at the foot of the Girnar hill, towards
the southwest of the Kathiawar peninsula. It is an ancient city, one
of the few places in India where the stone edicts of Asoka (250 BC)
have been found. In the twelfth century it was ruled by the
Chudasama rajas. According to legend, the last of these rulers, Ra
Khengar, pledged to his dying father to carry out four acts of
revenge against neighbouring kingdoms for the insults he had suffered. To carry out the last two of these tasks, the Ra attacked
Anhilvada, the Solanki capital; the king, Siddhraj, was not present,
but the Ra managed to destroy the eastern gate of the city and take
away Siddhraj's betrothed, whom he married. There followed a war
that lasted twelve years, at the end of which Ra Khengar was killed
and Junagadh fell to the Solankis. The queen, formerly betrothed
to Siddhraj, committed sati, joining her husband in the funeral pyre.

In 1467, the intrepid Sultan Mahmud Begada wrested Junagadh
from its Rajput rulers, thus making it the first of the two "ghads,"
the mountain fortresses, he conquered (the other being Pavagadh).

363
–

Subsequently he invited the nobility and scholars from other places to settle in the city, built his own palace there, and changed its name to Mustafabad. The older name, however, prevailed after his death. Mughal rule, beginning in 1573 with the defeat of the Gujarat sultans, lasted a long time, until the mid-eighteenth century, when one Sher Khan Babi took control and started a dynasty that later received protection from the British as an independent princedom. Its modern history is contentious. Although overwhelmingly Hindu in its population, its ruler, known as the nawab, opted to join Pakistan in 1947. This would make the state a Pakistani territory surrounded on three sides by India, with the Arabian Sea on the fourth. Intense agitation followed; neighbouring areas of Kathiawar began a boycott of Junagadh, and there were threats of an armed struggle. Finally the dewan, the prime minister, of Junagadh handed over control of the state to the Indian government. The nawab fled to Pakistan, taking with him the state treasury, and Junagadh came under Indian rule.

The last dewan of Junagadh was the father of the future prime minister of Pakistan, Zulfikar Ali Bhutto, who was hanged by the generals in 1979. His granddaughter Benazir was assassinated in 2007 by Muslim extremists.

×

Junagadh, at 7 a.m. from my hotel balcony. It's dark grey outside, a sliver of moon in the sky, the rest of the disc dimly perceptible. It all looks rather drab down below, at this intersection on the Ring Road called Kalwa Chowk: walls blackened with age, cars hunched in the shadows, pavement broken, no sidewalk. Ten-foot doors, wood or metal, grimly protect the stores. Litter lies thick on the ground.

Last night, though, we arrived in the midst of an explosion of noise and light, the streets thick with traffic and people, the shops brilliantly ablaze; restaurants, sweet shops, at least ten barbershops, dolled-up pavayas, eunuchs, standing at corners. African-looking men, who must be the Sidis. This is a pilgrim town, which explains this conglomeration of people.

Women—of the sweepers' caste, I surmise—appear, sweep the litter up outside the shops. Soon the street looks neat, but for the broken paving. The shops begin to open. Traffic slowly picks up, heading for the tumult and climax of the evening.

The hotel is modest—somewhat dark, and the hot water has to be brought in buckets for the private bathroom.

Delhi is far away (as the Sufi said to the sultan). In this quietude, every place seems far away. I have brought papers from Delhi, but they are like news from another planet. "Women on Top: Breadmaker to Bread-earner, Here's Looking at You, Lady!" says the front page of the *Times of India* in one of its tabloid moods. The *Hindustan Times* gives the results of a poll on adultery. Seventy per cent of Delhiites would give their spouses a second chance. What segment of society does this represent? There is excitement about an impending cricket series between India and Pakistan. Hindu women activists in Gujarat are protesting against the observance of Valentine's Day.

✂

Four roads leave the Kalwa Chowk junction, heading parallel to each other up the length of the city, through its heart. The closest one to us passes the old palace, then proceeds through an elaborate and decorative arched gate into a decrepit wonderland with the stately name of Diwan Chowk. This is a circle with three gates leading out, described by once-elegant buildings that could have been the administrative offices of the old regime, now in grimy disrepair, or gracelessly rebuilt. The principal motif here, where not vandalized, is the pointed arch, flanked by circular Indic emblems. One imagines state processions, guards of honour, foreign dignitaries greeted, under the handsome facades now blotted by parking sheds, warehouses, and small stores. Reinforced metal doors and square windows occupy arches like ill-fitting false teeth. The left gate leads into a neighbourhood street of old decaying buildings with trellised balconies bespeaking an age long gone. A crowd of young men stands intently around some roadside gamblers throwing dice. We return to the main road—across from us a balcony where dignitaries might have stood; underneath, a bank. We proceed through the third gate, and turn into a crossroad.

Ambling along, we sight an old faded board announcing a cemetery. The entrance is behind a sidewalk stall, and in answer to our curious inquiry the vendor comes out to tell us brusquely there is nothing there. What to make of this? But he's only whetted our interest. A man sitting at the entrance says certainly we may enter and opens the gate. Behold, then, a beautiful necropolis, sad as a widow in purdah. It takes the breath away. An overgrown graveyard, some of the graves ancient and covered with chaddars, a few recent; from their midst rise faded, discoloured monuments, among them two ghostly mausoleums wonderful in structure, ornately carved, tragically going to seed. One of them is that of the "first nawab," a woman with a child tells us, and is dated in the seventeen hundreds. We come back out into the street, feeling dejected. My friends tell me perhaps the neglect we've seen represents a different sense of history than I am used to. Different in what way? In North America we treasure the past, strive to preserve it; but perhaps there is not that much of it anyway. Here, there is a glut, enough to be neglectful, or selective. The last nawab of course did not endear himself to much of the population here.

There is the city library close by, an impressive structure, built about 1900, but otherwise a disappointment. Most of the books—dusty, broken-spined, aged in content—stand behind glass, inside locked cabinets. There is a newer shelf of Gujarati novels, and of course the newspapers are current. That's where the public goes.

The former palace, now the museum, is closed today.

It's not hard to conclude that for all its ancient history and its renown to my young ears in East Africa, this is a small city that time has left behind. Its population, when I check, has grown far less than the national average over the last hundred years. The present population is less than two hundred thousand. This is a city, or town, you abandon eventually, for Ahmedabad, Bombay, Africa. My antecedents left here and developed Dar es Salaam and Nairobi almost from scratch. Now the populations of those cities outnumber Junagadh's ten to one. The Indian downtown core of Dar es Salaam, where I spent so much of my young days, was, I am convinced, simply another Jamnagar or Junagadh. And it is not surprising anymore to realize that my people, the Khojas, with their odd, syncretistic faith, would thrive here in relative isolation, far away from the political and commercial centres of the land.

—

We stop to chat with a friendly chap who describes himself as a sayyid (a descendant of the Prophet) and says yes there is a settlement of Sidis in the area. The Sidis are African Indians. Their origins are steeped in legend, which is not surprising because they came to India in a variety of ways, over land from the north with the armies, as soldiers and musicians, and by sea as servants, slaves, and perhaps also as sailors and traders. The connection of Gujarat with the East African coast across the Indian Ocean is ancient, of course, and the 1901 census shows some three hundred Swahili speakers here. The features of the Sidis are so distinctly African they are startling. In Nairobi I was told an amusing story about how a group of visiting Sidis was detained by Kenyan authorities, who would not believe them when they said they were Indians, regardless of their passports. I can imagine them saying contemptuously, *"Eti, mnajidai Wahindi,"* "So, you think you are Indians."

We follow the sayyid into a warren of streets turning progressively squalid—dilapidated structures, open drains, one being cleaned by a woman, animals and animal shit and refuse on the narrow road, no businesses—until we reach the end of the maze. We walk through a corridor to the back of a house, where there is a rather modest shrine: a grave inside a small enclosure of unpainted brick, with a grille door. It has been in the keep of a succession of women, the current one of whom is called Haluma, a friendly woman of dark though not completely African features, with henna in her hair, prominent brown teeth, smiling mouth. There is a tin box by the shrine for donations; it does not seem much used.

We ask Haluma if she can tell us about the history of her people. I tell her that I come from Africa, near Zanzibar, but my pardada—my ancestors—were from around here. Did hers come from Africa? She doesn't know what I am talking about. She speaks in Gujarati and Hindi. Another woman comes by, says a brief prayer in the direction of the shrine. She looks more African and is an in-law. The two tell us their history is in India and Pakistan. Their ancestors, some seven generations before, came from near Surat, in southern Gujarat.

There are children about, home from school. A woman in a colourful sari arrives, and I could swear from her features she could be from Zanzibar, where one finds people of African, Indian, and Arab blood combined. Similarly a man, right down to his white singlet and brown trousers and curly hair, his very posture. I imagine this, partly, of course. I cannot help feeling a rather silly closeness with these people.

A cart of small-scale items indicates their trade, peddling on the streets.

To the right from the main road, a branch climbs up to Uppar Kot, the massive old fort of Junagadh on a hill, conquered in the twelfth century by Jaisingh Siddhraj and three centuries later by Mahmud Begada. At the entrance below, we have to give our names and addresses to two men seated at a rickety table with a register; women have been abducted and brought here, they tell us, and so everyone who goes up has to be accounted for. Much of the fort area is overgrown, though the thick grey crenellated walls and towers are visible standing intact and strong in the midst of bushes when viewed from the upper levels; outside the walls and partly surrounding the fort lies the modern city of Junagadh. The principal structure inside is a former mosque, now a mere husk and no longer in use, its three domes collapsed, the three mihrabs mere shadows on the western wall. A staircase leads up to a terrace, from which is visible the entire city clothed in a haze; on the opposite side, the imposing sacred hill of Girnar looms up through a gap in the raised foreground. Outside the mosque entrance, occupying a part of the courtyard, are some graves covered in chaddars and a small shrine with a lonely-looking man sitting outside on the ground, for no one seems to visit it. The man tells us the grave in the shrine belongs to the pir of the last nawab of Junagadh. The nawab's family is in Pakistan and does not come here. The man is the voluntary caretaker of the shrine, though he tells us he himself is a Hindu.

At this fort site there is also an ancient Buddhist cave, two millennia or so old, its meagre sculptures on walls and columns almost erased with wear; and a very deep medieval step-well open at the top. There is nothing here to explain them, put them in a context; the visitor must come armed with his own information.

Finally, the climb up Girnar, a pilgrimage to the gods. This is why most people come to Junagadh.

Four in the morning at Kalwa Chowk; cows and dogs sleep side by side on the roadside; the restless among the dogs are already trotting about. A man prepares to open his stall in the distance, another heads off on a motorbike; otherwise, the street, the intersection further away, are empty. The air is cool yet somehow feels exhausted.

Later, as we turn in to the road that heads towards Girnar, a furiously barking dog breaks the stillness and chases us for a good couple of hundred yards. What offence have we caused? Before us a formation of bright lights marches up into the sky, an awesome ladder-galaxy, the path to the various peaks of the mountain.

We stop at a tea stall by the roadside, next to a Rajput hostel. The area is full of such hostels, or dharamshalas, belonging to various communities whose members regularly make the pilgrimage; it is more convenient and economical to stay in them than in the city. There is an air of anticipation about, where we sit with a bunch of other people in a silent fellowship. After tea and biscuits, we drive on towards the entrance to Girnar. Whereas the city streets are only just astir, over here hundreds are walking up to the entrance. It's still dark, 4:30 precisely, as we take our first step up. A stall shrine is open to our left, playing a well-known bhajan that's a film staple.

Lampposts light our way up; it's these lights that make the ladder-galaxy seen from a distance. It extends now ahead of us, winding along. Noisy kids go racing past us. People barefoot, in chappals, girls in sandals, some even in heels. My companion, only a year younger than I, is straining at the leash; I on the other hand would like to keep a steady pace, not get breathless too soon. The steps are numbered at intervals; the journey up is ten thousand steps, we have been told, and takes eight hours, there and back. It's cool, but at eight hundred steps I am sweating. The city lights are visible below, and the path seems endless.

A group of girls climbs with us in the care of an uncle of sorts, who has a whistle and carries a staff for good measure. He is answering questions, doling out advice: "What side of the road do we stay on?" "The mountain side!" comes back the answer, in a chorus. He scolds mildly: "Then what are you doing on the other side?" The other side borders on a sheer drop. It seems that this chattering mob with its shrill whistle is intent on keeping pace with us, stopping to rest as we do, always disturbing our peace.

"Already tired, Uncle?" a Marathi woman asks me jovially when I sit to catch my breath. As I search for an answer, she goes panting past, adding, "He'll not admit it."

The refreshment stalls are beginning to open; people trudging up or having paused to rest, kids racing and noisy. The chattering troupe is still with us, their avuncular captain keeping up spirits with his endless advice. "*Jai Girnar-ji*," chant the girls as instructed. Even the mountain is a god. Now there's a relationship with nature.

We keep going, along a steep, black mountainside—at times almost a vertical wall—zigzagging back and forth, and we wonder at the time taken, and the devotion, and the numbers it took, to carve out this stone path, as we look down the parapet from a landing into a dark abyss. The city lights appear in a broader expanse the higher up we go, forming a tender gauze of light spread over the dark countryside, and the road coming up to Girnar, through a pass between two hills, is a thin golden strand.

We pause to take a long break and have a cuppa, the voices of our noisy companions disappearing above us, perhaps having attached themselves elsewhere. Starting again, we soon reach a complex of stone temples. Could this be the top, so soon? The heart leaps in anticipation. But it's the Jain sanctuary, only halfway up; we are told we are too early, it will be open on our way down. Now we are onto another mountain face. The city lights show themselves in greater number, far below. Above us the bright stars, the Milky Way carelessly and lightly spilled, and we are headed directly for them at a forty-five-degree angle.

Dawn has approached. On the side sometimes, on a ledge jutting out into open space, are the meagre signs of habitation—a mat—on which a yogi must have sat or slept, in the proverbial fashion. Plastic and foil litter some of the hillsides, and occasionally we see large numbers of discarded plastic slippers. Perhaps on the way down the pilgrims wish to carry the dust of this sacred mountain with them on their bare feet.

Faces beam at you; the old struggle up with brave looks and pained smiles, the middle aged trudge along, the kids chatter incessantly. Some people carry staffs, and we already wish we had taken one each, to assist us on our climb, and also to make us look like real pilgrims. The mood is pleasant but not exactly jovial. The climb up Pavagadh was easier, gradual. This one takes an obvious toll.

Finally we reach the first of the mountain's several plateaus, where sits the goddess Amba's temple. It's a squat, dark stone building, with a modern, rather incongruous, tall white superstructure topped by a red flag. At a flat ground across from it, our former chattering companions have gathered with other school groups. It appears that the uncle with the whistle is a teacher, after all. One school group has come all the way from Navsari in south Gujarat.

We keep going. A deep ravine separates this peak from the next, the highest one on the range, the steps towards it leading down, then dauntingly going back up. At the bottom, on a ridge between the two peaks, we pause to look upon a vast vista: the city, the highways, vehicles like pinpoints moving along them, the villages beyond. And then, finally, we are at the shrine of the famous yogi Gorakhnath, of kanphata ("torn-ear") fame. The Kanphata Jogis are a well-known order of ascetics who split their ears for their large earrings to go through; they also blow horns at various times and put ashes on their forehead. Gorakhnath was their founding guru and he is supposed to have spent time at this peak on Girnar; here, apparently, the Sufi Baba Farid of Lahore, master of Nizamuddin of Delhi, came to visit him. The shrine consists of a small structure with a decorative tiled surface, beside a couple of flags and a bell, on a rock platform that looks out at the world below in all directions.

And then, the sheer exhilaration on the way down. (There is a third plateau further up, beloved to Marathis, but we've had enough.) The feeling is one of triumph over the mountain and over the night. The morning is cool, pure, hazy. Going down looks easy, the breathing effortless. People whom we meet coming up need encouragement—"it's only a short way, now"—and some of the older women look beat, taking time to collapse on the steps, but we know they will keep going, no one gives up. We pass the woman who had taunted me earlier, subdued now, slowly, silently climbing up. We stop at the Ambaji temple and pay our respects. The grumpy priests seem scornful of our stinginess, expecting donations of ghee and oil.

Halfway down, we return to the Jain complex, a magnificent medieval site of grey stone temples, exquisitely carved. At the main entrance, crowded with worshippers, we are summarily told by a guard that only Jains can go in today, a ceremony is in progress. As we proceed down, disappointed, we pass numerous Jain men and women climbing up, some of them of them struggling in the growing heat, others carried up in hammocks dangling from poles supported on the shoulders of two men, one at either end, each bearing a thick staff for support. Every few yards they pause for a break. The passengers on these rocky rides must be prosperous, more often than not they are soft and flabby, and look embarrassed, avoiding your eye. It's a somewhat pathetic sight. Yet it's a pilgrimage, and some need to be carried and others to carry for money. The fare depends on the weight of the passenger and could amount to a few thousand rupees.

By now our knees, thighs, calves can tell; going down may be easy on the lungs, but it's painful on the leg muscles. My ebullient companion has to be cautioned twice when he almost slips, for the steps are smooth. An old Marwari man—proverbially miserly—receives a taunt from a stall keeper for quibbling about the price of a cup of tea. An old Marathi woman is hanging onto the side wall, smiling. "Far?" she asks. "You'll reach there, Mother," we tell her. And she has to go beyond where we turned back. A young man with a child passes us; he went up last night, spent the night at the Ambaji temple. "It was cold, but there were blankets." A youth, a student from a middle-class family, is here because the exams are only a couple of weeks away. A girl, barely fourteen, is a porter and carries up her load painfully. A boy scarcely one hundred pounds does the same. This is how the dried milk for the tea, the ghee for frying, go up.

Finally, 2000 steps left; 800; 500; 50. And we are home. As we stumble out the entranceway, rickshawallahs are ready to take us anywhere; a masseur is prepared to massage our legs. But we first plonk ourselves down at a stall and have two sugarcane juices each. Our driver finds us and convinces us that a massage is a good idea, and so we surrender to the able hands of the masseur, who knows where exactly on the calf to press and squeeze out the pain. The driver watches with satisfaction: clients of substance reflect well on him.

Back on the streets of Junagadh. We have been told that there are some Khojas doing business at the town's vegetable market, and that's where we proceed. The market is like any other: shady, damp, and cool inside, rows of raised stalls selling carrots, spinach, tomatoes, squash, among a dozen other vegetables, sellers calling out; bustling activity on the aisles. A consignment of red chillies is the focus of attention. Several Khoja men are pointed out to us, young and old—all very busy, unpacking, arranging, selling, hurrying between stalls—one with the surname Kutchi, though he claims he does not speak the language, then proceeds to do exactly that with his relations. He escorts me up the road to the khano: a broad, one-storey building with a tall, narrow, and handsome section of the front set off emblematically at one end. There is a large arched entrance here, with a blue door that is closed; but it has a smaller door that opens.

I take off my shoes, go upstairs. Some repairs are in progress; the mukhi, who is present and supervising the work, tells me that the damage was incurred in the earthquake of a few years before. While being repaired, the place is also being modernized. We are on an upstairs terrace, at one end of which is an office, traditionally called the daftari. It has a large desk, behind which sits a woman; there are cabinets and shelves; a ceiling fan is on. There is a similar office in Dar es Salaam, another one in Nairobi. A visitor could go there and make inquiries about the local "vata-varan," the situation, and about relatives; he might even meet the marriage committee. Here I have a friendly chat with the woman, and with a man sitting to one side of the desk, evidently here to chat. There are always those, too, people who come by to pass the time, have a cup of tea. And once again, the trust, the comfort. My manner, my way of speaking, what I say, completely identifies me. And so I take the only chair, my friends stand. They are the outsiders. We too are given tea.

I tell the woman I am looking for a place called Gadhada, where my ancestor came from. This does not surprise her; others have come by with similar requests. This must be Gir Gadhada, she says; the other Gadhada is Swami na Gadhada, where the Swami Narayan people have their headquarters.

I learn that there is a community policy to move from villages to larger centres, for social reasons like marriages, for educational opportunities, and for safety. There is also a trend for young men to go away to Kinshasa, exactly what I was told in Dhroll, which I think of now as Somani Town. These young men set themselves up overseas and return like big shots, the woman says; but they also send for other youths from the area and employ them. History repeating itself, for this is exactly what the people who left a hundred or more years ago for Zanzibar and Mombasa did, though the east coast of Africa was not a desperate place, as the Congo is now. In Zanzibar and Mombasa, communities were established, traditions preserved and developed, generations progressed. These new entrepreneurs will probably head off somewhere else from Africa.

Gir Gadhada, my ancestor Nanji Lalji's birthplace, is near a town called Una, which is where we proceed. The woman says she will make a phone call about us to the office in Una, where there is a khano.

⋈

In Una, a market centre for the local villages, it is easy to find the local Khojas. We ask for the khano at a shop, are pointed to a boy selling fruit at a stand. He is the mukhi's brother's son, a young man who has just finished school, he informs us, after the initial greetings. Behind him is the mukhi's fruit and vegetable store. The young man tells us to go straight, turn right, then right again at the "vadalo," which turns out to be a large banyan tree.

The mukhi's house is across from the khano, which is represented as elsewhere by a large gate. A quiet place, closed, unprepossessing. There is an entrance across the street that leads into a yard, at the end of which is the open door to the mukhi's house. We have disturbed his siesta, and he doesn't look very happy, the first time I have seen such a reaction from a Gujarati Khoja, let alone a mukhi. There is a daughter of about eighteen around, the mukhi himself is seated on a chair. The house looks prosperous, a new-looking television on a stand is showing a movie. We are given tea and uncomfortably try to make conversation. Yes, he says, there is a village called Gadhada . . . Very soon a well-dressed young man in his twenties arrives and rescues us from our ordeal; he is the local Khoja administrator contacted by the woman in Junagadh regarding my inquiries concerning Nanji Lalji Bhimani. This is a good pretext for departure and we hasten out with the young man to his office.

He opens the khano gate and we enter a paved courtyard above which stands a quite magnificent structure. Not the Taj Mahal, of course, we are in a village. But the contrast with the outside, and with the house we have just departed, is striking. It is a tall, two-storey building, with arched doorways and decorative details. There are two flights of stairs, one for the men, the other for the women. We take the former to the second floor, where the congregation hall is, as well as the office.

The young man tells me, when we are alone in the office (my two companions, "outsiders," are waiting downstairs), that he has taken a census of the community in the region. He shows me his results, tabulated in a ledger-style book: names, numbers of persons in each family, levels of education. A full report on each family, the last names, I notice, all with the typical ending, -ani. He travels by motorbike regularly to the villages, collects his data in Gujarati and enters it into a computer, also in Gujarati. His salary is three thousand rupees and is hardly enough; in Bombay, he is aware, the salary is five times as much for the same job. He has a wife, and a child in nursery school. He confirms that Khojas are moving to the larger centres, and that many young men are going to Africa. He has his own passport prepared. I ask him about the recent violence. He says Khojas were spared personal attacks, but property was burnt down. A Khoja boy was surrounded at a bus station by a mob. But they spared him when he identified himself as a Khoja, walking him home just to make sure he was who he said he was. In the Muslim area two Hindus were killed. But, he is convinced, as are many in Gujarat, that there is an active campaign to keep the Muslims economically backward. After every so-called riot they are set back.

He comes with us to Gir Gadhada, leading the way on his motorbike with us following in our taxi.

We arrive at a large, rather messy-looking village: untidy narrow dirt roads, abandoned dwellings. There are a cobbler shop, two tailors, some clothing stores, a barber, a provision store. The khano has been recently closed, the blue door firmly padlocked. It seems to be a large building. There are one or two Khoja families around, including one with a provision store, attended by a young woman. We inquire about local history at a few shops and are directed to the home of someone called Baap Bhai, a turbaned, mustachioed man—at not much more than sixty hardly the aged person we expect, but very much with the bearing of a chief. We are in a courtyard, entered from the street, and there are two women about, one of whom is Baap Bhai's mother. There is a low bench-swing on the verandah, on which, at his invitation, I come and sit next to him. He can't tell me much except that this was a Khoja village once. The village accent is caustic, and the speech fast, not so easy to follow, but his manner is kindly. His people, the Vanyas, had come later and been welcomed, he says. When he was young he had heard of a place called Nanji Khoja's house, from where, presumably, this Nanji Khoja had departed. He could tell the history of his own community up to ten generations, but how could he tell mine? he asks. Why, I ask myself, could my people not preserve records like their neighbours did? Could it be due to the initial conversion, the first exile, as I see it, then the consequent uncertainties? I can hardly assume that Nanji Khoja was my ancestor Nanji Lalji; perhaps he was, perhaps not. But that Nanji and Vassanji are Khoja names in this village does not lack significance. Gujarati names are regional, communal, generational.

It pleases Baap Bhai no end that I have returned to the village of my ancestors. After tea and water, we go to what looks like a square or crossroads and sit down outside a shop, on chairs brought out for us. People gather, drawn to the strangers. Kids play around. A bearded man in a green shirt goes inside his house, returns wearing a new white shirt for the benefit of the camera. There is talk of Nanji Khoja; people point to where the shop had been, but are vague. Nobody seems to know exactly. The village had been smaller once, and all the Khojas, it appears, had farmed and run shops.

There is no Kunta Kinte moment; I did not come looking for one. If there ever was one close to it, it was when I first stepped on Indian soil, undertook that quick tour of the country that began with a train ride, the Puri Express.

It is dusk when we return to Una, which, like all Indian towns at night, thrums with busy life—noisy, dusty, brilliantly lit, people out to buy their necessities. We pause at a food stand for a meal. The khano is in progress; something is being sung that we can hear all the way down here, and it sounds nice, but I can't recognize it. We have omelettes and scrambled eggs made for us by a Makran—a Baluchi whose family came here some generations back. His way of making scrambled eggs is to put oil and onions into his large pan, throw in red chili powder and salt to create a stinging mist, to which he is immune, then add more spices and mix them in before adding a whole egg and scrambling it. The omelettes are cooked similarly.

We depart for Baroda via Bhavnagar on the coastal road. Our young driver, who may soon be off to Dar es Salaam, is as reckless as ever, the music on his tape a hip, modern mix, very much popular with the young, though he does not realize that its main refrain is a line from a well-known Sufi qawali, an ode to Imam Ali. The night is thick and dark, lit periodically by lonely roadside shrines to Shiva awaiting the upcoming festival of Shivratri.

During this trip, while asking for directions, I have learned a new Indian English expression, "road to road," meaning a direct route, one road leading to another, more or less.

More Road-to-Road: Gujarati Fragments

THERE ARE THE OTHER PLACES in Gujarat that I passed through, or stopped at, or visited briefly out of curiosity or whim, all memorable nevertheless, some intriguing, some literally wonderful; and there are the people who touched my life momentarily, the driver, the greengrocer, the priest, the doctor. Places and people that would make a much longer narrative, but I turn away from them reluctantly and move on in this madness that has become the endless quest for a place.

1. The Mohammedan

Your next driver is a Mohammedan, I am told by the long-legged youth bringing me back from Champaner. I did not know the term was in use any longer anywhere in the world, it sounds medieval, but in Gujarat, much to my surprise, it is current. The Mohammedan driver turns out to be one Sharif Bhai, a middle-aged man (a surprising contrast to the near-teenagers I have had before) who lost his home during the violence and lives in the Tandelja area of Baroda with his brother-in-law. His house was gutted and even his safes were mutilated, he complains forcefully. It's the latter offence that irks him more. He seems rather dense at times but knows his way around the state because he used to drive a "luxury" (a tour bus) for ten years, and he takes Raj Kumar and me to a few more places of interest in Kathiawar. The frequency of his swearing increases the more he gets to know us. His taste in hotels runs to dharamshalas, in the search for which, once at Somnath, he lands us in a ditch; and he has a predilection for stopping at the worst eating places. As soon as we've eaten some tasteless food at a desolate dhaba, we drive past restaurants bustling with custom. He acknowledges with a kiss of the hand and touch to the forehead any roadside shrine we pass.

2. The African Indians

Jambur is a village in the back of beyond, almost at the end of a coastal road from Somnath. The town just before is Sasan, and already here we see the presence of the Sidis—a few young men sitting at a roundabout (it's Sunday), a man in the pilot seat of a tempo full of people. And as we proceed further along an old and narrow road, we know we are in Sidi territory. So as not to seem inquisitive—which is what we are—and rude, we ask for a dargah, a shrine; there's bound to be one.

We head off towards where we are directed, and come to a green and white building, people walking in and out the courtyard through a gate. A "maanta" is in progress, we are informed, and we throw off our shoes and hurry into the courtyard. A crowd has gathered, through which African-looking boys run chasing each other. In the middle of the crowd a black goat wearing a garland of marigolds and roses is being prodded towards the dargah entrance by a Sidi man. The majority of the people are not Sidis, however; they have come from outside with a maanta, a prayer to be answered and offerings for the pir, Hazrat Nagarchi Baba, who is buried here. Now the doorway to the mausoleum is crowded with women offering prayers to him, while outside the reluctant goat is being cajoled towards the steps. If the goat goes up, the pleaders' desires will be fulfilled, the maanta will have been accepted. But this goat refuses to budge. A young boy pushes it with some violence and is scolded.

Four black men appear at the outside gate, two playing drums, one, who is blind, playing a flute, all smiling and laughing. An old black woman among the bystanders begins to dance by herself, in slow and understated but very deliberate motions. The fourth man, who is without an instrument, also begins to dance; as he does so, making leaps and bounds, he collects money from the people, snatching bills in his mouth, handing them to one of the drummers, who seems to be the leader. People give money to their kids, from whom this young man accepts them; if the child is small, he picks it up, dances with it. Some people now place bills on the ground, which with a somersault the dancer snatches in his mouth, hands them to the leader.

The drumbeat is loud, the compound now packed with people.

A small white goat is pushed in through the gate, washed at the taps, garlanded. It steps up to the mausoleum.

We learn that the goats will be slaughtered and eaten. A young man sits down to chat with us outside the gate on a stone bench. His name is Abdulrazak, his family is from Junagadh, and he is doing his FYBA at a college in Veraval. What's that? First-year B.A.

3. Ghadiali Bawa—The Pir of the Clocks
Sharif Bhai our driver brings us back to Baroda through Rajkot. On the way we treat ourselves to Kathiawari cuisine: bajra rotlo, bhinda, daal, bateta, khichdi, and papad. Later the driver stops at a place at a highway junction which he says makes the best burfi in Gujarat. Gujaratis living in America buy kilos of it to take back. And so we buy a couple of pounds.

The final stop before we reach Baroda in the night is the roadside dargah of Ghadiali Bawa. It's dark and raining, the traffic heavy, headlights hurtling past reflecting off the tarmac. The shrine is modest, open at the sides, consisting of a green latticed fence around a grave. Above, in a haze of incense, hangs a tube light, and still higher, from the beams under the corrugated metal ceiling hang a few square and many round clocks of all sizes; in their midst a framed photo of a bearded man, the Bawa. You can buy garlands and such to place on the grave, but many people give clocks. Some of them have been placed on shelves further from the grave. This Bawa is a favourite of taxi and truck drivers—perhaps because they work to time, in a sense they live by it.

4. And on and on, this endless quest. Dholera, Jaffarabad, Somnath, Karimabad, Rajkot, Siddhpur, Bharuch, Navsari, Sarkhej, Godhra . . . Dholera, once upon a time a thriving port that boasted eighty thousand souls; now with a mere three thousand. Its harbour silted up, and the once-elegant, now tottering wooden houses tell the tale of its demise. A solitary Khoja family plies its vegetable trade and has its own private shrine. We can't refuse to share a meal. *Jaffarabad,* a thriving fishing village of picture-postcard beauty. The young Khoja mukhi begs us to spend the night, but we can't. *Somnath,* a late-night arrival, when Sharif Bhai through sheer obstreperousness runs into a ditch. *Karimabad,* a Khoja colony in a large city, guarded by two vicious dogs; the friendly retainer at the gate lets me in quickly enough, tells me to go to the khano, but confesses a niggling doubt to Raj Kumar, who is waiting outside, that my beard looks somewhat Christian to him. *Rajkot,* the great city where I once spent only a few hours, and another time missed an appointment I needed to keep. *Siddhpur,* the ancient and lively city where a wedding procession is on when we enter, a uniformed band playing at the main intersection and a young man lip-synching to an old film song; sitting in the verandah of a house, some Momins tell me the story of their banishment here by the Mughal emperor Aurangzeb (for heresy, what else). *Bharuch,* once a great port, now famous for the peanuts sold outside. *Navsari*, where a Hindu group (if labels mean anything in the context) worship a medieval Ismaili missionary in a modest temple; a ginan book lies open on a podium; the furtive priest says they have to worship with some caution. *Sarkhej*, a great complex with marvellous buildings, containing the tombs of Mahmud Begada and the Sufi Ahmed Khattu. It's hot, and the marble floors burn our bare feet. *Godhra*, the tinderbox that set off the Gujarat violence; I visit three schools, feel much apprehension, see some hope, and fear.

In East Africa my community and other Indians, mostly Gujaratis, were scattered around similarly, sometimes a family or two to a village or town. Thus, endlessly: Babati, Mengo, Tororo, Mpwapwa, Songea, Singida, Kilosa, Lamu, Machakos, Kibwezi . . . We were a small minority, sometimes fearful. My ancestor Nanji Lalji left from Gadhada for Africa. Did he know, I wonder, that the Sidis living nearby were from that same part of Africa he was heading for?

Kerala:
The Goddess's Footprint

Everything there is different from what it is with us and excels both in size and beauty. They have no fruit the same as ours, no beast, no bird. This is a consequence of the extreme heat. They have no grain excepting only rice. . . . All that a human body needs for its living is to be had in profusion and very cheap with the one exception of grain other than rice.

MARCO POLO

The Malabar Coast

> Three days later we reached the land of Mulaybar [Malabar], which
> is the pepper country. It extends for two months' journey along the
> coast from Sandabur [Goa] to Kawlam [Quilon]. The road over the
> whole distance runs beneath the shade of trees, and at every half-
> mile there is a wooden shed with benches on which all travellers,
> whether Muslims or infidels, may sit. . . . On this road . . . there is not
> a foot of ground but is cultivated.
>
> IBN BATTUTA (1304–1368)

THE VEGETATION IS GLORIOUSLY TROPICAL and the sea is never
far off in Kerala. The people are polite and reserved—proud, is their
own description—and the houses are beautifully painted in shades
of blue, green, and pink, many of them with the traditional red-
tiled sloping roofs. There is a sense of the small here, and a slower
pace, yet any shopping area in the evening is as busy and noisy as
anywhere else in the country. In the capital, Trivandrum,
prominently facing each other at a busy intersection next to the
university stand a mosque, a temple, and a church, a coexistence
that is emblematic of the state's cordial diversity. It is pointed out
to me with a barely suppressed pride. At the beach, fishermen and
-women, of strikingly beautiful and unusual dark brown complex-
ion, sell their catch next to their boats; groups of men play cards
further away; and women sell tea under an ancient stone pavilion
once used by the royal family. A persistent rolling sound on a busy
street suggests to me balls or some other soft objects bouncing
about in a closed box; when I inquire, it is identified for me, much

to my embarrassment, as a voice on a loudspeaker reciting lottery numbers in a musical, typically southern voice. It all feels wonderfully foreign, yet, equally wonderfully, not quite so. This is still India.

Elsewhere in India, in the north, it is the people and language, the sight and sound of a place—a residential neighbourhood in Delhi or a street in Jamnagar—that have reminded me of the East Africa of my childhood. Here, it is the balmy salty air and the trees: the groves of coconut palms waving in the breeze, the banana stands, the mango giving shade to a house. Standing at the beach I cannot help but throw a glance out across the ocean, half expecting that other homeland to loom distantly in the mist. It was from there that the first European had arrived at this shore in India, brought across the ocean by two Indian guides soon after Columbus's blunder and discovery of America. And speaking of people and distant connections, I've realized after coming to Kerala that some of the Indian teachers at my school—a string of Thomases, Johns, and others—were in fact Keralan Christians.

They say of Kerala that it's the gods'—and perhaps also, for the monotheists, God's—country, and they boast a 100 per cent literacy rate. Book and magazine stores abound, selling mostly Malayalam literature, which is impressive. The communists are often in power, but there is a free economy, and during my later visits the effects of the current economic boom are evident. Among the newly affluent, I am told, weddings can draw two thousand or more guests, and the gold passing hands is measured in kilos. The dowry custom persists among all the three major religious groups. There are churches everywhere, though the recent upsurge of Christian evangelism is a cause of some resentment. The population is 21 per cent Christians, 25 per cent Muslims, and the rest Hindus. During my first trip, a nationwide leftist student congress was in progress and there were the red flags and banners of protest everywhere on the main highway leading out of Trivandrum. As I write this, in Cochin, some two thousand Christian college students have gathered outside my hotel to protest a contentious government measure. They include both men and women, some chanting, many bearing flags, and all shepherded by their teachers, priests and nuns in cassocks and habits. This is a highly politicized state, and that goes with the literacy. At such a rally the typical Keralan reserve seems to yield a little.

The thin stretch of palm-fringed land along the Arabian Sea in the southwest called Kerala forms but 1 per cent of India's land mass. To the east, on the other side of the Western Ghats, lies Tamil Nadu, with which it shares a common ancient Dravidian past. The region of Kerala comprised in ancient times a number of small independent kingdoms that were all part of a larger South Indian Dravidian culture. The name itself (pronounced "Kair-al-ah" by the natives) means, according to one version of its origin, the land of the coconut. Another version has the region named after the Cheras, kings who ruled this narrow strip in ancient times, from a few centuries BC to the ninth century. The early history of that rule is cloaked in legend. In later centuries, the southern kingdoms on the coast were consolidated into Travancore, its capital Trivandrum; to its north was another kingdom, Cochin, and further north, Malabar, which included the cities of Calicut and Canganore. By the time the British ruled India, Travancore and Cochin had joined the ranks of the Indian princely states—ruled by local dynasties but under British protection and dominance—and Malabar was part of the Madras Presidency, ruled directly by the East India Company, and later the British government. Kerala obtained statehood in its present political and geographic form in 1956, made up essentially of these three territories.

Kerala's language, Malayalam, like Tamil, is Dravidian, and at first encounter sounds as different from the North Indian family of languages as Swahili. But its vocabulary is heavily influenced by the northern Sanskrit, and it takes only a little tutoring to discern the Sanskrit-based words: puram (pura), dasan (dasa), thiru (shree). Malayalam and Tamil have similar-looking scripts, both from the same family as Devanagari, in which Hindi and related northern languages are written, though this is far from obvious to the uninitiated eye. The ancient Brahminism of the Aryan Vedas was native to the north of the subcontinent and did not penetrate much to the south. Jainism and Buddhism both thrived here in ancient times, believed to have arrived from the north in the third century BC during the period of the Maurya empire, which extended all across India except a small portion at the southernmost tip. Statues of Jain Tirthankaras and the Buddha continue to be discovered to this day in rural areas of Kerala, sometimes standing in for Hindu deities. Hinduism arrived with the emigration of Brahmins from the north. It was in the eighth century AD that it properly took hold, and by the ninth century the other two faiths had almost vanished from the land. Many of the old Hindu temples are believed to have been Jain and Buddhist in origin. The great synthesizer of Hindu philosophy, Shankaracharya, was born in Kerala, though presumably of northern ancestry.

Facing the Arabian Sea in the west, Kerala has since ancient times had seafaring contact with other lands across the ocean— Greece, Rome, Arabia, and China. From the fifteenth century onwards, the Portuguese, Dutch, and British, in that order, successfully rounding the formidable Cape of Good Hope at Africa's tip, arrived on its shores and dominated the region. Islam had already arrived by the eighth century, brought soon after the death of Muhammad by the Arab merchants already trading on the coast, at a time when, interestingly, Hinduism was still taking hold. Thus the advent of Islam in Kerala is remarkably different from its arrival in northern India. Sufism, though present, was never a big force as it was in the north.

Christianity, according to legend, was brought by the Apostle Saint Thomas, who landed in 52 AD, near the town of Muziris; in the fourth century arrived a group of Christians from Syria, giving rise to the distinct group of Syrian Christians of Kerala. There is a tiny community of Jews left in Kerala; they could have come here very early, and travellers through the centuries have commented on the existence of Jewish communities, but details of their arrival vary. The synagogue in Cochin is from the sixteenth century.

This unusual provenance of its several faiths—Christianity and Judaism predating Hinduism proper, an Arab presence predating the advent of Islam—and the arrival of diverse peoples upon its shores must surely have contributed to the more accepting attitude among the Keralans. For one thing, there is no single villain to easily point to. Indeed for many southerners it is the northerners who are the villains. The communal strifes of the north, therefore, do not hit Kerala with the same savagery, if they do at all. On the other hand, the viciousness of Kerala's traditional caste system has been noted in the past by many travellers. The great reformer Vivekananda, passing through the region in the early twentieth century, called it a "madhouse of caste."

Immediately after my arrival in Trivandrum, once, I receive a phone call in my room. A very warm and rich voice welcomes me with familiarity. It is the doyen of Malayali literature, K. Ayyappa Paniker. A little more than a year ago, upon hearing that I edited a literary magazine, he called me from Boston and told me about the Oriya poet Jayanta Mahapatra. Since then I have had the opportunity to visit Mahapatra at his home, and met a man as graceful as his sinuously beautiful poetry, which I published, along with an article by Paniker on the great Malayali novelist Thakazhi Sivasankara Pillai. I meet Paniker the following day at his office. He has recently retired from the local university and is compiling a Malayali contribution to a national project on the Indian literatures. He is a short dark man with a milk-white beard and a wide toothy grin, and surprisingly (I was expecting a South Indian professor in a grey suit) is attired in a black shirt over a traditional white dhoti, with slippers. He has a wonderfully understated humour, delivered in his low voice and easy manner of speech, keeping me on constant guard against his meanings. (Complaining about Indian typesetters: "If they can't find a letter, they will substitute another . . . after all, there are all of twenty-six letters to choose from.") Tongue always in cheek, eyes twinkling, and a mysterious man, too, difficult to know even after several meetings. A Keralan trait. It takes me some years to discover that this man, who looks like a pilgrim, completed his graduate work in the United States, in Indiana, and is a modernist poet in English of no mean stature. And yet he is constantly promoting other writers, never attempts to press his own publications upon me, a tendency very much present in the north. He has a much younger, though not very glamorous-looking, woman assisting him on his project, the mention of whom brings smiles of tolerant understanding among his admirers. During one of my visits he invites me to see his village in the famous Kerala backwaters, and to meet Thakazhi Sivasankara Pillai, who comes from the same area as he does.

My guide in Trivandrum is Hussein, who first brought me on a two-day train journey across the subcontinent to this city on my first visit. He is a student of Michael Ondaatje, who, he is convinced, has based one of his books on the life of the playback singer Muhammad Rafi. His one ambition is to make it to Canada on one of those fellowships that entice scholars to study Canada. One has the impression with him of a life burdened by a limited village background, a traditional family, and responsibility for growing children, with an underpaid job in a drab college in a small town. But he has this one ambition for a shot at excitement and freedom, to elaborate his thesis on Ondaatje's book while visiting faraway Canada—to rise above his poor Muslim background just this once and be somebody in the wide world. The contrast between him and the better-placed academics from wealthier backgrounds is touching.

><

Buses blaring their horns, grinding their way along highways that were streets once, through towns that were villages, racing back and forth past each other. Even over long distances it's standing room only, and more difficult getting off than getting on, because you work against a clamouring incoming tide. One understands overpopulation in such a setting—town upon town thronged with people. Poor fishing villages with large new structures built with Gulf money from émigrés working abroad—mosques, houses, a brick factory along the beach. New Muslim houses tend to use arches where they can, and sometimes boast a decorative crescent and star; Hindu houses seem more square. These are pointed out to me by Hussein on our way to Allepey from Varkala, the urban centre near his village. We pass a village that seems more together than most, more residential, less split apart by the highway and attendant business; less crowded. Here, my friend tells me, the Muslims have a matrilineal system; their neighbours are Nairs, who traditionally have the same system. The Muslims must have converted, I say. He is reluctant to admit that, says they just copied their neighbours. I point out to him that Muslims don't drop fully formed from the sky, they grow from the same soil.

There is a certain reluctance to speak about Muslim conversion (as there is among Hindus to talk about caste). It's like a family secret. Yet the outward manifestations of Muslim-ness I've been shown here are so few. No *salaam alaykum*, no cap, no beard. No sign of Arabic script. Their kids' names—Sophia, Sonia, Sarin, Suja—are hardly the traditional Muslim names, which, Hussein tells me, are considered old-fashioned. I get a sense of an identity without root, a certain insecurity.

If Keralan reserve extends to the Muslims keeping mum about who exactly they are, the literature about them is also essentially uninformative. One imagines the Keralan Muslims as different and detached from the North Indian Muslims, with whom they share only a little of language and literature, roots and history. The northerner is associated, directly or otherwise, with the religious traditions of Iran and Afghanistan. He is linked—in my opinion, often very dubiously—to the conquering Turks and Mughals, and can point to the monuments and shrines among which he lives, and the poetry and music of high culture and draw real or fanciful pride from them. The Keralan Muslim has little of that calibre to point to; the Muslims had a very strong commercial and seafaring presence in Kerala but produced no court culture. Perhaps here lies the root of the embarrassed silence. I interpret, of course.

M. Mujeeb's tome *The Indian Muslims* spares but two lines for the Keralan. The old, detailed, though flawed survey by Murray Titus, *Islam in India and Pakistan*, gives them a paragraph, only to illustrate their backwardness and fanaticism, referring to a revolt of 1921. The eminent Aziz Ahmad's *Studies in Islamic Culture in the Indian Environment* has not even a word. These are all books from the north.

A good number of Keralan Muslims are descended from a mix of the early Arab merchants and local Keralans; others are descended from those who converted. A caste system of sorts has also existed, the fisherfolk and barbers, for example, lower down on the ladder. Keralans of the Brahmin and Nair castes are also known to have converted.

The term "Mappila," or "Moplah," has been used to describe Keralan Muslims. Unfortunately the exact definition of the term is elusive; it is sometimes used to refer to the earliest Keralan Muslims, but then slithers into a vagueness defining all of them, and one learns that there are also Mappila Christians. The Keralan Muslims have been associated with a martial tradition (as have some of the Christians) and a certain element of militancy, which gave rise to the "Moplah Rebellion" of 1921 in the northern parts of the state. One of the main causes of the "rebellion," which lasted six months to a year and involved more than a million people, is said to have been poverty.

I can not imagine a less militant group than that of Hussein and his friends from Varkala.

We arrive at the bus station in Allepey, where my local host, a young college teacher called Rajan, picks me up and Hussein says good-bye and returns to Varkala. I get on behind Rajan on his motorbike and we head off to his suburban house; on the way we wait for a temple procession with an elephant to pass. Rajan is a Brahmin with two young children, and that evening at his house there is shyness all around. English is our common language; but that's an exaggeration, for English in Kerala can sound foreign if you are not used to it.

The next morning Rajan and I go to Kavalam, Paniker's village, by boat.

Like Venice—with which it's been compared, Rajan tells me— the Allepey district is full of canals that connect inland lakes and are used for rural travelling. We take one of the boats, which function like buses on a rural route, transporting people to and from their villages. Hardly Venice, but beautiful all the same.

There are paddy fields on either side of us. We pass a few modest houses and shacks. Occasionally, men and women washing themselves on the banks; it's an art to do so without exposing oneself. In India sometimes, after the throngs and bustle of the city, filled with life to the brim, one yearns to escape into solitude. This boat ride through a quiet tropical paradise is a wonderful interlude. My companion is unobtrusive. Coconut palms loom overhead. There are red mangoes just ripening, bananas hanging from trees. And flowers, red, orange, yellow, and blue, bougainvillea, hibiscus, water lilies. At regular stops a few people get off onto a small jetty, and soon disappear. Habitation is sparse, such a huge contrast from the bus route on which I came hurtling to Allepey. Now and then the canal opens into a large body of water, then becomes a canal again. Narrower channels head off, perhaps for local use. Then a few entire villages appear—a church, a school, a banner for a Marxist splinter group.

Our destination is the farthest village on the route, two hours distant, the family home of K. Ayyappa Paniker. It's a quiet place, hardly a business in sight. We follow a trail through a thicket, stop at a country restaurant for lunch, and arrive at a large dilapidated house, where we meet Paniker's sister and her husband. There's nothing much to say, we don't have a language in common, and the woman evidently doesn't know what to do with us. We have imposed. We decline tea and walk back to the jetty, await our ride. It's a disappointing visit. Perhaps some communication was lost somewhere. What did I expect here, except to see something different?

The next morning, looking out from the balcony, I watch an elephant plodding on the road on its way to the temple. It's one of those moments of solitude and silence when I wonder whether I am in the real world or in a dream; if there truly is another world I have left behind. How distant it seems. After breakfast we go by taxi to Thakazhi, but first we stop at the Shrikrishna Temple of Ambalapuzha. The temple, situated in a complex next to the waterside, is several centuries old and quite modest, with a sloping slate roof. It is famous for its milk porridge, but this is not the time for it.

We arrive in the village of Thakazhi, still in the Allepey district, where Paniker has sent me to meet the famous writer.

Thakazhi Sivasankara Pillai is one of the most celebrated of the older Keralan writers, and we sit with him in his living room, which faces the street. "I am a farmer," he says modestly in response to my question as to which of his books is his favourite. A silly question, really, which he doesn't answer. "I felt like writing, and so I wrote." There is still mud on my feet, he is reported to have said to the guests at the ceremony where he received the Gyana Pith, the country's highest award. The citation, on a wooden plaque, is brought for me to see.

At more than eighty, he is suffering the effects of diabetes. Weakness in the bones, bad eyes and ears. He is barefoot and bare-chested and sits straight up, wearing a blue dhoti round the waist, his cropped hair, abundant chest hair, and face stubble all white. There is a string of beads around his neck, a caste mark on his forehead. He is a fairly big man, fleshy though not fat, and has a strong, impressive head. He speaks clearly, and like his friend Paniker's, his English is better expressed and better pronounced than that of the younger generation. Of the Nair caste and a small landowner, he was trained as a lawyer, his biography says, and his father was a gentleman scholar. His uncle was one of the great Kathakali dancers of his time. So he is not exactly a peasant; the modesty is a typically Indian one and not to be taken seriously. This ancestral village where I have come to meet him is, like most villages, hostage to heat and dust and modest circumstance, not unlike the area I grew up in; unpaved or partly paved streets, boys playing in the dust, small shops selling small items, bunches of bananas hanging on display from their door frames, poster ads on the walls outside. Only four years ago he stopped working on his farm. Now "it lies fallow"; the son can't or doesn't want to manage it. As we sit, a nurse comes to administer insulin. The son is visiting from Trivandrum, a doctor. A daughter and granddaughter arrive.

He represents the old India and is its quintessential revered wise old man, the pride of the village and the state. India has seen much, he says, it's an old country. So it will survive. Troubles come and go. There are stop points in the country beyond which troubles—disturbances—don't move, so that the entire country doesn't flare up. But in his younger days, like many other Indian writers of his generation (including Bhishm Sahni, whom I met in Shimla), he was attracted by Marxism and its promise of social and economic reforms in an India for which there seemed little other hope.

Now he is a Gandhian. "He is still there [in India]," he says in answer to my question whether the Mahatma is relevant anymore. "When we are in trouble, despair, we think of Gandhi-ji." Changes have been good for the country. The invasions, the religions, the mix. Indians have one ethos, in spite of north-south differences. The mix is extensive. It is when I ask about north and south that he gets a little impassioned, perhaps irate. He talks defensively, mentions other countries where differences still exist—the United States and France—but his knowledge and memory seem imprecise.

"Posterity will judge my work," he says. "If they find it useful, they'll keep it." His influences are the Russians, mostly Dostoevsky, Tolstoy, Turgenev, and Chekhov, and therefore, not surprisingly, his work tends to be epic in its concerns about land, families, and traditions, and the changes wrought upon them over time. He mentions Tagore among the Indians. And he is working on a book about the Indus Valley civilization and the arrival of the Aryans.

Ever the vain writer, in spite of the modesty, he wants to give me a book to take, despairs that I can't read Malayalam. He possesses only one copy of the English translation of the classic *Chemmeen*, in a recent edition. I settle for a signed Malayalam novel.

><

It is quite surprising that the use of pepper has come so much into fashion. . . . [It] has nothing in it that can plead as a recommendation to either fruit or berry, its only desirable quality being a certain pungency; and yet it is for this that we import it all the way from India!

PLINY THE ELDER, *Natural History*

Colonial education inevitably influenced my generation's perception of the world, how could it not? It bequeathed to us an inner compass, a bias to live with. The world was in its own image, London was its centre. In my schooldays Vasco da Gama's voyage loomed large; he was the first European to round the Cape to reach India, arriving by way of Mombasa and landing somewhere close to Calicut.

I am in Kerala, I have to see Calicut

In medieval times this city on the northern Kerala coast was one of the great entrepôts of the Indian Ocean, the others being Cambay, Bharuch, and Veraval-Somnath in Gujarat, Hormuz in the Persian Gulf, Aden at the entrance to the Red Sea, and, on a smaller scale, Mombasa and Kilwa in East Africa. Because the Arab route to Malabar was from the north, Calicut always had a strong Muslim presence. The rulers of Calicut, called the zamorins, had cordial relationships with the Muslims, among whom were the prominent merchant princes of the domain, customs officials, and sailors. The great Chinese mariner and diplomat Zheng He, who visited Calicut in the early 1400s, observed,

Many of the king's subjects are Muslims, and there are twenty or thirty mosques in the kingdom to which the people resort every seventh day for worship. On this day, during the morning, the people being at the mosques, no business whatever is transacted; and during the latter part of the day, when the services are over, business is resumed.

Zheng He himself was a Chinese Muslim, whose other name was Haji Mahmud Shams.

In 1340, before Zheng He's, and more than a century and a half before da Gama's, arrival, the Moroccan traveller Ibn Battuta, who had visited the East African coast ten years earlier, arrived in Calicut from Delhi as an envoy of Sultan Muhammad Tughlaq. His mission was to board a junk for China with a message for the emperor of the Mongol Yuan dynasty. When the Moroccan arrived, the town's dignitaries, Hindu and Muslim, came to greet him with "drums, trumpets, horns, and flags on their ships. We entered the harbour amid great ovation and pomp, the like of which I have not seen in these parts." Tughlaq's ambassador became a guest of the zamorin.

Calicut, says Ibn Battuta, "is . . . one of the largest harbours of the world. It is visited by men from China, Sumatra, Ceylon, the Maldives, Yemen and Fars [Persia] and in it gather merchants from all quarters." Arriving at the port, Ibn Battuta saw thirteen Chinese ships in the harbour awaiting the end of winter. Only Chinese ships, he says, could travel through the Sea of China. The largest of them, the junks, came equipped with twelve towering sails, their four decks "containing rooms, cabins, and saloons." Each junk carried a thousand men, "six hundred of whom are sailors and four hundred men-at-arms," in addition to the merchants, their families, and retainers. So wealthy were the merchants of the city that "one of them can purchase the whole freightage of such vessels put in here and fit out others like them." The captain of such a ship was like "an amir" and went around on shore with a retinue of archers and men playing drums, trumpets, and bugles.

Today, Calicut is a modest little port city of roughly half a million inhabitants; it is Cochin, its ancient competitor to the south, that is the larger port, is more developed and attracts more tourists. Calicut has the added disadvantage that it is further away from the capital, Trivandrum. But its compactness makes it accessible, and it has a bustling market downtown which you have to wade through to get to the ancient spice market, the famous Big Bazar.

In the Big Bazar this late afternoon, just before sunset, the spice wholesalers relax outside the shops and warehouses. Business is over for the day. The Big Bazar has existed at this place for centuries. The spices sold in this market were craved by the Europeans. Pepper was like black gold. Towards the end of the street, and all along the beach road which it meets, are parked dozens of trucks in a row ready to take away the produce. But that will be tomorrow morning. There is a Gujarati school on the beach road and a few Gujarati businesses. Gujarati merchants, in numbers small and large, like the Arabs, have been ubiquitous in the Indian Ocean ports for centuries. I imagine the antecedents of the local Gujaratis going to welcome Vasco da Gama as he arrived, in 1498. Portuguese accounts mention the "Guzaratis" in various places as far as Macao. Vasco da Gama's last stop before arriving here in India was Mombasa, where my mother grew up, where, according to legend, he picked up two Indians, presumably Gujarati, to guide him to their homeland. If not for them, would he have arrived here? There is a small, nondescript stone plaque to commemorate his landing on a beach called Kappad further up from the city. In Mombasa, the Portuguese built Fort Jesus and fought against the Arabs and the Swahili. In Malabar, too, they carried on a bitter rivalry against the Arabs.

As I walk along the road out of the Big Bazar and next to the beach, there occurs a coincidence, a personal little epiphany: two of the businesses facing the sea bear, as their proprietors' last names, my own surname. What's in a name? For me, much. Vassanji is not a common name, not even in Gujarat. What does it signify, here, on the signs of two businesses in this Malabar port? It is not a family name, being my grandfather's first name, so I cannot claim a clan connection. The connection must be regional (Kathiawar, Gujarat) and generational (my grandfather's). Calicut, the ports of Kathiawar, and those of East Africa were all linked through the Indian Ocean trade. In my grandfather's generation there were other Vassanjis, a few of whom travelled from Kathiawar to Calicut, others to East Africa.

The sun is setting and people are arriving to stroll down the boardwalk, or sit on the parapet looking out, as citizens of beach towns everywhere have always done. The ocean conveys a sense of faraway places. Young Muslim couples, the women in loose hijab, sit close to each other; this is their private space. Some of them couldn't be more than teenagers. There is no abashedness, I observe; a couple fondle each other, another stare long into each other's eyes. It's only the headcover that gives them away. The sun goes behind clouds, sets, the crowds begin to thin.

A little further south from the Big Bazar is the Muslim area called Kuttichura. It is a quiet old village around a large pond; there is hardly any traffic, and the place seems curiously untouched by the bustling life outside. The only commercial activity is the odd village shop, a coconut stand, a fish market. The ocean is visible in the far distance. Here, the women are in full black burqa, many of the men wear white lunghis and Muslim caps. Features vary from the very fair to the typical dark that one associates with the south.

There is a mosque close by, a few hundred years old, I am told by a young man from the area who walks along with us. The sloping roof is red-tiled and flat-topped, in traditional Keralan style, which is unlike the typical Middle Eastern domed and arched style now common to new mosques in Kerala, and indeed everywhere. We go to another mosque, where the tops of the walls are trimmed with colourful floral designs. There are Quranic inscriptions etched on the walls inside. On one wall, however, an unpainted area of one by two feet contains an inscription. No one can say what the script is, what the language. No one cares. But we are brought an old Quran with beautiful calligraphy, partly coloured, on yellowed paper. A thousand years old, I am told, but it looks, to my admittedly untrained eye, not more than two hundred. The young man with us, fair, handsome, and of medium height, is called Aziz. He sounds cynical about the old folk, sings a popular Hindi film song as we walk, though his knowledge of Hindi and of English is next to none. At the mosque, he easily introduced my companion, a Hindu, as Abdullah, thus avoiding complications.

He takes us to his house, which is a traditional one, I gather. It is walled, and the entranceway has a red-tiled roof. Inside the entrance is a courtyard, beyond which is the house, which also has a red-tiled roof. The house has a verandah, and large spacious rooms, some of them empty of furniture, and it is cool and dark compared to the sun drenched street outside.

From here he takes us to the home of a prominent local family. There is a somewhat surreal quality to the experience. The young man speaks in Malayalam, my companion translates in the simplest of terms, and I follow where I'm taken. For the guide I am a "foreign," someone special, and perhaps this is how he gets us admitted to the house of an eminence. At the entrance there are two photos of ancestors proudly displayed. On the verandah wall are more photos, and framed letters. The verandah has chairs to sit on, and a telephone. There is a mosque adjoining the house. We meet here a father and son, both very fair, wearing lunghis. They claim descent from the Prophet, their ancestors having arrived from Aden about a thousand years ago to preach.

There is an old bench in the courtyard, where, it is claimed, the eighteenth-century Mysorean Muslim ruler Tippoo Sultan once sat. The old shaikh whose home we are in is some kind of a doctor, who heals mental cases.

The Sultan of Beypore, as he is affectionately called, is the other grand old man of Keralan fiction: Vaikom Muhammad Basheer. There is a photo I have seen showing Thakazhi grabbing Basheer in an affectionate armhold around the neck, from behind; another shows these two and a few other writers all seated, wearing milk-white lunghis and overshirts, staring at the camera. This would be after India's independence, the writers are in their forties. Basheer sports a black moustache.

His fiction is modernist, with dialect and multiple voices cutting into the narrative. The stories and novels are short and full of humour and irony. There is a facility in his style, an easy grace, that makes even the presence of a goat in a story into a revelation about family and communal life in Kerala. In his stories he scorns convention, albeit in his charming way, and perhaps this is not surprising, for it is convention and tradition of which he has been a victim. In their backgrounds and life experiences, the two friends, Basheer and Thakazhi, could not be more different. If Thakazhi has the mud of his ancestral land on his feet, Basheer has on him the dust of city streets, British jails, and the highways of India.

Beypore is a settlement a little to the south of Calicut, where I arrive at mid-morning on the passenger seat of a motorbike to pay my tribute. A single telephone line leaves the main road, goes to the writer's house, which is typical of the area, with a garden and a raised verandah in the front. He sits bare-chested on the verandah on a makeshift bed with sheets and three pillows, looking emaciated, all skin and bones, the collarbones bulging. The very sight of him is intimidating. "I am about to die," he says matter-of-factly. He is quite bald, with only a few hairs at the back of the head and a grey stubble on the chin. He leans forward as he sits, his long arms outstretched, his knotty fingers spread out. He reminds me so much of Gandhi. Every little while, he stops, looks distracted, and seems to hum a tune; but it is to breathe that he does this. He suffers from acute asthma.

We sit facing him. Behind us is a breathing apparatus with some odds and ends. Beside him is an oxygen tank. A built-in cabinet in the front room of the house is full of medicine bottles. The smell of medicine predominates.

His wife brings us some tea. He barely manages to gulp down a couple of sips, spits out some, puts down the glass partly full.

He's been here about thirty years, he says, having moved from Vaikom, the family home. This is his wife's home. Her parents had died and there were her siblings to care for. The house is nice outside, but inside it is very modest—no rug or linoleum, old, makeshift furniture, no fancy lighting or artifacts.

He says there are two books he would still like to write. One, a book of stories; another, a book on creation. But he can't, physically. He's on the verge of dying.

He brings out a spray and inhales. It's not much use, his wife says.

No, he's not travelled much outside India, except for the Middle East and the coast of Africa—he's vague about this, reluctant to say much, I sense. But he travelled ten years throughout India, up to the Himalayas, became a sanyasi, someone who's renounced ordinary life. Then he returned and became a freedom fighter, followed Gandhi. He went to prison several times, many times spent nights in the lock-up, was beaten and tortured. For that, along with other freedom fighters, he receives a monthly pension from the Indian government.

I ask him about the recent "disturbances," the violence following the destruction of the Babri Mosque at Ayodhya.

"I didn't give it a thought," he says. "Fifteen years ago, when the question of Ayodhya came up, I said give it back to the Hindus. No Muslims live there. In Spain, Muslims ruled for some hundred years, what happened to the mosques? Ayodhya is a silly affair."

"There's no difference between northern and southern Muslims," he says.

How mistaken he is, I think; there are different kinds of Muslims even in Kerala. But perhaps this is what he would like to believe. Like Thakazhi saying there is no difference between the north and the south. A refrain repeated much more in the south than in the north.

"Muslims are fools," he goes on. "Out of one country they are now in three countries which are enemies with each other. Jinnah was not a Muslim. He drank, ate pork; he came from the Bohra community, who can marry their own sisters . . ." Here he displays an ignorance and a prejudice. Jinnah was not a Bohra, and the Bohras in any case do not marry their sisters.

"God bless you," he says, as we take our leave.

On my last day in Calicut I go to visit my companion's family. The father is a simple middle-class engineer, fair and lean, somewhat proud to be a Namboodiri Brahmin. According to him, many of the Muslims in Kuttichura are converted Namboodiris, the conversion having happened as recently as the early twentieth century due to a conflict. He proudly shows me the special features of his house, designed by him using basically sound principles: windows without frames but with bars, inner doors decorated with a laminated printed cloth, tiles on the ceilings, a high ceiling in the centre of the house to let the warmer air rise up. The dining area is a raised platform at which the three of us are served, vegetarian of course, the women keeping to themselves.

Fifteen minutes to my train's departure time, my companion is ready to take me on his motorbike to the railway station. We seem to be cutting it close, but to my great surprise and irritation the father brings out his own bike and suggests we stop on the way to listen briefly to a music concert. I am the type who arrives at a train station half an hour early, he is obviously the type who arrives just on time, and I get anxious. This last-minute plan seems to court

disaster; if I miss my train, I will have to re-book, spend another night in a dingy hotel, and delay or cancel my plans in Trivandrum. But there is no choice, and so we race through the evening traffic on our impossible venture.

The concert turns out to be in a school hall, and it's a Carnatic recital of songs by Thyagaraja. And I, who came to it impatient and a little angry, not expecting much from such a setting and ready to depart as soon as I took a peep inside, am completely bowled over by the beauty of the singing and the music, performed by three or four musicians in the far front of the hall. It is a lesson in humility, patience, and sense of humour. We stay longer than intended, and at the station I have to run to catch my overnight train. But once I have deposited myself in my second-class seat, staring out at the darkness and listening to the clackety rhythm of the rails, I feel an overwhelming sense of elation. Trust a bit of music to lift you up in the most unexpected of circumstances.

I learn later from an amused and happy Paniker, who shared a room with him once, that Basheer was an excellent cook and loved tea. He listened to Paul Robeson and K. L. Saigal.

Thakazhi, on the other hand, was a miser.

I finish reading Thakazhi's *Chemmeen* in an Indian edition I have picked up in Trivandrum. It's a slim novel, one of his shorter ones, a story about the romance between a girl from a Hindu fishing village and a Muslim boy. A tragic tale, simply told, in which customs and taboos—internalized taboos, as well as those enforced through family and neighbours—work with the immutability of fate. Breaking a taboo in such a setting is to court disaster, which for fisherfolk is meted out at sea. What would have happened if the young couple had run away together to live in a city? *Could* they have run away? I have met many Hindu-Muslim couples, but there are few fictional and hardly any cinematic treatments of this phenomenon, even though in Bollywood Muslim actors regularly play upper-caste Hindu men, and in their real lives marry Hindu women. This is a subject fraught with sensitivities. Recall the phenom in Gujarat who uses goons to break up mixed marriages in order to save the Hindu nation. Why, I was asked passionately once, could Muslim men marry Hindu women, and not the other way around? This seems a common perception, especially since orthodox Muslim women live sheltered lives and could not possibly come into contact with Hindu, or indeed any, men. Among the mixed couples I have come across, however, the women have been of either community.

Basheer, it turns out, had a passionate love affair with a Hindu Nair girl. This I discover much later after my visit to see him, in a brief biography introducing an English edition of his stories. The young woman's parents threatened to kill themselves, and Basheer pleaded with her to give him up and marry the man of her parents' choice. The experience took its toll on Basheer, "leading him to intemperance of an alarming nature," says the introduction to

Basheer Fictions. What form this intemperance took, the introduction doesn't say. Basheer married later, when he was fifty.

⋈

Every year from November to January thousands of men, many of them wearing black lunghis round their waists and bare-chested, are seen on the railways on their way to make pilgrimage at the Sabarimala temple of Lord Ayyappa. When I suggest to my friend Hussein that we undertake this journey, even though the pilgrimage season is over, and he consults with his friends in Varkala regarding my crazy-sounding proposal, there is a deal of objection. Climbing the mountain in the heat is hazardous, I am warned; if I go, I should leave early in the morning and take plenty of rest on the way; and so on, until I am ready to give up the idea. But finally they agree, they will indulge my wish. Hussein thinks much of me. My letters to him from Toronto, I have learned from his friends, are a source of pride for him.

We leave from Varkala at 4:30 a.m. With us is a railway station master, who has called in sick to accompany me and see the site for himself. He tells me that a Muslim (he is one, too) from Varkala had done the pilgrimage and been ostracized afterwards by his mosque. And so I am his ready excuse, it's for my sake he's going there.

The full pilgrimage requires a kind of preparatory ritual of forty-one days—a fast, abstention from sex, meat, alcohol, etc., sleeping on a hard surface. The pilgrims are required to take a black bundle, carried on the head and representing their sins, which will be left behind at the temple. The bundles contain offerings, usually rice and coconut, so the value of the collections during the pilgrimage must be enormous.

Ayyappa, born of the gods Shiva and Vishnu, the latter of whom had taken the female form of Mohini to give birth, was found by the childless King Rajasekara as an adorable baby on the bank of the Pampa river. He was brought up as Manikandan, a gifted child, and considered the heir to the throne; but meanwhile the queen gave birth to her own son. Encouraged by the prime minister, she pretended to have a sickness which could be cured only by drinking a tigress's milk. An impossible proposition, who would milk a tigress? The foundling Manikandan, as expected, volunteered to go to the forest and fetch the milk. He would have met certain death had he been an ordinary prince. But he was not. On the way he met and killed the evil Mahishi, a deed that accorded with prophecy, and returned to the palace in the company of gods and goddesses, who had all taken on the forms of tigers or tigresses. Manikandan's identity as the god Ayyappa was thus revealed. The king had been a father to him and therefore Ayyappa told the king to ask for a boon. Rajasekara requested him to indicate a place where a temple could be built in his honour. Ayyappa drew his bow and let fly an arrow. It fell on the hill where the ascetic Sabari had once lived, where Rama had once passed. This became the site of Sabarimala.

Rajasekara, of the Kulasekara empire of Kerala, lived in the ninth century, so this legend of Sabarimala is quite recent. Hundreds of thousands of pilgrims visit the site every year. Any male, and any female not in her childbearing years, irrespective of caste or creed, can go up to glimpse the god and attain his darshana. Before going up, the pilgrims are required to visit a mosque in Erumeli, a nearby town. And up on the mountain, beside the main temple, there is a shrine to a Muslim saint called Vavar that the pilgrims attend.

Why then would Hussein and his friends hesitate to take me up to Sabarimala? The answer lies in the recent hardening of attitudes.

Our taxi climbs a steep hill on a quiet, winding highway. There's not a soul in sight. On one side of us, a forest valley, the meandering Pampa river sometimes visible. On the other side, thick vegetation; at one point columns of tall rubber trees, at another, straight, sleek-trunked teak. Parallel to us, at the same height, puffs of cloud across the valley. We realize that we are in a cloud ourselves. The visibility is low, some seventy yards at most. Sharp, clear calls of the birds. The Pampa flowing below in the valley.

The natural Keralan reserve I had seen among my companions now dissolves, and there is, in the small-town companionship of friends, much giggling and teasing. The driver, near retirement—he's fifty-five—has jet black hair, presumably dyed. He can't see well but will not wear glasses. He spent fifteen years working in the Gulf, and upon his return, flush with money, bought this car. He also has another job.

The station master, who generously put me up for the night, giving me a room probably used by someone else, has a nice large two-storey house. But it has such rudimentary furniture as would suit a mud house, giving me the impression that nothing more can be afforded for the time being.

In olden days the journey to Sabarimala was undertaken on foot, through the forest. Legend has it that those who had not observed the preparatory rituals would be picked off by the tigers and leopards. But now there is this road, smooth except for the odd interruption, which takes us straight to the town of Pampa at the foot of Sabarimala.

The town has numerous "hotels," canteens roofed with thatch for the pilgrims to rest at and purchase refreshments. Two of them are open but almost empty. In the distance, rows of public toilets, one rupee per head, as a large sign says.

The place has not been cleaned since the last pilgrims left about a month ago. Litter lies all over, plastic and paper of all kinds. There is a stench of rotting fruit. The alleys between the hotels serve as garbage dumps, and the ground is covered with animal turd. It's not obvious at first what animal is responsible, then comes a braying sound accompanied by rhythmic groans, and we realize that it's donkey turd around us and a copulation is in progress. The donkeys are used for carrying sand for building in the area, and perhaps also for carrying up pilgrims.

There are flies in abundance. The pilgrims may have left, but the flies have only multiplied. And how they cling.

Two of my companions now spend an hour hiring a tractor to take us up the mountain. A noisy tractor with four chattering people going up to a pilgrimage site somehow doesn't sound attractive to me. I tell my companions that I prefer to hike up. The time factor is mentioned to deter me, but I persist, saying they have already wasted an hour. Finally the station master and I walk up with a guide, the other two drive away ahead of us.

There are canteens, now empty, to either side of us as we walk, the path littered with plastic wrappers, paper, cardboard, juice boxes. But the climb is relentlessly steep, so that one has to rest. After a mile or so, the track flattens, and there are fewer stalls around. The land drops steeply away on either side here. The guide points to a ravine, saying, Sabari peed there once with such great force that the land gave way. There is indeed a fast-moving stream below; I don't know if it signifies anything. All around us, green dense forest. There are sounds in the bushes and trees— birds, wildfowl, a brown furry-tailed thing of which only the tail is glimpsed, a red and black squirrel. The trees are huge, the red earth soft. Two stones, one large and one small, are kept in an enclosure, and they symbolize the story that Sabari was once turned into a stone by a rishi, until Rama on his journey in the forest came upon her and released her. I have not been able to corroborate these stories about Sabari since. Across the valleys, other mountains. No sign of habitation, but an electric cable has discreetly followed us and becomes visible. After a couple of miles, tube lights appear at regular intervals on the trees to light the way of the pilgrims in the dark. The sight of thousands walking, clad in black, carrying two bundles each, chanting to Lord Ayyappa must be inspiring, electricity and juice boxes notwithstanding.

We finally come upon the pilgrimage site. It is a modern village, with recently constructed blocks of flats, a bank and other businesses, and public toilets, one rupee a head. There are flies without number, and smells, and unpicked litter. The path now has railings on both sides to hold in the crowds, and it leads directly to the temple and Ayyappa's shrine. The temple is constructed of wood and looks rather small and strangled, the modern concrete jungle pressing in all around. The government has plans to build a road up, in order to convert this into an even bigger tourist site. Impressive as the number of pilgrims would be at this enlarged shrine, I cannot imagine what spiritual comfort it could give. But I have not gone through the rituals, the expectations; perhaps the experience would reside in one's anonymity among other black-clad pilgrims, the humility that would impart.

We are unable to climb up the famous eighteen steps to see the icon of the god; it is the off-season, and besides, we have not gone through the forty-one-day ritual. We do not carry on our heads black bags with our offerings and our sins. Instead, we see a smaller shrine with two pictures of Ayyappa, one with him on a tiger, in the company of a few other tigers, another with him sitting in a sort of Buddha pose. Since 5:30, hymns have been sounding here, over a loudspeaker, one to Lord Ayyappa, in which the devotee-singer falls to the god's feet, saying, "*Swami sharanam Ayyappa*," the same chant the pilgrims sing on their way here.

It's time to go. The tractor not having returned, all four of us walk down. The time factor is again forgotten as the walk turns into a lazy stroll. But in an hour we are down, and after a dip in the Pampa river, considered sacred, we depart.

It is not the tigers, snakes, or elephants who ultimately scare me, but the driver, who is so reckless he misses our turn and consequently has to take a longer route. This bothers no one. We stop for lunch. Then we stop at a village where Hussein was brought up. It is more a town now, a previously small street having become a highway spewing fumes, having taken over part of the sidewalk. A street has been nicknamed Pakistan Street because of its quarrelsome Muslims. But Hussein's former home is a ruin, the back destroyed and covered with junk for sale—bottles, shoes, cardboard. The front is a proper junk store, called Seconds. It belongs to his younger brother, who is not around. The older brother, living next door, comes out in shirt and dhoti and gets someone to climb up a coconut tree and drop a bunch of fruit, which are then shaved and cut for us. We stop at his sister's house next, which is nice, the husband working as a caretaker in an expatriate colony in Abu Dhabi. Then we leave.

On the way, some customs are explained to me by the station master. Most Muslims, he says, tuck in their dhoti on the left side, Hindus on the right. There are exceptions, he being one. The Hindu women have the tikka on the forehead and let their sari fold fall on a shoulder.

They talk about dowries. An engineer or doctor is the most preferred groom. When a girl's family (she has to be educated) finds such a boy, they will make their offer, something like two hundred thousand rupees for "pocket money" for the groom's family, and a car (three hundred thousand), a hundred and twenty-five gold sovereigns (a kilo), and a nice house for the couple. Such a dowry is being contemplated by Hussein's brother-in-law, who is in the Gulf, for his daughter. I don't know what to make of the figures. Hussein himself received a dowry of six thousand rupees; but that was a different time, a modest family.

A family they know has seven sons. Six are physical therapists working abroad. The seventh is pursuing the same training. Getting into college is not easy. Hussein's son is also training as a physical therapist.

✐

During a subsequent visit I learn that Hussein has moved to the more civilized Trivandrum from the backward Varkala—actually the beautiful cottage by the sea where I stayed once. But his wife suffers depression in the city. Still later I hear that he suffered a heart attack while on a train and died. He had found a better job as a school inspector. His dissertation was incomplete, his dreams of Canada unfulfilled. The translation he began of one of my novels also remains incomplete.

Whenever I think of him I cannot help but recall my first visit to his home: the waves pounding at the shore, the wind rustling through the coconut palms; the outside door open and his wife, cooking in the kitchen, too shy to come out and meet me; Hussein telling me of Raja Rao. I also think of our relationship, fraught with misunderstanding as it was, due to the partial language barrier. He respected me, in the way Indians traditionally respect teachers and writers; I think he also felt affection for me because I was accessible. And I responded with affection in return.

Vaikom Basheer, too, has died, as has Thakazhi; and more recently, Paniker, who was sick but did not reveal it until finally, as I am told, when the pain became too hard to bear. Three literary men of a generation.

><

He who has served and helped one poor man seeing Siva in him, without thinking of his caste, creed, or race, or anything, with him Siva is more pleased than with the man who sees Him only in temples.

SWAMI VIVEKANANDA

Trivandrum is far south on the Indian subcontinent, but not quite at the tip, the apex of the upside-down triangle. I have always harboured a desire to visit that tip, called Kanya Kumari, and simply stand there, looking away. There is something romantic about the idea, something symbolic about that point where India ends so abruptly. All that tumult, all that land mass, all that history behind you, the silent sea ahead of you.

It is not quite like that.

The road to Kanya Kumari rips through town after roadside town. On the way, rice and banana fields, the occasional hospital or college, and temples, churches, and makeshift shrines consisting sometimes of nothing more than a stone, or three stones, or some god's pictures. Fifty-six miles take all of three hours to traverse. India's economic boom is apparently reflected, in 2007, in the fact that several times I have to tell the driver to turn the air conditioner down; I had to make a similar request in my hotel. We arrive finally in Kanya Kumari. A long, straight cheerful street leads us into the town, restaurants on either side serving veg or nonveg, and delivers us to the beach, where rows of shacks sell cheap plastic goods, electronics, and articles made with seashells to local tourists. The feel of the place is that of a rustic funfair.

From the beach one takes a ferry to two little islands close by; they form the tip of India, as it were. The sea is choppy but the attendants very adroitly help the passengers into the rocking vessel thus keeping the ferry service brisk. The first island we come to has two handsome mandapas (halls) of stone, one quite dwarfing the other and blocking it from the open sea. The smaller, squat structure houses a rock with an outcrop upon it that is in the shape of a human foot. It has a garland of flowers around it and is apparently the footprint of the Goddess, who is supposed to have once visited here. The larger mandapa is a hollow rectangular block of grey stone, with a layered red-brown roof flanked by cupolas and black columns of marble at the entrance, the whole raised upon a pedestal and reachable by some two dozen steps. Impressive and beautiful—one might well call it intellectual in design—it is the memorial to Vivekananda (1863–1902) and was built in 1970. Swami Vivekananda, born in Calcutta, was a spiritual teacher of the Vedanta philosophy and practice of self-realization, which is based on the Upanishads. He is said to have sat at this spot to meditate before heading out for Chicago to attend the World's Parliament of Religions in 1893. He became famous as a teacher and now has an international following through the Ramakrishna Mission, which he founded. The simply stated features of his memorial, compared to the richness of a typical temple, are striking and indicative of the esoteric nature of his teaching. Inside is a statue to him, in a large austere hall, and there's a room for meditation at the side of the building, where a few people have come to contemplate in silence; on a screen in front of them is displayed the symbol Om.

The swami's memorial easily steals the thunder from the Goddess's foot. And ironically it seems that Vivekananda himself has been turned into a god.

Walking around this rock islet, looking back upon the mainland, the Nilgiri mountains are visible on the right, to the east; and, somewhat surprisingly, the most prominent and tallest structure in the town of Kanya Kumari is seen to be a white cathedral. On the opposite side, facing south, you see the horizon and the point where the two seas, the Indian Ocean and the Bay of Bengal, meet and the sea changes colour from green to blue.

The ferry takes you to the second little island. Here, atop a pedestal which is itself a full-scale building, is an immense statue to the Tamil poet-guru Tiruvalluvar that, at 133 feet, dwarfs even the Vivekananda memorial. Just the toe of the statue is a foot or more in height. Tiruvalluvar is the author of the 133-chapter Tamil work *Thirukural*, considered by his followers to be the best among the world's masterpieces of literature or philosophy. His dates are before the Christian era, but not much more about him is certain. It took five hundred sculptors nine years to complete his statue, which was inaugurated in 2000. It is undoubtedly a magnificent achievement, though one wonders what the point of it is, here, blotting the view of the sea from the mainland.

And so, two new idols at a symbolic spot. They stand high and aloof, stony and sterile, celebrating supposedly poetry and philosophy, yet in reality human vanity and political power.

More satisfying for me is the visit to the temple of Kanya Kumari, the Goddess. The temple is reputed to be three thousand years old and you enter it bare-chested along with the crowd that has been waiting for the door to open, having left your shirt and other belongings at a stand outside. If one wants a god or goddess, they had better be ancient and distant.

To Finish: Back on the Himalayan Foothills

On naked feet Akbar came,
A canopy of gold on Mother he placed
bhajan

IT IS SAID THAT THE GREAT MUGHAL EMPEROR AKBAR walked barefoot uphill from the pilgrim town of Kangra to pay respects to the goddess Jawalamukhi here at this temple, where she is represented by a perpetually burning flame. Proud Akbar, Protector of the World, who desired so much a convergence of faiths in his empire; Akbar who had beautiful, defiant Anarkali buried in a cave (legends say) for refusing to deny her love for his heir, but released her, for he had promised a boon to her mother and he always kept his word; Akbar the Great (as the history books taught) brought with him a canopy of solid gold to place over the flame that is the goddess Jawalamukhi. But next morning when they (it's not clear exactly who) opened the temple door, they saw that the emperor's gold had turned to base metal and darkened. This was the goddess's way of showing Akbar that he was still a mere mortal. Her name, Jawalamukhi, means "the one of the flaming face."

The other form of this goddess is a very beautiful and very Indian woman.

In a worship mandap next to the main temple, a woman in a trance jerks on the ground; a group of chanting women surround her. Over the loudspeaker, stories are sung about the goddess, who is a form of Durga.

Kangra, a short distance from Dharamsala in the western Himalayan foothills, where I am on a visit long promised to a friend I met on my second day in India, on the Puri Express, fourteen years ago. Much has happened since then.

Dharamsala is a simple little town, though now also a resort for some Delhiwallahs. More fashionable, for Westerners at least, is McLeod Ganj, a short distance up a steep hill. Movie stars visit here, bhang is available, and moksha. It reminds me of a fashionable American college town of the sixties and seventies, young people meandering about, a few bookstores, questionable but trendy restaurants, bookstores and signs offering faddish Orientalia—lessons in Tibetan, reiki, yoga, fortune-telling. The lineups outside the ATM are but a modern twist; the monks are a local attraction. The town is the exiled Dalai Lama's headquarters, and his temple has some beautiful sculptures and other art which was brought along from Tibet. In the morning, in the very colourful temple complex, you can see some of the younger monks in their maroon robes practising their debating skills, finishing each argument with an emphatic clap of the hands, the traditional way. An exclamation mark of sorts. You wonder how much of this is a show for the tourists. Relationships between the Tibetans and the locals are not always the best, and the Tibetans are not all monks, many run businesses.

The Bhagsunath temple, a short walk from the Dalai Lama's centre, at the end of the crafts market, was the official temple of the First Gurkha Rifles, which had its headquarters in this area from 1861 until it was moved recently. Further down the road back to Dharamsala is the Anglican church with a cemetery. Many of the British officers buried there died fighting in Afghanistan.

"There is much to see . . . you should have stayed longer," scolds one of my hosts.

"I should have," I confess, regretfully. "It never ends."

Two weeks ago I was at India's southernmost, tropical tip looking out towards Africa; now, here I am in the north in the Himalayan foothills, where numerous conquering armies camped, including the Turkish, the Mughal, and the British; where they still remember the Mughal Akbar as a great emperor but remind him of his mortality.

"Have you seen all parts of India?" ·

"Hardly." I sound rueful. "I'll have to keep coming, I guess . . ."

In my mind, I imagine a map with large swaths of not-yet-visited India.

"You must stay longer next time."

Meanwhile, photos; coffee at one of those new bars that have sprung up everywhere in the country, where we have to tell them to switch the teenage music off—there is nobody else here anyway on this monsoon day—and I wonder aloud if the roads will bear up to take me back to the heat of Delhi.

Yes, there is more to discover, there will always be more, the journey is endless, as I knew, as I had been forewarned.

But for now I must stop here, conclude this token of pilgrimage.

Select Glossary

Banya	a member of the traditional trading caste
bhajan	devotional song
bhakti	devotional worship
Brahmin	a member of the traditional priestly caste
dargah	a shrine where a holy man is buried and worshipped
fakir	mendicant
ginan	religious songs (bhajans) of the Khojas, and other sects
kafir	heretic, in Islam
khano	a Khoja prayer house and community centre (from *jamat khana*)
Khoja	a Gujarati ethnic-religious group with elements of both Ismailism and Vaishnavism
Kshatriya	a member of the traditional warrior caste
mandir	temple
masjid	mosque
pavaya	a transvestite eunuch
pir	a Muslim holy man or saint
qadi	an Islamic judge
qawali	a form of Urdu poetry, often devotional
sadhu	an ascetic
sepoy	private soldier
Sufi	an Islamic mystic
Vaishnavism	worship of the god Vishnu and his avatars, especially Rama and Krishna
yogi	an Indian ascetic

Bibliography

Delhi: The Burden of History

Ahmed, Firoz Bakht. "Anglo Arabic School: A Three-Century Old Academic." *Milli Gazette*, www.milligazette.com/Archives/15062002/1506200256.htm

Albcruni. *Alberuni's India*. Translated by Edward C. Sachau. Abridged. New York: Norton, 1971.

Ali, Ahmed. *Twilight in Delhi*. London: Hogarth Press, 1940. Reprint, Bombay: Oxford University Press, 1966.

Baba, Hazrat Nawab Gudri Shah. "Hazrat Nizamuddin Awlia, R.A." Canadian Society of Muslims, www.muslim-canada.org/sufi/nizamud.htm#notes

Babur. *The Baburnama: Memoirs of Babur, Prince and Emperor*. New York: Modern Library, 2002.

Barani, Ziauddin. In *The History of India as Told by Its Own Historians*. Vol. III. Edited by H. M. Elliot, John Dowson. Allahabad: Kitab Mahal, n.d.

Battuta, Ibn. *Travels in Asia and Africa*. Translated and edited by H.A.R. Gibb, 1929. Reprint, New Delhi: Low Price, 2004.

Brahmbhatt, Preetee. "Who Was Mangal Pandey?" Rediff.com, August 10, 2005. http://us.rediff.com/movies/2005/aug/101p.htm

Dalrymple, William. *City of Djinns: A Year in Delhi.* New York: Penguin, 2003.

———. *The Last Mughal: The Fall of a Dynasty, Delhi, 1857.* London: Bloomsbury, 2006.

Dunn, Ross E. *The Adventures of Ibn Battuta, a Muslim Traveler of the Fourteenth Century.* Berkeley: University of California Press, 1986.

Foster, Peter. "Rough Reception for 'Mutiny Tourists.'" Telegraph.co .uk, September 25, 2007. http://blogs.telegraph.co.uk/foreign/peterfoster/sept07/mutinytours.htm

Guha, Ramachandra. "India's Internal Partition." *The New York Times,* August 15, 2007.

Habib, Mohammad, and Khaliq Ahmad Nizami. *A Comprehensive History of India: The Delhi Sultanate.* New Delhi: People's Publishing House (with the Indian History Congress), 2006.

Habib, Mohammad. *Hazrat Amir Khusrau of Delhi.* 1927. Reprint, New Delhi: Cosmo, 2004.

Hardy, Peter. *Historians of Medieval India: Studies in Indo-Muslim Historical Writing.* Westport, Conn.: Greenwood Press, 1982.

Hibbert, Christopher. *The Great Mutiny: India 1857.* London: Allen Lane. 1978. Reprint, New Delhi: Penguin, 1980.

Hosain, Attia. *Sunlight on a Broken Column.* London: Chatto & Windus, 1961. Reprint, New Delhi: Penguin, 1992.

Kaul, H. K., ed. *Historic Delhi: An Anthology.* New Delhi: Oxford University Press, 1996.

Khusrau, Amir. In *The History of India as Told by Its Own Historians.* Vol. III. Edited by H. M. Elliot, John Dowson. Allahabad: Kitab Mahal, n.d.

Peck, Lucy. *Delhi: A Thousand Years of Building.* New Delhi: Roli Books, 2005.

Peer, Basharat. "Anti-Sikh Riots a Pogrom: Khushwant." Rediff.com, May 9, 2001. www.rediff.com/news/2001/may/09sikh.htm

Percy, Clayre and Jane Ridley, eds. *The Letters of Edwin Lutyens.* London: Collins, 1985.

Ramesh, Randeep. "Protests Force India War Grave Visitors to End Tour." *The Guardian.* September 27, 2007.

Russell, Ralph and Khurshidul Islam. *Ghalib Life and Letters.* Cambridge, Mass.: Harvard, 1969.

Schimmel, Annemarie. *Mystical Dimensions of Islam.* Chapel Hill: University of North Carolina Press, 1975.

Sharma, Sunil. *Amir Khusraw: The Poet of Sultans and Sufis.* Oxford: One World, 2006.

Sharma, Y. D. *Delhi and Its Neighbourhood.* New Delhi: Archaeological Survey of India, 1990.

Singh, Khushwant, and Raghu Rai. *Delhi: A Portrait.* New Delhi: Oxford University Press, with Delhi Tourism Development Corporation, 1983.

Singh, Khushwant. *The Vintage Sardar.* New Delhi: Penguin, 2002.

———. *Big Book of Malice.* New Delhi: Penguin, 2000.

———. *Train to Pakistan.* Reprint, New Delhi: Roli Books, 2006.

Singh, Upinder. *Ancient Delhi.* New Delhi: Oxford University Press, 1999.

Sobti, Krishna. *The Heart Has Its Reasons.* Translated by Reema Anand and Meenakshi Swami. New Delhi: Katha, 2005.

Thapar, Romila. *A History of India.* Harmondsworth: Penguin, 1966.

Shimla: A Spell in the Mountains

Anand, Mulk Raj. *Coolie.* 1937. Reprint, New Delhi: Heinemann Educational Books, 1981.

———. *Seven Summers.* 1951. Reprint, New Delhi: Arnold-Heinemann. 1987.

———. *Seven Stripes.* 1968. Reprint, New Delhi: Arnold Publishers, 1993.

———. *City of Dreadful Nights.* 1968. Reprint, New Delhi: Arnold Publishers. 1993.

Bhasin, Raja. *Viceregal Lodge and the Indian Institute of Advanced Study.* Shimla: IIAS, 1995.

———. *Simla: The Summer Capital of British India.* New Delhi: Viking, 1992.

Barr, Pat, and Ray Desmond. *Simla: A Hill Station in British India.* New York: Scribner, 1978.

Buck, Edward J. S*imla: Past and Present.* Calcutta: Thacker, Spink, 1904.

Grewal, J. S. *The Sikhs of the Punjab.* New York: Cambridge University Press, 1990.

430
–

Jalal, Ayesha. *The Sole Spokesman.* Cambridge: Cambridge University Press, 1994.

Kipling, Rudyard. *Kim.* 1901. Reprint, New York: Dell, 1959.

Manto, Saadat Hasan. *Mottled Dawn: Fifty Sketches and Stories of Partition.* Translated by Khalid Hasan. New Delhi: Penguin, 1997.

———. *Kingdom's End and Other Stories.* Translated by Khalid Hasan. New Delhi: Penguin, 1987.

Nirala. Translated by David Rubin. *The Toronto South Asian Review* 4, no.1 (1985), p. 4.

Sahni, Bhisham. *Basanti.* Translated by Jaidev. Shimla: IIAS, 1997.

———. *Tamas.* Translated by Jai Ratan. New Delhi: Penguin, 1988.

Sharma, Rajendra. "A Life of Commitment: Bhisham Sahni, 1915–2003." *Frontline* 20, no. 15 (2003). Online edition, www.hinduonnet.com/fline/fl2015/stories/20030801003612900.htm

Singh, Harbans. *The Heritage of the Sikhs.* Columbia, Missouri: South Asia Books, 1983.

Singh, Khushwant. *The Sikhs.* London: Allen & Unwin, 1953.

———. *A History of the Sikhs.* 2 vols. Princeton: Princeton University Press, 1963, 1966.

Gujarat: Down Ancestral Roads, Fearfully

Bolitho, Hector. *Jinnah: Creator of Pakistan.* London: John Murray, 1954.

Briggs, George Weston. *Gorakhnath and the Kanphata Yogis.* 1938. Reprint, New Delhi: Motilal Banarsidass, 1973

Burns, James. *A Sketch of the History of Cutch.* 1839. Reprint, New Delhi: Asian Educational Services, 2004.

Chaube, J. *History of Gujarat Kingdom, 1458–1537*. New Delhi: Munshiram Manoharlal, 1973.

Commissariat, M. S. *Mandelslo's Travels in Western India*. 1931. Reprint, New Delhi: Asian Educational Services, 1995.

———. *A History of Gujarat, 1297–1573*. Bombay: Longmans, 1938.

Dosabhai, Edalji. *A History of Gujarat*. 1894. Reprint, New Delhi: Asian Educational Services, 1986.

Eaton, Richard M. "Gates of Discord." *Times Literary Supplement*, May 5, 2006.

Forbes, Alexander Kinloch. *Ras Mala: Hindoo Annals of the Province of Goozerat in Western India*. 1854. Reprint, New Delhi: Low Price, 1997.

Gandhi, M. K. *An Autobiography: The Story of My Experiments with Truth*. Translated by Mahadev Desai. 1927. Reprint, Ahmedabad: Navjivan Trust, 1940.

Jalal, Ayesha. *The Sole Spokesman*. Cambridge: Cambridge University Press, 1994.

Mehta, R. N. *Champaner: A Mediaeval Capital*. New Delhi: Heritage Trust & Archaeological Survey of India, 2002.

Kamdar, Mira. *World Policy Journal*. XIX, No. 3, 2002. http://www.world policy.org/journal/articles/wpj02-3/kamdar.html

Misra, R. K. "Cowboy of the Faith." *Outlook*. February 26, 2007, p. 22.

Misra, S. C. *The Rise of Muslim Power in Gujarat: A History of Gujarat from 1298 to 1442*. New Delhi: Munshiram Manoharlal, 1982.

Munshi, K. M. *Gujaratno Naath*. 1917. Reprint, Ahmedabad: Gurjar Prakashan, 2005.

———. *Jaya Somnath*. 1940. Reprint, Ahmedabad: Gurjar Prakashan, 2005.

———. *Patanni Prabhuta*. 1916. Reprint, Ahmedabad: Gurjar Prakashan, 2005.

———. *Rajadhiraja*. 1922. Reprint, Ahmedabad: Gurjar Prakashan, 2005.

Rajan, K. V. Soundura. *Junagadh*. New Delhi: Archaeological Survey of India, 1985.

Sheikh, Nazir Ahmad. *Quaid-i-Azam: Father of the Nation*. Lahore: Qaumi Kutub Khana, 1968.

Siddiqui, Muhammad Ali, ed. *Quaid-i-Azam Jinnah: A Chronology*. Karachi: Quaid-i-Azam Academy, 1981.

Padmanabha. *Kanhadade Prabandh.* Translated by V. S. Bhatnagar. New Delhi: Aditya Prakashan, 1991.

Thapar, Romila. *Somanatha: The Many Voices of a History.* New Delhi: Penguin Viking, 2004.

———. "Somanatha and Mahmud." *Frontline* 16, no. 8 (1999).

Tod, James. *Travels in Western India.* 1839. Reprint, New Delhi: Munshiram Manoharlal, 1997.

Varadarajan, Siddharth, ed. *Gujarat: The Making of a Tragedy.* Delhi: Penguin, 2002.

Watson, J. W. *History of Gujarat.* 1876. Reprint, New Delhi: Cosmo Publications, 1983.

Wolpert, Stanley. *Jinnah of Pakistan.* New York: Oxford University Press, 1984.

Yagnik, Achyut, and Suchitra Sheth. *The Shaping of Modern Gujarat: Plurality, Hindutva, and Beyond.* New Delhi: Penguin, 2005.

Kerala: The Goddess's Footprint

Ahmad, Aziz. *Studies in Islamic Culture in the Indian Environment.* London: Oxford University Press, 1964.

Basheer, Vaikom Muhammad. *Basheer Fictions.* Edited by Vanajam Ravindran. New Delhi: Katha, 1996.

Battuta, Ibn. *Travels in Asia and Africa.* Translated and edited by H.A.R. Gibb. 1929. Reprint, New Delhi: Low Price, 2004.

Bayly, Susan. *Saints, Goddesses, and Kings: Muslims and Christians in South Indian Society, 1700–1900.* Cambridge: Cambridge University Press, 1989.

Dunn, Ross E. *The Adventures of Ibn Battuta, a Muslim Traveler of the Fourteenth Century.* Berkeley: University of California Press, 1986.

Kunhali, V. *Sufism in Kerala.* Calicut: Publication Division, University of Calicut, 2004.

Menon, A. Sreedhara. *A Survey of Kerala History.* Madras: S. Viswanathan, 1991.

Miller, Roland E. *Mappila Muslims of Kerala: A Study in Islamic Trends.* 1976. Reprint, Hyderabad: Orient Longman, 1992.

Mujeeb, M. *The Indian Muslims.* London: Allen & Unwin, 1967.

Pillai, Thakazhi Sivasankara. *Chemmeen.* Translated by Narayana Menon. Bombay: Jaico Publishing, 1992.

Pliny the Elder, *The Natural History of Pliny.* Edited by John Bostock and H. T. Riley. London: II. G. Bohn, 1855-57. See www.perseus. tufts.edu/cgibin/ptext?doc=Perseus%3Atext%3A1999.02.0137&query=head%3D%23741

Prange, Sebastian R. "Where the Pepper Grows." *Saudi Aramco World* 59, no. 1 (2008).

Randathani, Hussein. "Genesis and Growth of the Mappila Community." Jaihoon.com, November 25, 2007. www.jaihoon.com/genesis-and-growth-of-the-mappila-community.htm

Titus, Murray T. *Islam in India and Pakistan.* Calcutta: YMCA, 1959.

Woodcock, George. *Kerala: A Portrait of the Malabar Coast.* London: Faber and Faber, 1967.

433
–

Sources and Credits

The epigraphs in this book have been used from the following sources.

p. 1. Homer, *The Odyssey XXIII.* Translated by Robert Fitzgerald. *The Norton Book of Classical Literature.* Edited by Robert Knox. New York: Norton, 1993. p. 43. T. S. Eliot, "Gerontion." *The Complete Poems and Plays 1909–1950.* New York: Harcourt, Brace & World, 1971. p. 45. Edward Fitzgerald, *The Rubaiyat of Khayyam.* The Folio Society, London, 1970. p. 79. Ibn Battuta. *Travels in Asia and Africa.* Translated and edited by H. A. R. Gibb. (1929), reprinted New Delhi: Low Price, 2004. p. 90. Christopher Marlowe, *Doctor Faustus and Other Plays.* Oxford: Oxford University Press, 1998. p. 99. Allama Iqbal. From *The Vintage Sardar,* Khushwant Singh. Delhi: Penguin, 2002. p. 113. Octavio Paz, *The Collected Poems of Octavio Paz 1957–1987.* Edited by Eliot Weinberger. New York: New Directions, 1990. p. 129 Krishna Sobti, *The Heart Has its Reasons.* Translated by Reema Anand & Meenakshi Swami. New Delhi: Katha, 2005. p. 153 Octavio Paz, *The Collected Poems.* p. 155. Rudyard Kipling, *Kim.* New York: Dell, 1959. p. 187. Faiz Ahmed Faiz. *100 Poems by Faiz Ahmed Faiz.* Translated by Sarvat Rahman. New Delhi: Abhinav Publications, 2002. p. 203. Saadat Hasan Manto, "The Price of Freedom." *Mottled Dawn. Fifty Sketches and Stories of Partition.* Translated by

Khalid Hasan. New Delhi: Penguin 1997. p. 215. W. B. Yeats, "Why Should Not Old Men Be Mad?" and p. 233. "Meditations in Time of Civil War," *Selected Poems and Two Plays of William Butler Yeats*. Edited and introduced by M.L. Rosenthal. New York: Collier, 1962. p. 233. Avinash Vyas, popular song, freely translated from Gujarati. p. 235 Ali Muhammad Khan, *Mirat-i-Ahmadi*. p. 258. Quoted in J.W. Watson. *History of Gujarat*. 1876. rpt. New Delhi: Cosmo Publications. 1983. p. 273. Quoted by Alexander Kinloch Forbes, *Ras Mala*. 1854. rpt. Delhi: Low Price, 1997. p. 307. M. S. Commissariat. *Mendelslo's Travels in Western India*. 1931. rpt. New Delhi: Asian Educational Services, 1995. M.K. Gandhi, *Autobiography*. 1927. rpt. Ahmedabad: Navjivan, Trust, 1940. p. 337. Homer, *The Odyssey XXIII*. Translated by Robert Fitzgerald. *The Norton Book of Classical Literature*. Edited by Robert Knox. New York: Norton, 1993. p. 363. James Tod. *Travels in Western India*. 1839. rpt. New Delhi: Munshiram Manoharlal, 1997. p. 387. Marco Polo. In George Woodcock, *Kerala: A Portrait of the Malabar Coast*. London: Faber and Faber, 1967. p. 389. Ibn Battuta. *Travels in Asia and Africa*. p. 401. Pliny the Elder. *Natural History*.

The material quoted in this book has been taken from the following sources. Full publication data can be found in the bibliography.

DELHI. THE BURDEN OF HISTORY

pp. 46–47. Upinder Singh. *Ancient Delhi*.

p. 55. Frederick Treves. In H.K. Kaul, *Historic Delhi: An Anthology*.

pp. 59–60 Mohammad Habib and Khaliq Ahmad Nizami. *A Comprehensive History of India: The Delhi Sultanate*.

pp. 69, 70. Ziauddin Barani. In *The History of India as Told by Its Own Historians*.

p. 71. Mohammad Habib. *Hazrat Amir Khusrau of Delhi*.

p. 72. Mohammad Habib and Khaliq Ahmad Nizami. *A Comprehensive History of India*.

p. 79, 80. Mohammad Habib. *Hazrat Amir Khusrau of Delhi*.

p. 81. Ziauddin Barani; Firoz Shah. In *The History of India as Told by Its Own Historians.*

p. 87. Ibn Battuta. *Travels in Asia and Africa.*

p. 87. Ross E. Dunn. *The Adventures of Ibn Battuta.*

p. 88. Ziauddin Barani. In Mohammad Habib and Khaliq Ahmad Nizami, *A Comprehensive History of India.*

p. 88, 89. Ibn Battuta. *Travels in Asia and Africa.*

p. 90. Firoz Shah. In Mohammad Habib and Khaliq Ahmad Nizami, *A Comprehensive History of India.*

p. 90. Timur. In *The History of India as Told by Its Own Historians.*

p. 91. Timur. In H.K. Kaul, *Historic Delhi: An Anthology.*

p. 96. Sauda, Mir. In Khushwant Singh and Raghu Rai. *Delhi: A Portrait.*

pp. 103–110. Ralph Russell and Khurshidul Islam. *Ghalib Life and Letters.*

p. 110 Christopher Hibbert. *The Great Mutiny: India 1857.*

p. 111 *The Guardian* (London).

p. 113–115 Ahmed Ali. *Twilight in Delhi.*

p. 136. Clayre Percy and Jane Ridley, ed. *The Letters of Edwin Lutyens.*

p. 137–138. Edwin Lutyens. In H.K. Kaul, *Historic Delhi.*

p. 138–141. Khushwant Singh. *Big Book of Malice.*

SHIMLA. A SPELL IN THE MOUNTAINS.

pp, 158, 159. Raja Bhasin. *Simla: The Summer Capital of British India.*

p. 160. Emily Eden. In Pat Barr and Desmond Ray, *Simla: A Hill Station.*

p. 160. Rudyard Kipling. In Raja Bhasin, *Simla.*

p. 161. Rudyard Kipling. *Kim.*

p. 175. Rudyard Kipling. In Raja Bhasin. *Simla.*

p. 178. Nirala. Translation by David Rubin. *The Toronto South Asian Review.*

p. 198. Peter Coates. In Raja Bhasin, *Simla.*

p. 200. M. K. Gandhi. In Raja Bhasin, *Simla.*

p. 205. Khushwant Singh. *The Sikhs.*

p. 212. Saadat Hasan Manto. Tr. Khalid Hasan. *Kingdom's End and Other Stories.*

p. 218. *Coolie.* Mulk Raj Anand.

GUJARAT. ALONG ANCESTRAL ROADS, FEARFULLY.

p. 236–237. Mira Kamdar. *World Policy Journal.* XIX, No.3, 2002.

p. 246. Quoted in S.C. Mishra. *The Rise of Muslim Power in Gujarat.*

p. 247. Amir Khusrau. In *History of India as Told by Its Own Historians.*

p. 278. Prahlada Shastri. http://youtube.com/watch?v=p4FvGap_eh8

p. 327–328. Esther David. *The Walled City.*

pp. 339–340. Alexander Kinloch Forbes. *Ras Mala.*

p. 358. K.M. Munshi. In Romila Thapar, *Somanatha.*

p. 360. Romila Thapar. *Somanatha: The Many Voices of a History.*

KERALA. THE GODDESS'S FOOTPRINT.

p. 393. Swami Vivekananda. In George Woodcock. *Kerala: A Portrait of the Malabar Coast.*

p. 401. Zheng He. In George Woodcock. *Kerala.*

p. 402. Ibn Battuta. *Travels in Asia and Africa.*

p. 417. Swami Vivekananda. http://www.ramakrishna.org/universl.htm

Acknowledgements

This book would not have been possible without the warmth, the hospitality, and the companionship I was offered from various people across India. Their welcome and friendship altered my world; to thank them here is a mere formality and hardly any indication of my gratitude. In no particular order,

Alka Kumar, Neerja Chand, "MC" Chand, Harish Narang, Pankaj Singh, Kishan Singh, Jaidev, Charu Sharma, Bhishm Sahni, Sheila Sahni, Chandra Mohan, Om Juneja, M. F. Salat, Raj Kumar Hans, Sudha Pandya, Sharifur Rahman, Jameela Begum, K. Ayyappa Panikar.

Also:

Mrinal Miri and the Indian Institute of Advanced Study.

Sanjay Talreja, Rikhav Desai, Achyut Yagnik, Suchitra Sheth, Amritjit Singh, Devika Nirula, Hariharan, Krishna Kumar, Vaikom Muhammad Basheer, Thakazhi Sivasankar Pillai, Mulk Raj Anand, Balwinder Singh Dhillon, Sherali Aziz, Abualy Aziz, Madhu Mehra, Asgharali Engineer, Shirin

439
–

Kudchetkar, Roshan Sahani, Govind Sahani, Raj Mohan.

Maya Mavjee, my publisher for her enthusiasm, her comments, and her sense of humour; Bruce Westwood, my agent; Susan Burns, Alex Schultz, Martha Leonard, Cathy Paine.

Diya Kar Hazra, Khushwant Singh, Shantanu Ray Chaudhuri, Rakesh Batabyal.

Stella Sandahl, Alok Mukherjee, Arun Prabha Mukherjee.

And finally Nurjehan, Anil, and Kabir.

About the Author

M.G. Vassanji is the author of six acclaimed novels: *The Gunny Sack*, which won a regional Commonwealth Prize; *No New Land*; *The Book of Secrets*, which won the very first Giller Prize; *Amriika*; *The In-Between World of Vikram Lall*, which also received the Giller Prize, and *The Assassin's Song*, which was shortlisted for the Scotiabank Giller Prize and the Governor General's Award for Fiction. He lives in Toronto with his wife and two sons.

A NOTE ABOUT THE TYPE

A Place Within is set in a variation of the classic Bodoni type known as "Oldface." The original Bodoni font family was designed by Giambattista Bodoni of Parma, Italy, at the end of the eighteenth century, and continues to be a touchstone of the so-called "modern" style of type design, with its marked difference in thick and thin letter strokes, and extremely delicate serifs and hairlines.